MW01166537

THE GRANDCHILDREN OF TRIANON

HUNGARY
AND THE HUNGARIAN MINORITY
IN THE COMMUNIST STATES

RAPHAEL VAGO

EAST EUROPEAN MONOGRAPHS, BOULDER

DISTRIBUTED BY COLUMBIA UNIVERSITY PRESS, NEW YORK
1989

Contents

Preface   1

Chapter I. Hungarian Communists in the Shadow
            of Trianon   5

Chapter II. The Years of Silence:
             Stalinism and Its Aftermath 42

Chapter III. The Hungarian Revolution and the
              Hungarians in the Neighboring States . . . 59

Chapter IV. Socialist Internationalism in Crisis:
             Hungarians in Romania and Czechoslovakia
             1958–1968 68

Chapter V. Winds of Change from Budapest 103

Chapter VI. The National Minorities in Hungary 128

Chapter VII. Socialist Internationationalism in Practice:
              Hungary and the 'Bridges of Friendship' . . 155

Chapter VIII. Between Crisis and Detente: Hungarian–
               Romanian Relations 1969–1977 201

Chapter IX. A Decade of Crisis: Hungarian–Romanian
             Relations 1977–1987 214

Footnotes 261

Bibliography 290

Index 295

Preface

This work is an attempt to analyze one of the most significant developments in interstate relations in Eastern Europe: the effect of the Hungarian minority on the relations between Hungary and the neighboring communist states. My main objective has been to follow the pattern of Hungary's relationship with the Hungarian minority in the Successor States, and to trace its involvement in the lives of the Hungarians abroad from the end of World War II until 1988.

Hungary has shown a growing interest in the fate of the Hungarian minority in Czechoslovakia, Romania, and Yugoslavia since 1968, which was bound to have an immediate influence on the interstate relations among the states involved. Hungary introduced the notion of the minorities playing the role of "bridges of friendship" between neighboring communist states, a concept accepted, albeit often with some reservations, by Czechoslovakia and Yugoslavia. However, the thorniest and most intricate divisive issue was and remains the fate of the Hungarians in Transylvania and Hungary's policies vis-à-vis the line pursued by Romania.

The study does not intend to survey chronologically the history of the Hungarian minority in the respective states, but rather concentrates on those aspects, especially in the cultural field, which have been at the center of attention in Hungary, and thus have influenced the interstate relations. Naturally, the seemingly everlasting polemics between Hungary and Romania, which reached a new climax by 1987, is treated more extensively considering that the issues involved between the two states are more complex.

The study also analyzes Hungary's favorable policies toward the national minorities living in Hungary, as these minorities, which are ethnically linked to a neighboring communist state, are playing a major role in Hungary's attempts to achieve reciprocity with the respective states.

Ultimately the study also reflects upon the relationship between nationalism and communism, on aspects of ethnic survival under assimilatory pressures, and ethnic loyalty to Hungary.

The Hungarians in the communist states are, as Hungary is keen to underscore, the largest national minority in Europe. These grandchildren of Trianon, especially the Hungarians in Romania, are at the forefront of contemporary Hungarian foreign policy, constituting in Hungary itself a clear divisive issue between the regime and its opponents. The bitter polemics raging between two communist states testify to the failure of the communist regimes to solve the nationality questions. The past, unfortunately, is alive and well in the Danube Basin, and old enmities, best forgotten, continue to shape the attitudes of the peoples in Eastern Europe, in the fifth decade of the communist rule.

This author's doctoral thesis on the "History of Hungarian–Romanian Relations Since 1945" has served as the basis for this study. He is most grateful to his two supervisors, Professors Yaacov Ro'i and Zvi Gitelman, who provided valuable insights into the dynamics of the communist regimes, and the nationality policies in the area. Some of the sources were gathered in Munich, at the excellent collection of Radio Free Europe, and in academic centers and libraries in that city. Two research trips to Germany in 1976 and 1977 were made possible by the generous support of the Aranne School of History, Tel–Aviv University, and the Deutscher Akademischer Austauschdienst (DAAD).

Additional source material was supplemented in London in 1980–81, during a year spent as British Council Scholar attached to the School of Slavonic and East European Studies. Special thanks are due to the British Council, which enabled me to broaden my horizons on the complex nationality problems in the history of Eastern Europe and on the British perspectives of the issue.

Part of the manuscript was written in 1986–87 in Calgary, Canada, during a year spent as a Visiting Associate Professor, a Scholar of the Canada–Israel Foundation for Academic Exchange. I am grateful to the Foundation and to my colleagues at the Department of History at the University of Calgary, where the stimulating atmosphere added yet another dimension to the understanding of my topics of research.

The Russian and East European Research Center and the Department of History, Tel–Aviv University, have been home base since 1972. A debt of gratitude is owed especially to Professor Zvi Yavetz, Head of the Department of History, and to Professor Michael Confino, who have followed my academic career from an early state, supported and encouraged me in pursuing the teaching and the research into aspects of modern East European history.

Thanks are due particularly to Distinguished Professor Randolph L. Braham, Director of the Institute for Holocaust Studies at the Graduate School and University Center of the City University of New York. Since providing me in 1973 with the first forum for publication, he has followed and encouraged my scholarly endeavors with keen interest and friendship.

Last, but not least, warm thanks to my family: to my mother who devotedly ministered to my linguistic needs, and to my father, who until his grave illness had accompanied my academic studies and research, providing me with the necessary tools of the trade. And of course, to my wife, Gaby, and the children, Idit, Lior, and Eyal, who patiently endured with me the labor throes of this study and of my other publications.

Needless to say, any errors, shortcomings or inadequacies of exposition are to be debited entirely to me.

Raphael Vago

July 1988

Chapter I

Hungarian Communists in the Shadow of a New Trianon

There is no doubt that more than forty years after the end of World War II, "Trianon and its results continue to haunt Hungarian opinion, both the intelligentsia and the broader public, too."[1] Recent Hungarian historiography emphasizes the negative aspects of the treaty, which raises some heavy eyebrows in Bucharest, as Romania continues to see in the Treaty of Trianon an expression of the right for self–determination rather than an arbitrary deal between the victors of the war.

To a great extent the shadow of Trianon has been looming over Hungary since the end of World War II, as it did between the two wars, when the Treaty was the daily fare of Hungarian nationalism and revisionism. It was a living myth, a trauma that had to be perpetuated and sanctified. Hungarian nationalists needed Trianon to justify their greed for power and expansion, while Hungary's neighbors needed it to legitimize their regimes, to rally their nations around the menace of Hungary.

Hungary's revisionist policies drove the area into a vicious circle—fear of nationalist agitation among the Hungarians living in the Successor States, Hungary's militant policy, and an interminable chain of minority grievances. Democratic Czechoslovakia, autocratic Romania, and Yugoslavia were natural allies for what seemed to their politicians a formidable unity of forces—the Little Entente, which of course, as all edifices of international relations between the two wars, inevitably crumbled when put to the test of national survival in the late thirties.

Communists should always beware of the pitfalls of nationalism, for they are bound to open Pandora's Box. This is precisely what happened to the Communists in Hungary and elsewhere. The Hungarian Communists, whose top leadership was always in desperate need for ethnic Hungarians, found themselves for a short time after World War II championing for Hungarian national rights, fighting revisionism with something not unlike it. As long as Moscow tolerated the game, or rather as long as the game served Moscow's purposes, Hungarian Communists presented themselves as the true defenders of the Hungarians living beyond the yet undetermined and disputed borders. This was certainly the case with Czechoslovakia and Romania, where the Hungarian minority found itself under pressure immediately at the end of the war.

The dangers of a new Trianon were very evident in the minds of those Hungarian politicians who had secretly attempted to extricate the country from its alliances with Nazi Germany, and among Communists, both the "Muscovites" and the home membership. All sides about to be engaged in the struggle for power in postwar Hungary soon realized that by and large history was bound to repeat itself; once again, Hungary would have to pay for its allegiance to a losing side; once again, the Hungarian nation would find itself divided among the states of the Danubian Basin.

Communist logic presupposed that national and territorial problems should be solved under a Communist regime. In principle, nothing seemed more simple than the idea that with a friendly Czechoslovakia, Romania, and Yugoslavia, nationalism would lose its place, and territorial disputes would belong to the past. This communist euphoria is aptly expressed in the memoirs of Frigyes Puja, Hungary's Foreign Minister in the seventies, who reminisced about his activities in Battonya County near the Romanian border in 1945: "At the time we still naively believed that national frontiers will be unimportant in the future."[2]

Puja's illusions at the time were a reflection of the official Communist line, which by the end of 1944 had to be defined according to the vital territorial issues to be faced by Hungary upon its liberation. Radio Kossuth, the clandestine Communist station broadcasting from Soviet territory, expressed the Party line—approved, of course, by the Soviet supervisors of the broadcasting station—on the eve of Romania's exit from the war, in August 1944:

> There is no point in entering into argument with Romania over the future of Transylvania. This land is Romanian from an ethnic point of view, and Hungarian from a historical one. But, in the new democratic Europe we shall be free wherever we are. The fate of Transylvania will be settled by its own inhabitants. If they will wish union with Romania then, as a national minority, the Hungarian inhabitants will have to ask for equal rights with those of the Romanian population.[3]

In the interwar period, as well as after the annexation of territories by Hungary between 1938 and 1941, Hungarian Communists often used the term of "right to self–determination, up to secession" from the states that have annexed them. Such a position assumed different meanings under the changing conditions: it supported the rights of Hungarians outside the Trianon borders before the annexation of the territories, just as it left open the future status of the territories after they were annexed to Hungary.

The Hungarian CP found itself in a most embarrassing position during the heydays of Hungarian revisionism, in 1938–1940, when it had to take an unequivocal stand on the Nazi–supported process by which about 5,400,000 people were added to Hungary's population, out of whom 2,700,000 were Hungarians. The Party had for quite a time before the annexation supported a so–called "democratic revisionism" of Trianon, which, if cleared of its Marxist jargon, stated that "revision yes—if it does not entail the denial of rights of Hungarians in the annexed territories, and of the other nationalities living there. Today, this is the situation."[4] The Hungarian Communist line always achieved better results when using vaguer terms and shorter–range commitments. During the war years semantic acrobatics reached new heights, as the Communists had to formulate a line that would fit Moscow's policies while ensuring a certain degree of support among the growing forces that opposed Hungary's participation in the war as an ally of Nazi Germany. The annexation of territories from Slovakia and Sub–Carpathia in 1938 and 1939, from Romania in 1940, and Yugoslavia in 1941 brought the Hungarian Communists into contact with local Communists, of Hungarian and other ethnic origins. Suddenly, the small underground movement had to take into consideration not only the changing views from Moscow, before, during, and after the German–Soviet Nonaggression Pact of August 1939, but also the incorporation into Hungary of nationals of the Successor States, among them Communists.

The Hungarian Communists never denied that they had started the race for power, following the Liberation by Soviet forces, under very difficult conditions. They had to cope with the burden of war guilt which the Allies—including the Soviet Union—had induced into Hungarian national consciousness. Even before the early stages of the process of liberation, the Hungarian Communists were already expounding the notion that Hungary would have to pay for the deeds of its leaders. It was a very difficult point. The Communists had to hammer it into public opinion—as the Party had to present itself as the defender of national rights—while justifying the correctness of the anti–Hungarian atmosphere among the victorious Allies, and the sanctions against Hungary in the form of harsh conditions in the Peace Treaties.

It was easier to explain the guilt of the Hungarian ruling classes than to justify the collective punishment of the "other Hungary, of the

Hungarian people," who now had to pay the price for their leaders'
adventurism. Recent Hungarian historiography strongly emphasizes
this point, as part of the current reassessment of Hungary's contemporary history.[5] Rákosi, Révai, and the other Communist leaders indoc-
trinated the Hungarian public for years about the price that Hungary
had to pay, but only in recent years have questions been raised as to
the consequences of these measures on Hungary's postwar history.

The first action program of the Hungarian Communist Party
(HCP), on November 20, 1944, blamed Hungarian reactionary forces
for the country's ostracism from the "community of free nations,"
and stated that "since Mohács the country has never been in such
a grave situation"; nevertheless, the Party program went on, "there
shall be a Hungarian renaissance." This motto would be endlessly
repeated during the HCP's struggle for power, as it was meant to
play up Hungarian national goals alongside the ideological objectives
of the communist movement.

The future of Hungary, and especially the fate of the annexed
territories, remained an open issue as the Soviet forces advanced into
Hungary. However, several developments already indicated the shape
of things to come. Romania's exit from the Axis and its participation
alongside the Soviet forces in the last stages of the war as well as the
position of the Allies, left no doubt in the minds of all realistic political forces in Hungary that the country's future would not be much
different from the fate that had been meted out to her in Trianon.

Romania's self–extrication from the Axis in August 1944 continues to be an object of envy in Hungary to this day—a living proof
that the Romanians were "shrewder," more realistic, and one step
ahead of the Hungarians—a step which proved to be fateful for Hungary's future. Hungary had missed the opportunities to withdraw
from the war at the right time under the right circumstances. The
secret contact with the Allies (well documented by now in Hungarian and Western historiography) failed to lead to the results achieved
by the Romanians. On the morrow of the Romanian coup, Radio
Kossuth could only state the truth with some measure of candor:

> Let's say it openly, the Romanians were braver than us,
> more sober than us. . . . by continuing the war against the
> Soviet Union we shall only add to the stupidity of allowing
> the Romanians to overtake us.[6]

The future of Northern Transylvania, annexed to Hungary in 1940
by the Second Vienna Diktat, was only one aspect of the wider issue
of the future of Hungary's borders, and the fate of the Hungarians
living there. Following the withdrawal of Romania from the war, the

Hungarian Communists openly explained that the political affiliation of the territories inhabited by Hungarians would be solved in the light of Hungary's role in the war.[7]

For years, until well after Stalin's death, there were very few references in Hungary to the linkage between Hungary's wartime role and the fate of the areas inhabited by Hungarians. After all, officially, nationality problems had ceased to exist, and the neighboring states, Czechsolvakia and Romania, supposedly pursued "a correct 'Marxist–Leninist' nationality policy." Gyula Kállai attempted to tackle the problem in a very modest way in his book on the Hungarian Independence Movement published in 1955. But it was not until the 1970s that the problem received more objective treatment—spiced, of course, with self–criticism—and critical of those leaders ousted in the wake of the Revolution of 1956 as well as those still active.

Among the issues debated and linked to the fate of Hungary's borders was the failure to set up a Hungarian military unit in the Soviet Union, similar to the Romanian "Tudor Vladimirescu Division." The Hungarian Communist leadership in Moscow rejected any idea of cooperating with willing Horthyst officers who were already planning Hungary's withdrawal from the war. The main obstacle in the way of the Hungarian corps came from Moscow, which treated any Hungarian attempts with suspicion. This issue was dealt with for the first time in the memoirs of Zoltán Vas, who touched some raw nerves and sparked off debates when the first volume of his memoirs was published in 1970.[8] For him, the failure to set up a Hungarian corps on Soviet territory was bound to become a factor in determining the country's future:

> My belief is, that if we had got the permission, the corps would have been set up. Thus, the Czechs, Poles, and Romanians overtook us. . . . If the corps had been formed in time, Hungary's ethnic borders may have been different.

Vas's message boiled down to a simple inference: as the Soviets had rejected the formation of the Hungarian corps, to a certain extent they were also to blame for Hungary's ethnic borders—a fact well known to the Hungarian public but a taboo until it was raised by Vas.

To the participants of the provisional four–party Debrecen government, formed with the advance of Soviet forces into Hungary, it was clear, from previous contacts with the Soviets and the Western allies, that the starting point of Hungary's postwar history would be the annulment of all territorial awards. And, indeed, the armistice agreement with Hungary, signed in Moscow on January 20, 1945, decreed that principle, and Hungary agreed to rescind all the legal steps taken after the annexation of territories from Czechoslovakia, Romania, and Yugoslavia. At that point, in the winter of 1944–1945, the picture was not as clear as stated in the armistice agreement with Hungary. The case of Northern Transylvania indicated that Hungry's return to the Trianon borders would not go smoothly and that changes might occur among the various elements involved, including oscillations in the Soviet position. Article 19 of the armistice agreement with Romania, signed on September 12, 1944, left an opening on the future of Northern Transylvania:

> The Allied Governments regard the decision of the Vienna Award regarding Transylvania as null and void and are agreed that Transylvania, or the greater part thereof, should be returned to Romania.[9]

This article served as the opening salvo in Hungary's battle to change in her favor the upcoming payment for its wartime policies by attempting to reduce the number of Hungarians to be included in Romania's borders. That battle was lost from the beginning.

The First Test: Hungary and the Hungarians in Transylvania

The fate of the Hungarians in the first years of postwar Romania and Czechoslovakia is depicted bleakly in today's Hungary. The historical journal of the Hungarian Socialist Workers Party (HSWP) referred to Hungary's "going under"—*lesüllyedés*—and provided two examples for that situation: the atrocities of the "Maniu Guards" in Transylvania under the pretext that all Hungarians were Fascists, and the collective responsibility laid by the Horthysts.[10] Both examples indicate some recent trends in Hungary's treatment of those problematic years.

The fate of the Hungarians in Transylvania, especially in Northern Transylvania, was the first case to which all the active political factors in the as yet occupied Hungary had to relate by the autumn of 1944. Following the formation of the Provisional Government in Debrecen, the new emerging Hungary was faced with the embarrassing developments in Transylvania, which jeopardized her relations with Romania even before the character of their regimes had become clear.

By the end of October 1944 the whole of Transylvania had been liberated and the Romanian administration entered Northern Transylvania. Irregular Romanian troops—actually mobs—so-called Maniu Guards, committed atrocities against the Hungarian population of the area as a reprisal for the sufferings of Romanians at the hands of the Hungarian regime following the Vienna Diktat of 1940. In the middle of November 1944, the Soviets—expressing their worry that the disturbances could endanger their routes—expelled the Romanian administration, which at the time was under anti–Communist control led by Iuliu Maniu's men. Thus, the vacuum left in Northern Transylvania was to be filled by local Communists, mostly of Hungarian origin, under Soviet control. While on paper the expulsions were encouraging to the Hungarians, inasmuch as they promised Soviet backing in their gievances against the excesses of irregular Romanians, in practice they constituted a clear step toward an intensification of power struggle in Romania. The Soviets led the Romanians to understand that they would be able to return to Northern Transylvania only when and if the government became truly "democratic"—that is, under Communist control. As the democratization of Hungary was also to become a major Soviet goal, the Soviet, intimated to the Hungarian Communists that a prompt takeover of Hungary might yet change the fate of Transylvania. There is no doubt that under the specific conditions Romania was of higher strategic value to the Soviet Union than was Hungary, and as the Romanian "timetable" of liberation was ahead of Hungary's by several months, the democratization of Romania was a more urgent business. At the same time, however, promising hints could be bestowed on the Hungarians. Thus the Soviet expulsion of the Romanian administration from Northern Transylvania tempted both Hungary and Romania.

Romanian sovereignty over the whole of Transylvania was restored upon the formation of the Groza government on March 6, 1945. The four months between the expulsion of the Romanian administration and the establishment of the Groza government were a strange interlude in the history of Transylvania. It was a period in which a *de facto* autonomous Communist state of Northern Transylvania was established under a joint Hungarian–Romanian administration, in which the MNSz—the Hungarian People's Alliance—was holding the most important positions in that area of the province. Some Hungarian Communists in Transylvania nurtured the hope, or rather the illusion, that an autonomous Communist state could be established in Transylvania under a Hungarian leadership. Hungarian historiography is mostly silent on this chapter of postwar Transylvanian history, and the matter still seems to be very delicate to elaborate upon. Dániél Csatári's monogaph on Hungarian–Romanian relations during World War II, still the most authoritative source on this subject, does refer to

> some groups among the working class in Transylvania who interpreted the decision of the Allied Control Commission (on the withdrawal of the Romanian administration), as an

authorization for the formation of the dictatorship of the proletariat, a kind of Soviet Republic of Northern Transylvania.[11]

Romanian sources are also silent on this issue, as Romanian historiography is interested in proving that Hungarian and Romanian Communists cooperated in seeking the complete return of Transylvania to Romania.[12] Since the late sixties, in the various phases of Hungarian–Romanian polemics, Hungarian sources have often mentioned the withdrawal of the Romanian administration from Northern Transylvania until the instauration of the Groza government. Hungary's consistent policy has been to occasionally remind the Romanian side of its past—like the acts of cruelty of the Maniu guards—in order to counterbalance the Romanian writings on the atrocities committed by the Horthy regime during the Hungarian occupation of the area.

In one such Hungarian reminder, published on the occasion of the hundredth anniversary of Petru Groza's birth, a Hungarian newspaper wrote that

> it is a historical fact that in the villages inhabited by Hungarians in the reoccupied [sic: not "liberated"] areas, the Maniu Guards committed bloodbaths. Then the ACC ordered the removal of the Romanian reactionary apparatus and the installation of a democratic administration to be elected by the population with the support of the Soviet forces.[13]

The Hungarians in general were more cooperative with the Soviet forces than the Romanians in some areas. As appraised by a British military representative, Major W. R. Young, "by changing their colors the Hungarians hope to retain Transylvania at the expense of the Romanians, or at least to create an independent state under Hungarian influence."[14] The Romanian Communists made it clear that the territorial integrity of Romania depended on the good will of the Soviet Union. The secretary of the Romanian CP, Vasile Luca, of Hungarian origin, who was removed by Gheorghiu–Dej in 1952, wrote in *Scânteia*, the Party organ, that the Romanian public should keep in mind that Northern Transylvania would be returned to Romania only when a democratic regime was formed which would be able to safeguard the free development of each nationality.[15]

The Romanian Communists intensified their struggle for power against the "historical Parties," so that the issue of the country's territorial integrity was one of the main problems on the agenda of the various political parties. The Communists claimed to be the only political force which could ensure the territorial integrity of the country.

This point was especially essential from their point of view because of the linkage that existed between the fate of Transylvania and that of Bessarabia. The Soviets used the return of Northern Transylvania as a compensation for the loss of Bessarabia, but also as a weapon in the "democratization" of Romania.

The Yalta Conference of February 1945 was interpreted by the Romanian Communists as another step toward the democratization of the country, and Silviu Brucan, the editor of *Scânteia*, reminded the Romanian public that the Maniu Guards' anti–Hungarian excesses went counter to the spirit of the Yalta agreements, and that the formation of the Groza government of the National Democratic Front was a necessity for the rebuilding of Romania's international standing.[16]

In Transylvania itself the Romanian CP had to fight a battle on two fronts. It confronted the political forces outside the NDF, and at the same time had to eradicate any aspiration for an independent or Hungarian Transylvania. This was no easy task, as the great percentage of the local Communists were of Hungarian origin (as a matter of fact, many of them of Hungarian–Jewish origin), who harbored ideas of an "independent Transylvania." Thus the Romanian CP's emphasis was bound to focus on the common legacy of a common anticapitalist struggle, in a common homeland—Romania. The MNSz (often referred to by its previous name, MADOSz) became the transmission belt through which the Romanian CP pushed its line among the Hungarians in Transylvania. On the eve of the final thrust toward the formation of the NDF government, a conference of the MNSz for Northern Transylvania adopted a decision in February 1945, emphasizing the need for Romanian–Hungarian cooperation and the formation of an NDF government to assure the return of Northern Transylvania to Romania. The decision ended in a call which represented a combination of the various views voiced at the time, "Long live the free and democratic Transylvania, integrated in a free and independent Romania."[17]

Andrei Vyshinski, who orchestrated the Soviet moves for the formation of the Groza government on March 6, 1945, could sum up one result of his stay in Romania: "When I arrived in Romania I expressed my view that under certain conditions Romania would return to administer Transylvania. Those conditions did not exist then, but they do exist now." The Soviets emphasized, of course, that Romania would treat the national minorities in a positive way, and as Vyshinski expressed it at the festive session of the Romanian government celebrating the return of the Romanian administration over the whole of Transylvania, the "Soviet public is satisfied over the pledge of the national minorities."[18]

Once Romania had been rewarded for her correct behavior and progress in the process of democratization, the Soviet Union could go on and play the Transylvanian card until May 1946, when the Conference of the Foreign Ministers in Paris decided on the frontiers between Romania and Hungary.

The Romanian Communists presented themselves and their front organizations as the only force that could prevent Iuliu Maniu from achieving his aim of transforming Transylvania into a "bloodbath of Hungarian workers, peasants, and intellectuals."[19] While there is no doubt that Romanian irregulars committed atrocities against Hungarians, the Communists had every reason to deepen the hatred existing between the Romanian bourgeois parties and the leftist Hungarian elements in Transylvania. The new Groza regime took great pains to present the anti-Communist factors in Transylvania as the main obstacle in the way of a Hungarian-Romanian rapprochement in the region. The trials and the heavy sentences passed upon Maniu Guardists were aimed at defusing tension among the Hungarians, as well as a convenient means of eliminating political opponents of the new regime. There can be no doubt about the sincerity of Petru Groza to safeguard, or rather widen, the rights of the Hungarians in Romania. A Transylvanian of Romanian origin, he had a clear record of pro-Hungarian sentiments during the difficult interwar years, at which time he had shown a keen interest in Hungarian culture and believed in Hungarian-Romanian coexistence in that troubled land. The numerous articles published in Hungary in 1984 commemorating Groza's hundredth anniversary should be seen in this light—the message of today's Hungary being that the Romanian regime had not implemented the correct ideas of Groza.

With his pro-Hungarian reputation Groza was received with enthusiasm by the Hungarian inhabitants of Cluj shortly after the formation of his government.[20] In his speeches and public appearances he promised a new beginning in the troublesome Hungarian-Romanian relations, full rights for the Hungarians, and equal participation in the administration. However, the developments in Transylvania did not exactly follow Groza's ideas. After the formation of the Groza government, a list of Hungarian grievances was published by Hungary's Foreign Ministry in 1946 with a view to presenting Hungary's case before the Paris Peace Conference.[21] This official Hungarian document, often quoted by researchers of Hungarian-Romanian relations, did not reflect the position of the Hungarian Communists, although— given their influence in the governmental decision-making process—it must have been approved by them at the time of publication, when the Communists were playing the role of defenders of Hungarian national goals. The Hungarian document pointed to a process of "Romanization" in the administration in Transylvania, and the removal of Hungarians from their posts.

Some of the grievances of the Hungarians in Transylvania were documented not only by the official publications of the Hungarian government during 1946, but also through various means by the Hungarians living in the area. Diplomatic representatives of the U.K. and the U.S. frequently mentioned in their reports appeals transmitted by various groups of Hungarians in Romania. One such appeal was made by several groups and organizations which warned that they were about to be taken over by the communists through the MNSz–NDF. The appeal was signed by the Bishops of the Catholic, Reformed, Unitarian, and Evangelical Churches in Transylvania, the Chairman of the Hungarian Agricultural Association of Southern Transylvania, and the Vice President of the Transylvanian Museum Association,[22] an odd assortment of bodies, although perhaps no less peculiar than the mostly fictitious ones that made up the various front organizations of the Communist Party.

After April 1945 Hungarian–Romanian relations entered a new phase. The power struggle in Hungary, already manifest during the activities of the Provisional Government in Debrecen and the Provisional National Assembly, took a new turn. The Hungarian Communists intensified their pressure for the rapid "democratization" of the country, and it was only natural that the Romanian pattern should repeat itself as the real guarantor of the "Hungarian revival." Soon, the Communists were making use of the Hungarians in the neighboring states as a weapon for furthering the Communist takeover. Their line was a very delicate one, as the Party had to follow the Soviet policy very carefully.

The Hungarian CP decided to establish relations with the Romanian CP in May 1945,[23] an indication of the lack of communication between the two Parties in the period following the withdrawal of Romania from the Axis in August 1944. Rákosi's line in the wake of the liberation of Hungary was to give credit to the attempts of the "young Romanian democracy" to solve the nationality issue in Romania. At the National Conference of the Hungarian CP on May 20–21, 1945, Rákosi praised Groza's policies and referred to his optimistic assessments on the prospects of developing friendly relations between the two states. The decision of the Conference constituted the first official statement of the Communist Party on the nationality issue since April 1944. The Hungarian CP greeted "heroic Yugoslavia, Czechoslovakia, and Romania," their Communist Parties struggling against reaction, and it welcomed the pronouncements of Petru Groza on the question of the Hungarian population in Transylvania. The Hungarian Communists emphasized in their document that they would do everything to deepen the relations with the neighboring states on the basis of mutual respect and as good neighbors.[24] According to the armistice agreements the relations between Hungary and her neighbors were not considered as interstate relations until the formal signing of the Peace Treaties. In the words of Hungary's Foreign Minister, the developing relations with the neighboring states were "platonic," in which the sides concerned could only express their policies. In spite of the limitations, there were in fact several contacts between Hungary and Romania, most of them on interparty levels, especially between the two Communist Parties and the Social Democratic Parties.

The leftist press in Hungary praised the Groza regime through most of 1945 and the beginning of 1946. Groza was frequently interviewed and quoted by the communist *Szabad Nép* and the Social Democratic *Népszava*. The interviews and the articles painted a very optimistic picture of the future Hungarian–Romanian relations, stressing the correct line pursued by the Groza government in Romania.

However, parallel to the development of "platonic" ties between Hungary and her neighbors, including for example the first trade agreement signed with Romania in August 1945, the public in Hungary was aware that not everything was rosy in the life of the Hungarians in Transylvania. The Hungarian Communists just could not sweep under the carpet the disturbing news from Transylvania and the persecution of the Hungarian minority by the Slovak Communists in Slovakia.

The promises from the Romanian side of open borders between the two states, in a spirit described some 25 years later by Frigyes Puja in his book, remained only on paper. Groza was interviewed by *Népszava* in August 1945 and asked why severe measures had been adopted by the Romanians along the border, which "hindered communication between the two countries."[25] Groza cited cases of financial speculation and smuggling, which necessitated stricter measures of control. Such issues marked the beginning of steps which actually loosened the contacts between the two states, and eventually led to the growing isolation of the Hungarian minority in Romania from Hungary. For years, sources in Hungary kept silent about this process, and only during the last few years have some details come to light, including the reaction of the Hungarians in Romania to the strained relations between the two states. One such publication in Hungary was an article on Gyárfás Kurkó, one of the leaders of the Hungarian

National Alliance (MNSz) and a populist writer of renowned reputation in Hungary. The article described the disappointment of Hungarians in Transylvania when the promised customs union between the two states was not announced during Groza's visit in Hungary in May 1947.[26]

As the future of Transylvania was becoming an acute problem in the relations between the two sides, the Hungarian Communists took a more critical line toward the Romanian policies in Transylvania. The Party's official position was that the Groza government, although sincere in its policies, was often incapable of acting against reactionary elements among the Romanian "historical" parties. The Communist press frequently published evidence of the gap between the good will of the "democratic forces" in Romania and the slow implementation of promises made to the Hungarians. According to the HCP, the Hungarian and Romanian reactionary elements went hand in glove in their efforts to thwart the advances of the democratic forces. Hungarian Communist criticism of the situation in Romania became more outspoken during the "final battle" for the future of Transylvania's borders at the Paris Peace Conference.[27] By then, in 1946, Hungary could claim that "democrats in Transylvania" had foreseen the current developments in Transylvania a year before, and had warned of the difficulties of the Romanian regime in coping with the forces of reaction.

The Hungarian Communist media condemned some aspects of Romania's nationality policy; in one such criticism, *Társadalmi Szemle*, the HCP theoretical monthly, observed that "lack of confidence is starting to show itself among the Hungarians in Transylvania" when facing a democratic regime which has frequently given up before the reaction's pressure.[28] Moreover, criticism was leveled not only against the reactionary forces in Romania but also at the Groza regime, which was not pursuing a consistent line on the issue of the Hungarians' civil rights. The Hungarian Communists' critical position vis-à-vis the Romanian regime should be seen against the background of the competition for the future of Transylvania, and Hungary's diplomatic campaign to achieve even limited changes in the emerging borders proposed, or rather pressed, by the great powers. Considering that the fate of Transylvania—just as the situation of the Hungarians in Slovakia—had clear repercussions on the political map of Hungary, the Hungarian Communists were interested to appear as defenders of the Hungarian minority abroad. As it was clear that the vast numbers of Hungarians would find themselves once again living outside the borders of Hungary, the Communists had to maintain their line, and at the same time even to justify the positions of the neighboring

Communist Parties. It was certainly a difficult road to take, and with all the servitude to Moscow, the local Communists had to maneuver in order to advance their own position in the struggle for power. Thus it was in the Hungarian Communist interest to discredit to a certain extent the Groza government for not acting firmly enough against the forces of reaction.

The "public relations" of the Romanians were better in the eyes of the Soviets for obvious reasons, and all that the Hungarian Communists could do was to point out that the "democratization" of Romania had not proceeded as smoothly as the Romanian Communists would have liked to present it, and the situation of the Hungarians in Transylvania was an indication of the state of affairs in this respect. At the same time, the Hungarian Communists, who were pushing for the "democratization" of Hungary, had to expose the still-active voices from Transylvania advocating autonomous solution for the area.

The leftist forces in Romania acted firmly to silence any such voices, and the uproar created by a small group of Hungarian Social Democrats in Transylvania may well illustrate this point. The Social Democratic Party's section in Cluj, or rather the Hungarian leadership of the section, discussed at the beginning of 1946 the frequently raised possibility of an independent, autonomous Transylvania. Such speculations, in line with the situation that had prevailed during the months of the political vacuum following the expulsion of the Romanian administration by the Soviet military authorities, were out of touch with the new realities created by the formation of the Groza government. The Political Office of the Romanian Social Democratic Party and the Party's Chairman, Titel Petrescu, branded the position of the Hungarians in the Cluj branch of the Party as "thoughtless actions of a few Hungarian chauvinists . . . interested in stirring up disturbance aiming at the disintegration of Romania."[29]

By the beginning of 1946, international contacts were intensified in preparation for the various phases of the Peace Conference. This process ended in the Paris Peace Treaties, and with Hungary's reluctant acceptance of the new diktat imposed first of all by the Soviet Union.

After years of attempts by Hungarian historiography to present the results of the Peace Conference as an inevitable consequence of Hungary's war guilt, some new assessments have recently been voiced in Hungary, proffering a more realistic picture of Hungary's lost battle in 1946. Such was the sharp criticism of some aspects of the Paris Peace Treaties by Mihály Korom, one of the more prolific writers on Hungary's postwar history.[30] He pointed out that Hungary's proposals for a modification of the Hungarian–Romanian border along a more ethnic line were not supported by "any of the great powers," and he left to the reader to guess that the Soviet Union was among those great powers. According to this view Hungary could not reach any "positive modification," and consequently a quarter of the Hungarian nation remained outside the borders of Hungary, without adequate guarantees for the protection of their national rights. This was, in Korom's view, a "grave shortcoming" of the Peace Treaties, even though the great powers did not approve the collective expulsion of the Hungarians from Czechoslovakia. A similar view was upheld in several other Hungarian works belonging to this "new wave" in Hungarian historiography, such as Sándor Balogh's studies on the foreign policy and political strifes in postwar Hungary.[31] These studies underscore the activities of the Hungarian Communists at the time in seeking to achieve a more favorable decision at the Peace Conference. The Communist perception that all Hungary had to do was to win the confidence of the Soviet Union by demonstrating her resolute struggle against the reactionary elements, is being more and more criticized by Hungarian historiography.

The Hungarian Communists participated in the frantic diplomatic activity to assure better conditions for Hungary at the Peace Conference. In the high ranking delegations that toured Moscow, London, and Washington in spring 1946, the Communist representatives played a prominent role. Thus Ernö Gerö seemed very satisfied as Prime Minister Nagy and Foreign Minister Gyöngyösi were bewildered by the warm welcome the Hungarian delegation had received in Moscow in April 1946. Stalin's magnanimous gestures were received with great relief by the Hungarian delegation.[32] The highlight of the visit was the understanding—or what seemed to be the understanding—on the part of the Soviets of Hungary's arguments in regard to the borders with Romania. The Soviets reminded the Hungarians that Article 19 of the Romanian armistice agreement left the issue of at least a part of Transylvania open. The Soviets urged the Hungarians to open direct negotiations with the Romanian side before raising any specific demands. This was also in agreement with Hungary's position, but previously rejected by Romania on grounds—phrased diplomatically—that there was nothing to discuss with Hungary on the future of Transylvania.

The Hungarians returned from Moscow in an almost "revisionist" mood, and the Communists could present, for the first time, what seemed to them to be a solid Soviet backing for eventual Hungarian gains at the Peace conference. The euphoria in Hungary was shared by all political factors and parties participating in the coalition gov-

ernment. Headlines, such as that in *Kis Ujság*, the organ of the
Smallholders, that "Hungarian democracy could count on the support of the USSR in all issues," were characteristic of the Hungarian
press, including of course the Communist Party.

For a short period, the Communists could reap at home the results of the Moscow meeting: the majority of the Social Democrats
approved closer relations with the Communists—after all, who would
oppose such a winner, supported by the Soviet Union? Rákosi and
Szakasits appeared at a joint mass rally in Budapest and described the
fruitful results of the Moscow visit. Both leaders expressed in their
speeches Hungary's thanks to the Soviet Union, which "dealt a fatal blow to Hungarian reaction." József Révai, naturally, was elected
as Deputy Chairman of the Parliament's Foreign Affairs Committee,
which was in charge of formulating Hungary's case for the forthcoming Peace Conference. At the time, albeit for a short period, Révai
presented in his public appearances an irredentist line, which the in
words of Stephen Kertész "would have satisfied even the League of
Revision of the Horthy regime." The Communist Party carried verbatim the optimistic post–Moscow line. Révai declared in one of his major speeches at the Budapest Academy of Music that while Hungary
could not demand ethnic borders, it would raise territorial demands
and would strive to safeguard the Hungarians wherever they lived.
He outlined the state of relations with Romania and Czechoslovakia,
emphasizing that Hungary had no territorial demands from Slovakia,
where the main issue was the danger of expulsion of the Hungarians. Speaking on the relations with Romania, Révai praised Groza's
policies, and amidst cheers from the audience stated that in regard to
Romania, Hungary was not pursuing a policy of "all or nothing" but it
"wants something from Romania, and shall reach it by consolidating
our friendship and good neighborhood."[33]

It should be noted that the Communist leaders expressed themselves more in rhetorical terms rather than presenting detailed, concrete proposals on the future of Hungary's borders and the fate of the
Hungarians living in the neighboring states. They were also cautious
in capitalizing on Soviet support, which, as they must have known,
was only temporary. Rákosi, for example, presented the Moscow talks
as the "manifestation of the achievements of the Hungarian people in
one and a half years, raising from the abyss to rebirth,"—a phrase
frequently used by Communist speakers.[34]

The Communists could now become the main element that brought
an improvement in Hungary's foreign relations, but at the same time
they intimated that Hungary should be "realistic"—in less euphemistic
terms, she should be prepared for a debacle. Enjoying, what seemed

at the time Soviet support for Hungarian demands at the Peace Conference, the Communists began to tackle the various issues of Hungary's future foreign policy. The line was to be, no doubt, an echo of Soviet policy, but the Hungarians could get some leeway to raise issues which served their specific interests. One such case was the issue of regional cooperation among the states of the Danube Basin, a favorite theme of Hungary's foreign policy in several periods since the end of World War II, especially after 1966. The editor in chief of the Communist Party's theoretical monthly, Béla Fogarasi, depicted the prospects for regional cooperation, emphasizing the need to solve the nationality problem in the area under a regime which would erase all remnants of nationalism.[35] Hungary was looking forward to the new era of fruitful cooperation as an equal partner, freed from the policies of the exploiting classes. However, the author went on, the states of the area would have to solve the nationality problems in a spirit of friendship. He could only praise Yugoslavia's nationality policy, hinting that not everything was correct in Czechoslovakia's and Romania's policies toward the Hungarians. Fogarasi quoted Endre Ady's verses on the common grief of the nations of the Danube, a grief which under the new conditions should be transformed into a common goal. On this issue of the Danubian regional cooperation the Communists adopted a common line with the Smallholders. One of their leading politicians, Pál Auer, emphasized the need for "institutional cooperation" not only in the economic field but on the nationality issue as well. The nations of the area should acquaint each other with their culture, and the minority problems should be solved by mixed committees.[36]

While all of Hungary's political parties that were participating in the coalition government looked forward optimistically following the Moscow visit of the country's leadership, the decisions of the Council of Foreign Ministers in Paris of May 7, 1946 struck a Hungary that was quite unprepared for the "new Trianon" agreed upon by the Great Powers. On the eve of the decision in Paris, following the "advice" of the Soviet leadership, Hungary did try to negotiate with Romania, or at least to air the problems between the two states. Pál Sebestyén, a senior official of the Hungarian Foreign Ministry, held talks in Bucharest with Prime Minister Petru Groza and Foreign Minister G. Tătărescu. The Two Romanian leaders explained to the Hungarian guest that Romania's position was based on solid Soviet support for the country's territorial integrity. It was more than ironic that the Hungarian diplomat should have come to Bucharest with the presupposition of the same support from the Soviet side. Actually, the Romanian refusal to negotiate with Hungary on the territorial problems was based on Soviet promises.[37]

Romania's reaction to the decisions in Paris were enthusiastic, and cut across political lines. The jubilant Communists could only wink at the headlines in Iuliu Maniu's paper: "Transylvania Is Ours Forever,"[38] a style echoed in all the Romanian press.

Hungary reacted as if she had been dealt a fatal blow. Perhaps most embarrassed were the Communists, who only days before had portrayed the Moscow visit of Gerö and Nagy as "victory for Hungarian democracy." Hungary's initial tactic, shared by the Communists and Smallholders, was to play down the true meaning of the agreement reached in Paris, which meant the actual return of Hungary to the prewar Trianon borders. While Romania presented the decisions as definitive, Hungary viewed them only as a recommendation from the Peace Conference.

The deep disappointment felt in Hungary placed Rákosi—Stalin's most faithful disciple—in a rather difficult and delicate situation. For a short time, the Communist Party did not automatically follow Moscow's line, as it needed time to adjust itself to the rapidly changing situation, and to explain away the Paris debacle. The Party "reorganized" its Foreign Affairs Committee, removing its chairman and the editor of *Társadalmi Szemle*, Béla Forgarasi—as if the problem had to do with the functioning of the Party rather than the double dealing policy of the Soviet Union. The Central Committee now branded the Moscow visit as having been effectuated "too late"[39] and criticized high expectations from Moscow talks.

A major, but unsuccessful, Hungarian diplomatic thrust took place in May 1946 with the visit of a Hungarian delegation led by Prime Minister Nagy and Rákosi to London and Washington. The Hungarians failed in both places to enlist support for the various proposals for the Peace Treaties.[40] Hungarian historiography claims that the visit resulted in a further isolation of Hungary in the international arena, as Romania and Czechoslovakia bitterly complained about Hungary's unfriendly attitude in trying to win Western support.[41]

In the two Western capitals, members of the Hungarian delegation, including Rákosi, spoke as if they firmly believed that the issue of Hungary's borders, especially with Romania, should not be closed.[42] Rákosi repeated several times that Stalin had encouraged him to try direct negotiations with the Romanians. From the various diplomatic reports on Rákosi's visit to Washington and London, Rákosi by no means appears as one still dedicated to following Hungary's pre–May 7th line. The Hungarian delegation's only achievement in Washington was the U.S. promise to support Hungarian territorial and ethnic claims if the Soviet Union would agree to reopen the issue,[43] which, at the time, the U. S. was almost sure would not be the case. Whether Rákosi and his fellow Communists were privy to the Soviet intention not to reopen the case still remains an open question. In any case, both in Washington and London, where they received even less support, the Hungarians made a good impression. Indeed, Rákosi appeared as one of the staunch champions of Hungarian national goals. At a news conference after his return, Rákosi emphasized one main aspect of the delegation's visit to the two Western capitals—their presence there had been a blow to the "myth of the Iron Curtain."[44] Rákosi clearly aimed to place the visit against the background of the wider aspects of international relations rather than on the critical issues that preoccupied Hungary at the time.

Following the May 7th decision at the Council of the Foreign Ministers in Paris, and during the visit of the Hungarian delegation to the Western capitals, the relations between the Communists and the Smallholders entered into a critical phase, culminating in what Hungarian historiography describes as the "1946 summer crisis." Brewing for a long time between the coalition partners, the crisis naturally spilled over to the issues of the "Hungarian Peace," as the problem of the Peace Treaty with Hungary was termed. The Communists—who themselves did not, and perhaps could not, formulate a clear plan of their own on Hungary's future borders—accused the Smallholders of sabotaging all attempts at outlining a well–defined plan based on a realistic assessment of the situation. Moreover, the Communists, who felt the coming blows that Hungary was about to suffer at the formal convening of the Peace Conference, intensified their fault–finding propaganda about Hungary's too–slow process of democratization, which was falling short of the Soviet expectations. They stressed that now Hungary would be penalized for the reactionary elements still active in her political life. Their presence, the Communist Party press stated, was the reason why Hungary did not enjoy international support for her cause. As the crisis with the Smallholders intensified, the Communist press asked rhetorically:

> if the conditions for a Hungarian Peace not only have not improved, but actually are worsening, should not the blame be laid on those who are responsible for the Hungarian democracy having stepped one or even two steps backward, after it had stepped one step forward with great difficulties?[45]

The Hungarian Communists' adjustment to the realities emerging from the opening of the Peace Conference was slow and hesitating. Eventually, they stepped in line with Moscow, and made overtures for a reconciliation with their Romanian counterparts, but not before

they had gone to great lengths to inclucate the notion that they were
the real champions of the Hungarian minority rights in the neighboring countries. It was becoming clear that at least one–third of the
nation would go on living—once again—outside the boundaries of the
country.

Hungarian criticism of Romania's nationality policies became frequent and overt. The Hungarian Communists treated their Romanian
comrades very cautiously in all issues regarding Romania's nationality policy, and it seems that the Rákosi leadership was not convinced
that Romania would pursue a policy which would earn the praise of
the Hungarian Communists in face of local public opinion.

The Romanian Communist Party published its guidelines for
the nationality policy in July 1946, while formulating the Party's
line toward nationalities living in Romania.[46] *Szabad Nép* analyzed
Gheorghiu–Dej's presentation of the decisions in a fairly cool tone,
and remarked that in regard to relations with Hungary, Gheorghiu–
Dej had not reached Groza's perspectives, and was treating the issue
only in a superficial way.[47] The Hungarian press, including Communist-
controlled publications, led a last–ditch attempt to attract Western
eyes to the situation of the Hungarians abroad, especially in Romania and Czechoslovakia. Thus, *New Hungary*, published in English in
Budapest, devoted almost entire issues to the plight of Hungarians
in the neighboring states. In June 1946, coinciding with the formal
opening of the Paris Peace Conference, the journal wrote:

> Despite Premier Groza's decidedly pro–Hungarian policy,
> Hungarian democracy does not consider that Hungarians
> living in Romania are in safety. There is a lack of freedom
> from fear.

The article emphasized the gap between the official pronouncements and reality in the Romanian authorities' attitude toward the
Hungarian minority. It also criticized the state of relations between
the two countries, and hinted that the negative attitude toward the
Hungarians living in Romania was also manifesting itself in relations
toward Hungary. According to the Hungarian journal,

> the Groza government contents itself with theoretical em-
> phasis on the necessity of relations with Hungary, whereas
> in practice it sanctions numerous decrees which are anything
> but propitious to the interests of the two nations.[48]

Hungarian–Romanian relations were at their lowest ebb during
the days of the Peace Conference, especially in July–September 1946.
The Romanian press, including the Communist organs, described the
Hungarian delegation to Paris as made up of "revisionist–diversionist

elements,"[49] and minimized or completely ignored the fact that a leading Communist, Ernö Gerö, was one of the top members of the Hungarian delegation in Paris. In this war of words, the Hungarians on their part reacted with dismay to the tough Romanian position at the Paris Peace Conference as presented by Foreign Minister Gheorghe Tătărescu, who rejected talks between the two states in order to solve the territorial dispute. *Szabad Nép* wrote that the "voice we heard at the Peace Conference was not the voice of the new Romanian democracy but that of Tătărescu, the Prime Minister of the old reactionary Romania,"[50] a reference to Tătărescu's premiership between 1933 and 1937. Hungary, the paper continued, did not expect such an attitude from the representatives of the new Romania, and it rejected the Romanian position that Hungary did not have the right to interfere in the lives of the 1.5 million Hungarians living in Romania.

Romania, supported by the participants, rejected the two Hungarian plans presented to the Conference. By September 5, 1946, the Conference had reached an agreement on the border between Romania and Hungary: the borders of Trianon were restored.

The Hungarian Communists were still attempting to save at least something. *Szabad Nép* carried a dramatic last–minute call to Romania to "give up something"—if only symbolically—which would enable the Party to present some achievement to the Hungarian public.[51] For the first time the Hungarian Communists were openly declaring that the same principle which guided the Romanian Communists not to give up territories while fighting the Romanian reactionary elements was valid for Hungary as well. Thus, *Szabad Nép* emphasized that it should be in the interest of Romanian democracy to support the minimal demands of Hungarian democrats. The Hungarian paper admitted that Romania's record at the end of the War had been positive, but for the sake of the "Hungarian workers and peasants" who had aided the Soviet Union, the clause on Transylvania should be reconsidered. The article concluded that Hungary's desire that even a small part of Transylvania with its 1.5 million Hungarians should belong to Hungary was a "legitimate one and Hungary deserves it." The issue of collective war guilt had to be coped with by the Communists, and the article in *Szabad Nép* rejected the policy that the bill for Hungary's wrongs in the past should be now presented to the nation.

The formal decision of the Peace Conference was received with great shock in Hungary. Once again the Communists were in the most delicate situation. Now, they had to "strengthen Hungarian democracy under stern conditions of peace,"[52] and the organ of the Communist Party wrote in a desperate tone that Hungary had put

forward only limited and minimal demands at the Conference, hopeful
until the last moment. Regarding the future ties between Hungary
and the Hungarian minority abroad, the Party promised that

> we shall not allow ourselves to be cut off from a million
> and a half Hungarians [in Romania], and the relations with
> them will be stronger as we shall build a happy and more
> democratic home for our people living in the territory that
> has remained ours.

It was a promise that the Hungarians quickly learned would not be
kept, and soon the Hungarians living in Hungary were cut off from
those living beyond the new–old borders.

Budapest and Prague

There is no doubt "of all the difficult substantive issues the postwar government of Hungary had to face, none was more intractable
than the relations between Budapest and Prague."[53] After World
War II the Hungarian population in Slovakia, as in Romania, had to
pay the price for the past: in Czechoslovakia yet another account was
added to the long historical accounts that many Slovaks felt had to
be settled with the Hungarians—that of Hungary's participation in
the dismemberment of the state in 1938–1939. Those Slovak nationalists who had championed the dismemberment of the state between
the two World Wars were of course the most vociferous in opposing
Hungary's interests in Slovakia. After World War II, the mantle of
anti–Magyarism was taken over by the Slovak Communists who rode
the wave of anti–Hungarian sentiment, a very popular issue. The
Communist support for measures denying the rights of Hungarians
and expelling a large number of that minority from Czechoslovakia
should be seen against this background.[54]

In a broader perspective, the presence of Germans and Hungarians became the main issue through which the Communists could
press for the "democratization" of the country. Like the Germans,
the Hungarians were to pay a collective price for having stabbed the
Czechoslovak Republic in the back. The formula of "collective sin-
collective punishment" seemed very logical to the Slovak Communists,
who pursued a nationalist line, while of course paying lip service to
the "correct Marxist–Leninist nationality policy." It was clear to the
Slovak Communist leadership, in particular to Gustav Husák, that
the Slovak peasant, while not quite familiar with the principles of
correct Marxist–Leninist nationality policy, nevertheless appreciated
the expulsion of the Magyars from his village.

Overtly accused by the Communists in Hungary in 1946 of being
a "Slovak nationalist," Husák left no doubt as to the policies that his

party would pursue immediately after the Liberation:

> The Magyars should understand that no territory will be relinquished to Hungary, and we shall not even discuss the topic with anyone. The Slovak peasant and worker who was shoved out from the rich counties and for centuries forced into mountainous corners, must again return to those ancient Slovak territories, and gain opportunity for a suitable life.[55]

Although recent Czechoslovak and Hungarian sources have been critical of the position taken at the time by Slovak communists on the issue of the 600,000 Hungarians living in the country at the end of World War II, without implicating Husák personally, it would be superficial to see the policy of Czechoslovakia as purely that of "Beneš' leadership" which initiated the collective resettlement of the Hungarians,[56] as some Hungarian sources still describe the events of those years. The leadership was that of Beneš, but the hands were clearly of the Communists, even though they did not become complete masters of the situation until February 1948. In the struggle for power in Czechoslovakia, the nationality issue—both the German and the Hungarian—played a significant role in the internal and external policies of the country, and the Communists were at least one of the major forces in shaping the respective policies toward the two nationalities.

The history of the Hungarian minority in postwar Czechoslovakia is clearly divided into the period before and after 1948, when the Communists reversed, albeit slowly, their line of discrimination against the Hungarians.[57] Until February 1948 there were several main features to the Communists' policy toward the Hungarians: resettlement, expulsion, re–Slovakization, and, in addition, an agreement on an exchange of population between the two states was signed in February 1946.

The ultimate dream of the Slovak Communists, and others, may have been to expel the Hungarians from Slovakia, but this was more wishful thinking than a realistic plan, as the major powers were opposed. The Soviets were certainly involved in the same double game that they were playing in relations between Hungary and Romania, but in spite of Slovak boasting that Moscow supported their steps toward the Hungarians, the USSR could not support the expulsion of the Hungarian minority from Slovakia. It could, and did, reject any Hungarian territorial demands from Slovakia.

The Slovak Communists cannot be accused of too much discrimination, as they treated *all* Hungarians in an equal way. Thus, when following the Košiece program, the Slovak Communists implemented a set of legal restrictions on the Hungarians, and contemplated their removal either by resettlement or expulsion, these measures included Hungarian Communists as well, a fact critically appraised by later Slovak historiography.[58] According to later Slovak sources, the Slovak Communists did not consider the need for further participation of Hungarian "progressive" elements in the political life of the country,[59] but preferred them to build a new life somewhere else. In October 1946, for example, the Slovak Communist Party consisted of 514 Hungarian members and 150,079 Slovaks.[60] In a review of the Slovak work in which this statistic was published, a Hungarian commentator remarked on the ironic circumstance that it was the Hungarians who had built up the Slovak Communist Party between the two world wars. The low number of Hungarians in the Slovak CP was due not only to deportations and the population exchange with Hungary, but also to a policy of rejecting Hungarian participation in the Party. After the Communist takeover of 1948, this aspect of not so fraternal discrimination gradually stopped.

Legally the expulsion or rejection of the Hungarians from the Slovak CP was explained by a whole legal edifice which started from the decree on the loss of Czechoslovak citizenship by all Hungarians residing in the state. Likewise, the Praesidium of the Slovak National Council decreed in May 1945 that Hungarians could not be members of political parties and bodies participating in the Slovak National Council. Slovak sources writing on the period stress that some Slovak Communists, especially those who had been active in the Party during the interwar years alongside their Hungarian comrades, were not content with these discriminatory steps. Well tested in patterns of behavior during emergency, some Hungarian Communists "left immediately for Hungary, not waiting for the general expulsion." Others joined later either by force or by choice the re–Slovakization campaign and were active in Southern Slovakia in "furthering the victory of the working class in our Republic."

Hungary repeatedly called the attention of the Allied Control Commission (ACC) to the anti–Hungarian steps taken in Slovakia, and also turned directly to the three major powers. The 184 notes sent by Hungary to the ACC between April 1945 and July 1946 do not seem to include the delicate aspects of conflict between the two Communist parties. But there were other problems related to the daily harassment and forceful steps against Hungarians in Slovakia to which Hungary tried to call the attention of the major powers. But the issue of the treatment of the Hungarian "progressive" elements in Slovakia loomed over the relations between the two Communist parties, each of them in desperate need for support by the masses. From early 1946 the Communist press in Hungary took to task the Slovak democratic elements, chiefly the Communists, for having committed a mistake in "not choosing the brave way of opposing chauvinism," as Tito had done in Yugoslavia and Groza had promised to do in Romania.[61] The Hungarian Communists warned that Czechoslovakia was pursuing a policy of collective punishment for all Hungarians. Rakosi and his colleagues clearly understood that the same rules of the game applied in Slovakia as in Hungary—the Communists needed to present themselves as loyal defenders of national interests, but in the case of Slovakia it was the Hungarians who had to pay the price. Rákosi's struggle to "democratize" Hungary was obviously hampered by anti–Hungarian steps taken in Slovakia, at a time when the conflict with Romania was still very evident.

Lacking clear Soviet statements, or perhaps understanding the double game played by the Soviet Union, the Hungarian Communists tried to present evidence of Soviet reservations about the anti–Hungarian steps taken in Slovakia. Such evidence was rather scanty and, judging from the tone of some articles in the Hungarian Communist press, the authors themselves did not seem utterly convinced of what they were writing. For example, *Társadalmi Szemle* mentioned that Radio Moscow and some articles published in the *Moskovskii Bolshevik* praising Yugoslavia's and Romania's nationality policy toward the Hungarians and other minorities "clearly highlighted the Soviet position in this respect"; the point was that the Soviets expressed their reservations by way of omitting Czechoslovakia from their praise.[62]

One aspect on which the Hungarian Communists seemed very keen was their reaction to the attitude of the Slovak Communists and others toward the Hungarians and the Germans, who were, in the words of *Társadalmi Szemle*, "placed under the same hat." While Hungary was expelling its German population (some 136,000 Germans were transferred from Hungary to the U. S. occupation zone in Germany during 1946) it was counterproductive for the Communists to apply the same yardstick for the Germans and the Hungarians in Slovakia. The expulsion of the Germans from the liberated areas of Eastern Europe created a triangle by which the Beneš government sought to transfer the Hungarians from Slovakia in place of the Germans expelled from Hungary, and at a later stage attempted to resettle Hungarians from Slovakia in Bohemia, in place of the expelled Germans. The Hungarian government was certainly annoyed at this linkage between the German and the Hungarian problem, as it proved the Czechoslovak government's determination to place both issues "under the same hat."

Yet another angle to the problematic relationship between Czechoslo-

vakia and Hungary was the situation of the Slovaks in Hungary. They
were the logical candidates for a population exchange from a Hungarian point of view. The Hungarian government formulated its policy
toward the Slovaks very slowly. On the one hand it tried to prove that
the Hungarian regime would not react with anti–Slovak measures as a
reprisal for the steps taken against the Hungarians in Slovakia, but on
the other hand there was clearly tension building up as the Hungarian authorities reported on the developments in Slovakia. Until the
population exchange agreement was signed in 1946, the Communist
line in Hungary sought to stress that not too many Slovaks would
wish to leave Hungary for Slovakia. The Communist front organization among the Slavs in Hungary, including the Slovaks, was the
Antifasticky Front Slavonov, whose organ, *Sloboda*, which reflected
the Communist line, frequently expressed the Slovaks' trust in the
"new Hungarian democracy."[63] in marked contrast to the reports on
the disappointment of the Hungarian leftists in Slovakia with the new
regime's policies toward them.

In December 1945 the first of two series of negotiations took
place between Hungarian and Czechoslovak high–level officials with
a view to reaching an agreement on an exchange of populations involving Slovaks from Hungary and Hungarians from Slovakia. The
talks ended in deadlock as Czechoslovakia insisted on a one–sided expulsion of the Hungarians, but eventually a framework was worked
out for an exchange by which equal numbers of Slovaks and Hungarians would leave the two states. Statistical differences have made it
almost impossible to calculate the numbers involved, as there are various estimates about the actual size of the two nationalities. Hungary
claimed that in the 1941 census there were 75,920 Slovaks in Hungary,
while the Slovak authorities maintained that their number reached as
many as 450,000. At the same time the Czechoslovak regime spoke of
652,000 Hungarians in their country, while the Hungarian estimates
were between 700,000 and 800,000.[64]

The agreement on the exchange of populations was reached following the second round of negotiations between the representatives of
the two states, and was signed on February 27, 1946. The Czechoslovak side was very keen on its final goals, and Clementis, who headed
the Czechoslovak delegation, declared that his country wished to become a national state by relocating the German and Hungarian minorities. According to the agreement, Slovaks from Hungary were
called upon to register voluntarily for transfer to Slovakia, while the
same number of Hungarians would have to register for resettlement in
Hungary. The Hungarian Communists refused to accept any proposal
which would transfer the whole Hungarian population of Slovakia to

Hungary,[65] and had serious reservations about the process by which Hungarians were to be selected by the Slovak authorities for resettlement in Hungary.[66] The Hungarian Communists attempted successfully to make capital out of the strained relations with Czechoslovakia. They not only appeared as champions of the Hungarians in Slovakia but also tried to limit the number of Slovaks who volunteered to leave Hungary. There were two reasons for this attempt: to prove the loyalty of the Slovak minority to the new Hungary, and to lower the number of Hungarians who would be resettled from Slovakia. The Communists initiated a Hungarian government statement of March 21, 1946 which complained of the "pressure" on the Slovaks to sign up for transfer by the members of the Czechoslovak Committee which was dealing with this matter among the Slovaks, in accordance with the agreement between the two governments.[67]

The agreement on the exchange of populations did not immediately solve the problems between the two states. Indeed, to a certain extent it complicated them. During June–July 1946—a time when the Hungarian Communists were busy explaining away the debacle on the borders with Romania—a new crisis erupted with Czechoslovakia, when the latter asked the support of the Peace Conference for the expulsion of an additional 200,000 Hungarians from Slovakia. In other words, the Czechoslovak authorities were determined to solve once and for all the question of the Hungarian presence in the Czechoslovak national state.

In June 1946 a new element was added to the complicated issue between the two states: the Czechoslovak authorities had started a campaign of "re–Slovakization," whose essence was to re–award the Czechoslovak citizenship to those Hungarians who would declare themselves as Slovaks, and to transfer to Hungary those who refused to adhere to a supposed "Slovak ancestry" and would cling to their Slovak roots. Although the campaign was to be carried out on a "voluntary basis," and supposedly no pressure was applied on the Hungarians to help them discover or rediscover their Slovak roots, some 400,000 Hungarians, many of whom did not even speak the Slovak language, declared themselves as Slovaks.[68] The methods of persuasion were of such a nature that later Slovak sources could aptly describe the campaign as one of the "most delicate" actions undertaken in that period.[69] The authorities attempted to portray it as "due process of law," and in the wake of Hungarian government complaints about the process of re–Slovakization the Czechoslovaks frequently published details on the files of those who had declared themselves Slovaks on a "voluntary basis." Some 81,142 such requests were turned down on the grounds that the applicants could not prove genuine Slovak roots, and during 1947 there was a further slowing down of approvals. Following the rejection of this considerable number of files, the Czechoslovak statistics turned out some 326,679 "re–Slovakized" persons.

The Slovak historiography emphasizes to this day that in Southern Slovakia there were indeed many "superficially Magyarized" Slovaks who had to be "helped to return to their original Slovak nationality," but these sources cannot deny that the majority of those who underwent the process of re–Slovakization were in fact of pure Hungarian extraction. Some 533,900 Hungarians reappeared in the 1960 Czechoslovak census, which is seen by Slovak studies as an indication that actually the process of re–Slovakization did not bring any substantive changes in the area,[70] but did "cause grave damage to the relationship between the Slovak and Hungarian population." This cynical game played with a national minority, not unlike the fluctuations in the status of the Macedonians in Bulgaria, was bound to embitter for years to come the already heavily burdened delicate patchwork of Hungarian–Slovak relations.

A Slovak study stresses that "even if it sounds strange," the situation of the re–Slovakized Hungarians actually improved because they could join social and political organizations and enjoyed full rights.[71] It was certainly one of the bizarre ironies of the emerging postwar realities in Eastern Europe that Hungarians were able to join ranks of the Slovak Communist Party, of course as Slovaks, and contribute to the building of a new and democratic Czechoslovakia. Some comrades certainly found it hard at the time to swallow such an implementation of the Leninist nationality policy.

The reaction of the Hungarian Communist Party to the campaign of re–Slovakization was one of dismay. The Communist press reported scathingly on the attempts of the Slovak authorities, including the Communists, to "eliminate the Hungarians as a national group."[72] The conflict between the two Communist parties was entirely overt, as the Hungarian Communists found it impossible to account for the fact that the Slovak rightist elements were embracing solutions propagated by the Slovak Communists, as borne out by the campaign for re–Slovakization. At the same time the Hungarian CP could not but support the anti–Slovak attitudes of the other political parties in Hungary. In this regard they rode on the wave of opposition to the policies of neighboring Slovakia. Their delicate situation was clearly influenced by the events in Slovakia. Judging from the Hungarian press at the time, the attitude of the Communists was no less bellicose toward all the political parties in Slovakia than that of their coalition partners. The Communists did try their best to emphasize the anti–Hungarian attitudes of the Slovak bourgeois parties—the Democratic Party among others—but they could not ignore the simple fact that it was the Slovak CP, led by Gustav Husák, that was pressing for the re–Slovakization campaign, the resettlement and expulsion of the Hungarians.[73]

Yet another heavy blow to the relations between the two Communist parties was the process of forceful resettlement of Hungarians within Czechoslovakia. According to the Government's policies, former members of the Hungarian Fascist parties, war criminals, and those elements who tried to eschew productive work were to be transferred to the Western borderlands, especially to replace the expelled Germans. Hungary agreed reluctantly to these steps; naturally it could not defend former members of the fascist movements, yet it expressed reservations about the process by which candidates were singled out for resettlement. There was no doubt in the eyes of the Hungarian authorities that the resettlement measures also applied to persons who did not fall within the category of war criminals and members of fascist parties. Thus, while expressing their approval for the steps taken against former Fascists, the Hungarian Communists also publicized that even "progressive elements" were included in this forceful resettlement, a fact acknowledged by Slovak authors some twenty years later, admitting that "in many cases anti–fascists and communists were among those removed from their areas."[74] On the whole some 44,000 Hungarians were removed from 393 various localities in Southern Slovakia and transported to Western Czechoslovakia.

In February 1947 the authorities put an end to the resettlement of the Hungarians, to a large degree in response to pressure from Hungary and its complaints to the Paris Peace Conference. After the Communist coup of 1948, the Czechoslovak authorities allowed the return to their former homes of those who had been resettled. About half of them returned, thus causing new problems as they reclaimed their property confiscated during the difficult years of 1946–1947.

In 1954 the Slovak CP severely criticized retroactively its policy toward the Hungarians and the Germans, accusing the "national bourgeois group" that had been active in the Party at the time. As Gustav Husak was among those condemned in 1954 for such a deviation, the regime presented a clean slate with regard to the years of persecution of the Hungarian minority. According to the enlightening explanations, the Party had been correct in its policies until hostile elements managed to infiltrate it, manipulating it along a mistaken course. Now these elements had been unmasked and the culprits were caught. However, within several years the line changed, along with the personal fate of some of the leading actors of the early postwar years. In its Twelfth Congress in 1963, and in the ideological plenum held the same year, the Czechoslovak CP presented a new version of the errors committed against the Hungarians until 1948. The Congress rejected the assumption that a "bourgeois nationalist" group had been active in the Party, denying in fact the very existence of such a group. According to this version the activities of Gustav Husak were in the spirit of the Party's line at the time. The 1963 resolutions severely criticized the main features of the Party's policies toward the Hungarians, namely the re–Slovakization and the resettlement. The documents of 1963 also acknowledged that after 1945 there had been "nationalist, anti–Hungarian trends, which also raised their head in the Party."

Gustav Husák published his own version of the events in his book, *Aspects of the Slovak National Revival,* published in 1964, in which he—justly—claimed that the mistakes of the past in regard to the Hungarians were not his own personally but a reflection of the Party's line, for which he took personal responsibility—but not as a culprit. Extensive reviews of Husak's work in Hungary, which appeared in 1969, emphasize Husak's position, condemning the "falsification of evidence" and other misdeeds by means of which Husák and other Party leaders were personally blamed for the mistakes committed with regard to the Hungarians. One such review of Husák's book by Endre Ara'to was published in both a full and an abridged version in *Párttörténeti Közlemények* and *Társadalmi Szemle*[75] and in the Hungarian language newspaper in Bratislava, *Új Szó.* It is of course significant that the Hungarian reviews appeared after 1968, which should be seen in the context of the relationship between the Kádár regime and the post–August 1968 ruler of Czechoslovakia, Gustav Husák, who had indeed been responsible for the policies toward the Hungarians after 1945. Husák, observed the Hungarian reviewer, adopted in 1958 a "true internationalist position" in taking the responsibility for the mistakes committed. The Hungarian reviews quoted speeches and remarks made by Husák in 1968, in which he acknowledged the mistakes of the past by means of a certain degree of self–criticism. Such was the case in an interview given by Husak to the Bratislava *Új Szó* in June 1968 and in his speech before the plenum of the Cultural Association of Hungarian Workers in Czechoslovkia (CSEMADOK) shortly after the Soviet invasion, on September 8, 1968, in which he spoke about the injustices against the Hungarian minority in 1945–1948.[76]

The late sixties brought about a new flareup in the discussions in both countries about the "delicate" issues involved in the fate of the Hungarians in Czechoslovakia in 1945–1948. The dramatic changes

in Czechoslovakia, the position of the Hungarians during the events
of 1968 on the one hand and Hungary's growing involvement in the
fate of the Hungarians abroad after 1968 on the other, provided the
backdrop for numerous publications in both countries. The writings
of Juraj Zvara should be noted. He published in 1965 *Solution of the
Hungarian Nationality Question in Slovakia,* followed by numerous
other writings on this issue. While Zvara outlined the policy of injus-
tice toward the Hungarians, to which the Communists were privy, he
also underscored the negative role of the Slovak right, especially the
Slovak Democratic Party, which pursued a vehement anti–Hungarian
policy. Zvara's covert message was that the Communist attitudes toward the Hungarians should be seen against the background of the
tough competition for power in Slovakia—in other words, if the bourgeois parties were anti–Hungarian, how could the Communists not
participate in settling accounts with the Magyars?

The final stage in the Communization of Czechoslovakia made
the population exchange "obsolete," and after April 1948 the process
was slowed down. However, it was not until June 1949 that the last
family crossed from Slovakia to Hungary[77] All in all, more than 73,000
Slovaks left Hungary, and 68,400 Hungarians left Slovakia. In fact the
number of Hungarians who left Slovakia was higher, as some 6,000
left of their own free will, and another 20,000 to 30,000 lived in areas
to which they had moved after the annexation of areas in Slovakia to
Hungary in November 1938.

The signing of the Treaty of Friendship and Cooperation between
Hungary and Czechoslovakia in April 1949, the last such Treaty signed
between Hungary and a Soviet Bloc state, evinced—at least on the
formal level—the normalization of the relations. In Czechoslovakia
itself there was a gradual improvement in the situation of the Hungarians after 1948. Through a series of steps taken between 1948 and
1958, citizenship was restored to those Hungarians who had lost it
earlier. The formation, in 1949, of CSEMADOK was also indicative
of the changes in the attitude of the regime toward the Hungarian
minority.

Yugoslavia

In contrast to the situation in Romania and Czechoslavakia, the
fate of the Hungarian minority in Yugoslavia after World War II did
not cause special friction between the two states, and neither was
there an open clash between the Communist parties of the two states
until, of course, the rift between the Soviet Union and Yugoslavia in
1948. In Yugoslavia's first two postwar censuses, in 1948 and in 1953,
some 496,000 and 502,000 Hungarians were reported respectively.[78]

Around 90 percent were concentrated in Vojvodina, and the rest in
Croatia and Serbia. Following the war there were two major demographic changes in Yugoslavia—especially in Vojvodina—which had
repercussions on the ethnic map of the area: the expulsion of some
450,000 Germans and 47,500 Hungarians. In contrast to the policies
pursued by the Slovak authorities, the Yugoslavs did not try to "solve"
the Hungarian question in Yugoslavia with expulsions. It seems that
most of those expelled to Hungary were members of the Hungarian
administration who had moved into the area annexed by Hungary
during the war. Other expellees were Hungarian citizens who had
been resettled from Hungary into the annexed areas. Hungary moved
the expelled Hungarians from Yugoslavia into areas from which Germans had previously been expelled westward, and did not make an
international issue out of the incidents, which were seen as a settling
of a bill well deserved by Hungary for its past actions. The Hungarian media in that period also did not make too much of a case of
the imprisonment and even some executions among the 30,000 Hungarians who had been arrested in Yugoslavia. Such steps were not
part of an anti–Hungarian policy, as in Slovakia, but should rather
be seen in the framework of the period of the consolidation of power
in Yugoslavia.[79]

The Hungarian Communist Party often praised the new Yugoslavia's nationality policy, and until 1948 the Rákosi leadership
could feel comfortable with a "quiet front" with the neighboring state,
unlike the problems encountered with Czechoslovakia and Romania.
The Communist press singled out Yugoslavia's attitude toward the
Hungarians as friendly and favorable. For their part, the Hungarian
Communists were eager to elaborate on the favorable developments
in the life of the national minorities living in Hungary. The situation, or rather public attitudes toward Slovaks, made this task more
difficult, but in the case of the South Slavs, as the Slav minorities in
Southern Hungary are called, there were no special problems. The
Communists condemned those elements who opposed the expansion
of cultural and educational facilities to the South Slavs, and promised
to safeguard the right of this minority, which actually was made up
of Serbs, Croats, and Slovenes.

The only disputed issue between Hungary and Yugoslavia was the
exact number of the South Slavs in Hungary. In 1946 the Hungarian CP complained that "some circles in Yugoslavia claim a very high
number of South Slavs in Hungary, on the grounds that all the people
in Hungary with a South Slav name were actually Magyarized Serbs,
Croats or Slovenes."[80] As there were no exact Hungarian statistics,
the problem remained an open issue for several years. The Hungarian

census of 1949 reported 39,000 South Slavs, but taking into consideration the anxieties of South Slavs at the time because of the conflict with Yugoslavia, their numbers may have been higher.

Treaties of Friendship

In the wake of the decisions of the Paris Peace Conference, a new chapter started in Hungary's relations with its neighbors. The Communists had to adjust themselves to the changing realities, or rather had to play the tune that was dictated from Moscow. This was not an easy task as the results of the Peace Conference and the ensuing problems, especially with Czechoslovakia, made it very difficult for the Communists to proceed with the "democratization" of the country. Having received a mere 17 percent in the November 1945 elections, the Hungarian CP intensified its struggle for power, using more brutal force and cunning tactics, but it was unable to present to the nation any practical gains from the results of the Peace Conference. While an article in the Party's theoretical monthly praised the "Soviet peace policy's victory" at the Conference, the same article had to admit that in the "territorial aspects of our peace plans, even the Soviet Union did not support us, and this has surprised many people in Hungary."[81] Of course, the explanation had to be that Hungary not only paid for its crimes in the past, but did not proceed fast enough on the road toward "democratization."

Following the decisions of the Peace Conference, the issues that faced Hungary with Romania and Czechoslovakia were different, and while the "question of the borders was closed," and Hungary had to adjust itself to the territorial aspects of the decisions, the nationality question remained unsolved: the expulsions and the population exchange with Czechoslovakia and the drifting apart of the Hungarians on both sides of the border with Romania. Parallel to the disappointments and the tension with Czechoslovakia, relations with Romania did not basically improve, although both Communist parties, struggling for power in their respective countries, emphasized the new stage in their relations.

The last time the Hungarian Communists overtly criticized Romanian policies toward the Hungarian minority came around the Third Congress of the HCP, in September 1946, when along with praises for the achievements of the new Romania, Ernö Gerö called for the "removal of negative measures by which the friendship between Hungarian and Romanian democracy will be strengthened."[82] Vasile Luca, the Secretary of the Romanian CP—himself of Hungarian origin—represented the Party at the Congress. He expressed the belief that Romania would do everything to assure the rights of the

Hungarian minority in Romania. Luca also said that he was aware of the anxieties in Hungary regarding the fate of the Hungarians in Romania, but the Hungarian public should not worry too much.[83]

With the approach of the crucial November 1946 elections, the Romanian CP stepped up its activities among the Hungarians in Transylvania. The Party line was that only a clear victory for the forces of the Bloc of Democratic Parties (BPD) would assure the equality of the minorities. Gheorghiu–Dej also emphasized this position of his Party to the public in Hungary in an interview with *Szabad Nép*,[84] in which he called for the expansion of relations between the two neighboring states.

The Hungarian CP not only lowered its previous tone of criticism toward the Romanian comrades but also stressed the necessity of un-equivocal Communist victory. "It is time to deal Romanian reaction a decisive blow which will be a victory in the struggle for complete equality," wrote the Hungarian CP daily,[85] comparing the Party's own, rather modest achievement at the polls of November 1945. The Romanian CP did indeed fare much better than the HCP had done a year earlier, with the bloc of Democratic Parties receiving 79.86 percent of the vote, which constituted a major victory for the Communists. *Szabad Nép* warmly greeted Romania, stating that now "it has taken the correct road to solve the nationality question."[86]

As to the Soviet factor in the web of Hungarian–Romanian relations, the HCP continued to emphasize the Soviet support for Romania, as a clear hint that it would be meaningless for anyone in Hungary to hope for a Soviet change in policy in view of its complete support of Romania. *Szabad Nép* quoted an article in *Pravda* based on a correspondent's visit in Transylvania, praising Romania's nationality policy,[87] and recalled that before the Romanian elections the political right had spread rumors that Transylvania would be returned to Hungary. Certainly readers of *Szabad Nép* must have found this allegation rather amusing, as several months before, not the Romanian reactionary elements, but Stalin and Molotov had hinted in Moscow to the Hungarian leadership that the question of Transylvania was still open, and Hungary could raise territorial demands from Romania.

In 1947 the Communist struggle for power was in high gear in both states. Romania was several steps ahead, while Hungary almost envied what the Communist press was labeling the "achievements of Romanian democracy." As to their interstate relations, both tried to normalize them; and the signing of the Peace Treaty by Hungary and Romania in February 1947 gave a new impetus to these attempts. Mutual contacts became more frequent. For example, on the occasion of the Romanian cultural week held in May 1947 in Budapest, Romania's Prime Minister, Petru Groza, visited Hungary with a party of 80 persons. Groza's personal style, his fluency in Hungarian, and his long record of friendship with Hungarians in interwar Romania scored good points among the Hungarian public. In numerous speeches and interviews in the Hungarian language, Groza gave his assurance that Romania had embarked on a new road, based on complete equality of all nationalities living in the country. It was in this atmosphere that *Szabad Nép* praised Groza's line and the RCP's resolute fight against "remnants of the old regime." [88]

Groza's visit to Hungary was reciprocated in November 1947, by Hungary's Prime Minister Lajos Dinnyés. By then there were several fundamental changes in the power structure of the two states: in Hungary, Dinnyes had replaced Ferenc Nagy (who was forced to resign following prolonged Communist pressure against the Smallholders) and in the August 1947 elections the leftist bloc mastered 60 percent of the votes. On the eve of the elections the Communists accused the bourgeois coalition partners of sabotaging Hungary's relations with the neighboring countries.

In Romania the Communists had completed their routing of the National Peasants' Party, and in November 1946 the Party's leader, Iuliu Maniu was sentenced to life imprisonment for having, among other things, collaborated with Western intelligence services. Foreign Minister Tătărescu, who had also represented Romania at the Paris Peace Conference, was replaced by Ana Pauker of the RCP, after having suggested that Romania would benefit from the Marshall Plan.

As the Hungarian Premier acknowledged, not everything was rosy in Hungarian–Romanian relations, and during his talks in Bucharest several issues were discussed which "hindered the development of relations of friendship and cooperation." The main achievement of Dinnyés' visit was the signing of a cultural cooperation agreement between Hungary and Romania—the second such treaty signed by Hungary with an East European state (the first one had been with Bulgaria). Considering that cultural relations between Bulgaria and Hungary were not a top priority in either country, there was certainly more significance to the emerging patterns of Hungarian–Romanian relations. The interesting aspect of the cultural cooperation agreement was that it also contained reference to the advancement of Hungarian culture in Romania and that of the Romanian minority in Hungary. Although the role of the respective states in promoting the culture of their ethnic minorities in the neighboring country was not specified, its significance lay in the very mention of the national minorities in this interstate agreement. Another notable point was the reference to the Romanian minority in Hungary—one of the rare instances when Romania linked in a document the Romanians in Hungary and the Hungarians in Romania. According to Hungarian estimates in 1946 there were 15,000 to 20,000 Romanians living in Hungary,[89] and the Communist Party paid special attention to the welfare of this small community, in an apparent attempt to gain reciprocity in the treatment of the Hungarians in Romania. (In this respect there is a certain parallel in this document of 1947 to the agreement reached thirty years later, by Ceauşescu and Kádár, in 1977, when once again, after years of hushed–up silence, national minorities were mentioned in a document between the two states.) In the following years there were no significant steps in developing cultural relations between the two states, and it took a long time until Hungarian sources unmasked the stagnation in the relations, which had been so warmly outlined in the Groza and Dinnyés visits.

Along with the process of Communist takeovers, the East European states entered into the Soviet led alliance system, formalized by the Treaties of Friendship and Cooperation.[90] Often the timing of the signing of the Treaties was significant, as it indicated difficulties—such as unsolved problems in the relationships between East European states. For example, there was no special significance that the Romanian–Polish Treaty was signed in January 1949, but it was relevant that Hungary signed its last Treaty with Czechoslovakia in April 1949, well after a year following the Communist coup in Prague.

The Treaty of Friendship and Cooperation between Hungary and Romania was signed in January 1948. Romania had already signed similar treaties with Yugoslavia and Bulgaria. The Hungarian–Romanian Treaty was signed in Budapest, with the participation of a high level Romanian delegation led by Premier Groza and Foreign Minister Pauker. The leaders of both states did not miss any opportunity to emphasize the guiding role of the Soviet Union in formalizing the new relations of friendship between the East European states.[91] Hungary, according to the version of the Communist Party, had buried the hatchet with Romania over Transylvania forever and, as *Szabad Nép* expressed it, Transylvania was no more a bone of contention between the two states but a home for the nationalities living there. With the signing of the Treaty with Romania, Hungary would no longer mention its future role in the shaping of the lives of the Hungarian minority in Romania (just three months before, with the signing of the cultural cooperation agreement, the feeling had been that Hungary would play a role of an interested party vis-à-vis the Hungarians over the border). *Szabad Nép* also condemned in strong terms the policies pursued by former Premier Ferenc Nagy, which had hindered the expansion of relations with Romania. Thus, in the beginning of 1948, the Communists could blame their former partners, the Smallholders, of sabotaging relations with the neighboring states, ignoring the simple truth that exactly two years before, the Smallholders and the Communists had competed for the claim to represent Hungarian national interests, by blaming Romania and Czechoslovakia for their nationality policies.

The euphoria in Hungarian–Romanian relations, at least as they were manifested in the official documents, was also carried over to wider regional aspects: the joint statement between the Hungarian and Romanian leaders, issued along with the Treaty of Friendship, emphasized "regional cooperation in the Danube Basin," which represented an "important factor in defending peace in the Danube Basin and the Balkans." This vision disappeared very quickly from the scene, and Hungary was not to return to the notion of cooperation in the Danube Basin until 1966, and then under different circumstances, as part of its rapprochement with Austria.

The signing of the Treaty of Friendship with Yugoslavia, Romania, and lastly with Czechoslovakia in April 1949 clearly marked the end of the first postwar period in Hungary's attitudes toward the Hungarians over the borders. The period ended with an optimistic perspective as drawn by the Hungarian Communists, by now the sole rulers of the country. Praises were lavished on the solution of the nationality questions by the neighboring countries: Czechoslovakia was marching along the correct road—as seen by Budapest—following the gradual steps which improved the situation of the Hungarians; Romania was pursuing a correct Marxist–Leninist–Stalinist policy; Yugoslavia was praised (at least until the break with the Cominform, following which there was, on the whole, a taboo on the issue of Yugoslavia's Hungarians); and last but not least, Hungary praised the Soviet policy toward the 90,000 Hungarians in Subcarpathia— the area which was incorporated into the Soviet Union after World War II following a long and problematic history.[92] In fact, the picture was so optimistic that Hungary disengaged itself from the fate of the Hungarians abroad, and then a long period of silence ensued—broke, albeit for a short time, in 1956. The life of the Hungarians, or rather the cultural, social, and demographic trends among them, became a taboo. About 18 years had to pass before a different picture emerged of the years before and after 1948.

Chapter II

The Years of Silence: Stalinism and Its Aftermath

For years the subject of the Hungarian minorities was taboo, broken for a short time by the events of 1956, only to be veiled once again until the mid-sixties.

Officially the nationality question was solved in the spirit of Marxism–Leninism by the socialist states, and there were no more bones of contention after the signing of Treaties of Friendship and Cooperation. The expulsion of Yugoslavia from the Cominform ushered in a prolonged campaign against "nationalist, chauvinist elements"—which were to be found in abundance. They became victims of merciless purges, only to be rehabilitated—some posthumously.

Years were to pass before a more realistic presentation emerged from publications in Hungary, which shattered some of the myths Rákosi's regime was feeding the people of Hungary. Problems that were not supposed to exist were now raised as grave issues that had been hampering the development of the Hungarian minority abroad.

The Stalinist years were years of Hungary's disengagement from any involvement in the fate of the Hungarians abroad. Unmentioned were the Hungarians in Yugoslavia as any criticism of Tito's nationality policy could have constituted in itself a "nationalist deviation"—nor were those in Romania and Czechoslovakia. Hungary applauded every report on the full minority rights allegedly enjoyed in the respective countries.

Hungary and the Developments in Romania: The Hungarians and the Purges

A rare glimpse into the continuing problems of Hungarian–Romanian relations was given by Imre Nagy when he wrote on the lack of communication and the absence of any initiatives in interstate relations, which had induced him, in the early fifties, to appeal directly to Gheorghiu–Dej in hopes of improving relations.[1] The Stalinist pattern of interstate relations between the socialist states prescribed a steady dose of high-level meetings, mostly organized by the Soviet Union within the framework of the Cominform, the CMEA, and the other emerging bodies established for the furthering of socialist integration. One can well understand a Romanian criticism of the policies of that period—namely, that as a "consequence of I. V. Stalin's cult of personality there were negative influences upon Romania's foreign policy activities and on relations with some socialist states.[2]

In the wake of the rift with Yugoslavia, Romania along with the other East European states launched its campaign against the "national bourgeois" elements, which in practical terms meant the intensification of the power struggle within the Romanian Workers Party (As the RCP was renamed after its unification with the Social Democratic Party). The purges affected the nationality policies, as the Party was in the process of communizing the minorities and their front organizations. In December 1948 the RWP issued its most important document on the nationality question.[3] It was to become the guideline for the nationality policy of the new regime. The document called for the rapid takeover of all the bodies representing the national minorities—Hungarians, Germans, and Jews—by purging the "nationalist" elements who had "infiltrated" the organizations of these nationalities. Their leadership was severely censured and branded as incompetent in the face of the tasks demanded by the new realities in the country. The "Magyar Népi Szövetség" (MNSz)—Hungarian People's Alliance—was the successor of the MADOSZ. The latter had acted between the wars and shortly after the war as the main front organization of the Hungarians, and was reorganized according to the Party's guidelines in December 1948. "Bourgeois elements" were sought out among the Hungarian intelligentsia who hoped to transform the MNSz into a genuine representative body of the Hungarians in Romania.

Hungary welcomed these steps in its fight against "Titoism and its allies."[4] Hungary's support was natural, as both Rákosi and Gheorghiu-Dej were waging a power struggle against their opponents. Rákosi seemed very satisfied with Romania's steps, which eliminated in a short time a whole generation of Hungarian intellectuals who had been active in the interwar years and now seemed to challenge the new regime by demanding more rights for the Hungarian minority.

The newly reorganized MNSz with a new leadership could report to the CC RWP by the end of December 1948 that the organization would act to "strengthen the love and respect of the Hungarian working masses towards the RWP."[5] A more extensive clampdown on Hungarian activists in Romania came with the arrest and the trial of László Rajk in Hungary. This drive lasted until the culmination of the power struggle in Romania with the arrest of the Muscovites, including Vasile Luca, an ethnic Hungarian.

Rajk, who had family roots in Transylvania, often visited the area and kept up very good personal connections with the leaders of the MNSz.[6] Ironically, dozens of activists of the MNSz who were accused of backing Rajk's national communist line were staunch supporters of Hungarian–Romanian cooperation. They had worked for years—even during the war—for a genuine rapprochement between the two nations. In the dark years of suspicions, arrests, terror, and show trials that characterized the atmosphere surrounding Rajk's downfall, no one could recall that just a few months before his arrest Rajk, as Hungary's Foreign Minister, had praised the state of Hungarian–Romanian relations, as contributing to the "strengthening of the peace camp under the leadership of the Soviet Union in its struggle against the imperialist warmongers."[7]

There is no doubt, as recent Western research has pointed out, that the move to liquidate the MNSz was "as much a step against an autonomous political organization with genuine grassroot support as an anti–Hungarian, nationalist decision."[8] Details about the tragedies transpired only years later, when sources in Hungary started to lift the veil from the events of those years following the Rajk trial's repercussions in neighboring Romania. Having been posthumously rehabilitated on the eve of the Hungarian Revolution in 1956, Rajk could later well serve as a starting point for Hungarian criticism of Romania's nationality policy. While details were being published in a very selective and discreet way in Romania itself, the bitter lot of Hungarian intellectuals and activists in Romania was revealed by publications in Hungary. The fates of such persons as Gyárfás Kurko, József Méliusz, Edgár Balogh, and Lajos Csögör were often mentioned. Gyárfás, one of the main leaders of the MNSz, and a close supporter of Petru Groza's Ploughmen's Front during the interwar years, was arrested in November 1949 and jailed until 1964. Having been released from jail in a very poor mental state, he worked for several years as a worker in a factory, and later received a writer's pension. An article in Hungary could bitterly remark that "the years spent in Monarchist Romania's jails did not help him, nor did the fact of his alliance with Petru Groza in 1935."

Likewise, numerous publications in Hungary recalled the fate of Edgár Balogh, the grand old man of Hungarian thought in Transylvania, and one of the leading progressive activists in interwar Czechoslovakia. At the time of his arrest he was serving as Deputy Chairman of the MNSz (1945–1949), a member of the Grand National Assembly since 1948, Lecturer in History and Rector of the Bolyai University in Cluj. Balogh was held in jail until the spring of 1951, only to be rearrested in the wave of persecutions against Hungarian leaders in Transylvania in 1952. He was released in 1955, and rehabili-

tated and exonerated of all charges within a year. It is noteworthy
that Balogh's later writings were widely published in Hungary, where
at times he seemed more popular than among Romanian publishing
houses. Balogh's perceptions of the need for solidarity and cooperation among the nations of the Danube Basin were often quoted by
the media in Hungary. Until his retirement in 1971 from the deputy
editorship of the Cluj-based *Korunk*—the most prestigious and influential Hungarian language periodical in Romania—and in his later
activities as a publicist, Balogh rarely touched on the sensitive issues
of his persecution. Actually, much more biographical details were
published in articles and studies about him in interviews in Hungary.

The purges in the Romanian leadership signaled a further tight-
ening of Romanian control over the life of the ethnic minorities in the
country.[9] Petru Groza lost his job, although not linked directly to the
purges, while some prominent Party activists of Hungarian origin,
most prominent among them Vasile Luca, were purged. Moreover,
the purges hit a further layer of leaders of the Hungarian community
in Romania. The arrests and internal exiles of prominent intellectuals were a heavy blow to the life of the Hungarians. (In a wider
context the purges of 1952 also manifested themselves in the life of
the Jewish, German, and Slav minorities, whose leaders were at best
removed, but arrested in most cases.)

In January 1953 Gheorghiu-Dej declared that the nationality
question had been solved in the Romanian People's Republic, a statement which since then has often been reiterated by Ceauşescu, whenever facts do not seem to justify the statement. Georghiu-Dej's statement conveyed the message that there was no more place for any open
discussion on the nationality issue—which in fact had ceased long before 1953—and any such reference would be considered as chauvinism and nationalism. Along with the clamp down on all the national
minority organizations, the MNSz was rapidly disbanded, as it had
completed its official task: to "strengthen the friendship" between
the Hungarians and the Romanians. There was no more need for the
organizations of the national minorities which, although completely
communized, could request rights and facilities for the very reason
they had been set up—to serve the national minorities. The disband-
ing of the MNSz took place in a manner similar to that of the Jewish
Democratic Committee: arrests of the leadership and the nomination
of a new leadership which would disband "voluntarily," but not before the local activists had exerted severe self-criticism confessing to
"national bourgeois" deviations.

There is no doubt that there was friction between the Hungarians
and the Romanians during the various phases of the establishment of

the Communist regime and the ensuing power struggle between the factions of the Romanian CP. There may have been attempts, albeit not thoroughly documented in Western research, on the part of some of the Hungarian leaders in Transylvania to press for rights and autonomy. Thus, in 1949 there were demands by the Hungarians for 75 percent representation in the newly formed People's Councils in areas densely inhabited by Hungarians, while the Romanian authorities agreed to a 50 percent representation.[10]

One of the most important steps taken by the Romanian regime to prove that the solution of the national question in the country was close or had already been reached was the establishment of the Hungarian Autonomous Region in 1952. The setting up of the region, outlined in articles 19 and 20 of the Constitution of 1952, encompassed an area which, according to the 1956 census, was populated by 77.3 percent Hungarians and 20.1 percent Romanians. It can be argued to what extent the region was indeed "one of the most symbolic indications that the Hungarian minority was given special recognition by the Romanian government."[11] Its creation should be seen more as a legitimization, or the formalization of steps pursued by the regime with a view to curtailing minority rights and not giving in to pressures for more. Until its abolition by the administrative restructuring of Romania in 1960 and 1967, the HAR never served as a true center for Hungarian life, and especially not as an expression of true autonomy. Geographically, the region was far away from the predominantly Hungarian regions near the border with Hungary, so that there was no territorial proximity between the HAR and Hungary. Some of the main urban centers with a large concentration of Hungarians, such as Cluj, Brasov (renamed at the time Oraşul Stalin), and Oradea, were in regions bordering the HAR. There was certain logic in this, as these centers were in areas sparsely populated by Hungarians, as compared with the smaller number of Hungarians in the HAR, but more concentrated in a delimited area. The number of the Hungarians in the Region, more than 560,000, comprised about one–third of the Hungarians in Romania, which should also be seen as a significant aspect in assessing the impact of the HAR on the life of the Hungarians. As the HAR included some of the main areas inhabited by Széklers, it can be argued that the facade of autonomy granted to the Hungarian and Hungarian–Székler populations of the area shifted to a sidetrack the more crucial issues of the Hungarian minority in Romania at the time—the limited opportunities allowed by the regime for developing means of national self–expression along genuine national lines.

In fact the establishment of the HAR served as a pretext not to allow the expansion of Hungarian cultural facilities in other parts of

Transylvania, while in the HAR itself no significant steps were taken to transform it into a center of Hungarian life in Romania. From its very inception the HAR functioned administratively as any other region of the Romanian People's Republic, so there were no indications that the province was indeed "autonomous." Naturally a large part of the local administration, People's Councils, and the Party apparatus were made up of Hungarians; but on the national level, and in the national decision-making process, no special treatment was granted to the region. While the Romanian media were describing the "flourishing" of the HAR, steps were being taken by the regime to limit the contacts between the Hungarians living in Romania and Hungary. There were reports on the banning of newspapers from Hungary and the curtailing of travel to Hungary. Along with the campaign against "nationalist" elements, and the removal of a whole generation of Hungarian intellectuals from the scene, the evidence points to a worsening in the situation of the Hungarians in Romania at the time.

Hungary's reactions to the developments in Romania were mixed. On the one hand Hungarians acclaimed the witchhunts prevalent in Romania, while on the other hand they adopted a policy of presenting the Rákosi regime as a champion of Hungarian rights in brotherly Romania. While the frenzy of the Rajk affair was reaching its peak, and there were waves of arrests among Hungarian "supporters" of the Rajk line in Romania, the Party organs in Hungary were quite reticent in reporting the parallel events in Romania. The reason is to be sought in the absence of a showcase trial in Romania in the style of the Slansky's and Rajk's. Besides, among those purged at the time in Romania there were no leading personalities, only lower level "scums who collaborated with Rajk." With no archvillains exposed, Hungary only expressed its support for the steps taken in Romania, but could not speak of the spread of "Rajkism" in Romania.

There are indications that the 1952 purges in Romania—especially the removal of Vasile Luca and the extensive purge of the leadership of the MNSz and the arrests of Hungarian intellectuals—caused some uneasiness in Budapest. Not that Rákosi could be accused of supporting Hungarian minority rights in Romania, but once in a while the regime had to present to its public some optimistic reports on the life of the Hungarians in the socialist states. There was apprehension in Budapest over the removal of Petru Groza from the premiership, as Groza had the record of a staunch supporter of minority rights in Romania. Officially, Hungary reacted to the purges in Romania by praising the "successful struggle waged by RWP against the opportunist, rightist elements within the Party. The plans of the cornered imperialists have been foiled."[12]

In Hungary there were rumors that Rákosi may have intervened in Moscow over the matter of the anti-Hungarian purges in Romania at the time of Luca's removal.[13] Rákosi did indeed have good reason to do so, as the emerging Romanian nationalist line was also counterproductive to his own regime in Hungary. Rákosi may have used his influence in Moscow to press the Romanians into establishing a Hungarian autonomous region, which could be passed off as an indication of the good relations between the two socialist states. Following the establishment of the HAR, Hungary claimed that Rákosi had contributed to its formation as

> The success of building socialism in Hungary, and the fact that the Party of the Hungarian Communists and Comrade Rákosi have been educating the Hungarian people in the true spirit of patriotism and Stalinist proletarian internationalism— had an important role in the broadening of the rights of the Hungarian nationality in Romania.[14]

The unexpected formation of the HAR—as there was no previous indication or discussion in Romania—does indeed point to the possibility that outside interference, from Moscow, was instrumental in the Romanian decision-making process. Internal calculations also played a role, as the Romanian regime intimated that the victory of Gheorghiu-Dej over the Muscovites, Ana Pauker and Vasile Luca, would not change the Romanian PR's adherence to a correct "Marxist-Leninist nationality policy."

In the light of later Hungarian criticism of the true state of Hungarian culture in Romania in those years, some aspects of the cultural contacts between the two states should be reviewed. The first cultural cooperation agreement was signed in November 1947, which served as a main framework for the developing cultural relations. In November 1951 an agreement was reached on joint book publications, which would aptly be labeled in later years by the Hungarian press as an agreement "first of its kind in the world."[15] According to the agreement, mutual exchanges of books published in the two countries would take place. By 1954, Hungary had sent to Romania 360,000 copies of 296 different titles, while Romania had sent to Hungary 430,000 copies of 79 titles.[16] Among the books exchanged was a very large number of editions of the Marxist-Leninist classics and other standard books of the period. The agreement did not expose the Hungarians in Romania to Hungarian classics, or even to much of Hungarian writers of the Rákosi era, and neither was the Hungarian public exposed to writings by Hungarians from Romania. Thus, a Hungarian complaint in 1970, that for years the public in Hungary had known more about the literature of the awakening nations in Africa than about the Hungarian literation in Romania would seem plausible.[17] As the restrictions on the import of publications from Hungary into Romania were being tightened, the cultural exchange agreements at the time were devoid of any meaningful content.

The Romanian authorities were rather circumspect in allowing the Hungarian minority to be exposed to cultural activities originating from Hungary. Curiously enough, such activities were usually restricted to areas inhabited mostly by Romanians rather than by Hungarians. Thus, the annual Day of Hungarian Culture was always celebrated in Bucharest and Hungarian book exhibits were held in Bucharest,[18] but not in Cluj as might be expected. There were some mutual visiting tours—the Budapest National Theater traveled to several Romanian cities in 1948, including some in Transylvania, and artists from the HAR performed in Hungary—but by and large, few Hungarian artists from Romania performed in Hungary, and few artists from Hungary performed before Hungarian audiences in Romania.

In the wake of Stalin's death and the beginning of the "New Course" in East European states there came a marked expansion in the direct contacts between the socialist states, yet this did not bring about a fundamental change in the interest shown by Hungary in the fate of the Hungarians in Romania. Parliamentary delegations and more contacts between scientists and artists of the two countries certainly improved the quality of the interstate relations, yet the taboo against discussion of Hungarian minorities remained in effect, only to be cracked on the eve of the Hungarian Revolution.

After the Storm: Hungarian–Slovak Relations

The situation of the Hungarians in Slovakia after 1948 can be best characterized as a "gradual, though uneven improvement,"[19] with the emphasis on the "uneven improvement." The period preceding the Hungarian Revolution, and to some extent until the territorial reorganization in Slovakia in 1960, was marked by the regime's determination to bury the hatchet between the Hungarians and the Slovaks, after the traumatic relationship that had developed in the wake of the process of expulsions, resettlements, and re–Slovakization. However, this determination did not include the required practical steps for drastically changing the basic relationship between the Hungarians and the Slovaks in the area. It seems that the events of 1945–1948 were too fresh to be erased in such a short time. Moreover, the Slovak Communists could always continue to cynically exploit the friction between the two nations for their benefit, as they had been doing so well.

With this possibility in mind, the Hungarians were perhaps treated very cautiously, as potential hostages. One can speak of a gradual improvement in the situation of the Hungarian minority, but hardly of a genuine rapprochement. The Hungarians could enjoy more rights without eliciting overt Slovak criticism, and the framework for a more active participation of Hungarians in the sociocultural and political life of Czechoslovakia was being established. This delicate balance was drastically upset during the Prague Spring of 1968.

On the agenda of the Slovak Communist Party there were several grave issues which had to be treated immediately after 1948. The Party had to change course, to adapt itself to the new realities, and to welcome the Hungarians as potential partners in building the new socialist Czechoslovakia. The very same leadership that had pursued an overt and popular anti–Hungarian policy had to retreat from its previous line, find some scapegoats for the mistakes of the past, a process in which Husak was personally condemned, and prove the correctness of its new line by presenting satisfactory results in the situation of the Hungarians. These were emphasized in the field of developing Hungarian schools, cultural activities, as well as the Hungarian–language press.

In contrast to Romania, where the only time the Communist Party criticized its own "nationalist" deviation, was in the case of Pătrăscanu, the Czechoslovak Communists started quite shortly after the 1948 coup to reveal the mistakes they had committed with regard to the Hungarians. This process was clearly aimed at clearing the slate after years of discrimination initiated and perpetrated by the Communists. Communist self–criticism was usually exercised in a veiled manner. Karol Bacilek, the First Secretary of the Slovak Communist Party, condemned in 1951 the "excesses of Slovak bourgeois nationalism." He failed to mention that the Communists were those who actually guided the policies of the "bourgeois nationalists."[20] The re–Slovakization was one of the most delicate issues, and when in 1952 Karol Bacilek called upon the Hungarians to "demand the use of their fine old Hungarian names," referring to the Slovakization of Hungarian place names,[21] it sounded as if everything depended on the Hungarians' demanding the revived usage of Hungarian place names, and not on the good will of the Slovak Communists.

In fact, the process of eliminating the anti–Hungarian steps taken until 1948 was long and arduous. The starting point was a negative one, as immediately after the 1948 coup, the Communists seemed reluctant to give up the achievements of the re–Slovakization campaign, a fact criticized by Czechoslovak publications and Party decisions during the sixties as a "half–solution."[22] Instead of annulling the effects of re–Slovakization, the Party devoted its attention to such other is-sues, albeit important ones, as the restitution of confiscated property and citizenship to Hungarians. The CC SCP decided on several such measures in September 1948. As a result of the deliberations in the Party hierarchy on the Hungarian issue, a "Hungarian Committee" was formed. The participants were leading Hungarian Communists who hoped to aid the central Party Organs in implementing the new policies toward the minority. The Committee, and other committees acting on a local level, were to assure that the messages from above were clearly brought home to both the Slovaks and the Hungarians of Slovakia. Prejudices, especially if they were fostered by the Com-munists themselves, were not easy to erase, so in 1951 the Slovak CP found it necessary to stress the need to implement the correct Marxist–Leninist nationality policy among those who "are still under bourgeois–nationalist influences."

While in Romania, the early fifties were the years of purging "Hungarian nationalists" and other "chauvinist" elements among the Hungarian leadership in Transylvania, the Slovak CP was busy in building up a loyal Hungarian Communist following which would as-sure the implementation of the Party line. This was not an easy task, as Hungarian Communists had been discriminated against until 1948, and in this respect one can say that equality prevailed; often old–time Communists were treated no better than the ordinary type of "class enemies." The planned incorporation of Hungarian Communists into political activity was being hampered by the purges in Czechoslo-vakia, which, although they did not specifically hit the Hungarian Communists, certainly paralyzed the activities of the Party organs. According to the guidelines of the CC of the SCP from September 1948, Hungarians were to be drawn into the Party gradually. How-ever, the implementation of this policy was a very slow process, and only from 1950 were candidates approved for membership. Taking into consideration the very low number of Hungarians in the SCP in 1948, one can understand that the Slovak Communists faced a vi-cious circle; they could not advance the "strengthening of the friend-ship" between the two peoples without the solid backing by Hungar-ian Communists, but because of the previous policies of the Slovak Communist Party itself, there were not enough of them.

The enmity between the Communists of the two nations was highlighted by the foot–dragging in sorting and accepting application files of Hungarian candidates. In this protracted process, files were often "lost" by the Slovak Communist authorities,[23] which necessi-tated the intervention of the CC of the SCP in 1950 in order to speed up the admittance of Hungarian comrades. The education of Hungarian cadres became an important task, as the training of educational cadres as teachers, and functionaries of local administrative bodies was hampered by the dearth of trained activists. According to later Czechoslovak sources, the integration of the Hungarians into Party life was slow in spite of the facilitation of their acceptance. For example, in 1952 in the Bratislava region only 1.3 percent of the SCP members were Hungarians, while their percentage in the population was 20 percent.[24]

Under these circumstances the Slovak CP had to intensify its criticism of those "remnants of nationalism" still influencing the relations with the Hungarians. This was the essence of the decision of the Presidium of the CC of the SCP in January 1950, which called for the elimination of the "shortcomings" and the correction of the mistakes affecting the situation of the Hungarian minority. Later Czechoslovak assessments of the period, especially after the 1963 deliberations on the policy toward Hungarians, emphasized that while the CzCP had gradually corrected its mistakes, it had not openly discussed the period between 1945 and 1948. The reason was that in its attempts to look forward, the Party did not realize that more attention should be focused on the mistakes of the past.

A positive development was the elimination between 1950 and 1952 of administrative steps which until then had not encouraged the "re–Magyarization" of the re–Slovakized people. As a byproduct of the process of re–Slovakization, those among them who had genuine Hungarian roots, expressed—albeit very cautiously—their desire to return to their original identity. Until the early fifties, the Slovak Communists were anxious not to lose this achievement of re–Slovakization, but once it had become clear that no effective improvement could be forthcoming in the relations between the two nations as long as such issues remained unsolved, they agreed not to discourage this process of re–Magyarization. The problem of the "Magyarized," formerly Slovakized people was more complex, as the authorities were trying to shut them off from the emerging Hungarian educational and cultural life. For example, it was not until 1950 that their children were allowed to enroll in Hungarian–language schools or classes in Hungarian. The final blow to the whole chapter of re–Slovakization was not dealt until April 1954, when the CC of the SCP annulled all steps linked to the campaign, and decreed that every citizen could state his nationality according to the language he preferred or to which he felt himself closer.[25] The most important instrument in implementing the new line among the Hungarians was the establishment in March 1949 of CSEMADOK—the Social and Cultural Association of the Hungarian Workers in Czechoslovakia. The Association was,

and still is, the sole organization of Hungarians in the country cater-
ing to their cultural and educational needs. CSEMADOK represented
from its very inception a different approach to the organization of the
national minorities, as compared to the Romanian and Polish example. It was a front organization, but unlike the MNSz or the Jewish
Democratic Committee in Romania, CSEMADOK dealt with cultural
representation rather than political issues. Its membership is on an
individual basis, with fluctuations in the various periods. In 1987, it
was approximately 90,000.[26]

Between 1951 and 1971 CSEMADOK was a part of the Slovak
National Front. In 1971 it was excluded from the Front because of
"right–wing and opportunist" activities, but was readmitted in 1987.
CSEMADOK was the second such nationality organization formed after the Polish one. From its inception it encountered opposition from
various quarters—on the one hand from Slovak "ethnocentrists," who
resented the development of Hungarian cultural activities, and on the
other from Hungarians who regarded the activities of the association
as "traitors" to the Hungarian cause.

In 1952 CSEMADOK had 40,000 members organized in 430 local
groups. In fact, the organization was involved in political work, as it
was the only vehicle through which the Communist Party could relay
its message to the Hungarians. Cultural activities were conducted
only through the association, so that writers, journalists, and the
small Hungarian intelligentsia had to act within its framework. Being a Party creation, CSEMADOK could claim credit for several steps
which were important for the Hungarian minority. At the time of its
formation in 1949, in some areas of Southern Slovakia local authorities could not yet conduct their affairs in the Hungarian language;
but CSEMADOK's activities were in Hungarian from the beginning.
Thus, theoretically, a local official of Hungarian background had to
conduct his activity only in Slovak, but the very same person could
later in the afternoon appear as a speaker in Hungarian on behalf of
CSEMADOK.

The rising number of membership in CSEMADOK was also due
to the rising number of Hungarians in the country. This increase was
brought about by the gradual return of formerly re–Slovakized Hungarians to their original identity. Whereas in the 1950 census 367,733
Hungarians were reported, five years later their number reached
392,000, but some Czechoslovak sources estimated that in 1950 the
real number of Hungarians must have been 592,000. There is no evidence as to what role, if any, CSEMADOK played in encouraging
"closet" Hungarians to come forth, but there is no doubt that it was
instrumental in this process.

From its beginning the leadership of the association was rather mediocre, as the Hungarian community in Slovakia lacked a leadership. Most of the small number of intellectuals in the area renewed their activities under the tutelage of CSEMADOK, but those writers and journalists who so warmly praised the friendship between the Slovaks and the Hungarians were in no position to provide a leadership for the organization. This situation was very favorable to the Communists, as they did not have to cope with strong-willed and known personalities, as compared, for example, with the type of intellectual and political leadership that stood at the head of the Hungarian community in Translyvania. As a reflection of the changes and purges within the Czechoslovak system, CSEMADOK was not spared the occasional removal of those who deviated from the correct "Marxist–Leninist nationality policy." Hungarian chauvinists who opposed the "friendship between the two peoples" were often exposed and promptly removed and purged from the association.

CSEMADOK's contribution to the conduct of the country's nationality policy was evident in two main areas: the socialization of the Hungarian minority and the revival of Hungarian cultural life. Although by its very name and definition the association was supposed to deal with the cultural needs of the Hungarian minority, it actively participated in the social and economic restructuring of the Hungarian community. As a study published in Hungary and devoted to the Hungarians in Slovakia indicated, CSEMADOK "had an important role in the development of socialist agriculture in Southern Slovakia;" the reason was that the Hungarian peasants' will to work "had not awakened by the beginning of the fifties," and there was an urgent need for something which would convince the stubborn Hungarian peasants, long accustomed to a hostile environment, that they should adjust themselves to the winds of change blowing in the area.[27] As in all the socialist countries, coercion. of course, was the favorite weapon of persuasion; but CSEMADOK's task was to act as a transmission belt from the Communist Party, conveying the "good news" of the regime's carrot and stick policy—the possibility to return to a Hungarian identity, to speak and learn in the mother tongue and even to conduct their affairs with local Hungarian officials.

Ironically, Hungarian peasants joined the newly formed collective farms as members of the cooperatives more willingly than their Slav neighbors, as the land they had worked as new members was often their confiscated plot—a strange but logical solution to the problem of alienation. CSEMADOK's activities played a role in convincing the Hungarian peasants of these new facts of life, and of course, the agitprop activities they conducted were geared to this task: evenings of Hungarian folk dancing, preceded by speeches in Hungarian, urging them to play the new political tunes emanating from the Communist Party. As, "it was clear that without a politically active Hungarian peasantry there will not be a socialist transformation of the agriculture in Slovakia,"[28] steps were taken to involve them in political activity. Cadres were trained, and by 1954 Slovakia could boast of its successful nationality policy by pointing to some thirteen delegates elected to the Slovak National Council through CSEMADOK, certainly an increase over the two Hungarians prior to the 1954 elections.

The Hungarian cultural revival in Slovakia was to a large extent the product of CSEMADOK's activities. Such well-known writers as Zoltán Fábry—the foremost writer and idealogist of the Hungarians in Slovakia—worked enthusiastically for the much needed cultural revival. They started from scratch, as in the dark years of 1945–1948 there was no Hungarian literature and artistic creation, and the small Hungarian intelligentsia of the area had either been exiled or had left for Hungary. Those were the "years of silence" as defined by Fábry, who in a 1963 work spoke of the post–1948 period as the "third flowering." Before that year, Fábry, who had launched the first Hungarian paper in postwar Slovakia, *Új Szó*, in 1948, could not express openly the meaning of the "years of silence" for the Hungarian culture. His ideas did not find a more receptive ground until 1963, and in recent years studies published in Hungary have brought to light details of the sufferings of the Hungarian intellectuals in the early postwar years. Fábry's short essay, "A vádlott megszólal" (The Defendant Speaks Up), which was written in May 1946, was a heavy indictment against the mistakes committed by the Slovaks in their attitude toward the Hungarians. It had to wait until September 1968 to be published in full for the first time.[29]

How different was the atmosphere after 1948, when Fábry and his colleagues, among them Rezsö Szalatnai, Dezsö Györi, assumed a leading role. The change was certainly there, in the very fact that under the aegis of CSEMADOK the authorities allowed Hungarian cultural creation. But, as a much reviewed book published in Hungary in 1982 on the Hungarian literature in Slovakia since 1945 indicated, for years after 1948 no significant works emerged "from the products of amateurism and dilettantism."[30] It seems that Socialist Realism, which characterized the period, has finally come under fire by critics in Hungary who have been engaged for years in the study of the Hungarian minority in the socialist states. True, no significant work emerged from that period; but the contribution of the growing group of Hungarian writers was certainly there. CSEMADOK's offices in

Bratislava served as a center for the writers—before the Hungarian section of the Slovak Writers' Union was formed—and from there the writers and artists traveled to the countryside. As the writer József Macs later recalled, when the first writings appeared, the writers and poets went to lecture in the villages, where the audience "needed the word. They did not enjoy our stories or poems, but the fact that we spoke in Hungarian to Hungarians, is all that mattered to them."[31] The changes in the Slovak nationality policy after 1948 were also manifested in the development of Hungarian–language education in Slovakia. Until 1948 there was not one Hungarian language school, only some 154 classes with 5,400 pupils in Slovak schools, where the language of instruction was Hungarian. The educational opportunities granted to the Hungarians were later criticized by the Slovak authorities, and by 1960 it was fashionable to say that the Hungarians were not sufficiently exposed to the Slovak language and culture. It was a process very similar to the curtailing of the Hungarian educational system in Romania after 1957, especially in 1959–1960.

In contrast to the situation in Romania, in Slovakia there were no Hungarian language publications until December 1948, when the first issue of *Új Szó* (New Word) appeared as a weekly in Bratislava. The paper issued by the CC of the SCP became the only mouthpiece of the Party in Hungarian. Gradually more publications appeared, and by 1965 there were 21 Hungarian newspapers and periodicals. *Új Szó*, a daily since the mid–fifties, is still the most important, if not the most interesting, publication.

There was also a slow revival of book publishing in Hungarian, with the first six books of literature appearing in 1949, preceded of course by political literature at an earlier stage. From 1949, as a sign of rapprochement between Czechoslovakia and Hungary, books were imported from Hungary, especially for the benefit of the Hungarians. In 1949, there were 5,300 copies of Hungarian books brought in.[32] In 1953 a cultural exchange agreement between the two countries was signed, which regulated the exchange of books and their publishing, the emphasis also being on books by Soviet authors. With such an emphasis, it should not come as a surprise that Hungarian critics in recent years have stressed that there was not too much original thought in the Hungarian publications in Slovakia in those years.

Hungary reported with great enthusiasm on the new line pursued by the Czechoslovak regime after the Communist takeover. As the very recent past could not be erased (the expulsions, the resettlements, and the re–Slovakization being well–known), the Hungarian Communists emphasized the need to turn attention to the future. Reports from Slovakia on the steps taken to expand the rights of the

Hungarians were presented in Hungary as proof of the victory of the spirit of "socialist internationalism" in the relations between the two states. Between 1949 and 1951 a joint interstate commission handled all the issues linked to the population exchange agreement of 1946. According to the Hungarian press at the time, its activities were conducted in a spirit of "friendship and cooperation." With the signing of the Treaty of Friendship and Cooperation in March 1949, the two states officially buried the past, having removed all obstacles that hindered the development of the "new type of relationship" that characterized the Stalinist period.

Hungarian historiography had a difficult time to correct, or rather to place in a proper perspective, some of the problems of the Hungarian–Slovak relations, especially considering the accusations against Husák, who was found responsible for the anti–Hungarian excesses after 1945. In April 1954, when the Party condemned the re–Slovakization and called for the liquidation of all its nefarious consequences, Husák and others, including Novomeský, the well-known Slovak poet who had been in charge of education in Slovakia after 1945, was branded as a representative of the Slovak "national bourgeoisie." The accusations against Husák, remarked Endre Arató in his study, were at the time believed both in Czechoslovakia and Hungary.[33] What Arató did not elaborate on was that Husák's role in 1945–1948 was well documented, among others, in the Communist press in Hungary.

Novomeský's case was also illustrative of the ways in which the fifties have been presented and reevaluated in Hungary. Novemeský was purged in 1951, as the regime did not take into consideration the "years on the side of Gottwald, and his participation in the Slovak National Uprising." He was freed from jail in 1956, and rehabilitated in 1963. Novomeský's case, and that of Kurkó Gyáfás in Translyvania, are examples of individual tragedies of those years of rampant Stalinism in Eastern Europe. Along with the purge in 1954 of those allegedly in charge of the mistaken "national–bourgeois" line toward the Hungarians in the early postwar years, the Slovak Communists were careful not to allow the transformation of CSEMADOK into an organization which would truly represent the aspirations of the Hungarian minority. After all, this was not its original task when it was formed by the regime. There were reports in the Hungarian press in Slovakia that the Hungarians were showing disrespect for the local councils by complaining directly to CSEMADOK and to *Új Szó*'s editorial offices.[34] According to *Új Szó* the Hungarians tended to see the local authorities as "foreign bodies," preferred dealing with Hungarian officials, who, of course, did not have any practical authority, and could not function as a parallel or dual administration, as many Hungari-

ans seem to have considered them. The regime was also uneasy over
continuing signs of "nationalism" among the Hungarians in Slovakia,
and *Új Szó* condemned a demand by local officials in one of the small
towns to raise the Hungarian national flag beside the Czechoslovak
and Soviet flags. The reason for the request was that the majority of
the population was Hungarian.[35] The condemnation of such a demand
clearly indicated the limits of "socialist internationalism"—in other
words, too close a friendship toward the neighbor—even a socialist
one—may be counterproductive. Interestingly, *Új Szó* also published
some delicate issues—among them a report on rumors among Slovaks
to the effect that Hungarian Communist officials were turning for
advice to Budapest, bypassing the Czechoslovak CP's authorities.[36]
Such rumors were of course totally unfounded, as there was no reason
why a Hungarian Communist should seek advice from the comrades
in Budapest, considering that the Hungarian leadership totally approved and backed the Slovak policies. It is noteworthy that the very
publication of such rumors is indicative of the continued tensions and
mutual suspicions some seven or eight years after the Communist
takeover.

During the deliberations against the anti–Party group in the
spring of 1954, the CC of the Slovak CP published a decision on the
functions of CSEMADOK with a view to "strengthening the cooperation" between the Hungarians and the Slovaks, yet in fact aimed at
restricting the organization's activities by expanding the involvement
of non–Hungarian departments in the implementation of the regime's
nationality policy. An indication of the new line was the formation
of the Nationality Section of the Institute for People's Culture in
Bratislava, designed to "guide" the cultural work among Hungarians
and Ukrainians by coordinating the organization and financing of the
cultural and educational activities among the two minorities.

Considering the legal status of the Hungarian minority in Slovakia, a major positive change was the very mentioning of this minority in Slovakia for the first time in a constitutional law of July
1956, which stated that the Slovak National Council "assures the favorable conditions for the economic and cultural development of the
Ukrainian and Hungarian nationality."[38] In fact, subsequent legal
documents, such as the 1960 Constitution went no further in explaining the status of the minorities, but only elaborated on the type of
assurances previously given to them.

Chapter III

The Hungarian Revolution and the Hungarians
in the Neighboring States

The Hungarian Revolution had not only profound repercussions on the situation of the Hungarian minorities in the neighboring states, especially in Romania, but also long–range effects on Hungary's attitude toward the Hungarians abroad.

The intellectual ferment in Hungary on the eve of the Revolution naturally raised the issue of the Hungarians abroad. After years of silence and optimistic reports on the solving of the national question in the socialist states, the media in Hungary opened up the issue in a frank manner. Actually, the style of debate on the fate of the Hungarians in the neighboring states was more candid and blunt than the discussion on the other sensitive issues which characterized the very short–lived "spring in autumn" of September–October 1956.

The main target of complaints in Hungary was the situation of the Hungarians in Romania. *Szabad Nép* raised the issue unexpectedly in a long article written by Pal Pandi, one of the leading journalists in Hungary.[1] The article, "On Our Common Affairs," shattered the previous illusory image of the fate of the Hungarians in Romania. The author bitterly noted the taboo surrounding the situation of the Hungarians in Romania, an atmosphere in which any criticism of Romania's nationality policy was branded as "national deviation." In the words of the author, Hungary "had torn up the railroad tracks" between the two countries, thus creating a total lack of communication and understanding. Such a policy not only failed to eliminate Hungarian and Romanian nationalism, but actually fostered it.

The *Szabad Nép* article harshly criticized the main features of Romania's nationality policies. The dissolution of the MNSz was a "mistake," and the Hungarian Autonomous Region (HAR) was presented by Pandi as a fiction because it included only a part of the Hungarian minority in Romania. The article left no doubt that, as many Hungarians on both sides of the border felt, the HAR was neither Hungarian nor autonomous nor even a region. For the first time a Hungarian organ acknowledged that the Hungarians living in the HAR were not allowed to have contacts with Hungary, citing for example the ban on connecting Radio Budapest to the local relay systems in the villages.

The author also described the lack of cultural contacts: the press published in Hungary was not available in Romania, and the Hungarian–language press published in Romania was not available in Hungary. The superficial contact between artists and writers of the two countries was yet another sign of the deficient state of the the relations. Pandi's dictum that the "Hungarian culture in People's Romania is an integral part of Hungarian culture, and thus we are also responsible for it morally and intellectually," forecast the almost similarly worded resolutions of the Hungarian Writers Union in March 1968. The clear linkage, at least in the cultural sense, between Hungary and the cultural and intellectual fate of the Hungarians in the neighboring states was established, albeit only for a short time. In the aftermath of the Hungarian Revolution the issue of the Hungarians abroad once again succumbed to the same policies and attitudes that *Szabad Nép* had warned about in September 1956.

The nature of the nationalist Hungarian upsurge during October 1956 continues to preoccupy academic researchers who point out that "revanchism was simply not one of its objectives."[2] Considering the wide spectrum of forces which participated in the Revolution, generalizations should be avoided; and while there is no doubt of the activities of ultra–nationalist revanchist elements, the general impression is indeed that the main spokesmen of the political groupings and parties did avoid revanchist tones. The Revolution as a whole endeavored to win over the sympathies of the neighboring nations for the aims of the Revolution. Characteristic of such an attitude was a broadcast of Radio Miskolc on October 29, 1956:

> Slovaks, Romanians, Serbians, blood is flowing from our wounds and you are silent. . . . We see that you are groaning under the yoke we wish to throw off. Now foreign interests want to incite you against us. . . . We are for you too, for peace, for socialist truth.[3]

In the aftermath of the Revolution, Romania and Czechoslovakia sounded the alarm in the face of the revanchist character of the Revolution, and clamped down on "Hungarian nationalists," feeling reinforced by the apologetic attitudes of the Kádár leadership. In an ironical sense, the Hungarian Revolution served—especially in the case of Romania—as a means of promoting local nationalist policies.

Unrest was reported among the Hungarian minority in all the states surrounding Hungary, including Subcarpathian Rus, which geographically served as the main preparatory area for the launching of the Soviet military action against Hungary. The unrest in Romania, which was not limited to the Hungarian minority, was not reported by the media for several months, and when the first details were published, they were part of a well–orchestrated campaign serving Gheorghiu–Dej's policies. The Hungarian and pro–Hungarian demonstrations were as much in sympathy with Hungary as against the Communist regime.[4] *Scânteia* tried hard during the first stages of the Revolution in Hungary to emphasize the "fraternal relations" among the coinhabiting nationalities in the country.[5] In meetings of the Hungarian intelligentsia in Transylvania with high–level Party leaders, among them a three–day "marathon" in Cluj with such leading personalities as Miron Constantinescu, Iosif Chisinevschi, and Alexandsru Moghioroş among the participants, Hungarian intellectuals were typically accused of nationalism. The tense atmosphere and the mutual accusations were not reported by the Romanian media, except for the resolutions taken by the meeting on the need for "strengthening the fraternal relations of friendship between the Hungarian and the Romanian peoples."[6]

A tougher Romanian line toward the Hungarian minority emerged shortly after the Soviet crushing of the Revolution in Hungary. During November–December 1956, Romanian Party and state leaders, headed by Gheorghiu–Dej, visited various localities in Transylvania, especially Cluj and Tirgu–Mureş, the capital of the HAR. They accused the Hungarian intellectuals of fomenting unrest during the events in Hungary. Romanian nationalism rang through Gheorghiu–Dej's tough remarks on the need for resolute struggle against all manifestations of "nationalism and chauvinism."[7]

For almost a year the clampdown on alleged Hungarian nationalists in Romania indicated that there was indeed much work to be done for the strengthening of the "fraternal relations between the peoples." In October 1957, coinciding with the first anniversary of the Revolution, another round of antinationalist campaigning took place in Transylvania. A joint meeting of Hungarian and Romanian intellectuals in Cluj served as a forum for constructive self–criticism by Hungarian intellectuals who confessed publicly to their nationalist tendencies. The self–cleansing sessions were conducted by János Fazekas and Leonte Răutu, who calmly received the *mea culpa* of one such Hungarian intellectual who had "fallen prey" to Imre Nagy's views. Both Romanian Party leaders emphasized that in spite of "anarchist nationalist" views among some Hungarian intellectuals, they could look forward with optimism to the continuing fraternal relations between the two nations.

Tension in Czechoslovakia ran high too, especially in the Slovakian area inhabited by Hungarians. CSEMADOK's organ called upon the Slovaks and Hungarians to reject any "attempts by foreign reactionaries to weaken the unity of the peoples of our homeland."[8] Manifestations of solidarity with Hungary that took place in Slovakia had a similar character with those in Transylvania, not only raising the tension among the Hungarian population but also straining the relations between the Hungarians and the authorities. The Czechoslovak regime was no less anxious than the Romanian to nip in the bud any development which might lead to an upsurge of Hungarian nationalism, and the spilling over of the events from Hungary. As in Romania, the response of the Slovak authorities assumed the form of strengthening the Slovak grip on the Hungarians. After all, it was the Hungarians who had proved themselves disloyal to a socialist regime over the border. Accusations of "Hungarian isolationism" continued to be voiced in Slovakia in a similar pattern to events in Romania. The two Communist parties shrewdly took advantage of the danger of a Hungarian irredentist trend to thwart popular support for the Revolution in Hungary. Such a policy was bound to achieve positive results among the Romanians and the Slovaks.

Evidence is still very scarce as to the nature of the Hungarian behavior in Subcarpathian Rus, and although many Hungarians inhabiting the area were sympathetic to the events in Hungary, there are no indications that the reports about "serious outbreaks" among the Hungarians were truthful.[9]

Hungarian response in Yugoslavia could best be described as low-keyed.[10] Yugoslavia's attitude toward the Revolution in Hungary was generally ambivalent, and it seemed natural that Tito should be worried about—among other things–the emergence of a nationalist Hungarian regime in Budapest. There is no evidence that Yugoslavia clamped down on alleged Hungarian nationalists, and the Hungarian minority in Vojvodina did not become a scapegoat as did the respective minorities in Czechoslovakia and Romania.

For several months after the instauration of the Kádár regime, the media in Hungary did not specify the nature of the Hungarian reaction in the neighboring states during the Revolution. However, around May 1957 several articles appeared which mentioned the friction between the authorities in the neighboring countries and the Hungarian minority. One such Hungarian publication emphasized the friction at the time, but described the continuing relations of brotherhood despite the events of the "Counterrevolution in Hungary."[11] An integral part of the Kádár regime's drive for consolidation was its rapid disengagement from any feeling of responsibility over the fate of the Hungarian minorities abroad. This policy reached its peak at the time of the visits made by Hungarian leaders to Romania and Czechoslovakia, especially during Kádár's visit to Romania in February 1958. With a view to dissociating itself from the errors of the Rákosi–Gerö leadership, the new regime acknowledged mistakes committed in the past regarding relations with the neighboring states, including the nationality issue. One such occasion was an article written by István Szirmai, the leading Party expert on nationality issues, on Romania's Liberation Day.[12]

"During the last years," wrote Szirmai, "we did not fight resolutely and strongly against all remnants of nationalism and chauvinism," and in a direct reference to articles published in Hungary on the eve of the Revolution on the fate of the Hungarian minority in Romania, Szirmai wrote that

> during the last years articles have appeared on the implementation of the nationality policy toward the Hungarians in Romania, and if they found something wrong, it was artificially exaggerated. The publication of such articles was completely erroneous, because they contradicted the truth. Their aim has been unmasked: they nurtured chauvinism and nationalism.

Although mistakes were committed, according to Szirmai they were made during the implementation of a just nationality policy. Szirmai emphasized the achievements of the Hungarian minority in Romania, especially the Hungarian Autonomous Region. He attacked the machinations of the "revisionists" who tried to destroy popular power in Hungary as well as Romania. The Kádár regime was indebted to the "fraternal socialist help of Romania" during the dark days of the counterrevolution. He concluded:

> How can we reciprocate the brotherly, friendly aid of Romania? First of all by strengthening our popular power, our socialist state, for the sake of the Hungarian people and the socialist camp. Also, by steadily fostering the Hungarian–Romanian friendship of alliance.

The situation of the Hungarians being the most problematic in Romania, it was highlighted by the attention paid to their fate in post–October Hungary. In several articles the official Hungarian view of the life of the Hungarian minority in Romania was skillfully interwoven with the impressions of writers and journalists who visited Transylvania. Thus, József Horváth's reportage was composed of discussions with Hungarians in Romania, as well as remarks on Romania's nationality policies.[13] The author quoted a Hungarian worker in Transylvania as saying that outside interference in their lives would be rejected. The message was clear to the readership in Hungary:

> Nobody should worry about us, and whoever does so, should
> shed the burden of "trusteeship," as we live here as adults,
> masters of our destiny, and there is no need to worry as long
> as our fate depends on the Romanian Workers' Party.

One of the essential themes of the Hungarian stand in the wake
of the Revolution was that the lack of communication between Hungary and the Hungarian minorities abroad served as a hotbed for
misunderstandings and misconceptions about the life of the Hungarians in the neighboring countries. It was with this note that Horváth
concluded his article: "In the future we shall have to do more, so
that information about their life, work, and endeavors would reach
us more frequently." The lack of communication manifested itself also
in the ignorance of the Hungarian public about the cultural life and
achievements of the Hungarians abroad. The Hungarian regime had a
remedy for this problem too and, as Horváth wrote in another report
on the life of the Hungarians in Romania, "We in Hungary import
too few books by Hungarian authors from Romania, and should do
more in this respect."

The media in Hungary frequently published articles by leading
Hungarian intellectuals from Romania. These articles and interviews
presented Romania's viewpoint—namely, that Hungarian culture was
thriving in Romania. The weekly of the Hungarian Writers' Union
published two such articles by István Nagy and József Méliusz, both
well-known figures of Hungarian intellectual life in Romania.[15] Nagy
explained that Hungarian culture in Romania, albeit Hungarian in its
spirit and language, was the outcome of a long historical interaction
with Romanian culture. It should be emphasized that between 1957
and 1968 the media in Hungary often published such articles, but
these views were very rarely voiced by intellectuals from Hungary
itself. Interestingly, even in the period of Kádár's disengagement
from the issue of the Hungarians abroad, such voices were those of
Hungarians over the borders.

There was no doubt that the task of the Hungarian intellectuals
from Romania was to convince the Hungarian public not to worry
about the Hungarians abroad. Nagy wrote that

> any attempt to change our voices into nationalist or chau-
> vinist nuances was and is alien to us. Our literature rejects
> and condemns the attempts made by the imperialist circles
> to use once again Transylvania as a subject of dispute.

The Hungarian media did contribute its own products to the toning
down of the voices on the fate of the Hungarians abroad. *Népakart*

admonished the people of Hungary not to seek to make Hungarian citizens of all the Hungarians living abroad. "Such concerns and endeavors are non–productive when they are turned against friendly countries."[16]

In the wake of the mass meetings held in Transylvania against "nationalist and chauvinist" attitudes among the Hungarians in Romania, some high–ranking Romanian Party leaders of Hungarian origin were interviewed by the media in Hungary. Thus, János Fazekas, a member of the CC RWP, was interviewed by *Népszabadság*, where he emphasized the multilateral achievements of the Hungarians in Romania, especially those of the HAR.[17]

Within thirteen months of the beginning of the Kádár regime's consolidation, Kádár and Prime Minister Ferenc Münnich traveled abroad. They visited Romania, in February 1958, and Czechoslovakia the following December. The aims of the two visits were to renounce Hungarian territorial claims from those countries, and to praise their nationalities policy with respect to the Hungarian minority. Kádár's visit to Romania—his first visit abroad since assuming power in 1956, and Hungary's highest level meeting with Romanian officials since 1948—was opened with a series of articles in the Party daily, in which Istvan Szirmai attacked those who were seeking to abandon Hungary's friendship with the neighboring states and trying to revive the question of Hungary's borders.[18]

Officially, the Kádár visit was described as a return visit, reciprocating that of the Romanian delegation to Budapest in November 1956, during the first days of the Kádár regime. The Hungarian delegation visited several areas inhabited by Hungarians in Transylvania, especially in the HAR. The messages were very clear: Hungary had given up any irredentist claims on Romanian territory and supported Romania's nationality policy. In his main speech before a mass meeting in Bucharest, Kádár stated that the Hungarian People's Republic had no territorial or any other claims on any country.[19] Moreover, the Hungarian delegation reiterated several times that the events in Hungary in October 1956 had posed a danger to Romania as well. Gyula Kállai, the second ranking member of the Hungarian delegation, declared in a speech in Tîrgu–Mureş, the capital of the HAR, that the counterrevolution had overtly raised territorial demands on the neighboring people's democracies, while attempting to restore the old order not only in Hungary but in Romania as well. Amidst cheers from the audience, Kállai asserted that Hungary had enough land for its people in order to build its socialist homeland.

As to the endorsing of Romania's nationality policy, the statements made by the Hungarian leaders had a special significance inasmuch as they represented the highest ranking Hungarian approval of the steps taken by the Romanian authorities in combatting Hungarian "nationalism." Characteristic of this Hungarian attitude was the tone of a leading article in *Népszabadság*, which praised Romania's nationality policy as being loyal to the spirit of Marxism–Leninism. The "spectacular" development of the HAR is a proof of Romania's policies, emphasized the Hungarian paper.[20]

The "question of the borders," as the delicate issue of Hungary's frontiers was called, was raised repeatedly in the Hungarian media during and after Kádár's visit to Romania. In the wake of the new cordial relationship with Romania, the Kádár regime was determined to settle this matter once and for all. This was the gist of an article in *Népszava* appropriately entitled "Let's talk about the borders."[21] The writer supposedly answered two anonymous letters from readers defining themselves as "non-nationalists," who had raised the question why discussion about Hungary's frontiers was muted. Taking the challenge, the writer engaged in polemics with people wishing to broach the issue. After tracing the long history of Hungarian–Romanian enmity caused by the ruling classes and by the revanchist policies of Hungary's leaders, the author went on to describe the life of the Hungarian minority in Romania, praising their achievements under the Romanian Communist regime, and emphasizing the large-scale investment projects in areas inhabited by Hungarians and the promotion of Hungarian culture. As to the question of the borders, the author's conclusions were unequivocal:

> Who is really helping his own country and the Hungarians living in the other countries? Who is really contributing to the cause of peace in the Danube Basin and in the whole world? Only he who recognizes and feels that the question of the borders is completely closed.

It was in this spirit of the "closed question of the borders" that Hungarian scholarship treated various historical aspect of the Hungarian–Romanian relationship. In March 1958, coinciding with the Kádár visit to Romania, the first postwar monograph on the history of Hungarian–Romanian relations appeared in Hungary. Written by Dániel Csatári,[22] who became one of the major contributors in Hungary to aspects of Hungarian–Romanian relations and the nationality problem in the Danube Basin, the short monograph touched upon some sensitive issues between the two countries. Originally, the book was supposed to be published in the summer of 1956 but was overtaken by events. Some modifications were therefore introduced by the author. Kádár's new line of criticizing mistakes committed during the Rákosi–Gerö peiod were naturally highlighted in this outline of Hungarian–Romanian relations:

> Nationalist views were strengthened by the fact that the Hungarian Workers' Party committed mistakes in educating in the spirit of patriotism and proletarian internationalism, and neglected to answer the questions affecting thousands of people.

Hungarian revanchist feelings were still conspicuous in Hungary, warned Csatári, and these feelings might endanger the course of relations between Hungary and Romania. Csatári called for more realism in Hungarian–Romanian relations, and had some reservations about the all–out condemnation of "nationalists":

> Ignoring actual problems, branding the well–intentioned promoters of the cause as nationalists, as well as the one–sided exaggeration of the problems, can only harm Hungarian–Romanian cooperation.

Kádár's regime likewise emphasized the normalization of relations with Czechoslovakia through the solving of the nationality problem. In a carefully orchestrated visit to Czechoslovakia, Premier Ferenc Münnich praised Czechoslovakia's nationality policy and renounced all territorial claims against Czechoslovakia.[23]

Chapter IV

Socialist Internationalism in Crisis: Hungarians
in Romania and Czechoslovakia, 1956–1968

The Toughening of the Romanian Line Toward the Hungarian Minority

The emergence of nationalism as a notable, or rather the dominant, force in Romania's policies, along with the "maverick" line pursued by the regime in its relations with the Communist Bloc, had its inevitable impact on the fate of the Hungarian minority. There followed a period of gradual repression and curtailing of the rights of the Hungarians. Although it is doubtful what privileges the Hungarians had before the toughening of the Romanian nationality policy,[1] it is quite evident that beginning in the late fifties, Romanian policies toward the Hungarians underwent a change for the worse. The main manifestation of that line was the merging of Bolyai, the Hungarian language university in Cluj, with the Babeş, the Romanian university, in March 1959. This was the first step in the territorial reorganization of the HAR in 1960, and a growing process of Romanization in the educational system. All these intensified the assimilatory pressure upon the Hungarian minority.

Kádár's sanctioning of the nationality policies pursued by Romania during his 1958 visit enabled the Romanian leadership to carry on with its policies without drawing any criticism from Hungary. However, by the late sixties—especially in the wake of the emergence of the Romanian nationalist line—Hungary started to monitor more closely the fate of the Hungarians in its neighbor, signaling a slow shift in its policy toward the status and fate of the Hungarians in the Socialist states.

In February 1959 Gheorghiu–Dej set off a new "anti–nationalist" campaign, censuring the "reactionary elements among students" at the Congress of the Romanian Students' Union.[2] Representatives of the Bolyai University in Cluj asked for more Romanian–language classes, stating that the division between the two universities in Cluj on the basis of language was artificial and fostered nationalist agitation. In February 1959, after a series of so–called "auto–critical" sessions by the head of the various departments of the Bolyai University, the way was paved for the merger of the two institutions. It should be noted at this juncture that the media in Hungary had frequently extolled the activities of the Bolyai University in Cluj and of its medical school in Tîrgu–Mureş as evidence for Romania's positive nationality policy. The University had been opened in 1945 with the direct support of Prime Minister Petru Groza, and was regarded as a showcase for advancement and opportunities among the Hungarian minority.

For ten years, the media in Hungary remained silent about the implications of the merger of the two universities. Only in 1969 was the first remonstrance voiced, in an indirect way, in a book review on the minorities in Yugoslavia, published in *Valóság*.[6] The reviewer, Miklós Tomka, denounced the "assimilatory policies pursued since the fifties in some Socialist countries, manifested in the gradual elimination of minorities' rights, the closure of their universities and schools." As Bolyai University was the only Hungarian–language university in any of the Socialist states, there could be no doubt about what university the author was referring to.

The Romanian authorities were unusually forthcoming with Western correspondents in presenting their case for the merger of the universities. For example, it was explained to the *Times* of London correspondent that as a consequence of the division of the educational institutions, the young Hungarian generation in Romania was growing up with insufficient knowledge of the Romanian language.[4] Low–level officials, never previously allowed to speak with Western reporters, gave them frequent briefings during this public relations campaign, begun in the wake of hostile reportings in the Western media on Romania's assimilatory steps. The chairman of the People's Councils in the HAR explained to the correspondent of the *New York Times* the reasons why the institutions of higher learning in Cluj had been merged. Moreover, he disclosed that the merger of some high schools was also planned in order to better prepare the Hungarian youth for admission to the University.[5]

The Romanian campaign against "nationalist elements" was closely watched by Moscow, which apparently was at a loss to discern the road on which Gheorghiu–Dej had embarked. However, sensing the new direction of the wind, the Soviet leadership was quite apprehensive of the possibility of Romanian overtones regarding the fate of Bessarabia. Although this issue, along with Transylvania, was to become an integral part of Romanian–Hungarian–Soviet relations after 1964, Khruschev made a rare and curious remark on the national situation in Romania during a visit to East Germany in March 1959. In a speech in Leipzig, the Soviet leader estimated that the enmity between the nationalities in Romania, a policy pursued by the old regime, could not be entirely erased, and its consequences were still being felt. Though the question of the borders had been settled, Khruschev intimated that there were some people in Romania who claimed that Bessarabia belonged to Romania.[6] The implication of Khruschev's remarks was a piece of advice: the Romanian regime should fight resolutely against Romanian nationalism with the same vehemence as it was treating Hungarian nationalists.

Reports published at the time by Radio Free Europe that Hungary had raised the problem of the Hungarian minority in Romania with the Soviet Union during the spring of 1959 remain unconfirmed to this day, but it certainly seems plausible that Hungary started to surmise that the toughening of the Romanian line against remnants of "Hungarian nationalism" was becoming counterproductive, the more so since the Kádár regime proclaimed that the "question of the borders" had been closed.

From the summer of 1959 a very slow and cautious change in Hungary's attitude toward Romania's nationality policies became apparent. The merger of the two universities in Cluj was reported in Hungary merely factually, without comment, but it was more significant that in 1959, when the Hungarian media marked Romania's Liberation Day, August 23, the previous years' words of praise for Romania's nationality policies were conspicuously missing, or were subdued.

Prominent leaders from both sides used to publish articles in the leading newspapers of the neighboring country on each other's National Days or other festive occasions. Gheorghe Apostol, member of the Politburo of the Romanian Workers' Party published such an article in *Népszabadság*, concentrating more on bilateral relations and less on the life of the Hungarian minority in Romania.[7] Hungarian spokesmen were reluctant to discuss the fate of the Hungarians in Romania in view of the continuing campaign against "nationalism" in Romania. In a festive meeting in Budapest on the occasion of Romania's Liberation Day, the main speaker, György Aczél, the central figure in Hungary's ideological policies, avoided completely the nationality issue in Romania, merely referring to the friendship between the nationalities in Romania.

Although *Népszabadság* wrote that the "continuous struggle against all manifestations of nationalism was the best guarantee for the deepening of the friendship between the two peoples," there was a pervasive feeling of uneasiness on the part of the Kádár regime, reflected in the media, about the Romanians overdoing the "continuous struggle" against Hungarian nationalism. Once again, festive occasions may indicate the state of relations between the Communist countries, and in this context it was significant that the next year, 1960, the media in Hungary kept a low tone and made but scant references to Romania's nationality policies.[8]

In December 1960 the Romanian Grand National Assembly published plans for the administrative reorganization of the country's regions. The most significant change was the alteration of the character of the Hungarian Autonomous Region. By a virtually classic example of gerrymandering, two districts from the Region were removed, attached to the Braşov Region, while three other districts from neighboring regions were attached to it. The final result of the shifts was the splitting of the Hungarian population in the area, so that the region lost its predominantly Hungarian character. As a consequence of the changes, the Romanian population of the region increased from 19.9 percent to 34.8 percent, while the Hungarian population decreased from 77.6 percent to 61.7 percent.[9]

The administrative changes were accompanied by a constitutional adjustment to the new situation: the name of the Hungarian Autonomous Region was changed to Mureş–Hungarian Autonomous Region. This was not merely a semantic change adding the name of the river flowing through the areas but a clear political step deemphasizing the special character implied in the original name. Article 19 of the 1952 Constitution was amended; the clause specifying the Hungarian character of the area was deleted.

The media in Hungary kept a low profile in reporting the administrative changes in Romania. Radio Budapest quoted the official version of the new administrative distribution of the region, mentioning the changes in the HAR only in the sixth place.[10] One Hungarian paper supplied more details of the changes, but carefully remarked that because of the reorganization, the overall population was increased, overlooking the fact that the increase was in the number of the Romanians, while fewer Hungarians were included in the area.[11]

Hungarian leaders were undoubtedly aware of the nature of the redistribution of some regions in Romania. In a strange coincidence with the announcement of the changes, three leading personalities from Hungary, Premier Ferenc Münnich and Politburo members György Marosán and Sándor Rónai, chose to spend their vacation in January 1960 in Bucharest—a place not exactly renowned for mild climatic conditions at that time of the year. The visitors may have discussed the recent administrative changes with the Romanian leaders, and presumably expressed Hungary's concern over the alteration of the HAR.[12] Whether or not Hungary tried to intervene or to receive more exact details about the nature of the steps, it would also seem plausible that the three Hungarian leaders gave their consent to the changes affecting the HAR[13] No details were published in Hungary on their talks in Bucharest except for the laconic announcement that the three had spent their vacation in Romania.

The growing concern in Hungary over the curtailing of the Hungarian cultural activities in Romania was expressed in the literary-political weekly of the Writers' Union, *Èlet és Irodalom*, in an article titled "Mutual Acquaintance," published immediately after Gheorghiu-Dej's visit to Hungary in September 1961.[14] While emphasizing the positive results of the visit, the article took exception to the cultural relations between the two peoples, and set forth the assumption that relations between socialist peoples called for a deeper cultural relationship, involving more access to each other's cultures. What was needed, was more mutual acquaintance, as the achievements of the "past fifteen years have not been emphasized." The Hungarian call for each other's cultures came at a time when reports were circulating in Hungary on the gradual elimination of Hungarian language of instruction in schools and institutions of higher learning in Romania. Through a process of "unification," as highlighted in the merger of the two universities in Cluj, national minority schools and Romanian schools were fused together.[15] Western media reported at the time that Hungarian schools in Romania would be completely eliminated by 1962.[16] Such reports were rejected by the Romanians, yet the authorities could not hide the fact that Hungarian and Romanian schools were fused together.

At the time when the weekly of the Hungarian Writers' Union was calling for more cultural contacts with Romania, the main Hungarian–language publications in Romania were being purged of "nationalist" and "chauvinist" editors—among them *Utunk*, the leading Hungarian language cultural–literary weekly. Its editor, László Földes, was taken to task by Mihai Beniuc, the Secretary General of the Romanian Writers' Union, for furthering Hungarian nationalism: "Instead of absorbing the line of the Party . . . he wanted to guide the writers in a spirit alien to the Party. . . he tried to incite chauvinism."[17]

Anxiety over reports circulating in Hungary on the situation in Romania found expression in the *Hungarian Journal of Higher Education*, which warned about "nationalist attitudes toward Romania" among students in Hungary.[18] Hungarian intellectuals, especially some of Transylvanian origin, were quite overt in their efforts to bring about the intervention of the Hungarian government in alleviating the plight of the Hungarian minority in Romania. Romania reportedly pressured the Hungarian authorities to arrest those involved in such activities. In 1962, three intellectuals were indeed sentenced to four, three and a half, and three years in jail respectively. Although Budapest seemed to have yielded to Romanian proddings to clamp down on pro–Transylvanian nationalists in Hungary, the steps taken in Romania did not go unnoticed in Budapest, where official circles kept a watchful eye on the situation. Likewise, the deepening rift with the Soviet Union and the other East European allies, the growing anti–Soviet feelings fostered by the regime, and the intensification of the Romanian National Communist line were very closely monitored in Budapest.[19] Communist officials in Hungary reportedly complained about the fate of the Hungarians in Romania, and the issue was raised in Party meetings. Hungarian Party activists could react only by noting that the "Romanian comrades are not behaving correctly," promising that the issue would be raised with them.[20] Hungarian public opinion also found fault with the limitations imposed on tourists from Hungary visiting Romania and the virtually total ban of imports of newspapers and periodicals from Hungary into Romania.

Hungary's gradual shift toward intensified involvement in the fate of the Hungarians in Romania became an integral part of the Kádár regime's policies once it had embarked on the new National Communist line, especially in the wake of the conflict with the CEMA. From 1964 the historiographical polemics between Romania and the Soviet Union on the Bessarabian issue, and those between Romania and Hungary on Transylvania, were to become a constant feature of the Hungarian–Romanian relations. Hungary's total support for the Soviet line in Moscow's dispute with Romania added a new dimension to Hungary's role at the time as a Soviet proxy in opposing the Romanian line.

Between 1961 and 1964 Romania acted as a reluctant ally of the Soviet Union, growingly assertive in its policy of "partial alignment," culminating in the 1964 Statement of the Romanian Workers' Party. The dispute over "specialization" within the CEMA may serve as the first test case for Hungary's position vis–à–vis the Romanian line. As a result of the disagreements of opinion between Romania and the Soviet Union over the process of integration and specialization within CEMA, the Romanian line was first attacked by East Germany. The three more advanced East European states—East Germany, Poland, and Czechoslovakia—bore at first the main brunt of opposing, along with Moscow, the Romanian line. Hungary, which logically should have refuted the issue of specialization as proposed by the Soviet Union, joined the choir of disagreement with Romania, in what seemed at the time as the "warming up" of the conflict within CEMA. On the eve of the July 1963 CEMA summit held in Moscow, Hungary's representative to the organization, Antal Apró, praised at the Budapest International Fair products of the various socialist states manufactured in accordance with specialization, and condemned wasteful "parallelism" among the member states. Another indication of Hungarian criticism of the Romanian line was the fact that the Hungarian media deleted from its reports Soviet President Podgorny's appreciation of Romania's achievements in industrialization. At the Moscow summit Hungary, unlike the GDR, refrained from a forthright showdown with the Romanian position. Even so, Kádár took exception to the Romanian stand without his remarks being reported at the time by the Hungarian media. Nearly six months would pass before they were disclosed in a speech by Antal Apró at the Political Academy of the HSWP. Apró quoted Kádár as having stated in Moscow that in a "creative economy, just as in politics, there is no place for 'somebody's road.' There is only one way to reach new achievements, and that is the road of socialist-internationalist cooperation."[21]

Shortly after the Moscow summit, the newspaper of the Hungarian trade unions condemned, unnamed, "doctrinaire people" who opposed the strengthening of inter–CMEA ties under the label of "national independence." The paper contended that the age of economic isolation was over, so that it was not enough for a country to produce all its necessities to become independent. The country that produced goods needed in the international market was the one with true independence. The drive for autarky, concluded the Hungarian paper, recalled "some mistaken economic theories of the fifties."[22] It should be noted that during the East German–Romanian polemics, both sides had recourse to a highly specialized technical language to find fault with each other's position, and the East Germans made no attempt to overtly rebuke what obviously lay behind the Romanian line—the emergence of Romanian National Communism. Hungary's first references to the new Romanian doctrine of national independence, albeit in a veiled and discreet manner, were actually more vehement than the East Germans', inasmuch as it was the first time that the notion of rejecting integration under the pretext of "national independence" had come under attack.

Hungarian conformity with the Soviet line found expression in yet another new form: Hungary took the Soviet side in what was to become one of the major divisive issues between Romania and the Soviet Union—the circumstances of Romania's Liberation in August 1944. In one of the first major salvos of the polemics between the two sides, the Romanians criticized a Soviet book on this topic,[23] while the Hungarians completely ignored the exacerbating divergencies between Romania and the Soviet Union. Thus, Hungary took up the Soviet position and observed Romania's liberation by the Soviet Union on its eighteenth anniversary, without even mentioning Romania's reevaluation of the events with emphasis on the Romanian CP's role: "Eighteen years have passed since the Soviet Army liberated Romania from the Nazi yoke."[24] reminisced *Népszabadság*.

As the crisis within the Bloc deepened in the face of the Romanian challenge, and as the new style of Romanian nationalism was overtly practiced by Bucharest, the Kádár regime totally refrained from praising Romania's nationality policies. For the fourth consecutive year, the Hungarian media made no reference to Romania's nationality policies on the anniversary of the signing of the Treaty of Friendship and Cooperation in January 1964. The Romanian "Statement on the Stand Concerning the Problems of the International Communist and Working Class Movement" of April 1964 is certainly one of the most documented steps in the history of the communist movement. Its significance lies in the challenge the Romanian line presented to the Soviet leadership and the impact the Declaration had on the relationship between Romania and the other East European states. The Statement, which Western scholars analyzed and debated as representing little more than the reiteration of previous positions adopted by the Soviet Union, or as representing the "maturing" of the Romanian Workers' Party, did indeed serve as a landmark in "Romania's relations with the socialist countries.[25] Developments in post–1964 Romania and the line of "official nationalism" in Hungary[26] placed the two states on a collision course on several topics—first and foremost on aspects of nationalism and the national question in Romania. Hungary's determination to oppose any form of nationalism, especially Romanian, and Romania's policies toward its Hungarian minority added a new element to the strained relations within the Soviet Bloc. Romania's revival of the Bessarabian issue led to closer cooperation between Hungary and the Soviet Union, as the Soviet Union chose to support or even elicit Hungarian complaints against Romanian nationalism in response to Romanian pressure regarding the Bessarabian issue. There is no doubt that Hungary's emergence as the primary critic of the Romanian line became the most outstanding feature of Romania's relations with the socialist states from 1964 onward. Hungary spearheaded the Bloc's opposition to Romania and vicariously upheld Soviet attempts to keep Bucharest's maverick policies in check. Opposition to the Romanian line reached the boiling point after the nationality issue was included among Hungarian invectives launched against Romania.

The Warsaw Pact states initially reacted with restraint to the Romanian Statement of April 1964. Characteristic was the tone of one Budapest newspaper, implying that the Romanian statement was in accordance with the policies of the CPSU and the other Communist Parties.[27] No attempt was made at the time to analyze the various points raised by the Romanians, nor to explain the Romanian interpretation of the principles guiding the relations between the Communist parties and the respective Socialist states.

Subsequent Soviet endeavors to tone down the polemics with the Romanians failed to ease the tension in the Bloc. Hungary played an important role in the conciliatory high–level talks with the Romanian leadership during 1964. Among the main contacts between the Hungarians and the Romanians were the unusually lengthy stay of the Hungarian Foreign Minister János Péter in Romania in June 1964, the visit of the Romanian Party delegation in Budapest led by Ceauşescu in July, and Gyula Kállai's visit to Bucharest in August. The series of high–level meetings between Hungarian and Romanian leaders was evidently a part of a larger pattern of Romanian–Soviet meetings, such as Podgorny's visit to Romania in July 1964 and the Romanian Premier's visit to Moscow.

From the nature of the Hungarian responses to the Romanian line following some of the high–level contacts, it is evident that Hungary sent out feelers as to the aim of the Romanian challenge to Moscow's hegemony. The scarce press reports on the visit of the Hungarian Foreign Minister János Péter on June 9–19, 1964 described it as a return visit to the Romanian Foreign Minister's visit to Hungary in December 1963. Whether or not Péter informed his Romanian hosts of future steps envisaged by Hungary against the Romanian line, Hungary embarked on an ideological offensive some five days after Péter's return from Bucharest. The pronounced anti–Romanian line was elaborated by Politburo member Gyula Kállai, in a speech before the Political Academy of the HSWP, a favorite forum for the voicing of major Hungarian political statements. Kállai's speech outlining Hungarian foreign policy was the most explicit Hungarian stance on issues that had been up until then debated only between the Soviet Union and Romania.[28] Kállai dwelt on the dangers of "voices from abroad which advocated a 'neutral, non–committed' policy" and asserted that Hungary would reject policies based on "national sentiment." Referring to China—but hinting clearly at Romania–Kállai denounced "old and new forms of nationalism," mentioning nationalist endeavors aimed at denying the advantages of the socialist division of labor.

One week after Kállai's speech, which could not go unnoticed in

Bucharest, a high-level Romanian Party delegation led by Ceauşescu arrived in Hungary. There was no doubt that the crisis in CEMA was one major topic, but the state of relations between the two states was raised too. The Hungarian team to these talks consisted of some "old and new hands" in managing relations with Romania. Kállai was considered the foremost ideological and foreign policy expert, Béla Biszku served at the time as the head of the HSWP cadre department, and István Szirmai was the head of the Agitpop. It was significant that both Biszku and Szirmai were of Transylvanian origin. A newcomer to the Hungarian team was Zoltán Komócsin, chief editor of *Népszabadság*. A rising star in the Party hierarchy, Komócsin participated at the high-level talks between the Hungarian and Romanian leaderships in April 1964. If indeed Komóscin's participation in talks with the Romanians served as a "training" for him, as some analysts suggested,[29] it proved to have been a successful one. He would play a vital role in his country's relations with Romania in later years—especially in 1971.

At times it seemed that Hungary was positioning itself in the role of the "honest broker"—making some conciliatory overtures toward the Romanians, as if mediating between Moscow and Bucharest. However, as Romania continued to challenge Soviet policies, Hungary stepped up its criticism of Romania. Characteristic of this line was the warning in *Népszabadság* of "loosening up" within the socialist system on the part of those who "pursue a nationalist policy which undermines the unity of the Socialist states." Ferenc Várnai, the foreign affairs editor of the paper, suggested that the socialist states should close their ranks in face of manifestations of "narrow-minded nationalism."[30]

The growing cooperation between the Soviet Union and Hungary with regard to Romania was highlighted by the restraining effect that the removal of Khruschev had on criticism leveled at Romania both from the Soviet Union and Hungary. The relaxation in the Romanian–Soviet tension found expression, for example, in a *Pravda* article by Romanian Defense Minister Leontin Sălăjan, which presented the Romanian view on the country's liberation in August 1944.[31]

Hungary for its part praised some aspects of Romania's foreign policy. *Népszabadság* had warm words on Hungarian–Romainan cooperation as "both countries pursue a common foreign policy based on mutual interests, a policy which is also expressed by Hungarian support for Romanian initiatives, like those aimed at securing peace in the Balkans."[32] Actually, the two states did not exactly pursue a common foreign policy, but rather both were busily engaged at the time in regional initiatives, serving their national interests. Romania's traditional diplomacy in the Balkans, crystalized in the early fifties and reinforced after the rapprochement with Tito in 1955, became one of the backbones of the Romanian national Communist line, which was carried on by Ceauşescu, after Gheorghiu–Dej's death, in March 1965.

The evident similarity in regional interests between Romania and Yugoslavia, the good neighbor relationship with Bulgaria, and the expanding relations with Greece positioned Romania in a prominent place in Balkan regional politics.[33] Like the Soviet Union, Hungary usually refrained from commenting on Romania's Balkan policies— at least until 1968, when Budapest drew attention to Romanian attempts at reviving the "Little Entente," with reformist Czechoslovakia's participation, and the Balkan Alliance on the southern flank of the area. As both organizations were of an anti–Hungarian character, opposing interwar Hungarian revisionism, Hungary's sensitivity to the issue in 1968 was quite understandable.

Hungary's own regional policy on the Danube Basin had been pursued by the Hungarian Communists in the early postwar period, but was dropped on account of Soviet opposition to the various regional cooperation and federation plans. At the end of 1964 it was revived as part of Kádár's "national revival" line. It may well have been that the emphasis on regional cooperation and on the "community of fate" of the nations of the area was aimed at breaking Hungary's feeling of isolation and at appeasing public opinion over the lack of any independent Hungarian initiatives and the regime's servility to Moscow.[34] In that period distinctive Hungarian regional aspirations manifested themselves in two "waves": the first one from the end of 1964 until the spring of 1965, and the second lasting from the ninth Congress of the HSWP in November 1966 through 1967. However, it was eclipsed by the anti–reformist campaign in the wake of the developments in Czechoslovakia.

Kádár gave the opening sign for the Danube Basin cooperation policy in December 1964 at the Congress of the Communist Youth (KISz). He declared that the nations of the "Danube Basin share a common fate, they must unite or perish together."[35] The concrete foundation for such a highly emotionally charged statement was laid down in the course of the Hungarian–Yugoslav rapprochement reached during Tito's visit in Hungary in September 1964 and the later visit of the Austrian Foreign Minister, Bruno Kreisky, to Budapest. The euphoria displayed in the Hungarian media on the sudden rediscovery of Hungary's role and place in the area marked a complete break with the past taboo, under which the issue had been kept hushed up for years. As a Hungarian provincial journal noted:

> In our country any reference to cooperation along the Danube
> has been a taboo over the years, because of dogmatic pre-
> conceptions on the allegedly anti–Soviet implications of the
> idea. . . . The time has come to take up this legacy.[36]

However, Gheorghiu–Dej's death and the rise of Nicolae Ceauşescu
"stole the show" from Hungary's foreign policy initiatives. At the
ninth Congress of the RCP, held in July 1965, a major landmark in
the history of Romanian National Communism, Ceauşescu outlined
the main features of his country's policies. Moscow continued some of
its conciliatory remarks towards the Romanians, and Brezhnev even
praised Romania's drive for industrialization,[37] not mentioning, of
course, that this was precisely the issue that was dividing the two
Parties. In an apparent "socialist division of labor" with the Soviet
Union, Hungary was more restrained in its praises of the Romanian
leadership, and sent a lower level delegation to the Congress than the
other Bloc–member states. The two members of the Hungarian delegation had no previous experience in negotiating with the Romanians,
and it was also their first known official visit to that country.[38]

Hungary showed some signs of anxiety about the course taken by
the Romanian regime. Hungarian leaders made frequent statements
that tried to reassure Hungarian public opinion that national feelings
would not turn the socialist states against each other, despite temporary differences of secondary importance.[39] However, anxiety that
not everything was flawless in the nationality issues in the area, per-
vaded, clearly enough, these statements of reassurance. Under the
title "We have learned from history" one Hungarian newspaper recalled the tragic consequences of the nationalist policies of the ruling
classes for the peoples of Eastern Europe. The change under socialism, emphasized the author, was radical, as exploitation—the main
factor causing enmity among nations—had been removed. But, the
article went on emphasizing in italics: *under socialism the nations
have embarked on the road of national equality—though not always
with the same consistency and the same results.*[40] The author looked
forward hopefully to a bright and peaceful future of the cohabiting
nationalities of the socialist countries of the area:

> Walking among Hungarians in Pozsony, Ungvár, Szabadka,
> or reading the new Constitution of the Romanian People's
> Republic,one is filled with a very satisfying feeling that the
> time is near when the wounds of the past that have caused
> so much paid, will heal forever.

But in spite of this satisfying feeling the author felt that there were
still some things to be done:

> For the fostering and strengthening of socialist relations
> among brother nations it is essential to stand up resolutely
> against all forms of nationalism, even against the faintly
> heard, nostalgic recollection of feelings. History has taught
> us that there is no more dangerous thing than playing with
> this fire.

The references to walking among Hungarians in Czechoslovakia, the
Soviet Union and Yugoslavia (e.g., note that the place names are given
in Hungarian—Pozsony not Bratislavta), stand in contrast to the mere
"reading of the new Romanian Constitution." The author, it seems,
could not refer to the experience of walking among Hungarians in
Romania.

Interestingly, the article appeared several days after a visit of
the Romanian Premier, Ion Gheorghe Mauer, to Hungary. The visit,
which prepared Kádár's visit to Romania in March 1966, was strange:
Maurer came alone, and no announcement was made of the visit until
he had left the country. The talks were held in a "friendly atmosphere" and dealt with "topical questions of the international situation and relations between the two socialist countries."[41] It seemed
that there were some urgent problems between the two states, and
on the eve of Kádár's arrival in Bucharest, Zoltán Komócsin gave
an important and much publicized speech at the Political Academy
of the HSWP. His speech, "The Forces of Socialism and Peace Are
Stronger," also published in *Pravda*,[42] contained an attack on the imminent dangers of nationalist policies being pursued by some Communist parties. Overtly targeted at the Chinese, his references to the
dangers of nationalism hinted at an address much closer to home.

Kádár's visit in Romania, March 10–13, 1966, possibly designed
in hopes of arranging a Hungarian mediation between Romania and
the Soviet Union, failed to bring about any positive results. On
the contrary, following the high level Hungarian—Romanian dialogue
Hungary intensified its denunciation of the nationalist policies being pursued by some Communist parties. In a further policy statement, also at the Political Academy of the HSWP, Komócsin spoke
of "national interests and internationalism," attacking all forms of
nationalism, recalling the evils of nationalism as practiced by other,
unnamed parties. Komócsin rejected any alleged contradiction between national interests and the internationlist duty of the Communist parties—placing of course the internationalist principle above the
national interest.

While condemning all forms of nationalism, Komóscin praised,
without giving any specific details, the ways in which Hungary's
neighbors were solving their nationality questions. At that stage

Komóscin did not touch directly upon the fate of the Hungarian minority in Romania, but certainly the groundwork was being prepared for a more overt Hungarian criticism of the type of nationalism pursued by "some Communist Parties." Komóscin's speech was also a rebuke to the anti–Soviet nationalism that was raising its head in Hungary, reflecting the nationalist tensions within the Hungarian nation itself. The leadership of the HSWP understood only too well that there could be no effective combatting of the Romanian brand of National Communism, as long as undesired manifestations of Hungarian nationalism were occurring in Hungary itself.

The "National Revival" in Hungary and Relations with Romania, 1966–1968

The growing national awareness in Hungary and the policy of "official nationalism" became one of the most interesting features of the Kádár regime, which exerted their evident influence on Hungary's relations with Romania, and to a certain extent with Czechoslovakia and Yugoslavia. The search for national identity, the reappraisal of Hungary's past, the debates on the role of the national question between 1966 and 1969, the critical reexamination of Marxist notions about the nation, nationality, and the nationality question were to a large extent motivated by the leadership's search for legitimacy in face of the rising tide of National Communism in Romania. The Hungarian version of the synthesis between national traditions and national pride on the one hand, and socialist patriotism on the other was tacitly approved by Moscow. Positioned, as it had been from its inception, against Romanian nationalism, its toleration by Moscow was a calculated risk, taking into account the possibility that such a policy could potentially develop its own dynamism—thus assuming an anti–Soviet form.

The historiographical polemics between Hungary and Romania which took place in 1964, can be seen as an introductory stage for a long series of such seemingly never–ending rounds of polemics that have haunted the relations between the two states ever since. Such polemics have an intrinsic mechanism of involving various aspects of relations, centering on historical territorial claims as well as the nationality issue. In retrospect, the historiographical flareup of 1964 also served as an opening salvo in a prolonged dispute on the national question during 1966–1969. As Robert R. King noted:

> Discussions of history and the interpretation of history have been suitable vehicles for expressing differences on the national question. History has been made the principal basis for territorial claims in Southeastern Europe, and to debate

the interpretation of the history of certain areas is to debate
the validity of the current claim.[43]

The development of Romanian historiography is a classic example
of the process of nationalization of a communist historiography. At
least until 1962–1963 the mainstream of Romanian historical writing
followed a line which did not deviate from the standard Marxist and
Soviet theories. Until 1954, Romanian historiography had challenged
the very pillars of classical Romanian historiography by refuting the
doctrines of Romanian Latinity. Romanian historiography closely
followed the accepted Soviet line not only regarding the origin and
formation of the Romanian people, but also on such subjects as the
character of the historical relationship between the Romanian Prin-
cipalities and the Russian Empire, and on the issue of Bessarabia.

When Gheorghiu–Dej challenged the Soviet conception of the
role of the RCP in the liberation of Romania (and researchers trace
this challenge to as early as 1954)[44] this was the first evidence of an
independent Romanian course. It continued, and even expanded, in
a new version of *Istoria României*, the official history of the country. The emergence of Romanian National Communism was followed
step–by–step by a general buildup of a new historiography reflecting
militantly the course pursued by the Party leadership. Historiography has become since then one of the most effective weapons of the
new course, as it contests the tenets of the Stalinist school of historiography, while increasingly contending with Soviet and Hungarian
historiography—which became the natural targets of the emerging
Romanian line.[45]

The first politically motivated historiographical debate between
Romania and the Soviet Union and between Romania and Hungary
took place in 1964. The opening of the Bessarabian debate can be
traced to the Soviet pressure on Romania, on behalf of Hungary,
relating to the situation of the Hungarian minority in Romania.[46]
The new wave of publications in Romania on the role of Transylvania
and its place in the formation of the Romanian national state in 1918,
and on the first debates between Hungarian and Romanian historians
on the fate of the Habsburg Monarchy, were an integral part of the
political differences between the three states.

The first major debate took place at the international conference of historians in Budapest in May 1964, on the topic of "The
Historical Problems of the Austro–Hungarian Monarchy." It would
have a political importance as well as a scientific one. Historians
from Hungary, Czechoslovakia, Yugoslavia, Romania, and the Soviet
Union elaborated on the state of their historiographical research. The
marked dissensions between these outstanding Hungarian and Ro-

manian scholars were evident enough before the conference, but the meeting constituted the first forum in which the two sides engaged in an open debate that was covered not only by the specialized professional journals but also by the mass media.

According to the Romanian perception the Habsburg Monarchy had been a decaying body in all its aspects, and the emergence of the national states was a progressive step, natural, and a logical one.[47] The Hungarian position, as presented by Erik Molnár and László Katus, propounded the view—which since then has remained one of the basic tenets of Hungarian historiography—that the national movements of the period under discussion were not of a progressive characer, and that a federative solution (the orthodox Leninist position) rather than the breakup of the Monarchy into national states would have been the most viable solution for the nations of the area.[48] Referring to the quotations from Lenin, the Hungarian media noted with satisfaction that the Soviets supported the Hungarian concepts, and in some issues, unspecified by the Hungarian sources, even engaged in debates with the Romanian historians.

The Soviet support for the Hungarian viewpoint was expressed most explicitly by Turok–Popov, a Soviet historian of Hungarian origin, who condemned the Romanian position by clearly hinting at current events, and at the difficulty of assessing international developments when a nationality–centered view guided the researcher.[49] In a direct attack on the very core of the new line in Romanian historiography, the Soviet historian expressed the view that the new "national unitary states"—the favorite term of Romanian historians—were not really national–unitary, as they themselves were burdened by nationality problems.

The Hungarians characterized the debate as having been held between "dogmatists" and between historians holding more modern and liberal views,[50] and left no doubt as to who were the dogmatists. Perhaps some people were surprised to see the Soviets, along with the Hungarians, representing the more modern and liberal view.

The popular Budapest evening newspaper, *Esti Hirlap*, summed up the differences of opinion with the Romanians in an interview with Erik Molnár, who put forward a very critical assessment of the Romanian position at the historians' conference.[51] The Romanians answered in kind, in an article by Constantin Daicoviciu in *Contemporanul*.[52] The Romanian historian rejected Molnár's views as they appeared in *Esti Hirlap*. The "fallout" from the 1964 conference continued to feature prominently in Hungarian professional and popular publications in the years to come, in the form of a virtually incessant polemic between the historians of Hungary and Romania.

The Hungarian historians emphasized in particular the shift in Romanian historiography and the "national viewpoint" which guided it.[53]

The historiographical dispute of 1964 should be seen in a wider perspective, as it also included sharp differences of opinion between Hungarian and Czechoslovak historians, and to a certain extent between Hungarian and Yugoslav historians as well, centering around the issue of the national liberation movements in Eastern Europe since 1848.[54] The revival of the historiographical aspects of the Bessarabian issue came at a time of growing differences between Hungary and Romania and between Romania and the Soviet Union. The Romanian thesis on Bessarabia and Northern Bukovina, widely elaborated by Ceauşescu after 1965, was first raised by the publication of *Marx: Notes on Romania* in December 1964.[55] As research on the *Notes* had started in Amsterdam in the summer of 1964, it was more than a coincidence that Chairman Mao set off perhaps the first sparks of the Bessarabian debate by remarking in June 1964 to a group of Japanese socialists that the Soviet Union itself had occupied territories of other nations. Among them was Bessarabia, seized from Romania. The pattern that emerged in 1964—and it has prevailed ever since—was Hungary's tendency to refrain from any reference to the Soviet–Romanian dispute over the Bessarabian issue, but strong "circumstantial evidence" in the timing of the Hungarian–Romanian historiographical polemics leaves no doubt that there was a linkage between the political relations and the historiography of the three states involved.

The development of the official outlook in Hungary on nationalism, the national question, and the meaning of proletarian internationalism was a slow and arduous process marked by debates between the hard–line dogmatists and more liberal minded critics of the establishment. To a certain extent the vivid and spirited debates that took place on the pages of such periodicals as *Valóság, Új Irás, Élet és Irodalom,* and of course in such important Party newspapers and periodicals as *Népszabadság* and *Társadalmi Szemle,* contributed to the internal cohesion of the regime, and certainly to a greater degree of national consensus.

Some nondogmatic intellectuals—among them István Sütér, at the time President of the Hungarian PEN, and Aladár Mód, Vice President of TTIT (The Society for the Dissemination of Scientific Knowledge)—presented their case for rejuvenation, or rather rehabilitation of Hungarian national tradition, stressing the importance of the national culture in its socialist form.[56] In the course of the debates, some unexpected voices adhered to the more "liberal" line.

Erzsébet Andics, often referred to as the "high priestess" of Stalinist historiography in Hungary, defended the progressive nature of the 1848 Revolution in Hungary, while deeming as retrograde the Romanian and Slovak liberation movements of the period. The style and content of the Party officials' statements was more cautious, as if an internal division of labor existed between the hardliners and the liberals, with the latter overshooting the mark with greater emphasis on national values, and the former applying the necessary brakes to stablilzing the process at a desirable level.

One of the main objectives of the debates in Hungary was to combat internal forms of nationalism at home in order to pave the way for an assault on the Romanian brand of nationalism.[57] The Hungarian folk saying, "everyone must use the broom in front of his own gate first," was often repeated by Hungarian leaders. Writing in *Népszabadság*, László Rózsa warned that Hungary could not denounce external forms of nationalism as long as there was any indication of nationalism in Hungarian society itself.[58] Both Rózsa and Dániel Csatári, the leading expert on relations with Romania, condemned what they labeled as "Nationalism in a Marxist Veil."[59] They described the symptoms of nationalism evidenced in Hungarian society: excessive national pride and the demeaning of other nations.

The Romanian position, expounded through the years in countless articles and speeches, asserted that the national interests were in no way in contrast with internationalism. During one of his customary "working visits" in Transylvania, Ceauşescu declared that only by supporting and reinforcing the socialist construction of each specific country could the best contribution be made to the strengthening of the world socialist system.[60] The nation under, and being perfected by, socialism was a historic necessity. In the Romanian perception, the continuity of the Romanian people was one of the main pillars of the socialist regime, a continuity which justified the organic linkage between the past and the present.

Under these conditions, an open clash was inevitable. The first Hungarian overt criticism of the excessive emphasis by Romania on the role of the nation, in all its aspects, appeared in an article by Fehér E. Pál, entitled, "Together or Against Each Other," in which the author wrote that the Romanian theses reminded one of "inflexible Stalinist perceptions."[61] Fehér's article can be regarded as a direct Hungarian reply to Ceauşescu's militant speech on May 7, 1966, on the occasion of the 45th anniversary of the RCP. Although it is rather difficult to follow the almost daily duels, some of the exchanges were prompt responses to the other's claims. Such were the articles published by *Élet és Irodalom* in Hungary, answered in kind by the paper's counterpart in Romania, *Contemporanul.*

Several such exchanges of views took place in a wider context of the relationships between the two states and the Soviet Union, and especially as an echo to Romania's policies within the Warsaw Pact. It was not a coincidence that the crucial Warsaw Pact summit in Bucharest in July 1966 issued a clause in its final Declaration stating that the "Warsaw Treaty member–states declare that for their part they have no territorial claims with respect to any state in Europe" aimed at states in Eastern Europe, no less than at relations between East and West. Should anyone have missed the point, Kádár gave an interview to UPI's Henri Shapiro—one of the most candid interviews with an East European leader published at the time. *Népszabadság* carried the interview,[62] thus officially informing the Hungarian public of some delicate divisive matters existing between neighboring socialist states.

Kádár was asked for his comment on this point:

> the question of territorial demands was not raised officially, but there are some demands as those raised by China against the Soviet Union . . . and at the same time there were references to Bessarabia in the Romanian press.

The interesting point was not so much Kádár's evasive answer to the question but the very mentioning of the Romanian–Soviet differences in a period of polemics over Bessarabia. Another point which was raised in the Kádár–Shapiro interview was the "rumors and reports on nationalist phenomena among socialist countries, Romania being mentioned in this context." Once again, the airing of such delicate questions in the organ of the HSWP, was in itself noteworthy, irrespective of Kádár's replies.

Parallel to the upsurge in Romanian National Communism in 1967, there occurred a certain change in the regime's policies toward the Hungarian minority, which was to last, with some ups and downs, until 1971. Characterized as "resembling relative liberalization," this policy was followed from 1971 onward by more assimilatory pressures.[63] However, it seems that Romania's policies were not so much "liberal" as an attempt to find an accommodation with the Hungarians, assuring their loyalty to the policies of the regime. This was especially true in 1968, when Ceauşescu needed the total support of the Hungarian minority in face of the real or imagined threat posed by the Soviet Union against Romania, during the Prague Spring.

Ceauşescu's "working visits" in Transylvania during 1966 were aimed at reminding the Hungarians of the historical friendship of the two peoples inhabiting Transylvania at a time when the regime was pushing its policy on the importance of the historical continuity of the Romanian nation in its ancient homeland, and stressing the role of Transylvania—that "ancient Romanian soil" to use the favorite expression of the Romanian spokesmen—in the nation's history.[64]

While Ceaușescu did not try to hush up the "remnants of nationalism" that were still evident in certain areas of the country and admitted that nationalist manifestations among the Romanians toward Hungarians, and vice versa, could still be found, he characterized these instances as relics of the past which were doomed to disappear.[65]

As a part of this campaign there was an excessive emphasis on the historical traditions of friendship between the two peoples, a concept which unfortunately does not entirely correspond to historical truth. Perhaps to appease the Hungarians at a time of rising Romanian nationalism fostered by the regime, there were some concessions made to the Hungarian minority, especially in the cultural domain. There were more publications in the Hungarian language discussing the life of the minority, and a greater emphasis was laid on their cultural traditions. Numerous articles and essays published on the fortieth anniversary of *Korunk*, the leading cultural–political review in Transylvania, reflected this trend, which was also covered by the media in Hungary. However, there was no doubt that this line was aimed at emphasizing the special conditions and the special development of Hungarian culture in Transylvania. In the long run this line was aimed at justifying the curtailing of contacts between the Hungarian culture in Transylvania and the mainstream of Hungary's culture. The publications emphasized the strong ties between Hungarian and Romanian cultural traditions in Transylvania. Although at this stage Ceaușescu showed more willingness than Gheorghiu–Dej to allow the use of the Hungarian language and the development of the Hungarian culture,[66] the aim of this policy was to achieve maximum integration of the national minorities into the mainstream of Romania's political and cultural life.[67]

Hungary closely followed the wave of publications from Transylvania, reflecting a growing interest in the patterns of Hungarian culture abroad. Interestingly, some of the articles published in Hungary dealing with the life of Hungarians in Romania touched on some delicate issues, breaking for the first time some of the taboos in effect since the instauration of the Kádár regime. Such was the case of a short review article published in *Kritika* on the state of research into Hungarian literature published in Romania.[68] The reviewer, Mihály,

Czine, who published in the sixties and seventies numerous studies and essays on the cultural life of the Hungarians in the neighboring countries, wrote that for years Bolyai University in Cluj had carried out research on Hungarian culture, but

> later the Hungarian University stopped functioning, or rather merged with the Romanian University, and at the Babeş–Bolyai University there exists to this day a chair in Hungarian literary history.

Czine's reference to the fate of the Hungarian University in Cluj was much milder than the one in *Valóság* in 1970.[69] Czine also referred, perhaps for the first time in Hungary, to the fate of László Szabédi, the prominent Hungarian literary critic and lecturer who committed suicide following his "self–criticism" in the period of the purge of the Hungarian intellectuals in Transylvania in the wake of the Hungarian Revolution. Czine mentioned that the "tragically deceased László Szabédi was the author of the best study published in Romania on Hungarian poetry forms." No details were further mentioned as to the nature and reasons of his death, but its very mention was significant. It was bound to become known among colleagues in Hungary. One could also discern through Czine's lines several hints that the public in Hungary did not have enough access to the Hungarian culture from Romania. He remarked that on some books "we have information only through journals," noting that they were not available in Hungarian bookstores. Once again this was a mild reference. Compare this to Czine's remarks, four years later, that for years people in Hungary had known less about the Hungarian culture in Romania than about the literature of the awakening nations of Africa.

Attention was also drawn in Hungary to some Romanian publications on the progressive traditions of the intellectuals among the Hungarians in Romania and to their anti–Fascist activities in the interwar period in Romania, Czechoslovakia, and Yugoslavia. Czine and Pál E. Fehér wrote favorable reviews of the two books by Edgár Balogh.[70] One of them, *Hét próba*, was also published in Budapest by Szépirodalmi Könyvkiadó. Both reviewers stressed the importance of the books, which were Balogh's memoirs about his activities in interwar Czechoslovakia and later in Transylvania. No mention was made of the author's years of imprisonment and suffering. Such "delicate" aspects in the lives of some of the leading Hungarian intellectuals in Romania became known only gradually through the publications in Hungary.

The growing identification of the national history with the RCP, the militant nationalist tone in Ceauşescu's policies, and the contin-

uing differences between Hungary and Romania on inter–Bloc relations all had their impact on relations between the two states. The
Western media often reported on the strains in Hungarian–Romanian
relations, and such leading Western experts as Paul Lendvai linked
the worsening in Hungarian–Romanian relations to the nationality
policies of the Ceauşescu regime.[71]

Although from time to time Hungary took a conciliatory tone
toward the Romanian ideological and foreign policy line, criticism
of some Romanian steps pointed to the dissension between the two
states. Hungary criticized Romania's establishment of diplomatic relations with West Germany, her position during the 1967 Middle East
War, and her attitude toward proposals for meetings between representatives of Communist parties. Romania, for its part, showed
readiness to continue a dialogue with Hungary—perhaps to ease its
isolation within the East European system.

Ceauşescu's visit to Hungary in May 1967 was a landmark in the
contacts that nevertheless took place between the two sides. It took
place amidst media reports in Hungary aimed at refuting Western
reports on the worsening of relations between the two states. Radio
Budapest described the visit as a "surprise to bourgeois correspondents" so soon after the tension at the Karlovy Vary conference, and
the alleged divergences between the Hungarian and Romanian lines.[72]

In spite of Hungarian attempts to present a bright picture of
Hungarian–Romanian relations, the absence in the final communiqué
of any mention of the German question and the situation in the international Communist movement indicated that no agreement had
been reached. Nor was there any mention of the national minorities.
This omission stood in marked contrast to the atmosphere between
Hungary and Czechoslovakia. During Kádár's visit to Prague in October 1967, he declared the solution of the problems of the Hungarian
minority in Czechoslovakia to be completely satisfactory.[73]

Once again, as had become customary, Hungary expressed its
position vis-à-vis the Romanian line in greetings on the occasion of
Romania's Liberation Day. The Hungarian press reminded Romania
that the "key for further successes for the Romanian people lay in
belonging to the fraternal family of nations, and in pursuing a policy
of proletarian internationalism." This was also an appropriate time
to remind the Romanian leadership that the uprising of August 1944
had been successful because it was part of a vast anti–Fascist front
led by the Soviet Union,[74] an assertion minimized by the Romanian
line.

A more overt Hungarian criticism of the Romanian policies appeared in a full-page article by Kádár published in *Pravda*.[75] Indi-

cating the importance that the Kremlin attached to the Hungarian support for the Soviet line, Kádár, without mentioning the name of the main culprit, attacked those holding so–called "neutralist" views within the Communist movement, asserting that unity had been broken by unnamed "elements of national isolationism."

Inter–Party relations influenced various aspects of bilateral Hungarian–Romanian relations, as indicated by the approaching expiration of the twenty–year Treaty of Friendship and Cooperation, signed in January 1948. The Treaty would not be renewed until 1972—the last to be renewed among the socialist states. On the eve of the expiration of the Treaty, Paul Niculescu–Mizil, who had emerged as the professional troubleshooter in relations with Hungary, arrived in Budapest for short talks, linked to the situation in the Communist movement and the expiration of the Treaty. There was an atmosphere of crisis. The Treaty was not renewed, nor did Romania promise to participate in the forthcoming consultative meeting of Communist parties to be held in Budapest. It was symptomatic of the coolness in Hungarian–Romanian relations that the media in the two states did not mention when the Treaty was to be renewed. By contrast, close to the expiration of the Bulgarian–Romanian Treaty of Friendship, Ceauşescu spoke of its imminent renewal, and attended a celebration at the Bulgarian Embassy in Bucharest on the anniversary of the Treaty. A much less prominent representative, Iosif Banc, attended a similar ceremony at the Hungarian Embassy in Bucharest.

Romania finally did agree to send a delegation, led by Niculescu Mizil, to the Budapest consultative meeting. However, on the fifth day of the proceedings, on March 1, 1968, the delegation made a dramatic walkout, following Syrian criticism of the Romanian policies in the Middle East.[76] In spite of some conciliatory remarks, Hungary did not seek to conceal some of the differences with Romania before the Hungarian public. Zoltán Komócsin denounced "symptoms of nationalism and separatist trends within the Communist movement,[77] while Tibor Pethoe, a noted journalist and member of the National Assembly, contended that Romania's policies were governed by certain factors which caused her to "loosen ties with members of the socialist community." As for the future, Pethö expressed optimism, and in a mildly cynical tone remarked that he believed that the leaders of Romania "know where they belong." Romania, he added

did not want to defect—if I may say so—and leave the socialist community. I only want to emphasize that Romania is pursuing its own, in my view exaggerated, interests, to the detriment of the socialist community.[78]

Differences between Hungary and Romania were also highlighted by Kádár's speech at the fourth Congress of the Patriotic People's Front in April 1968, when he declared that "our public opinion was sorry to learn that the standpoints of our country and that of Romania diverged in appraising the German question and the Israeli aggression."[79]

Against the background of the strains in Hungarian–Romanian relations there was also an important development regarding Romania's nationality policy—the complete elimination of the Mureş-Hungarian Autonomous Region.[80] In January 1968 the government published the new territorial division of the country, after the draft program had been announced in October 1967. Although the "national composition of the population" was taken into account, as Ceauşescu had promised,[81] through a careful process of gerrymandering, parts of the previous HAR and the Mureş HAR were merged with areas from other counties to create Mureş County (a new enlarged area including Tîrgu–Mureş, the former capital of the HAR). Although Mureş and Braşov Counties had large Hungarian populations, the new divisions resulted in its fragmentation. The strengthening of Party control over local administration, as approved by the RCP National Congress, left no doubt that, even if the administrative changes were not initially aimed primarily at reducing the rights of the Hungarian minority, the very elimination of the words "Hungarian Region"—void of any real content, as many Hungarians claimed—was significant. As Robert R. King remarked, the changes meant the "breakdown of the sense of national isolation."[82] As such, this step was important in pursuing a policy of integration of the Hungarian minority, leading directly to more overt assimilationist pressures.

Hungary, it seems, was informed of the planned changes during Ceauşescu's visit to Hungary in May 1967, and shortly before the decision to carry out the changes was publicly announced, János Fazekas, Romania's Vice Premier, visited Hungary, where he gave reassurances that the planned changes would not affect the status of the Hungarians in Romania. The media in Hungary and official spokesmen virtually ignored the nature of the changes. The reason for Hungary's passivity in the face of several signs for a growing interest by Budapest in the fate of the Hungarians in the neighboring countries was Hungary's intention not to strain further the relations with Romania, at the time when it was becoming the foremost East European critic of Romanian policies on issues related to the Communist movement.

On the Road to the Prague Spring: The Hungarians in Czechoslovakia, 1957–1968

The lives of the more than 530,000 Hungarians in Czechoslovakia (according to the 1961 census) between the Hungarian Revolution and the Prague Spring of 1968 were affected by such internal events as the growing strains in Czech–Slovak relations, the opposition to Czechoslovak—or rather Czech—centralism in Slovakia, and the political changes leading to the rise of the reformist leadership. Externally, the Hungarian Revolution loomed large. We have already noted Czechoslovakia's satisfaction with the loyalty of its Hungarians during the Revolution. But twelve years later, during the events of 1968, when the Hungarians raised demands for more rights and complete equality, the Slovak press instantly uncovered some of the fears that had been underlying Hungarian and Slovak relations for many years— the strong support of the Hungarians in the country for the Revolution in Hungary, and especially the emergence of Hungarian irredentism during those days. Retrospectively, it seems that the misgivings about stirrings among the Hungarians were indeed more profound and even more justified than the pronouncements over the loyalty of the Hungarians regarding the building of socialism in Czechoslovakia. Yet it should be stressed that the Czechoslovak authorities did not proceed in their nationality policy in the panicky way that characterized the post–1955 attitude of the Romanian regime toward the Hungarians there, where the danger of Hungarian nationalism was indeed more menacing than in Slovakia. The antinationalist campaign in Romania leveled against Hungarian intellectuals was harsher and more protracted than the reaction in Slovakia during that period.

Developments in the shaping of Czechoslovakia's nationality policy with regard to the Hungarians in the years following the Revolution in Hungary indicated that some steps may have been a belated reaction to the fears imminent since 1956, as well as to the internal conflicts building up in the country. The first notable change was somewhat of a reversal in the policy favoring the Hungarian minority that came about in 1960. At that time a new Constitution was put into effect and the administration of Slovakia was reorganized, which affected the ethnic boundaries of several *kraje*. These changes certainly justify the delineation of a distinct period in the history of the Hungarian minority, as several Western scholars have suggested.[83]

The Czechoslovak Constitution of 1960, which to the surprise of observers announced the advent of the long awaited "stage of socialism" in the development of the country, also heralded the restructuring of some of the main pillars of Czech and Slovak relations that had prevailed since the Košice Program—namely, the official abrogation of all signs of local autonomy that supposedly had been held until then in the hand of the Slovaks.[84] Regarding nationality groups, the new constitution dealt only with their individual and not their collective rights. This was criticized several years later, both in Hungary and in Czechoslovakia, especially after the Prague Spring. Although the number of Hungarians in the higher legislative and executive bodies was proportionate to their number in the population, they could represent the Hungarians only as individuals, not a national minority. Moreover, certain clauses dealing with the general rights of national minorities had been omitted, so the Hungarians could have neither representative bodies nor executive institutions of their own.[85]

The consequence of the administrative changes in Slovakia in 1960 was the numerical reduction of the Hungarian population in several areas, while in only two districts did they remain a majority— Dunajska Streda and Komarno.[86] Economic considerations and the need for efficiency played a significant role in the administrative changes, but it seems that the changes also reflected the regime's determination to reduce the Hungarian influence in the areas where they still had a numerical majority, or constituted a considerable part of the population. After all, the same economic factors and the need for efficiency could have induced the regime to create predominantly Hungarian districts. It was hardly coincidental that in both Romania and Czechoslovakia, economic considerations served as a justification for a process that resulted in the minimizing of Hungarian influence. At least in Slovakia, in contrast to Romania, the leadership acknowledged during the Prague Spring that the administrative changes had increased the number of Slovaks, giving them a majority in most of the districts. Arató's study in Hungary also pointed out that while the justification for the 1960 changes was the furthering of closer cooperation between Slovaks and Hungarians, in some areas the changes benefited the Slovak majority.[87]

Both the publication of the new constitution and the administrative reorganization were preceded and followed by an intensive campaign elucidating the policies of the regime. Noteworthy was the line which sidetracked the nationality question, while emphasizing the importance of the main task—the building of socialism. To achieve this, greater significance was to be attached to the "deepening of Czechoslovak socialist patriotism."[88] In a similar tone, the Communist Party warned of the dangers of "national isolationism," intimating that the Hungarians might misinterpret the favorable policies developed after 1948 as a sign that they could develop their own institutions, separate culture, and ultimate isolation from the existing political, social, and cultural environment. This line was rapidly implemented in the school system.

An impetus was given to the learning of the Slovak language and to bilingualism as a *sine qua non* for Hungarian equal participation in the life of the country. This trend certainly ran counter to the previous policy, which had encouraged the development of facilities for Hungarians to learn and speak in Hungarian after years of discrimination following World War II. On the one hand, as expressed in the resolutions of the Congress of the SCP in 1958, the regime called for the creation of conditions which would allow the use of Hungarian in the "national committees"—the local administrative organs—but on the other, it emphasized that the study of Slovak was necessary for the implementation of the rights of the national minorities. In fact, as *Új Szó*[89] put it, the linguistic rights of the Hungarians and their learning of Slovak were inseparable.

The campaign aimed at intensifying the learning of the Slovak language was frequently accompanied by self–criticism, in which the Slovak CP organs admitted that the promises for free use of the Hungarian language had not been kept. Such shortcomings made it difficult to demand the study of the Slovak language by the Hungarians. At the same time, the more the regime expressed openness in recognizing its own mistakes, the easier it was to pressure the Hungarians into accepting the necessity of bilingualism. This campaign lasted for several years, and was often reiterated by the leading spokesmen of the Slovak CP. Thus, Karol Bacilek, the First Secretary, speaking before the eighth General Assembly of CSEMADOK in 1962, stressed that any division on ethnic lines in the state organs would "alienate us from one another and prejudice our common aim. First and foremost we must establish the principle of bilingualism in areas of mixed population."[90]

Understandably the Party emphasized education as a way to achieve its goals. The schools—and continuing and adult educations should be seen as part of the system—were given the task to deepen the "socialist patriotic consciousness" among the minorities. This theme was largely elaborated in one of the most important articles of the period, that of Jan Uher on the "Certain Questions Concerning the Life of the Citizens of the Hungarian Nationality in the CSSR."[91] Uher underlined the importance of mastering the Slovak language, and provided the Marxist–Leninist framework for the understanding of the trends of Czechoslovakia's national minority policy at the time.

From the end of 1958 there appeared growing signs to the effect that the regime was about to act for the merger of Hungarian and Slovak schools in order to foster the education for "socialist patriotism." The CC of the Slovak CP discussed the issues in January 1959 and proposed the "organizational amalgamation" of Hungarian and Slovak schools, called for the teaching of some subjects in the Slovak language and for an intensification in joint educational activities involving Slovak and Hungarian pupils at all levels of education. In a series of debates in the Party's forums, several shortcomings were highlighted, which needed urgent consideration by the relevant authorities. Thus the SCP pointed out that Slovak–language classes were inadequate, there were not enough opportunities for "practical implementation" of Slovak language skills, which resulted in a disadvantage for those Hungarian students who, lacking a working knowledge of Slovak, had difficulties in continuing higher education and could not integrate into the political, economic, and cultural life.[92] In other words, those Hungarians who took too seriously the right to speak Hungarian, were about to face some problems.

One of the practical steps taken by the authorities was to urge the educators and teachers to improve their skills in the Slovak language. *Új Szó* frequently complained and published details on teachers in Hungarian villages who did not speak Slovak, and thus were unable to implement the new line. *Új Szó* reported:

> The continuing political and professional development of these teachers poses a serious problem [as a] significant part of the Hungarian educational cadres do not have a good command of the Slovak language.[93]

The process of amalgamating Hungarian and Slovak schools had a far–reaching impact on the relationship between the authorities and the Hungarian minority, as it deepened suspicions on both sides. The Slovak authorities reported cases of Hungarian opposition to such steps, or lack of understanding of the goals of this policy. At the same time the Hungarians feared that the authorities were about to eliminate the Hungarian schools gradually. These anxieties were strengthened by what the Party later called "administrative interventions and misunderstandings,"[94] when more than the planned proportion of classes were being taught in the Slovak language, replacing the instruction in Hungarian.

The new educational policy had some positive results, though, as it enabled the number of Hungarians enrolling in higher education establishments to increase. The price to be paid for this was of course their closer affinity to the Slovak language and culture. The authorities pointed out that in the mid–sixties only 36 percent of the Hungarians went on to some form of higher education, while 60 percent of the Slovaks did so.[95] The evidence does not necessarily suggest that the regime pursued a deliberate policy of assimilating the Hungarians, but in the long run the effects of the policies amounted to an assimilationist trend—if not direct pressure. As in the case of the administrative reorganization of Slovakia, the campaign to learn the Slovak language and the amalgamation of Hungarian and Slovak schools was very similar to the process that was taking place at the same time in Romania.

From the late fifties the Party stepped up its efforts to enroll in its ranks more members from among the Hungarians. The starting point was difficult, as the discrimination practiced against the Hungarians was reflected at the Slovak CP. After all, the same Party which for years had rejected Hungarians was now eager to take credit for their integration within its membership and among its leading organs. During 1959–1962 numerous items in *Szabad Szó* dealt with the small number of Hungarians in the Party, especially in the rural committees and provincial towns. The situation in the town of Somorja was characteristic: while Hungarians constituted 85–90 percent of the population, they represented only about 15–20 percent of the Slovak CP members.

By the mid–sixties there was an increase in the number of Hungarians in the Party, but proportionally they were still underrepresented. In 1964 there were 25,000 Hungarian Party members, which accounted for less than 5 percent of the Hungarian population in Slovakia. Although the official statistics often reported on the rising number of Hungarians holding various posts in the Party organs and the local administrative authorities, in fact the regime did not formulate a clear policy as to the role of the Hungarian national minority in the country's life. After 1968 Slovak studies widely elaborated on what were termed mistakes with regard to the nationality policy, and these were periodically discussed and criticized by the Party. These mistakes were committed on what can be described as both the tactical and the strategic levels, and lacking a clear long–range nationality policy, as the Slovak CP analyzed it after 1963–1964, *ad–hoc* measures served as the basis for the country's nationality policy.

Although the Party did not mention at the time that the mistakes originated in the 1960 Constitution (which dealt with the linguistic–cultural aspect of the national minorities, and not with their collective rights as separate nationalities), after 1968 it was made clear by the Czechoslovak regime that the overall conception as reflected in the 1960 Constitution, had been wrong. This criticism, which was one of the results of the debate between the Hungarians and the Slovaks during the Prague Spring, also pointed to the fact that the Czechslovak government did not conduct any debates on the national questions of the country, so that, as time went on, the policies pursued by the regime became gradually outdated. Not that the Slovak Communists regretted the pressures exerted on the Hungarians to integrate into the system through bilingualism, but rather that not enough had been done to prove to the Hungarians that the regime meant to help their integration by these educational pressures.

Probably as an answer to complaints by Hungarians that they still suffered from prejudices and encountered difficulties with the authorities, the Party stepped up its efforts for bilingualism. As *Új Szó* stated, the "neglect of bilingualism is the root for the problems concerning the implementation of the nationality policy."[96] As frictions between the Slovak and Hungarian populations increased, and Hungarian anxieties over the policies pursued since 1960 made themselves felt, there were rising voices in the Communist Party to reassess the nationality policy and to discuss more openly the problems confronting the Hungarians. As usual, past mistakes were to be blamed, and Vladimir Kouchky, the Secretary of the CC of the CzCP, and one of the leading ideologists of the regime, declared that the resolutions on the development of the Hungarian minority had not been correctly implemented.

The internal debates led to the publication in December 1964 of one of the most important documents regarding the nationality question.[97] It harshly condemned past practices and excesses of Slovak nationalism, especially in the late forties, and took to task the entire Party and Government leadership and apparatus for these mistakes. The document also reviewed the decade since the 1954 purges and the decisions at that time concerning the nationalities, and clearly hinted that a Hungarian–Slovak rapprochement had still not been reached. Slovak nationalism was, of course, condemned and blamed for some of the problems, just as "isolationist, chauvinist" trends among the Hungarians were also highlighted.

The immediate result of the December 1964 resolutions was the beginning of a more open atmosphere in discussing mistakes of the past, and allowing Hungarian intellectuals to tackle in public some of the delicate issues, most of which were linked to the difficult forties. This new line found expression in the publication of studies concerning the national question, which represented the first serious attempt to cope with issues considered until then as taboo. This new wave of "mea culpa" also included details published in the non–Hungarian press, addressed to the general public in Czechoslovakia. Articles as those in *Kulturný Život*,[98] described for the first time manifestations of anti–Hungarian feelings, and referred to the process of re–Slovakization and the resettlement of Hungarians. The tone of the articles in the Czechoslovak press indicated that the regime was attempting to win over the loyalty of the Hungarian minority by reinforcements—such as the unmasking of Slovak nationalism after World War II, while at the same time also condemning Hungarian nationalism.

The Hungarian–language press in Slovakia, and in 1965 there were 22 newspapers and periodicals, discussed in detail problems of the Hungarian minority. They concentrated not only on the persecutions until 1948, but also on some more recent grievances. While all such publications were always in accordance with the Party line, the atmosphere was certainly more open, and the criticism levelled at the various authorities was constructive, not only in name, but also to a large extent in its content. The Hungarian publications, especially the literary *Irodalmi Szemle*, played a leading role in calling for the fostering of the "progressive traditions" of the Hungarian minority, and for the strengthening of "national pride, which should not be seen as bourgeois–nationalism." Such an attitude, stressed the Hungarian press in Slovakia, was in line with the campaign for socialist patriotism.

The most important contribution to the debates on the fate of the Hungarians in Czechoslovakia was the publication of Juraj Zvara's "The Solution of the Hungarian Nationality Question in Slovakia," in 1965. Zvara, who was to become the leading authority in Slovakia on the nationality question, detailed the phases of the country's nationality policy, and harshly criticized the anti–Magyar policies of the late forties and the mistakes in treating the Hungarians after 1948. Zvara's perceptions should not be seen as the "continuation of the well established tradition of double morality and double standards in Slovak thinking on the Hungarian question," nor did Zvara try to "work out a compromise between the nationalist view, so dear to the heart of Slovak historiography, and the Marxist ideology reigning officially supreme in a Communist society."[99] His sole aim was and remained in his subsequent publications (e.g., in "The Nation and National Consciousness" published in 1982) to interpret the Party line on the issue against the background of a keener presentation of the situation of the Hungarians. Interestingly and paradoxically, his book in 1965 appeared at first only in Hungarian, and when it later appeared in Slovakia, it drew criticism from dogmatic Marxists, who in fact represented a Slovak nationalist line. Such was the criticism by Maria Lavova, in the *Historicky Casopis* of February 1967, in which the notion of "rightful self–defensive nationalism" appeared as a justification for Slovak attitudes toward the Hungarians.

Zvara did break new ground in the presentation of a gloomier

picture of the patterns of postwar Hungarian–Slovak relationship under the Communists, and his revelations and tone of discussion were
innovative. As a review of his studies published in Hungary noted,
"to write all these in 1965 was a brave and internationalist deed." [100]
Important in the discussions in Czechoslovakia on the nationality
question were the growing references to the "bridge building" role
of the national minorities in the relations between the East European
socialist states, increasingly manifested in Hungarian–Czechoslovak,
Hungarian–Yugoslav, but not Hungarian–Romanian interstate relations. However, before this notion could be translated into practical
steps in the relations between the neighboring states, and in this case
between Hungary and Czechoslovakia, there was an urgent need to
"clean one's own house" of the remnants of unwanted nationalism.

Hungarian literature in Slovakia was immediately drafted into
the new critical reappraisal of the recent past. The literary press,
led by *Irodalmi Szemle,* as well as the literary pages of the other
periodicals bloomed with stories that only recently had been taboo.
The Hungarian reader could feel that justice was being done, and
that grievances were indeed aired by a more understanding regime.
Such leading intellectuals as Zoltán Fábry had first to adjust themselves to the changing atmosphere. which from their perspective was
a favorable development, as more artistic freedom was promised to
the nationality intellectuals. As in every socialist state, the intellectuals at the time had to adjust to the Party line, and thus it was
natural that the Hungarian section of the Slovak Writers' Union—
whose very formation was a sign of the relative thaw—should critically review their own past, condemning "Zhdanovist practices." [101]
While certainly not all the readers among the Hungarians in Slovakia
understood the meaning of such political jargon, there were more
down–to–earth pronouncements, which had a clearer appeal. Fábry,
who had a long account to settle with the Slovak Communist leadership of the years following 1945, wrote that "there was a time when
our existence, our word, our language was in oblivion. We had no
freedom of speech and of expression." [102]

CSEMADOK played a very active role in this relative thaw in
the attitude of the regime to the cultural rights of the national minorities, and in keeping within the limits of the 1960 Constitution,
numerous cultural activities were organized, especially in the smaller
villages. CSEMADOK's illustrated weekly magazine, *A Hét,* published in 37,000 copies, appealed to the wider Hungarian population,
while the more exclusive *Irodalmi Szemle* was published by the Hungarian section of the Slovak Writers' Union ten times a year. Along
with the Hungarian daily published in Bratislava, *Új Szó,* the minor-

ity press in the mid–sixties showed signs of revival and a marked thaw as compared to the late forties and the mid–fifties.

The Kádár regime followed with keen interest the developments in Czechoslovakia's minority policy.

The Kádár line was laid down by Premier Ferenc Münnich's visit to Czechoslovakia in December 1958 (the period of the post–November 1956 consolidation) in a manner very similar to Kádár's visit to Romania that same year. Hungary gave assurances that it was satisfied with the solution of the minority question in Czechoslovakia, and that it had no territorial claim to any part of the country. This line was reiterated numerous times on various occasions, as it is customary in the conduct of relationships between socialist countries. Against the background of the deliberations on the national question in Czechoslovakia, President Novotný visited Hungary in October 1964. The Hungarian leadership warmly praised Czechoslovakia's nationality policy, and Kádár declared that Hungary was satisfied that the Hungarians in Czechoslovakia had been granted "complete equality."[103] The approbation in Hungary of the "correct Marxist–Leninist policy" in Czechoslovakia was in stark contrast to the patterns of anti–Romanian criticism in that period. Yet another sign of the growing differentiation in Hungary's attitude to the solving of the nationality issue in Czechoslovakia, as compared to Romania, was Kádár's visit to Czechoslovakia in October 1967, in which he warmly praised the "satisfactory solution" of the issues of the Hungarian minority.[104]

Such voices differed widely from the frequent condemnation of Romanian nationalism. In point of fact, Kádár's pronouncement was rather ill–timed, as several months later, during the Prague Spring, the Hungarians expressed dissatisfaction over their place and role in Czechoslovakia, and there were even reports that when some Hungarian grievances were raised, the authorities rejected them invoking Kádár's praises.[105] Nevertheless, Kádár's words of praise conveyed the message that Hungary had no special objection to the policies pursued at the time by Prague, or rather by Bratislava, with regard to the Hungarians. During the numerous Hungarian–Czechoslovak interstate contacts, several forms of cooperation were expanded in which the Hungarians and the Slovaks were involved on each other's territory. Thus, in 1964 an agreement was reached to use some schoolbooks published in Hungary in the Hungarian schools in Slovakia, and a similar agreement facilitated the instruction in the mother tongue for Slovaks in Hungary. Joint book publishing was expanded, involving more translations from Hungarian authors and less emphasis on Marxist–Leninist classics or translations from Soviet authors, as was the case in the late forties. In 1965 Czechoslovakia brought from Hungary 181,000 copies of 127 titles.[106] The Madách publishing house in Bratislava, established in 1967, played a leading role not only in the promotion of Hungarian literature originating in Slovakia but also in marketing and distributing the books brought in from Hungary. Although no exact details can be obtained, it seems that periodicals and journals from Hungary were more available in Czechoslovakia than in Romania. The Czechoslovak regime was less apprehensive about Magyar irredentism and nationalism, and it interpreted correctly that while the media in Hungary were reflecting a growing interest in Hungarian national values of the past, and in the fate of the Hungarians over the borders, it certainly did not contain subversive items, as the Romanian authorities believed. Publications in Hungary stressed the positive cultural developments among Hungarians in Slovakia. Thus, *Kritika* wrote in 1965 that "in the last few years the Hungarian literature in Slovakia has become more lively, colorful, reinforced by new style and content."[107] Although in this respect there was a similar attitude between the publications in Hungary toward the state of Hungarian culture in Romania and Czechoslovakia, as for example in the case of the reviews published in Hungary about the renewal of *Korunk's* publication in Romania, overall, the attitude toward developments in Slovakia was more favorable.

With the emphasis on "socialist patriotism" in Hungary, and the internal debate there on the role of the nation under socialism, some aspects of Slovak historiogrpahy came under criticism, especially in 1964–1965. The Hungarian–Slovak historiographical polemics did not have a direct linkage with specific aspects of Slovak politics, unlike the Hungarian–Romanian polemic, which was linked to the strengthening of the nationalist line in Romanian historiography; but it was an expression of Hungary's rejection of a Slovak nationalist line as it emerged from the mid–sixties, until and including the Prague Spring. The debates concentrated mostly on aspects of the 1848 Revolutions, as the Slovak historians writing on the role of Ludevit Stur in 1848, expressed Slovak nationalist sentiments for which they were immediately taken to task by Hungarian historians.[108] Both sides, armed with their own interpretation of the correct Marxist line, brought mutual accusations of nationalism and revisionism.

The fact that Vladimir Mináč, a well–known author and essayist, who wrote some of the major polemic studies defending nineteenth–century Slovak nationalism against Magyar nationalism, was elected in June 1966 as candidate member of the CC of the CzCP, indicated that the polemics were carried on not only between leading academics, but also among those who held Party functions. The course of the

Prague Spring and the events following the Soviet invasion shifted the emphasis from the historiographical polemics to more up-to-date issues, and the debate between Hungarian and Slovak historians, unlike the one between Hungarian and Romanian historians, faded away, and has not been revived.

Chapter V
Winds of Change from Budapest
"Discovering" the Hungarians in the Neighboring States

The debate that took place in Hungary on the meaning of nation and patriotism under socialism and on the remnants of nationalism led to what can be described as a "higher stage" in the regime's tackling of such delicate issues—the rapid "discovery" of the Hungarians abroad along with a redefinition of Hungary's role with regard to the parts of the nation living in the neighboring socialist states. The Kádár regime underwent a marked change in attitude on this issue from late 1967 on.

The growing interest in the Hungarians abroad was bound to have immediate effects on the nature of interstate relations, as Hungary positioned itself—almost overnight—into the role of an "interested party" as regards the fate of the Hungarian minorities abroad. The regime was about to implement, to the growing displeasure of at least one neighbor, Romania, its perceptions on the constructive role that the national minorities were expected to have in the relations between socialist states—namely, that of serving as bridges of friendship and understanding. Moreover, by calling for a closer monitoring of the fate of the Hungarians abroad, Budapest also opened its doors for a reciprocal relationship between the minorities living in Hungary and the respective "mother–tongue" states of these nationalities.

In any Communist regime there is a constant search for legitimacy. The Kádár regime scored some very good points, as the issue of the Hungarians abroad was close to the heart of most of the Hungarian nation. For years the regime had been taken to task by its internal critics, including leading personalities of the intelligentsia for not doing enough, if anything, to ease the pressures on the Hungarians over the borders, especially in Romania and Slovakia, and now it was the HSWP itself that brought home to the nation the necessity to watch more closely the developments among Hungarians abroad, and made this concern into one of the main pillars of its policy vis–à–vis the neighboring states.[1]

The line proclaimed by Hungary between late 1967 and the spring of 1968 has in essence not changed to this day. One can attribute the subsequent development of strained relations with Romania, the often critical dialogue with Czechoslovakia (and to some extent with Yugoslavia), and the praises lavished on the Soviet Union's policies toward its small Hungarian minority to the guidelines formulated and publicized in that period. The keynote of this policy is Hungary's non-interference into the internal affairs of the neighboring states, while reserving the right to closely monitor the nationality policy of these neighbors and to criticize any repression or discrimination against their Hungarian minorities.[2] Budapest stressed from the beginning that the Hungarians abroad were—and should remain—completely loyal citizens of their respectives states, but neither they—nor especially their governments—should forget that their cultural and ethnic identity was to be preserved and fostered. Hungary would pursue the same line toward its own minorities. As later developments bore out—especially in the case of the never-ending polemics with Romania—this "interested party" policy was often received with reservations and even hostility, and although Hungary became a self-proclaimed "bridge builder" of friendship with the neighboring states through the nationalities, the pillars were not always there on the opposite bank.

Although the first official pronouncements on Hungary's new line came in late 1967, there had been intimations for some time that Hungary was about to enhance the significance of the national minorities. This became evident from the frequent publications on the nationalities in Hungary and their role in interstate relations, and from the stepping up of reports and the growing number of publications on aspects of the life of the Hungarians abroad. In its mutual contacts with Yugoslavia, and also in line with Yugoslav perceptions on this issue, Hungary emphasized the constructive role of the nationalities in their relations.

The first indication of the new line was given by Dobozy, the Secretary of the Hungarian Writers' Union, in October 1967, when he declared that "our solidarity and responsibility for the fate of the Hungarians outside our frontiers cannot be considered nationalism . . . but only the deeper and more exemplary practice of internationalism."[3] The essence of this statement was reiterated several times in various political and cultural forums by leading politicians and intellectual figures. Dobozy and other leading personalities openly appealed to the Hungarians abroad to preserve their national identity, and promised to pursue the fostering of Hungarian national culture abroad. The most outspoken position was taken at the Hungarian Writers' Conference in March 1968, when Dobozy declared that Hungarians abroad should not surrender their ethnic and national characteristics under any kind of compulsion.[4] Although such statements were startling, Dobozy disregarded or minimized the fact that the neighboring regimes, in whose internal affairs Hungary vowed not to interfere, were exposing the Hungarians to occasional pressures which displeased Hungary. Thus, it becomes self–evident that the preservation of Hungarian ethnic identity abroad does not depend solely on the determination of the local Magyars to do so, but also on the good will and understanding of the respective socialist regimes.

The Kádár regime was very careful not to insert too much implicit criticism of neighboring regimes into speeches and publications, and to emphasize the cultural dimension in Hungary's closer monitoring of the lives of the Hungarians abroad—hence the leading role of such cultural organs as the Writers' Union and of such literary journals as *Élét es Irodalom* in the campaign for cultural minority rights abroad. The resolutions of the Writers' Union reflected this line, as one of its clauses referred, for the first time in a Communist document, to the issue of preserving national identity and culture among the Hungarians abroad.

From the deliberations in the cultural forums the new line was carried over to debates in more politically significant institutions. The fourth Congress of the Patriotic People's Front (PPF) formed a subcommittee which dealt with the situation of the Hungarian minority abroad—yet another unprecedented step in Communist politics—and adopted a resolution to the effect that the "national minorities should become the agents and sources of closer relations, not of isolation among the socialist countries." Some linguistic formulations used by this committee, as well as by members of the Congress, were innovative. Frequently the speakers mentioned that one–third of the Hungarian nation lived abroad, a fact very well known to the citizens of Hungary but never mentioned in such a context by the authorities. The PPF stressed that any reference to the Hungarians abroad, as well as to the minorities in Hungary, should start from an "internationalist" point of view, implying that certain guidelines should be kept in mind when discussing the issue, lest nationalist argumentation should creep into the debates.

The next step following the discussions on the Hungarians abroad at the PPF Congress was a special session of the Hungarian Writers' Union in May 1968, devoted to the state of Hungarian culture in the neighboring countries. The deliberations marked the culmination of the keen interest shown by the Hungarian media in this issue for a number of years, but never had such a topic appeared as the theme of a full–scale discussion. The discussions aroused great interest in the media, reflecting the public's preoccupation with topics that until then had been regarded as taboo. Several points were singled out in the special session of the Writers' Union which were further expanded in the media coverage. One was Hungary's responsibility—and this word became more and more frequently used in conjunction with the role that Hungary was expected to play—to aid the Hungarians abroad in preserving their culture, and to strengthen their attachment to Hungarian culture.[5] Another point was the relevance to Hungarian culture of Hungarian literature published in the neighboring countries. The implication here was that Hungarians abroad should be urged to remain loyal to their countries while keeping in mind that their culture was an integral, organic part of the Hungarian culture. In order to bring home this point, numerous publications in Hungary stressed that until then references to the Hungarian culture abroad had been "sporadic and superficial."[6]

A characteristic presentation of the new Hungarian line was carried by *Élet és Irodalom*, in an article entitled "Double Ties—Double Responsibility," in which the author analyzed the nature of the relationship between the Hungarians in Hungary and those over the borders.[7] Hungary was striving for closer contacts with them on the premise that their culture belonged to the mainstream of Hungarian culture. The article anticipated some voices of opposition to this line from the neighboring states, and it preempted the criticism by stating that if a true Marxist–Leninist nationality policy had been implemented in a neighboring socialist state, there would be no reason why Hungary should not actively follow and support the developments among the Hungarians there.

As *Élet és Irodalom* had intimated, the new line was indeed criticized. Romania could not leave such a policy unchallenged at a time when the Romanian regime was making efforts to foster close contacts between the nationalities in Romania and was pursuing its own brand of national communism. The already strained relationship between the two states, involving issues linked to the international Communist movement and to foreign policy, was further put to test on this new front, which was about to become dominant in their relationship.

The major Romanian response came in the Bucharest *Gazeta Literară* in an article by the Transylvanian writer, János Szász, who rejected the themes advanced by the press in Hungary.[8] "We cannot agree with people who undertake to assume responsibility for our literature," wrote Szász, and deemed that such an attempt "can only be considered a violation of those tenets which should govern the relations between friendly and fraternal states." Szász also emphasized that Hungarian literature had common traditions with the literature in Hungary, and that there were "obvious common elements, parallel themes due to the fact that social reality in fraternal Hungary is similar to that of Romania." Thus, the Romanian position disputed the need of the Hungarians in Romania for the self–styled feeling of responsibility emanating from Budapest and also called into question the alleged common links between the cultures of the two states.

One of the main implications of the Romanian line was the tenet that the cultures of the national minorities in Romania were more closely linked to the Romanian culture than to those of the neighboring states. Such a perception was already evident at the time of the first deliberations in Hungary on the links with Hungarians abroad. Although in an interview with *Népszabadág*, Edgár Balogh did not react directly to the new line emerging from Budapest, he emphasized that the literature of the two brotherly states were linked with "thousands and thousands of threads." Balogh also gave an account of the excellent conditions in which Hungarian culture was flourishing in socialist Romania, as if implying that the Hungarians were in no need of the sort of protection offered by Hungary.[9] Balogh's intention was clearly to shift the center of gravity of Hungarians culture in Romania from the organic linkage suggested by Hungary toward closer affinity with Romania's socialist culture. Thus, Balogh propounded that the "Hungarian literature in Romania is a major force in the shaping of Romania's socialist culture, enriching the totality of Hungarian culture and that of Eastern Europe." Both Balogh and Szász agreed that cooperation between the two states involving the minorities should be strengthened and expanded, but clearly this should be done on Bucharest's terms and not along the lines suggested by Budapest.

Besides several such polemical articles, the Romanian CP also took action to assure the loyalty of the Hungarian minority against the background of the developments in Czechoslovakia and the Warsaw Pact threats at that country, which were followed with great anxiety. Ceauşescu and several other high–ranking leaders met with a group of Hungarian intellectuals in June 1968 to elicit a declaration of support for the regime's nationality policy. Hungary's self–styled "responsibility" for the Hungarian culture abroad was received with mixed feelings in Czechoslovakia and Yugoslavia. In Czechoslovakia the new Hungarian line was interwoven with the overall problematics of the situation of the Hungarians in Slovakia during the Prague Spring. There were no direct polemics with Hungary on this issue, but the strain in Slovak–Hungarian relations in the summer of 1968 was also linked to the new interest shown by Hungary in the Hungarians abroad.

Neither was there a direct polemic between Hungary and Yugoslavia on the new line from Budapest. But unlike the vehement criticism from Romania, there was a more reasonable argumentation by Hungarian intellectuals in Yugoslavia. *Új Symposion,* a rather avant–garde Hungarian periodical published in Novi Sad, rejected the Hungarian perceptions of the ties between the Hungarian culture in the various countries. *Új Symposion* stood up for the free development of Hungarian ethnic culture in Yugoslavia, implying that it was better to flourish in Tito's Yugoslavia than to live under the watchful eyes of the regime in Budapest.[10] Considering the specific problems of the Hungarian intellectuals in Yugoslavia, their small number, and their attempts to develop a Hungarian cultural life, the position as expressed by the Hungarian periodical was quite understandable. But overall there was no argument between the Hungarian intellectuals and the regime that close contacts should be kept up between the Hungarians living in Yugoslavia and Hungary. Yugoslavia, the first among Hungary's neighbors to accept Hungary's perceptions on the role of the national minorities as "connecting bridges," was not wary of a danger of Hungarian "intervention in its internal affairs," as the Romanian regime presented Budapest's new line from 1968 on.

Hungary's growing interest in the fate of the Hungarians in the neighboring states not only was manifested in the cultural domain but also found expression in a "statistical offensive." Before 1968, the mentioning of the Hungarian minority abroad was rarely accompanied by statistical data. This was considered a delicate issue, as any reference to the number of Hungarians abroad would have raised questions about the nationality policies in regard to the Hungarians– namely their assimilatory tendencies or the number of those who, for various reasons, concealed their nationality. In 1968 there appeared a sudden wave of publications dealing with the statistics concerning the Hungarian minority abroad. However, the first such studies tended to avoid implications and interpretations, concentrating rather on the raw data. Such was, for example, the article published in 1969 by Zoltán Dávid, who would later specialize in the statistical aspects of the Hungarians abroad.[11] Dávid concluded in 1969 that the number of Hungarians in the neighboring countries was 3,350,000. He attempted to correct some of the inaccuracies in the existing data, hinting at the more sensitive aspects of Hungarian life abroad. For example, he mentioned that

> as a result of the discrimination in Socialist Czechoslovakia, which has been since then eliminated, the 1961 census corrected to some extent the earlier inaccurate data and listed 534,000 people whose mother tongue is Hungarian.

In retrospect Hungary's new policy of monitoring more closely the life of the Hungarians abroad, and of fostering their relations with the motherland was timely, as the nationality issue became in 1968 an important factor in the shaping of its relations with Czechoslovakia, Romania, and Yugoslavia.

Hungary and the Prague Spring

The Prague Spring did not leave the Hungarian minorities in the neighboring countries untouched. In fact, Hungary's relations with the three socialist countries were deeply affected by the impact of the events in Czechoslovakia, not only over matters of bilateral relations, such as Hungary's criticism of Yugoslavia's and Romania's attitudes to the Soviet invasion, but also with respect to the Hungarians abroad. Budapest's new life on the Hungarians abroad was thus immediately put to the test. The limits of Hungary's role in influencing the lives of the Hungarians abroad were clearly highlighted in the role that Hungary sought to play in regard to Hungarian demands raised in Slovakia and vis-á-vis accusations by Czechoslovakia that Hungary had interfered in its internal affairs. Likewise, Hungary's position was tested in those days in view of the changes in Romania's nationality policy manifested by Ceauśescu's attempts to reach an understanding with the Hungarians in face of the crisis between Romania and the Warsaw Pact states. The nationality issue was also raised between Hungary and Yugoslavia in the wake of Tito's criticism of Hungary's participation in the invasion and its impact on bilateral relations.

Another aspect of Hungary's relationship with the Hungarians abroad was the problem of reciprocity between the treatment of the nationalities in Hungary and that of the Hungarians in the neighboring socialist states. This issue was also highlighted and Hungary's views probed during the crisis in Czechoslovakia and its immediate aftermath.

With the blooming of the Prague Spring came the awakening of Hungarian demands in Czechoslovakia for more rights and a better status. The intensity of the Hungarians' activity during that period may have startled Slovak leaders, especially as for years the nationality policy had been aimed at keeping the Hungarians well under control. They were given the permission and means for cultural expression, as the literary thaw from 1965 indicated, yet were always being watched for any unwanted signs of Hungarian nationalism. The leaders of CSEMADOK and other activists of the Hungarian minority very adroitly took advantage of the political turmoil in the country, especially the Czech–Slovak tensions, in order to further their demands. It was clear to them that the newly evolving patterns of Czech–Slovak relations, and the demands for the country's reorganization by according more rights to the Slovaks, were bound to affect the Hungarian minority as well. Any gain for Slovak nationalism was to be a net loss for the Hungarians, and this was a fact only too well understood by Czech leaders who opposed Slovak demands for greater autonomy. Reformist elements, including Dubček and other Czech and Slovak liberals, sympathized in general with Hungarian demands during the Prague Spring.[12] Such a support may well have been aimed at countering Slovak nationalist pressures. The Hungarian minority acted as a well-organized pressure group expressing some of the frustrations built up for years, and the resentments over the events following World War II. The Hungarian–Slovak tension during the Prague Spring brought into the open the unresolved issues of their relationship, and proved that nationalism was alive and well, and living among many Slovaks as well as Hungarians. The mutual accusations that the majority was attempting to impose its terms on the minority, while the Slovaks themselves were asking for a larger share of the national cake, shattered the Communist tenet propagated in the years before 1968 professing that a correct Leninist nationality policy had solved the divisive issue between Slovaks and Hungarians.

Hungarian demands raised during 1968 covered a whole range of issues: they called for the territorial reorganization of Slovakia which would annul the 1960 administrative changes, for the formation of a separate polical organization with wider authority than CSEMADOK, for more educational opportunities in the Hungarian language, and for greater cultural freedom. In sum, the Hungarian demands added up to an attempt at restructuring the whole framework of the Hungarian–Slovak relationship in the area. Encountering heavy Slovak opposition to their demands, the Hungarians could point to the irony of the situation—as they were practically requesting almost the same rights as the Slovaks were seeking in the framework of the Czechslovak state.

The first significant Hungarian proposals (and they were to be viewed by later studies published in Hungary as such and not as "demands"[13]) were put forward in the resolutions of the CC of CSEMADOK in March 1968, calling for the democratic implementation of the rights of the Hungarians by means of the reorganization of the local districts where Hungarians were in a minority as a result of the administrative reorganizations of 1960. The proposals suggested by the CSEMADOK meeting, and adopted in its resolutions, were reflections of the guidelines of the CzCP published in January 1968. As such, the CSEMADOK document supported the process of democratization from above, and in accord with the CzCP guidelines called for the acceptance of the national minorities as constituent parts of the state, and for the assurance of their rights not only as individuals but also as self–managing groups.[14]

In fact, the CSEMADOK proposals and the views presented in the Hungarian language press in Slovakia proceeded at that state almost hand in hand with the parallel developments in the Prague Spring. Other national minorities issued their own similarly worded proposals evincing a sense of responsibility and moderation.

Much of the ferment among the Hungarians during that period was led by the intellectuals. They were the ones who gave the tone, and often uncovered their frustrations in highly emotional articles. The Hungarian section of the Slovak Writers' Union discussed in March 1968 the situation of the Hungarians, and its Proclamation, issued some 10 days after that of the CC of CSEMADOK, was more strongly worded and left no doubt that the expectations of the Hungarian minority were rising. Slovak counterattacks were not late to come. It is rather difficult to follow the waves of mutual accusations on a day–to–day basis, but there was an evident escalation on both the Slovak and the Hungarian side. Each accused the other of heating up the atmosphere. The Hungarian–language press, led by *Új Szó* and *Irodalmi Szemle*, started to publish articles in a highly emotional tone, mostly on the postwar relations between the Hungarians and the Slovaks. Leading officials of the Hungarian community along with the intellectuals brought forth their bitter comments, and some published their personal memoirs. Gyula Lőrincz, the President of CSEMADOK and a leading activist in the Slovak CP, recounted how the Hungarians "were sold on the market as slaves" in the areas where they were resettled in the Sudentenland.[15] Likewise, Zoltán Fábry, whose voice was perhaps the most emotional among Hungarian intellectuals, described the situation as

> perhaps the first historical test, the test of maturity of the Slovak nation, of their ethical values. The Hitlerite Independent Slovak State was a prostitution, an adherence to the forefront of inhumanity. Slovak progressiveness must now prove whether it is worthy of victory.[16]

The Hungarian intellectuals described the bleak state of the Hungarian educational system, the lack of facilities, and the deplorable future waiting for the Hungarian youths, who were discriminated against in jobs and in general did not have the same opportunities as their Slovak neighbors. The Hungarian–language press attributed the economic difficulties facing the Hungarians to the social and economic discrimination practiced by the authorities. These reports reflected the Hungarians' adjustment to the changing realities in Czechoslovakia—the extensive use of the media for free discussion and reporting on issues that could not be raised before. Naturally, as Hungarian demands and complaints became more radical the more anti-Magyar the Slovak reactions became, thus generating a vicious circle.

Actually no spark was needed for the eruption of a prolonged spiteful debate between Hungarians and Slovaks. Elements that later were to be branded by each regime as "nationalist and chauvinist" hurled invectives at each other for having infringed on minority rights. When Hungarians complained of discrimination, the Slovaks alleged that in Hungarian–majority areas near the border, it was the Hungarians who denied full rights to the Slovak population. The reborn Matica Slovenska played a major role in heating up the atmosphere, and it was its activists who launched a campaign agains the "Nationalist" Hungarians. Symbols, always so dear to the hearts of the nationalist movements, had been cherished by the Hungarians and Slovaks alike. For example, in Kosiče there was a commemorative plaque honoring the Hungarian anti–Habsburg freedom fighter, Rákoczi. This was deemed a "Hungarian national symbol" by the Matica, who demanded its removal. In an atmosphere that some years later was branded by an article published in Hungary as "nationalist and anti–revolutionary,"[17] the Slovak papers wrote on the attempts of "Magyarization" in areas where the Hungarians were in majority, and depicted in dark colors the imposition of Magyar culture and language on the Slovaks. They made use of the same descriptions that several years before had served the organs of the Slovak CP to describe their own sins in the re–Slovakization campaign. Certainly, some Hungarians may well have wished to "Magyarize" the Slovaks around them; their ancestors had done so for generations under the Austro–Hungarian Empire. In practice, however, opportunities to do so were scarce, considering the nature of the Communist regime and its nationality policy.

The Slovak media not only rejected the Hungarian complaints but also stressed that the Hungarian minority was enjoying extensive privileges, so that any compromise was bound to lead to territorial autonomy. Even worse, it could cause the dismemberment of the Czechoslovak Republic and the "Magyarization of Southern Slovakia."[18]

The Czechoslovak press refrained for two months from publishing the resolutions of CSEMADOK and the proclamation of the Hungarian writers of March 1968, thus distorting the true picture of the range of the Hungarian proposals, or at least the proposals of the official bodies of the Hungarian minority. Slovak papers called for the dismissal of Gyula Lörincz from the Presidency of CSEMADOK, and for the removal of other leading Hungarian activists of the organization on the grounds that they were slandering the Slovaks. It was a deliberate attempt to bar CSEMADOK from acting as the spokesman of the whole Hungarian minority, as indeed had been the case.

Slovak attitudes toward the Hungarians differed between various newspapers and journals, reflecting the views of the emerging groups in Slovak society. Some papers kept to a more sophisticated tone, analyzing the situation according to the Party line, in a spirit of self-criticism, as the Bratislava *Pravda* stated: "In 1949 we thought that we had solved the nationality problems, yet we failed to notice the warning signals that this was not so." [19] Yet other papers, during those very same days, alleged that Hungarian separatism had even gone so far as to demand that a separate Hungarian currency be used in Slovakia.[20] Such an extremist presentation of the Hungarian line was mostly reflected by papers as *Praca, Semna*, and *Lud*, whose defamatory invectives were answered in kind by the Hungarian-language press in Slovakia.

A new element was brought in by the involvement of Hungary in the intricate web of Hungarian-Slovak relationship in Slovakia. The Slovak press drew attention to the situation of the Slovaks in Hungary, calling for a reciprocity in the nationality policies of the two neighboring states. The allegations against Hungary were quite serious—the Slovak press published numerous articles describing the decline of Slovak educational rights in Hungary, manifested in the small number of Slovak-language schools and teachers. These publications sought to arouse public concern for the "forgotten Slovaks in Hungary." Anti-Hungarian feelings, already rampant, received a new boost by the linkage created in the Slovak media between the Slovaks in Hungary and the Hungarians in Slovakia. The Slovak demands for a change in Hungary's policies toward the Slovaks left a bitter taste in the relations between the two states. As the Slovak allegations did not stop immediately after the invasion of Czechoslovakia, the media in Hungary continued its criticism of the Slovak line, condemning the "irresponsible accusations against the Hungarian PR—in matters shaping the internal affairs of our country." [21]

Hungary rejected the idea of reciprocity, and its media emphasized the regime's positive policies toward the Slovaks in Hungary all along the line. Hungary deliberately thwarted any attempt by the Hungarians in Slovakia to seek help in Budapest for their problems with the Slovaks. Any overt support by Hungary would have played immediately into the hands of the nationalist Slovak elements.

Hungary was assuming the role of an interested party, yet keeping as low a profile as possible. Its media kept a watchful eye and reported on the evolving pattern of Hungarian–Slovak polemics, but it refrained from any policy statement supporting the Hungarian proposals and demands from the Czechoslovak authorities. As Hungary bluntly discounted any Slovak criticism as to the state of the Slovak minority in Hungary, it could not act otherwise in face of the Hungarian complaints from Slovakia. Nevertheless, by monitoring and amply reporting on the Hungarian–Slovak polemics, Hungary unequivocally intimated that it was an interested party in the lives of the Hungarian minority abroad.

This line was also stressed during Dubček's visit to Budapest in June 1968, when the two sides renewed the Treaty of Friendship and Cooperation. Kádár seized the opportunity to advise the Hungarians in Slovakia to look to Prague and not to Budapest in search of solutions to their problems.[22] This suggestion may have disappointed the Hungarians in Slovakia who hoped for Hungary's intervention on their behalf. Officially the leaders of the Hungarian community in Slovakia disclaimed any suggestion that they expected support from Hungary, and as the President of CSEMADOK, Gyula Lörincz, put it: "We have always proclaimed that we must settle our problems within our fatherland."[23]

From its initial stages Hungary followed with great interest and with increasing concern the process of democratization in Czechoslovakia. Hungarian intellectuals with whom the regime was conducting a fruitful dialogue openly sympathized with the objectives of the Prague Spring. Leading Hungarian intellectuals, writers, and journalists warmly praised the "socialist humanist" experiment, while the regime was denouncing the "anti–Socialist" activities of the Czechoslovak intellectuals.[24] The intellectuals' endorsement for the developments in Czechoslovakia was tolerated by the Kádár regime for quite some time preceding the invasion of August 21, 1908, in which Hungary itself participated. The media were also reporting on Hungarian–Slovak tensions. As Hungary had only recently embarked on its new policy of following more closely the fate of the Hungarians in the neighboring states, intellectuals in Hungary interpreted this new line as an approval of their support for Hungarian aspirations in Slovakia. However, the media in Hungary carefully refrained from suggesting any interference by Hungary in favor of the Hungarians over the border, nor to advise them on how to proceed with their demands from the central authorities.

Hungary's somewhat hesitant support for the Soviet invasion ended any hope of Hungarians in Slovakia that Hungary would sup-

port their cause.[25] In fact, the appearance of Hungarian troops polic-
ing the Hungarian majority areas near the border was a cynical ex-
ercise in the practice of socialist internationalism, and it certainly
wasn't the kind of intervention that some Hungarians in Slovakia had
hoped for.

After the invasion, the media in Hungary became more critical in
condemning the anti–socialist views that had prevailed in Czechoslovakia during the period preceding it. Newspapers like *Népszabadság*
published stories on the alleged intimidation of true Communists in
Slovakia, hinting that this had taken place in Hungarian–majority
areas.[26] As a justification for Hungary's participation in the invasion,
the media in Hungary made a point of analyzing the counterrevolutionary trends during the Prague Spring, and depicted the imminent
danger of the socialist regime's collapse.[27] Hungary's "internationalist" support and the presence of Hungarian troops on Slovak soil
could not but awaken memories of the not so distant past, of Magyar
rule in the area.

Hungary's sensitivity to any criticism referring to its participation in the invasion was quite understandable. In this respect, as
late as at the end of September 1968, Hungary rebuked the Slovaks
for "slanders" against Hungary. The occasion for this renewal of the
polemics involving Hungary and Czechoslovakia was the tone of some
publications in Slovakia, which hinted at the parallelism between the
invasion of the Hungarian Soviet Republic's forces in 1919 during the
Béla Kun regime and the formation of the short–lived Slovak Soviet
Republic, and the present participation of Hungarian forces in the
invasion of Czechoslovakia. In both cases Hungary was fulfilling its
internationalist duty, of whose legitimacy parts of Slovak public opinion were not quite convinced to say the least. *Népszabadság* bitterly
rejected Slovak slanders in an article "Selections from Slanders."[28]
It discounted Slovak accusations that Hungary's role in 1919 had
been motivated by nationalist goals and not by internationalist sentiments. According to the image presented in Slovakia, and reported
by *Népszabadság's* correspondent, Béla Kun had pursued a line of national communism, and if he had been victorious, the Slovaks would
have received under Magyar Communist rule the same treatment that
they had received under the Habsburg Monarchy. Such voices from
Slovakia, aired in public on the occasion of the forthcoming fiftieth
anniversary of the Czechoslovak Republic, naturally did not please
Budapest, which was looking forward to a speedier normalization in
post–invasion Czechoslovakia, and without the unpleasant reminders
to Hungary's role in the invasion.

From the nationalities' point of view the most important result of the Czechoslovak drama of 1968 was the adoption of the Minorities Statute by the National Assembly on October 27, 1968. The Statute guaranteed the status of the minorities, treating not only their individual rights, as had been the case before, but also their collective rights.[29] They would now be allowed to develop cultural and social organizations and to have mass media in their own languages.[30] The new statute went into effect in January 1969, as the new Czechoslovak federal state came into existence. On paper it was a new beginning both for the Czechoslovak state and for the national minorities. Yet, as later developments indicated, although most of the demands CSEMADOK had presented during the short–lived Prague Spring were incorporated into the statute and other accompanying documents, there was really no significant change in the position of the Hungarian minority. After the removal of Dubček, the new Husak regime returned the Hungarian minority for better or worse to its former position. One of the first manifestations of this new reality was the curtailing of the possibilities of the Hungarian minority to voice openly their complaints and problems as they had been able to do for a short time.

CSEMADOK's role during the Prague Spring was one of the first Hungarian–related issues that the Husak leadership had to deal with. Various high–level leaders, including Husak, appeared before the CC of CSEMADOK and called for a new relationship between Hungarians and Slovaks. They denounced past mistakes, but expected that the organization be purged of its culprits, who had misled the Hungarians in crucial issues during the events of 1968. The authorities were principally apprehensive lest CSEMADOK, in the light of its resolutions of March 1968, would attempt to form a political organization of the Hungarians, a so–called Hungarian National Council. Although, in the wake of the invasion, the Ruthenians set up such a body—which in fact did not possess any practical power—the authorities were wary of the creation of such a political organization by the more numerous and influential Hungarians. As a matter of course, Husak's main case against CSEMADOK was its full support for Dubček's reforms. Thus, the new leadership pressed the organization for a purge of its "right–wing elements," and repeatedly called for CSEMADOK's endorsement of the leadership of the normalization era.

In 1970 the organization came under a heavy Party attack for "opportunism and revisionism" among its ranks, which was followed by the removal of its leadership. Moreover, CSEMADOK must have been regarded at the time as a serious threat to the stability of the Husak regime, at least in Slovakia, and the leaders of the organization gradually lost their seats in the Slovak National Council. In 1971 CSEMADOK was excluded from the National Front, which constituted a heavy blow for the further functioning of the organization.[31]

At least until 1970 Hungary showed some support for CSEMADOK, cautiously refraining from any interference in the internal affairs of Slovakia. Arato's study in *Társadalmi Szemle* in 1970 rejected any attempt, as apparently was made in Slovakia, to draw similarities between sanctions of the right wing of Matica Slovenska and CSEMADOK. Although there was no doubt that "right wing, nationalist elements held posts in CSEMADOK,"[32] Arató's article, published in Hungary, nevertheless referred to the "offensive Slovak press articles and the defensive Hungarian replies."

Hungary did not publish too many details on the assault on CSEMADOK by the Husak regime in 1970–1971. The frequent changes in the leadership of CSEMADOK, such as the tactical removal in 1972 of Zoltán Fábry, who had served as President for about a year, were reported without comment. However, the reports (which did not appear in the Slovak media) had a certain significance, inasmuch as they indicated Hungary was continuing to monitor the situation. As to the constitutional arrangements, Hungary expressed accord over the federative system and the Nationality Statute, but it hinted that a certain price had to be paid for the solution of Czechoslovakia's problems. "Without August 21, 1968, there would have been neither a Czech–Slovak federation nor a Nationality Statute." Arató surmised this in his study, while leaving the reader to wonder if indeed August 21 had been needed to achieve these two steps.

The Prague Spring and its shockwaves in Eastern Europe had caught Hungarian–Romanian relations in a transitional period marked by their polemics following Hungary's new policy on the Hungarians abroad, and Ceaușescu's successful attempts to rally the national minorities, the Hungarians, and the Germans around the regime in face of the threat from Moscow. It was in this period that the Romanian regime displayed a certain change toward the Hungarians. While it would be too far–reaching to characterize the period as the only one that neared "relative liberalization,"[33] there can be no doubt that the regime did introduce several concessions, mostly of secondary importance, which were later withdrawn.[34] Overall, the Romanian National–Communist line was neither weakened nor pushed aside, but there was a temporary shift toward boosting the unity of the peoples inhabiting the Romanian socialist state who, according to the regime, had just given proof of their cohesion in defending the regime in face of threats from Romania's Warsaw Pact allies.

Romania's support for Czechoslovakia had nothing to do with

Dubček's reforms, which were a nightmare to Ceauşescu's leadership. It had merely sought to defend the particular way of a member of the socialist community. Hungary condemned that support. Although Hungary was the primary critic of the Romanian line, its criticism of Bucharest was stepped up, as not–so–old historical memories were being revived: Hungary followed with apprehension not only the Romanian historiographical works praising the Little Entente of the interwar period, but also the revival of this concept in Romanian foreign policy and the favorable echo it received from the two other partners, Czechoslovakia and Yugoslavia.

Ceauşescu expressed his views on the day of the Soviet invasion in a mass rally in Bucharest:

> It has been said that there was a danger of counterrevolutionary tendencies. If so, our answer to all that is that the Romanian people will not permit anyone to violate the territory of our fatherland.[35]

Hungary's tone in criticizing the Romanian line was often very bitter, cynical, and even more hostile than the Soviet reprimand. The Kádár leadership was very keen in its condemnation of the Romanian line. This acerbity may also be accounted for by Ceauşescu's success in winning over the Hungarians of Romania, inasmuch as they shared with the regime their aversion to Hungary's participation in the invasion of Czechoslovakia.

In one of the first reactions to the Romanian stance the Budapest *Esti Hirlap* severely censured Ceauşescu's tough speech at the special session of the Grand National Assembly on August 22, 1968, labeling it "grotesque" both for its contents and its timing—the day before Romania's Liberation Day. The paper reminded Romania:

> Could the Romanian people celebrate this historical turning point, were it not for the Soviet Union, which at the time used its military might in World War II. And would Socialist Romania have reached its 24th anniversary were it not for the Soviet Union and the socialist states that have defended by all means, and yes, by armed strength their common achievements—including those of the Romanian people.[36]

Ceauşescu was accused of appealing to "nationalist passions,"[37] and the Hungarian media's treatment of the Romanian leader indicated almost a personal quarrel with him. The Hungarians carried the criticism of Romania further than the other members of the Warsaw Pact, as if trying to deal Romanian National Communism a decisive blow. In a cynical tone, unique in the style of the East European media, *Magyar Nemzet* reminded Ceauşescu that he himself knew quite well the laws of the class struggle, and the Romanian leadership did not hesitate to use the "necessary means when facing an internal enemy."[38] Romania's response to the invasion was compared with that of President Johnson, who verbally opposed the Soviets but took no action.[39] The "choir" which Romania joined, warned *Népszabadság* was sounding voices which might have grave consequences.[40]

Hungary, the foremost critic of the Romanian line, also shared in the attempts by Moscow to calm down the tension with Romania after Czechoslovakia had been taught its lesson. A high-level Hungarian–Romanian meeting took place five days after the invasion, when Politburo member and Nationalities' expert Dezsö Nemes visited Romania between August 26 and 29.[41] Nemes's visit was probably aimed not only at easing the tension between Romania and the other Warsaw Pact states, but also at warning Romania of the dangers of playing around with nationalism. Hungary could well bring up subjects that would harm the Romanian leadership, such as the issue of Transylvania. Following Nemes's talks in Bucharest, Hungary gradually lowered its scolding tone against Romania, yet continued its critical line toward Yugoslavia, only occasionally associating the Romanian with the Yugoslav opposition to the invasion of Czechoslovakia.

Hungary also tried to defuse the military tension rumored to exist on the Romanian border, and to assure Romania that it did not face the danger of an invasion. At the time there were unconfirmed reports from Hungary, on which the Romanian Foreign Ministry refused to comment, that there had been an incident along the border, following the straying into Romanian territory of several Soviet tanks from Hungary.[42]

Further Hungarian–Romanian contacts took place on the eve of the meeting of the Communist parties in Budapest, which Romania attended as a full participatory member. Paul Niculescu–Mizil arrived in Budapest a week before the meeting, on September 23, and held talks in a "frank and comradely atmosphere" with his Hungarian counterpart, Zoltán Komócsin. Hungarian–Romanian talks were held at an unprecedented pace, and at the beginning of November 1968, Paul Niculescu–Mizil arrived in Budapest for a "short and friendly visit"—his third in six weeks. The noteworthy aspect of Mizil's visit was its agenda: it was related not to the forthcoming second Budapest meeting of Communist parties but to ideological problems of mutual interest. Mizil held talks at the CC's Department for Culture, Science, and Education.[43] As a preparatory gesture to the ideological talks, a joint Hungarian–Romanian protocol was signed on cooperation in the field of book publishing. The document discussed the "accomplishments of earlier cooperation plans and the implementation of future tasks." Such talks, along with a series of agreements on interstate relations, suggested that both states were keen to reach a rapprochement after a period of tension linked to the invasion of Czechoslovakia.

The Hungarian media moderated its critical tone and avoided the discussion of some of the divisive issues with the Romanians. Thus, reacting to a speech by Ceauşescu, a Hungarian daily reported that "speaking on relations between socialist states, Ceauşescu said that there were differences of opinion, but expressed his hope that they were temporary."[44] The cordial atmosphere and the spirit of rapprochement lasted for several months, until the renewal of Hungarian–Romanian polemics on a whole range of issues linked to Romania's foreign policy, such as President Nixon's visit in Romania in August 1969, and the raising of the level of diplomatic relations between Romania and Israel. On the ideological front the polemics also covered Romania's National Communism, a topic which had direct implications on Hungarians views of Romania's treatment of the national minorities. One such occasion for direct and indirect Hungarian assault on Romanian National Communism was the fiftieth anniversary of the formation of the Romanian national unitary state. It was celebrated by numerous public events, focusing on the historical significance of the unification of Transylvania with Romania. Historical studies that appeared on this occasion reiterated the Romanian thesis of the continuity of the Romanian people in its historical homeland and the role of Transylvania in the nation's history. At mass rallies the leadership stressed once again its positions on the independence and sovereignty of the country, promising to strengthen the unity of the Romanian socialist nation. As the commemorative events were also linked to the issue of Bessarabia and Northern Bukovina, the Soviets carefully monitored the Romanian line. The pattern of the Soviet support for the Hungarian position that emerged then, and has continued ever since, was very clearly evident in the joint Soviet–Hungarian efforts to oppose Romanian National Communism. The Soviet foreign affairs weekly, *New Times*, did not see eye–to–eye with Bucharest as to the circumstances of the formation of the Romanian state in the wake of World War I, and put forward the thesis that the Western imperialist powers had supported Romanian aspirations at the end of the war only because such policy harmonized Western self–interest and not out of sympathy with Romanian national goals.[45] The media in Hungary on the whole ignored the numerous celebrations in Romania at the time, but *Népszabadság* chose to bring up the matter by publishing excerpts from the article in *New Times*, especially such as were critical of the Romanian presentation of the events at the end of 1918.[46] It was a silent, low–key, yet significant Hungarian contribution to the festivities in neighboring Romania.

Hungarian criticism of Romania increasingly covered topics which were more directly related to Romania's internal policies. This Hungarian approach had already surfaced before the Prague Spring, when Hungary contested the importance that Romania attached to the national interests vis–à–vis the internationalist obligations of a socialist state; but after the Soviet invasion of Czechoslovakia, this line in the Hungarian attitudes to Romania became more overt. In general, Hungary's media did not award high marks to Romania's "socialist construction," hinting that not everything was stable in its socialist edifice. Such a line could very well serve as a preparation for more vehement rebukes with regard to the nationality policy of the Romanian regime. In "Reflections on Romania's Internal Policies," Tibor Várkonyi, one of Hungary's best known journalists, settled a Hungarian account with some aspects on Romania's policies both at home and abroad.[47] The timing of the article's publication was intentional, three days after Kádár's visit to Moscow, where the Hungarian and Soviet leaders coordinated their activities in the Communist movement, and immediately after Paul Niculescu–Mizil's speech at the Congress of the Italian CP, in which the Romanian delegate condemned the invasion of Czechoslovakia. Another date linked to the publication of Várkonyi's article was that of the approaching elections to the Grand National Assembly in Romania, with the debut of the Socialist Unity Front, and the Councils of the Workers of German and Hungarian Nationalities formed at that time.

Várkonyi described the Romanian system as backward in its administrative and managerial methods, a fact which according to the author was also acknowledged by the Romanians. He also elaborated on the latest process of political rehabilitations in April and September 1968, at a time when this "process was already over" in the other bloc states. While Várkonyi referred only to the belated rehabilitations and not to their content, what really bothered the Hungarians was the posthumous rehabilitation of Lucreţiu Pătrăşcanu, who had been transformed overnight into the forerunner of Romanian National Communism. For the first time in the Hungarian media Várkonyi allowed himself the liberty of disputing the glorification of various Romanian personalities from the past. Nicolae Iorga, he claimed, "had flirted with Fascism," but failed to mention that Iorga himself had fallen victim to Fascism.

Várkonyi's article was also the first one to refer, if only in passing, to the newly formed Council of Workers of Hungarian Nationality (CWHN), along with the similar Council of the German nationality, in the framework of the newly established Socialist Unity Front. The Councils, the first minority organizations since the dissolution of the existing organizations in the early fifties, were expected to provide a representative body for the nationalities.[48] In fact, from their inception these organizations had no effective power, but they served as forums for the airing, not for the debating, of the major policy statements by the regime. Dissident voices from Transylvania, especially after the Károly Király letter to the Romanian leadership in 1978, gave details as to the impotence of these bodies and the fiction that they represented the national interest of the Hungarian minority. The formation of the CWHN was an important step in the Romanian regime's policy to mobilize the support of the minorities and to strengthen national unity. There is no doubt that in the circumstances that prevailed after August 1968, when there was certainly a better working relationship between the regime and the Hungarians, high hopes were attached to the Council.

Hungary was more skeptical about the reorganizations in Romania's policital bodies, such as the formation of the Socialist Unity Front and the nationality Councils. Várkonyi dryly remarked that "little is yet seen from the new directives" regarding the tasks of the SUF, and as to the CWHN, his only comment was that the "exact functions of the new body are yet to be defined." As a continuation to this type of comment on developments in Romania, the Hungarian media practically ignored the elections to the Romanian Grand National Assembly in February 1969, presenting the results very factually without significant comments about the debut of the CWHN. Overall, reports in Hungary on the nationality policies in Romania were rather scarce immediately following the invasion of Czechoslovakia. It seems that in the light of the Hungarian–Romanian polemics on the reports that Budapest was about to intensify its involvement in the fate of the Hungarians abroad, the Hungarian regime did not want at that specific point—in the wake of the crisis with Czechoslovakia—to push this point much further.

For a while Hungary refrained from insisting on its declared "responsibility" toward the Hungarian culture in the neighboring states. Budapest was also well aware that Romania's staunch opposition to the invasion had brought about temporary harmony between the regime and the Hungarians. The Romanian media continued to strongly emphasize the unity of the Romanian socialist nation in face of the dangers of foreign intervention. Public support on the part of the Hungarians was highlighted by the letter of some sixty leading Hungarian intellectuals in *Scînteia*.

Nevertheless, Hungary did not give up its newly formed policy in regard to the Hungarians abroad. About a year after the invasion, and parallel to various steps (including an agreement for the exchange of high school students) designed to strengthen interstate relations between Hungary and Romania,[50] Hungary intensified its criticism of certain aspects of Romania's nationality policy. It thus signaled that the the deep political differences highlighted during the crisis in Czechoslovakia should not obscure other divisive issues on the agenda of Hungary.

As in the case of Hungarian–Romanian relations during the crisis in Czechoslovakia, both Hungary and Yugoslavia attempted to restrain the vehemence of their polemics so as not to harm their relationship in the long run. Yet, the unpleasant tones that accompanied their contentions during those days were bound to leave a bitter taste for a long period. Yugoslavia's position on the invasion of Czechoslovakia, and its criticism of the Hungarian line, involved to a certain extent the minority issue—inasmuch as the Hungarians in Yugoslavia identified themselves with Belgrade and showed cohesion with the regime. They had actually done so since World War II, but this time they also adhered to their government's critical stance toward Hungary's policies.

The crisis in Czechoslavakia affected Hungarian–Yugoslav relations in a period when both states were trying to involve their national minorities—Hungarians in Yugoslavia and the South Slavs in Hungary—in "bridges of friendship." But at the same time, by showing keener interest in the fate of the Hungarians abroad, Hungary took a more critical approach to the existing trends in Yugoslavia's nationality policy. Hungary hinted that some negative developments were taking place in Yugoslavia, and such criticism was often linked to Hungarian condemnation of Romanian policies. Thus, one may find, according to a Hungarian article, that both in "Yugoslavia and elsewhere, some people who instead of meticulously putting into practice the Leninist principles, support the overt or concealed arguments of nationalism."[51]

These Hungarian remarks came in response to the claims by the Serbian writer Dobrica Kostic who, according to *Magyar Hirlap* delivered a sharp attack on the universal rights of the Hungarian minority in Yugoslavia. In fact, throughout the years, Yugoslavia's Hungarians were reproached for enjoying "too many rights," and the allegations on this subject were quite similar to charges brought by the Slovaks during 1968 that they were discriminated against by the Hungarians, and not vice versa. In the specific case of the Yugoslav writer's attacks on the Hungarians, the article in *Magyar Hirlap* contended that although the League of Yugoslav Communists "rejected these slanders," this phenomenon indicated that "there is still something to be done to further the *de facto* implementation of equal rights, not only with regard to the Serbian–Hungarian, but also the Croatian–Serbian, Slovenian–Serbian, and other relationships."

Reviewers in Hungary welcomed the publication of László Rehák's book on the nationalities in Yugoslavia, which appeared in Hungarian in Novi Sad in 1967, and served for years as one of the major studies on the topic. One such review by Miklós Tomka[52] estimated that the book was hailed because, in addition to the debates in Czechoslovakia in the years prior to 1968, it reflected a similar interest in Yugoslavia the topic of the nationalities. Tomka mentioned several shortcomings of Rehák's study—namely that the Hungarian author from Yugoslavia did not envision clearly the prospects for the nationalties' development in the future: Were the Hungarians facing a process of peaceful assimilation? Was the state keen to assure the safeguarding of the Hungarians' specific feature? In face of the publications in Hungary after 1968 about the process of assimiliation of the Hungarians in Yugoslavia, it seems that Tomka's review reflected Hungary's position—that the respective countries should not encourage the assimilation of the minorities.[53]

Yugoslavia's prompt condemnation of the intervention in Czechoslovakia sparked off a Hungarian–Yugoslav polemic in which the Hungarians were more moderate in their criticism of Yugoslavia than they were toward the Romanians. The Yugoslavs, however, were more eager to respond to the reproof from Budapest than were the Romanians. Moreover, the Hungarians were careful not to attack Tito personally, in contrast to their criticism of Ceauşescu. One interesting aspect of the Hungarian–Yugoslav polemics was the involvement of the Hungarian–language press in Yugoslavia in censuring Budapest's policies. In this respect the Hungarian–Yugoslav debate differed from the one between Hungary and Romania, as there was no difference between the Hungarian– and Romanian–language press in Romania in their attitude toward Hungary, while in Yugoslavia, the Hungarian–language press was more critical of Budapest than were the Serbo–Croatian media.

In one of the more acrimonious pronouncements in Yugoslavia, *Magyar Szó* declared in an editorial that

> It is no way possible to justify the presence of Hungarian troops on the territory of Czechoslovakia, where in both the Slovak and the Hungarian people it will awaken those extremely sad memories which not so long ago were left behind by certain other Hungarian troops.[54]

Such an utterance not only awakened memories in Budapest but also touched some very raw nerves, as Hungary had always been wary of such historical memories, and the behavior of the Hungarian occupation troops in Újvidék in World War II was a strong reminder to Budapest, even when coming from a Hungarian–language newspaper. *Népszabadság* immediately responded by stressing that *Magyar Szó* had slandered the army of a socialist state, and that Yugoslavia knew only too well that Hungary's army had "nothing, just nothing in common with the Hungarian troops that occupied Slovakia thirty years ago."[55] Still, the last word seemed to belong to *Magyar Szó* which stated that an "occupier is an occupier, and if he is a socialist, so much the worse."[56]

The rapprochement in Hungarian–Yugoslav relations a few months following the invasion of Czechoslovakia indicated that both sides were careful to limit their polemics, and to prevent a drastic deterioration in their relations. During the crisis following August 1968 both states continued and even intensified their interstate contacts in various fields, such as trade agreements and cultural cooperation. Yet, the mutual accusations at the height of the polemics along with the evoking of unpleasant historical memories, left a bitter taste, which was reflected in various publications in both countries in the years to come.

Chapter VI

The National Minorities in Hungary

Characteristics of the National Minorities in Post World War II Hungary

Hungary pursues a deliberately positive policy toward the national minorities, and by setting an example it hopes for a reciprocally beneficial treatment of the Hungarians abroad. This, all features of Hungary's liberal nationality policy are linked to a wider perspective—that of fostering its ties with the Hungarians in the neighboring countries. It seems that the Hungarian regime has been promoting the ethnic identity and the culture of the national minorities, encouraging their external ties with the "mother–tongue countries and homelands," thus also slowing down a natural process of assimilation. The emphasis given by the Hungarian leaders and the media to aspects of the regime's nationality policy clearly indicates that their aim is to establish a recognized linkage between the nationalities in Hungary and those in the socialist countries, and to use the national minorities as bridges of friendship and cooperation with the neighbors. Hungary's shift in its relationship with the Hungarians abroad could not have been translated into a long–lasting policy without the positive policy toward the national minorities in Hungary. By that policy, Hungary hopes to show the outside world both its freedom from nationalist attitudes and the new socialist–internationalist relationship it has developed between the majority and the national minorities—one which Hungary wishes and expects to be pursued in the other countries. This gradual evolution of Hungary's emphasis on the nationalities as bridges of friendship represents the most innovative feature of Hungary's relationship with the Hungarians in the neighboring states.

Following several changes in its borders in this century, Hungary has lost its multi–national character and has practically become a homogenous national state,[1] with only about 450,000 people belonging to the national minorities—a mere 4.5 percent of its population. This figure of 450,000 frequently referred to by the authorities[2] reflects some of the difficulties in assessing the number of the citizens belonging to the national minorities and the efforts of the regime to encourage them in asserting their identity.

In the 1970 census 155,861 citizens of Hungary declared their native tongue to be other than Hungarian. According to this breakdown there were around 36,000 Germans, 34,000 South Slavs, 21,000 Slovaks, and 12,200 Romanians—altogether some 1.5 percent of the population.[3] The criteria used in Hungary for determining which citizens belong to the ethnic minorities has become a subject of discussions and concern for the policymakers, in light of the regime's policy to encourage ethnic consciousness. The main criterion is that of the mother tongue, on which the above results of the 1970 census were based. However, language alone does not correctly reflect the number of those who could be regarded as national minorities. The second criterion in the Hungarian census is the interest and participation in the cultural life of the ethnic minority groups. When this aspect is taken into consideration, the national minorities comprise many more people. By estimating the membership in minority associations, the figures of 200,000 Germans, 110,000 Slovaks, 100,000 South Slavs, and 25,000 Romanians is derived.

The Gypsies and the Jews are considered ethnic minorities, while the others as national minorities. Until recent years Hungarian experts have avoided any candid discussion on their status. As to the Gypsies, their number ranges from 40,000 to 300,000.[6] That seems to be a rather exaggerated figure, while their position in Hungary is gradually becoming an issue of discussion because of their peculiar problems, characterized by one study published in Hungary as "requiring measures, first of all not of a political or cultural sort, but rather economic and social equality."[7]

Regarding the estimated 80,000 Jews, in spite of numerous publications dealing with the past and some reflections on the present, no discussion has yet taken place on the status of this community in relation to the other nationalities living in Hungary.[8] The Jewish problem in Hungary has no direct relevance to the relations with neighboring countries, nor could the regime's Jewish policy have any effect on the Hungarians living elsewhere.

Studies published in Hungary on the nationality issues strictly keep the divisions between Jews, Gypsies, and the national minorities. Very rarely do they mention the Gypsies—and when the do, they have emphasized the Gypsies are a special case. That, until recent years, has served as a poor alibi not to discuss the issue at all.

The official government position regarding all nationalities is to apply three main criteria. Described as "not a scholarly classification," these criteria include:

1. Anyone who is a Hungarian citizen but speaks only his native language and Hungarian is certain to belong to some native minority.

2. Some speak Hungarian and one other language with the proficiency of their native language. In their case it is a matter of their own subjective choice whether they consider themselves Hungarian, or members of some national minority.

3. There are some whose customs, traditions, and sympathies differ from the others' and on this basis their environment regards them as being members of some national minority.

It is elucidated in numerous Hungarian publications that people are clearly members of a certain national minority owing to their descent, traditions, and cultural heritage, even if they no longer speak the language of their parents and grandparents. Thus, the common origins of a national minority plays an important role in determining the national identity of a person.[10] From here the road to the organic ties that should link a national minority to the mother tongue country is very short, and it is a two-way road: it accounts for the basis of Hungary's perception of the ties that are expected to exist between the national minorities in Hungary and the respective mother-tongue countries on the one hand, and between Hungary and the Hungarians in the neighboring countries, on the other hand.

There are several characteristics of the national minorities in Hungary which are also reflected in the development of the regime's policies toward them, and which logically could be applied to Hungary's expectations from the neighboring countries' policies toward their own Hungarian national minorities. One such feature is the circumstance that Hungary's national minorities are there as a result of a long historical process, which under socialism has brought them to a close attachment to the land of their birth, Hungary, and to its language and culture, while at the same time they cling to their language and traditions. This factor has allowed them, under the guidance of the regime, a close integration into the system, as well as the fostering of their attachment to the unique characteristics of their specific nationality group.

Another characteristic is the dispersal of the national minorities in several regions. This characteristic determines the patterns of common life as they have developed in the mixed localities, many of which have a majority of ethnic Hungarians. In fact, there are few areas with homogenous clusters of one national identity. The national minorities in Hungary usually speak Hungarian. The younger generation usually are able to speak it better than their own mother tongue. This can be seen as bilingualism at its best, but it also indicates a growing assimilatory trend. By the end of the sixties the Hungarian authorities became worried about the fading away of bilingualism, at the expense of the minority language, as the Hungarian language gained ground among the younger generation. Thus, one of the fundamental objectives of the regime's cultural policy since then has been the fostering of the nationality languages by means of a series of educational measures.

Another characteristic of the national minorities in Hungary is the fact that they constitute a fragment of a larger nation, the mother tongue nation, to which the minority is emotionally attached. The question of assimilation, which looms over most of these characteristics, features prominently in the nationality policy of the regime. The geographical dispersion of the minorities, and the process of modernization—migration to the cities and industrial growth—have contributed to this process. In these conditions a "certain degree of natural spontaneous assimilation" is obvious,[11] but as the weekly *Magyarország* summed up Hungary's policy on this issue,

> Natural assimilation cannot be prevented, but it should not be sped up. Nevertheless, even this principle, if applied in the full sense of the word, would endanger the existence of the nationalities. Something has to be set up against the grinding mill of natural assimilation to enable the small number of ethnic minorities to preserve themselves.[12]

The Hungarian policy of encouraging the national minorities to assert their identity could be hindered by the process of spontaneous assimilation. But there is yet another danger in the process of assimilation: Hungary shows apprehension over the assimilatory pressures applied to Hungarians elsewhere, most of all in Romania, and any indication of the gradual fading away of the national minorities in Hungary, even through spontaneous assimilation, would also account for the developments among the Magyars in the neighboring countries. Thus, the equation that a Hungarian policy-maker would perceive is quite simple: every Romanian among the 25,000 living in Hungary who is encouraged and supported to read and write in the Romanian language and to dance Romanian folk dances may serve as an insurance policy that the Hungarians in Transylvania would also keep up their identities. But of course reality is harsher: Romania is not eager to reciprocate in its policy toward the 1.8 million Hungarians living in Romania.

Finally, among the main characteristics of the national minorities in Hungary is the social aspect of the issue, a favorite feature of any

Marxist analysis of the national problem. In Hungarian society the worker–to–peasant ratio is 58 percent to 15 percent, while among the national minorities it is still the reverse in spite of the rising number of factory workers.[13] Thus, the basis of national minority existence and the guardian of the heritage of the nationality groups remains the village, with its peasant population. This poses a dilemma: the regime fosters modernization, while migration to the cities loosens the links with the traditions and the language, thus speeding up natural assimilation, which the regime would like to restrain.

The Shaping of Hungary's Nationality Policy 1945-1968

After World War II every nationality in Hungary "had a cross to bear,"[14] which left a lasting imprint on the attitude of the national minorities to the new regime and to its policies toward the minorities. Some 170,000 ethnic Germans were expelled from Hungary, the Slovaks were affected by the turbulent Slovak–Hungarian relationship in Czechoslovakia, and more than 73,000 were transferred to Czechoslovakia in accordance with the population exchange agreement. The South Slavs bore the brunt of the worsening relations between Hungary and Yugoslavia after 1948. Only the situation of the small Romanian community in Hungary remained unaffected by the ups and downs in the relations between Hungary and Romania. As already indicated, officially, the policy of the Hungarian CP was to avoid any reciprocity in the nationality policy, and as the Party's theoretical monthly put it:

> It's the firm attitude of the Hungarian democracy that the country's Slav and Romanian nationalities should receive support for the national development and cultural needs, without taking into consideration the fate of the Hungarians in the neighboring states.[15]

By the end of the war the Hungarian communists were well aware of the imminent changes in Hungary's borders, as reflected in the emphasis on the demise of "Hungarian supremacy" in the program of the Hungarian CP issued in Szeged on November 30, 1944[16] There is no evidence of any long–range policy formulation on the nationality issue by the Hungarian Communists during their struggle for power. The Party concentrated on spreading its influence over areas inhabited by the national minorities, coping with such issues as the friction between Hungarians and Slovaks. The first systematic outline of the new regime's nationality policy was published in the program of the Hungarian Workers' Party in 1948, following the fusion of the Social Democrats into the Communist Party. The program had a striking similarity to the line that was to be pursued by Hungary after 1968.

The 1948 program assured the nationalities not only of equal rights and promotion of their "progressive culture," but also of the Party's support for "cultural exchanges and free contacts with their mother tongue nations in the neighboring countries."[17] The Party program on the nationalities' free contacts was never implemented, as relations with Czechoslovakia remained strained even after the 1948 coup, deteriorated with Yugoslavia after 1948, and the Hungarian minority in Romania was rapidly cut off from any contacts with Hungary, as was the small Romanian minority in Hungary.

The influence of interstate relations on the nationalities and on the national policy is clearly illustrated by the fluctuations in the regime's policy toward the South Slavs and their attitude to the regime. The South Slavs belong to at least four subgroups. The Croats are the largest with two subgroups of their own, the Bunyevaci and the Sokaci, and the remainder are either Bosnians, Serbs, or Slovenes. Most of them live along the southern and southwestern borders of Hungary, but many of them are scattered in several counties around Mohács and Budapest.[18] Following the Cominform break with Yugoslavia, the South Slavs were treated with "lack of confidence and discrimination"[19] and their situation became linked to the state of relations between Hungary and Yugoslavia. After the 1955 thaw, the Hungarian authorities ceased to consider the South Slavs as potential "Titoists," as the label itself had lost its evil connotation inculcated for years by Communist propaganda. The South Slavs could finally come out of the closet after a long period when many of them felt more secure by denying their ethnic origins. It seemed that a new era of Hungarian–Yugoslav relations was dawning. However, in the light of their 1948–1955 experience the South Slavs developed a sensitivity to any changes in Hungarian–Yugoslav interstate relations. Their apprehensions increased during 1957–1958, when Hungarian–Yugoslav relations once again became strained due to the Moscow–led criticism of Yugoslavia's "revisionist" line.

A major document dealing with the national question in Hungary was the October 1958 Resolution of the Politburo of the HSWP, which called the local Party organs' attention to fears among the South Slavs lest the restrictive measures applied after 1948 be renewed as a result of the tension between the two parties, the HSWP and the LYC. The HSWP's efforts to assuage the South Slavs reaped positive results; according to Hungarian sources they were convinced that the "ideological differences concerning the Programme of the LYC would not lead to the repeating of the restrictive measures ten years before, following the decision of the Information Bureau."[20]

The Slovaks, a large concentration of whom live in Békés County while the rest are scattered all over the country, were affected not only by the population exchange agreement but also by the tension between themselves and the Hungarians, who in turn were reacting to the mistreatment of the Magyars in Slovakia. The tension and the mutual suspicions in the areas where Slovaks and Hungarians came in contact lasted for long years, becoming a fact of life with which the Communist regime could not cope effectively. Nor could the Leninist phraseology about nationality policy erase the bitterness between the two communities—just as was the case north of the border in Slovakia.

The Romanians, concentrated along the Romanian border in the counties of Békés, Hajdú-Bihar, and Csongrád,[21] were not affected by the postwar divisive issues in Hungarian–Romanian relations, and in later years—when Hungary was still complaining of the lack of facilities for the development of the Hungarians in Romania—the Hungarian regime kept emphasizing the free development of its Romanian community.

Until the mid-fifties the largest ethnic minority in Hungary, the Germans were not even mentioned as one of the country's minorities. Their specific economic, cultural, and social needs were simply not being taken into account. Under such conditions it was natural that there was a strong tendency toward assimilation as a means of escaping the negative image of a German living in Hungary, an image reinforced by the Party's policy of collective punishment of the German nationality in the immediate postwar years.[22] However, by the mid-fifties a gradual change had become evident. There was an improvement of the educational facilities available to the Germans, and in 1954 the first issue of *Freies Leben* was published. The regime criticized its own German policy in the May 1956 policy statement of the CC of the HSWP on the nationality question. The document acknowledged that during the period when measures were taken against former members of the SS, the Volksbund, and other Nazi organizations, people who should not have been punished as such were included in the expulsions and affected by the restrictive measures.[23] These events would be highlighted later in various forms in Hungary— for example in the 1983 film *Living Together*, which depicted these expulsions.[24]

The building up of confidence between the Germans and the regime was a slow process. In 1958 the regime was still mentioning some friction between the Germans and the Hungarians who had been resettled from Slovakia into their areas. The HSWP document on the nationality question from 1958 noted the results of "enemy propaganda" among the Germans, following exchanges of letters with relatives living in the RFG, and the reluctance of many Germans to subscribe to the weekly *Neue Zeitung* for fear of being accused of nationalism if they were found reading German—even a newspaper issued by the regime.[25] The party document failed to surmise that perhaps the content and the style of the paper may have had to do with the reluctance of the Germans to read it.

Following the East European pattern, "democratic organizations" of the nationalities were formed, which, from their very inception served as Communist front organizations. Thus, the Anti–Fascist Front of the Hungarian Slavs was set up, which as already indicated, was active in the implementation of the Hungarian–Slovak population exchange agreement. The Democratic Association of Romanians, formed in 1949, became a smoothly running organization, as the Romanians were not involved in the delicate interstate issues between Hungary and Romania. The German minority's organization not founded until 1955, was at first labeled the "Cultural Association of German Workers in Hungary" in order to emphasize the strictly cultural character of the German minority's activities.

If the nationality organizations were designed to involve the nationalities in the building of the new socialist society, this goal was not achieved, as the non–policy of the regime on the national question was reflected in the activities of the associations. During the era of the "New Course" new vitality was injected into the nationality organizations[26] and in June 1956 the Party's Central Committee published what was its first statement in years on the nationality question. The document pointed to "shortcomings" and "mistakes" in the nationality policy, such as the influence of the rift with Yugoslavia on the regime's attitudes to the South Slavs.

The events of October 1956 affected the Hungarians in the neighboring states much more deeply than the nationalities in Hungary. There is no evidence of specific revolutionary activity among the minorities in Hungary, and certainly some of the minorities feared the rise of Magyar nationalism. Following the crushing of the Revolution, along with the reorganization of the Communist Party, the minority organizations were purged of allegedly nonloyal elements, and were reactivated in the consolidation of the Kádár regime.

Promoting the National Minorities Since 1968

The predominant feature of Hungary's nationality policy since the late sixties has been a function of the external goals set by Hungary— to provide an example by a correct and positive nationality policy that it hoped would be followed by the neighboring countries. Since the late sixties, and most noticeably in the mid–eighties, Hungary has proceeded to promote the cultural life of the minorities, encouraging them to assert their ethnic identity and to slow down the process of their assimilation. The shift in the regime's attitude toward the ties between Hungary and the Hungarian minorities abroad found expression in numerous publications in Hungary on the status of the national minorities in the country. These writings not only outlined the nationality policy of the regime, but also indicated new trends in fostering the minorities in Hungary. At the same time the regime pointed out the achievement of its policies, preparing the ground for the forthcoming linkage between the national minority policy in Hungary on the national minorities after the events of 1967–1968 brought forth public debates on aspects of national identity and the role of patriotism under socialism.

The first most significant contribution to the debate was a series of sessions at the Social Science Institute of the HSWP in July–December 1967. The tone for the debates was given by a comprehensive study by László Kővágó, the foremost authority on the subject in Hungary, followed by lectures and papers presented by the participants, who included high Party functionaries and leading representatives of the four national minorities. One version of the debates appeared in an edition marked "confidential."[27] An introductory remark justified the confidential character of the discussions on the grounds that the issue touched upon "sensitive international questions." Indeed, the work reflected the atmosphere in one of the first "workshops" of its kind dealing with the implication of the nationality question in Hungary on the state's relations with its neighbors.

The changes and the developments in Hungary's nationality policy are reflected in the legal framework relating to the rights of the nationalities. Hungary attaches great importance to the safeguarding of these rights, as reflected in the Constitution, which serves as the basis for the implementation of a correct Marxist–Leninist nationality policy. Hungarian experts on the nationality question stress that the Leninist nationality policy "considers the minority problem not as one which may be resolved and closed once and for all, but a problem requiring continuous attention and effort."[28]

Since 1968–1969 Hungarian experts have increasingly criticized the nationality clauses of the 1949 Constitution as not adequate in safeguarding the rights of the minorities.[29] Such experts as Kővágó warmly greeted the amended text of the Constitution in 1972, which emphasized the equality of the minorities as a collective and not only as private individuals. Moreover, the 1972 Constitution guaranteed the national minorities the use of their mother tongue and the "preservation and practice of their own culture."[30] This proved to be a significant legal guarantee as it expressed Hungary's policy of preserving the unique features and culture of a national minority, a clause which Hungary finds wanting in the Constitutions of some neighbors, as Romania for example, which never promised nor delivered the "preservation" of the Hungarian culture in the sense that the Kádár regime promised to Hungary's minorities.

One of the most important features of Hungary's nationality policy is the promotion of ethnic education and culture. The implementation (or the failure to do so) of such a policy would undoubtedly have an impact upon the external role of the minorities as "bridges of friendship" to the neighboring states. The furthering of ethnic culture was a blatant rejection of the theory of "automatism" according to which, until the late sixties, the Party had explained that there was no need to pay special attention to the minorities, as the problem would be solved by itself in the process of building the socialist society. Automatism was replaced by a deliberate policy of satisfying the educational and cultural needs of the minorities, which gave positive results from the Party's point of view. National–language instruction was greatly expanded, and the Hungarian media often gave details on the increase in the "demands for national minority education." One significant achievement of this policy of expanding the educational framework of the nationalities was the rise in the number of those attending the various establishments from kindergarten on, and a growing willingness of the younger generation to send their children to schools in their mother tongue. Overall, bilingualism is taken for granted. Indeed, many of the younger generation speak only Hungarian.[31] The fostering of the nationality languages was also highlighted at the Congresses of the nationality organizations. In 1978, for example, 85 percent of the speakers spoke in their own native tongues.[32]

Hungarian policy–makers recognized from an early stage that the learning of the "dear mother–tongue"—an age–old Hungarian expression—is the key for the preservation of the ethnic identity. The regime was apprehensive that the fading away of the national language might disrupt the policy of prompting the minorities. Thus, in the words of one study, Hungary's nationality policy "should strive to ensure the instruction in the mother tongue, to raise the standards and render it permanent. There is much to be done."[33] Secondary schools, in the nationality languages, and teacher training were established or expanded—yet another indication for the regime's struggle against the trends to assimilation.[34]

The media often report on the rising number of nationality pupils and students. Characteristic of this line of reportage was a report in *Magyar Nemzet* which highlighted the increase in student enrollment in Slovak schools, whose number reached 10,000.[35] The official report presents a constant rise in the number of students in educational facilities where the language of instruction is that of the minorities. Thus, between 1980 and 1985 their number rose from 32,000 to 52,000,[36] a rise so rapid that it may even elicit allegations that Hungary is practicing almost a forced policy of fostering the nationalities' ethnic identity and the preservation of their culture and language.

One significant aspect of Hungary's nationality policy, which also has direct implications on the desired relationship between Hungarians abroad and their host–nation is the policy of teaching the national minorities' languages to the young Hungarians, especially in the areas where they are present in large numbers. It was no coincidence that this line was explained by László Kővágó not only at home in Hungary but also at a symposium on ethnic education held in Slovakia in 1972 under the auspices of the Slovak Academy of Sciences. Kővágó, at the time head of the Ethnic Minorities' Department at the Hungarian Ministry of Culture, explained that

> One target—functionally connected with the educational policy vis–á–vis the national minorities is that as many young people as possible should master the language of our minorities— in other words, the language of neighboring friendly nations. Therefore, our cultural authorities urge the introduction of instruction in the Serbo–Croatian, Slovenian, German, Romanian, and Slovak languages in Hungarian secondary schools.[37]

Although it seems such proposals remained mostly on paper, in 1985 the Democratic Federation of the South Slavs "recommended the teaching of minority languages in Hungarian secondary schools in the Yugoslav border region."[38] The gesture or the intention was certainly innovative.

There is a great emphasis on book publishing in the nationality languages, one more area where international cooperation with the neighboring countries can be involved, and they have been involved for the last twenty years or so. In the period between 1981 and 1985, the publication of 157 books was planned in the nationality languages.[39] The diversity of publications is quite a contrast to the immediate postwar period, when the emphasis was on the publication of translated works of political significance, such as the Marxist–Leninist classics. The recent titles, however, reflect more the nationalities' own literary works and a growing number of sociocultural and historical studies. Among such works is the publication of the first anthology of Serb and Croat writers in Hungary[40] and a volume of Romanian folktales.

The numerous recent studies on the history of the nationalities in Hungary include a study of the Slovaks, published both in Hungarian and Slovak.[41] The Romanian publications have been enriched by several new types of books, an ethnographical journal, *Izvorul (The Source)*, published since 1982, and a Romanian almanac, *Timpuri (Times)*, with a print run of more than 1,000 copies—a high number in proportion to the number of the Romanians in Hungary.[42] The mass media have also been increased in the last few years. Currently four main nationality weeklies cater to what the authorities hope will be a widening readership—the Serbo–Croatian *Narodne Novine*, the German *Neue Zeitung*, the Slovak *Ludova Noviný*, and the Romanian *Foaia Noastră*.

Regional and national radio and TV broadcasts are yet another indication of the regime's eagerness to foster the language and the culture of the minorities. In 1983, Slovak TV programs were introduced. With this inauguration, every minority now had their own programs—albeit all of them with a limited time at their disposal. The Slovak TV programming, for example, was limited to 15 minutes per month.[43]

A great effort is being made to collect and safeguard the traditions of the nationalities. Teams of researchers from various related fields are involved. Much of the work is coordinated by the active nationality section of the Hungarian Ethnographical Society, which publishes the findings in books, pamphlets, exhibits, and other means. The Society is also in the process of completing a major work, the twelve–volume Nationalities' Ethnographical Encyclopedia. The expressed goal of this project is to emphasize the cultural relationship between the Hungarians and the national minorities over a long historical period.

Scientific conferences are being held periodically at which methodological problems, and research reports are presented. One such major conference was held in 1984 by the Intercultural Section of the Modern Philosophical Society, with the participation of top experts reporting on their research on such topics as "National Consciousness among Senior Classes in Nationality High Schools."[44] Some of these research projects undoubtedly support the regime's declared policy of promoting and encouraging the ethnic identity of the nationalities. A thorough survey entitled "On the Ethnic Groups in Barany County," which took fifteen years to complete, certainly serves such a purpose.[45]

The associations of the ethnic minorities play the most important role in implementing the regime's nationality policy. They function within the framework of the Patriotic People's Front, to which they are organically linked, as indicated by the resolution adopted at the sixth Congress of the PPF in 1976,

> We shall support the work of the associations of the ethnic minorities, which they perform among, and for the benefit of the various nationalities. In addition to the preservation and promotion of their traditional folklore, we must help them to learn more about their home country's (Hungary's) past and about its plans for the future.[46]

The congresses of the minority organizations are widely reported in the media, with reviews of the achievements of the specific minority through its organization. High–level Party and State leaders address the congresses, presenting the Party line and the expectations from the organizations. The ideological guidance to the minority organizations is provided by the CC of the HSWP's Department for Education, Science, and Culture, while the other Party organs lend their support and oversee their activities.[47]

The minority organizations in Hungary have had a less turbulent history since 1956 than the similar organizations in Czechoslovakia and Romania—compared to the periodical purges of the CSEMADOK leadership and the changes in the Council of Workers of Hungarian Nationality in Romania. In Hungary the minority associations never attempted to act as lobbies for the respective minorities, as was the case with CSEMADOK or with the MNSz in Romania until its dissolution in 1952. This not only indicates the strong and efficient Party control in Hungary but also implies a working relationship that has developed between the two sides. This has especially been true since the change in Hungary's policy with regard to the Hungarians abroad.

The more the nationalities in Hungary were being promoted, the more the range of the minority associations' activities was broadened. The associations often act to promote ethnic culture, thanks to the mandate given to them by the regime, and to its support. In this sense there is no doubt that the minority associations in Hungary function in a very different way from the style of CSEMADOK, and even more differently from the style of the Hungarians' organization in Romania. However, there is a certain resemblance between the activities of the organizations in Yugoslavia. The associations in Hungary, for example, conclude cooperation agreements with various public and governmental organizations—as was the case of a five-year agreement between them and the Society for the Dissemination of Scientific Knowledge (MTTT) for the propagation of material on the nationalities in Hungary and vice versa.[48] Likewise the Slovaks reported in their Congress in 1983 on their working arrangement with the Hungarian Press, TV, and its national news agency (MTI), with a view to fostering the dissemination of knowledge on the nationalities among the wide public.[49]

Such activities indicate that a certain degree of autonomy has been granted to the minority organizations. Within the limits prescribed by the regime, the minorities in Hungary have been geared not only to playing a positive role in the socialization of the minorities but also to promoting the external goals of the regime in relation to the Hungarian minorities abroad.

The External Role and Ties of the Minorities in Hungary

Hungary pursues a policy of open contacts between the nationalities and their mother tongue countries, and attributes a special role to their external relations with the neighboring states. This policy has two main pillars: first, the perception of the minorities in the role of "bridges of friendship" between peoples; and, second, Hungary's endeavor to set a further example, besides its liberal nationality policy, and achieve mutual contacts between Hungary and the Hungarians abroad. This policy of encouraging and promoting the external ties of the minorities with the neighboring countries has become one of the main features of the regime's line since the "rediscovery" of the Hungarians abroad.

The linkage between this aspect of Hungary's nationality policy and the expected policy from the neighboring states naturally raises the question of reciprocity in the nationality policy of socialist states. After all, as was shown in 1968, reciprocity is a two–way street, and the voices from Slovakia on the "forgotten Slovaks" in Hungary were met with deep indignation in Budapest, which rejected any reciprocity between the neighboring states. During the bitter disputes with the Romanian and Slovak comrades, the Hungarian CP indicated that it did not intend to pursue a reciprocal policy toward the minorities in Hungary, and rejected the suggestion of linking their fate with that of the Hungarians abroad. Nevertheless, at the same time the linkage was made, in the case of Slovakia by the population exchange agreement of 1946.

The theoretical basis for the "bridge" role of the nationalities was laid down gradually by the Kádár regime from the mid–sixties on. It appeared with growing frequency in the talks between Hungarian and Yugoslav, and later with Czechoslovak leaders, when in such high–level contacts both sides expressed the wish for their nationalities to play a role in the rapprochement between neighboring states. As a matter of course, the practical implementation of such a perception was linked to the readiness of the respective states to involve their Hungarian minority in interstate relations, just as Hungary proposed to do with those national minorities living in Hungary. While just before the Prague Spring both Yugoslavia and Czechoslovakia gradually agreed to the "bridge" theory, relations with Romania were not to be based on this perception until 1977, when for the first time the Romanians agreed to the mentioning of the respective national minorities in a joint declaration by Ceaușescu and Kádár.

By 1967–1968 the theoretical groundwork had been laid down in Hungary and explained to the wide public in numerous publications in the popular and the professional press. Hungary did not, at this stage, have enough experience on the possibilities of implementing the "bridge" theory in the interstate relations, nor was the notion that Hungary would set an example to be followed by the other socialist states put forward in an overt manner. The main ideological principle in developing the external role of the nationalities was the assumption that the nationality question in Hungary had been solved on a satisfactory Marxist basis, and that there was no tension whatsoever between the Hungarian majority and the minorities. However, the shortcomings in the practical implementation of the nationality policy were to be rectified—and the Party subsequently pointed to its own soul–searching process in pursuing a correct Marxist–Leninist nationality policy. The results of the internal debates in Hungary on nationalism and the role of patriotism were also emphasized at the time as an indication that Hungary had "cleared its own back yard" and that its people were free from nationalist chauvinist prejudices. Although in the years to come there were reports that such relics of the past still appeared in isolated cases, the overall picture as presented by the regime was one of self–satisfaction over the elimination of Magyar nationalism in respect to the national minorities.

It seems that questions were asked in Hungary as to the reasons why the national minorities, representing less than 5 percent of the population, were being given such a prominence. "What is all the fuss about?" was a question that the regime addressed. The answer was, as emphasized in the 1967–1968 debates on the nationality question,[50] that the "nationality question plays an important role in several socialist states," and thus Hungary considered that a positive echo to its policy abroad would bring about a favorable contribution to the cultural and economic relations with the neighboring countries. At the same time Hungary was also aware that a positive policy would enhance Hungary's prestige abroad.

From 1968 onward the nationality questions have been treated by Hungary not as isolated aspects of each country's internal policies, but rather as features with international impact and influences on the relations between states. Hungarian leaders have repeatedly emphasized that they do not intend to interfere in the internal affairs of other states, while Romania has frequently expressed its anxieties over Hungary's interference in its internal affairs.

One of the main means by which Hungary proposed to cope with the question of interference, or rather noninterference, in the neighbors' internal affairs, was the open–door policy to outside observation of the results of its nationality policy. In 1968, Hungary began to pursue a deliberate policy of "marketing" the national minorities, especially in the case of the Romanian minority in Hungary. Thus, the minorities—which no doubt benefited from such a shop–window display policy—were exposed to what amounted to an invitation to outside inspection by the neighboring countries.

Hungary is very much aware that the numerical factor belittles to a certain extent its efforts to "market" the national minorities. The minorities represent a very small part of Hungary's population, especially compared with the number of the Hungarians in the neighboring states. This factor explains the Romanians' rejection of any reciprocity in their policy toward the more than 2 million Hungarians in Romania, in return as it were for the promotion of the 25,000 Romanians living in Hungary.

The Hungarian response to the hints from abroad that it is easier to pursue a policy toward fewer people, and that quantity does have an impact on the shaping of the nationality policy, is that a liberal minorities policy is a matter of principle, irrespective of their number and their proportion to the majority nation. In order to emphasize this aspect of a policy based on staunch principles, of the need to grant equal rights to the minorities and to foster their culture and heritage, including their language, Hungary frequently makes a point of raising the status of the national minorities as an international issue through various forums, such as the conference on human rights in Ottawa, and other similar forums.

Hungary recognizes that the nationalities constitute a fragment of a larger nation both from an ethnic and linguistic point of view, and that they are attached to their mother tongue countries by natural ties that must be fostered. Thus,

> In the relations of Hungarian national minorities with their linguistic kin beyond the borders one has to reckon with clear emotional bonds, language, kinship relations, and concrete requirements.[51]

The logic behind this principle is quite clear—Hungary wishes that

the other countries would see in the same light the nature of ties between their Hungarian minority and Hungary itself. The more the
Hungrian regime rationalizes in this direction the more it indicates
its eagerness to establish a recognized and accepted framework for its
ties with the Hungarians abroad. The nationalities in Hungary, as
often reiterated by Hungarian leaders, "have found a home here and
are happy in their homeland, socialist Hungary,"[52] are well integrated
into their homeland, but at the same time their objective situation
"predestined them to play a role in the internationalist relations of
Hungary."[53] This sense of "predestination" is quite non-Marxist—
indeed it is a Calvinistic perception. It raises two main questions: To
what degree are the respective countries willing to accept their role
in fostering Hungary's nationality policy and at the same time to pay
a price in the conduct of their own policies with regard to the Hungarian minority in their country. Are the neighboring countries also
inclined to recognize this "predestined" role of their ethnic groups in
Hungary in fostering their relations with Hungary? Czechoslovakia
and Yugoslavia have accepted the main features of the Hungarian
line, while Romania tends to perceive the whole issue in very pragmatic terms, and there is no way for Ceauşescu to believe that the
25,000 Romanians in Hungary are predestined to play a significant
role in Romania's relations with Hungary, and neither would he see
the Hungarians living in Romania from the same perspective. As to
the second question, treated elsewhere in this study, Hungary has also
to cope with the developments among the Hungarians abroad, and it
seems that the

> Overwhelming majority of state–Hungarians find it extremely
> difficult to recognize that the national Hungarians are de-
> veloping an autonomous nationality–consciousness of their
> own—that they insist on being Hungarians culturally, but
> this is not the same as loyalty to the Hungarian state.[54]

Hungary often emphasizes that while it expects and wishes the Hungarians abroad to be loyal not to the Hungarian state but to their
socialist homelands, their loyalty should also extend to their Hungarian culture, heritage, and language. There are several main areas in
which the nationalities in Hungary can apply their predestination to
support Hungary's internationalist foreign policy. It is in the domain
of cultural and educational activities that Hungary has fostered the
external ties of the minorities in the last few years. Such ties, almost
always initiated by Hungary, and not by the respective states, are en-
shrined in interstate cultural agreements and local cooperation along
the border counties.

Interestingly, such local cooperation—very much supported by the central authorities[55]—serves as an alternate channel of communication between peoples over both sides of the border. These ties have been quite evident along the Hungarian–Romanian border, where Hungary has succeeded in developing, with the hesitant cooperation of the Romanian authorities, some more significant forms of border trade and other joint ventures.

As to the mechanism of the external cultural and educational ties between the nationalities in Hungary and their mother–tongue countries, the principles are always laid down in high–level discussions, in which—in the case of Yugoslavia and Czechoslovakia—the respective leaders agree that "nationality groups should serve as a bond of friendship and thus strengthening the external ties between the states." In this process of external marketing of the nationalities, the Germans are a special case. The issue is a double one: there are no Hungarians in German–speaking countries (except in the Burgenland in Austria) and Hungary has had to solve the question of whether the mother–tongue country of the Germans in Hungary have not been given much choice—the Hungarian regime has, of course, the GDR because of the ideological affinity to that state.[56] Matters have been complicated, however, by foreign policy calculations—namely, the interest shown by the FRG and Austria in the fate of the Germans in Hungary. This development was clearly presented by György Aczél, Politburo member and Secretary of the HSWP in his speech before the sixth Congress of the Democratic Association of the Germans in 1983:

> We consider it natural, welcome, and call for—in the case of Hungary's Germans—a multifaceted assistance by the GDR's institutions in improving the standard of satisfaction of their culture requirements, owing to the identity of our social regime. We also find natural the interest shown by neighboring Austria and the FRG in the life of Hungary's Germans.[57]

Hungary meets the cultural demands of the nationalities from its own resources, but as the head of the nationalities section of the Ministry of Culture has stated, "the high level support of the nationalities' culture is totally unimaginable without close relations with the mother tongue culture."[58] Such cooperation includes the training of teachers, librarians, and cultural leaders in the neighboring countries, while Hungary invites experts from these fields to visit and provide professional guidance among the nationalities in Hungary.

Recent Hungarian assessments on the results of this kind of cooperation indicates both achievements and frustrations. According to Ferenc Boros, head of the nationality section in the Ministry of Culture in 1977, there was intergovernmental and interdepartmental cooperation with the GDR, and intergovernmental links with Czechoslovakia and Yugoslavia. Romania was absent from this list, in spite of the agreements reached between Ceauşescu and Kádár in June 1977. Lászlo Kövágó was more specific about the modest success with Romania, as he gave the list of achievements in interstate cooperation involving the minorities: "the best results have been achieved with Czechoslovakia, Yugoslavia, the GDR, and to a lesser degree with Romania."[59]

The ties with Yugoslavia are very active, involving mutual visits by various experts from Hungary to the Hungarians in Yugoslavia and vice versa. The Democratic Association of South Slavs has signed agreements of cooperation with the cultural organizations of three Yugoslav Republics: Serbia, Croatia, and Slovenia. On the local level there are also several significant patterns of cooperation. The towns of Szeged and Subotica have concluded a "Charter of Friendship and Cooperation," described by the Mayor of Szeged as "even ahead of official diplomacy." Likewise, local border trade, a point very high on the agenda of the Hungarian nationality policy's foreign aspect, reached some $20 million in 1984, indicating mutual interest in such contacts, mainly involving the nationalities on both sides of the border.

The emphasis on Hungary's wish for other countries to follow its example became evident in the late seventies. The Hungarian regime felt that in spite of the positive reinforcements given to the nationalities in Hungary, some of Hungary's neighbors—especially Romania— did not intend to adjust their policies to the Hungarians on a reciprocal basis. At the twelfth Congress of the HSWP, Kádár elaborated the linkage from Hungary's point of view. He reiterated that,

> We are trying to ensure that the members of the German, Slovak, South Slav, and Romanian nationalities living in the neighboring socialist countries contribute to the deepening of the friendship and internationalist cooperation between our peoples.

And he added a more significant aspect to the question, namely that

> as a result of the history of our people about a third of Hungarians live outside the borders of our country. There are Hungarians in almost every part of the world. When we think of them it is good to realize that most of them, as far as possible, preserve and cultivate their mother tongue,

national culture, and traditions, and respect Socialist Hungary. What we expect from them is that, while nurturing their national culture, they would be decent citizens of their countries, and should serve social progress and friendship between peoples.[60]

The twelfth Congress served as a sounding board for the shift in the emphasis in Hungary's nationality policy. Summing up the deliberations of the Congress, in which several of the speakers discussed the country's nationality policy, Kádár returned once again to his main point in this issue, that

> Here in Hungary, people of different nationalities—in accordance with the principles of Lenin's policy on minorities, and with our law and constitution—live, work, and prosper as citizens with full rights. And as I said in the report and say it again, we want this for the Hungarians as well who live beyond our frontiers.

Certainly the reason for Kádár's repetition of this point was to hammer it into the Romanian neighbors who had different perceptions on the role of the nationalities in interstate relations, and especially on the role that the Hungarians in Romania should play in relations with Hungary.

In addition to the example set by Hungary, there is also another aspect which is seen as natural by Hungary in the relations between the nationalities and their mother–tongue countries. Thus, Kövágó argued that it was a "natural phenomenon" that the nationalities in Hungary should be interested in the life, the work of their mother–tongue countries, and Kövágó went on, "the same we can say about the Hungarian nationality in the neighboring states.[61]

From this period on it became clear that Hungary's relations with the Magyars abroad had entered a new phase, at least from Hungary's point of view, and that the external relations of the nationalities in Hungary with their mother–tongue countries were not fostered simply because of the deep desire to implement a Leninist nationality policy, but also as a pragmatic step to reach out to the Hungarians in the neighboring states and thus to satisfy pressures from the Hungarian nation in Hungary that the regime should act more on behalf of their brethren over the borders.

The Marketing of the Romanian Minority in Hungary

In the light of the strained relationship between Hungary and Romania, the small Romanian minority in Hungary receives special attention among the nationalities in Hungary, and its role as a bridge of friendship, or rather as a means to include the nationalities on both sides of the border, has been more emphasized. This policy amounts to a deliberate attempt to market the Romanian nationality and to secure reciprocal conditions for the Hungarians in Romania. If indeed the nationalities in Hungary are predestined to play a role in relations with the neighboring countries, the Romanian minority in Hungary was certainly geared up by the regime to play it. There is clear indication that the fostering of the Romanians is above and beyond that of the other nationalities, that they are, as it were, a "most favored nationality," in response to what many Hungarians feel: that the Hungarians in Romania are a "most unfavored nationality." The conditions for the fostering of the small Romanian community in Hungary are ideal: there is no danger whatsoever of a Romanian irredenta, and the Hungarians, so well–versed in the practice of nationalism and irredentist policies, know how to appreciate this aspect of their Romanian minority. There are no evident feelings of bitterness among Hungarians and Romanians in the mixed–population areas, and last but not least, the Romanian community in Hungary is traditionally a peasant one, without an intelligentsia, which at least theoretically would be prone to voicing dissident views.

The takeoff point for the special attention paid to the Romanians came parallel with the outburst of the first Hungarian–Romanian polemics linked to Romania's maverick policies in the Soviet bloc, and Hungary's growing role as the primary critic of Romanian policies. In the early sixties there was little mention of Romania in the context of the life of the Romanian minority in Hungary. The Kádár regime gradually expanded the educational and cultural facilities of the Romanians. Thus, at the first Congress of the Democratic Association of Romanians in Hungary, Péter Szilágyi, the Secretary of the organization, warmly praised the policy of the regime, and one of the guest speakers, Sándor Vendégh, the head of the nationality department of the Ministry of Culture, stressed that "never before has our country done so much for the development of the nationalities' culture."[62] Yet there were no direct references to the external role of the Romanian nationality, or, for that matter, of the other nationalities. This aspect became evident after the change in Hungary's attitudes to its relations with the Hungarians abroad, and the growing emphasis on the nationalities' policies.

At the third congress of the Democratic Association of the Romanians in Hungary held in Gyula, the center of the Romanian minority in Hungary, in April 1969, there were already enough references to the changing attitudes of the Hungarian regime as to the role of the minorities in its external policies. A mild attempt was made to draw the minority's attention to some divisive issues within the Communist movement, as Péter Szilágyi stressed the significance of the "Budapest Document" on the importance of the unity of the movement. In that period of the post–invasion interbloc diplomacy, this was a clear reference to Romania's reluctance to pursue a rapprochement with the Soviet Union and the other loyal Warsaw Pact states.

Szilágyi commended the "continuous strengthening of relations of friendship and good neighborship" between Hungary and Romania, as living together for centuries served as an indication of the two nations' determination to live in peace and cooperation. He expressed his trust that the friendship between the Hungarians and the Romanians in Hungary would also have international effects, contributing to the strengthening of relations between the two states.[63]

The nationalities' media have an important role in fostering the external ties of the nationalities. Thus, *Foaia Noastră,* the organ of the Romanians, which first appeared in 1951 under the name *Libertatea,* frequently publishes short news items about Romania, albeit rarely extensive analysis. At the same time *Foaia Noastră* reflected in a satisfactory manner the policies of the Hungarian government and the Party, and contributed to the "strengthening of relations of friendship" between the two peoples.[64] The interest shown by *Foaia Noastră* in Romania was a significant step in implementing the external role of the Romanian nationality.

At the fourth Congress of the Romanian association in 1973, and in the preparatory meetings held before it, more details were given on the nature of ties that the Romanians of Hungary were developing with Romania. Szilágyi defined their "international relations" with Romania as good and mentioned the mutual visits of folklore and other artistic troupes. More significant was the visit of Romanian specialists in the fields of cultural activities.

However, these forms of cooperation were not satisfactory from Hungary's point of view. The Hungarian complaints as expressed through the Democratic Association of Romanians in Hungary centered upon two deficiencies: the Romanians from Hungary were not invited to appear in Romania often enough, and second, the cooperation was limited only to the border counties. These two points cast light upon the small returns for Hungary's positive attitude to its Romanian minority. Romania showed very little, if any, concern for the Romanians in Hungary, as any manifestation of interest in them would have been interpreted by Hungary as a Romanian willingness to reciprocity in minority issues. *Népszava* gave expression to these Hungarian frustrations caused by Romania's silence on the nationality issue, by stating, emphasized in italics in the text that,

> Our Romanian compatriots would like by now that their artistic groups, teachers, instructors, would be invited to appear in Romania, and to acquire further training there. It would be desirable if the nationality cooperation, virtually limited to Békés and Arad counties, were expanded in content as well as geographically.[65]

From Hungary's point of view, the expansion of the contacts along the borders was an important aspect of the nationalities' role as bridges of "friendship and cooperation," but such steps had no long–range practical value unless followed by additional steps taken on a higher interstate level. Moreover, if the contacts were confined along the borders, it implied that Hungary was not in a position to reach out to the Hungarians in Romania, as it had intended to do, and had to limit itself to exchanges between Romanians in Hungary with Romanians over the borders—or in the best cases involving Hungarians on both sides of the border, but in a rather small geographical area.

Ironically, in 1978, following the apparently short–lived rapprochement between the two states reached during the Ceauşescu–Kádár talks in June 1977, both sides admitted that the possibilities for small–scale border trade had not yet been fully utilized,[66] and talks were held to increase them. Yet, no significant steps have been taken since then to expand the trade and human contacts between the nationalities along the borders, in marked contrast to the situation along Hungary's borders with Czechoslovakia and Yugoslavia.

The Romanian minority's leaders in Hungary were often quoted in remarks which indicated that cooperation between them and the mother–tongue country had not reached the desired level, from Hungary's point of view. In an interview with *Magyar Nemzet*, Péter Szilágyi reiterated that

> we aim at strengthening relations with Romania in keeping with the HSWP policy. In certain areas, mainly on the developing of the native language, we can rely on the help of the mother country. The development of such cooperation is essential for the Romanian minority to act as a bridge between the two nations, for Hungary is our homeland but our language and traditions link us with Romania.[67]

Romania had steadfastly opposed for years the mentioning of the national minorities as a factor in interstate relations with Hungary. It seemed, albeit for a short period, that there was a breakthrough in this respect during the meetings between Ceauşescu and Kádár in 1977. The final communique noted that,

> The two sides were unanimous in considering that the exis-

tence of the Magyar nationality in the Socialist Republic of
Romania and of the Romanian nationality in the Hungarian
People's Republic is the outcome of historical development
and accounts for an important factor in the development of
friendship between the two countries. . . . The sides consider that the existence of nationalities in the two countries
are turning to an ever greater extent into bridges bringing
closer the Hungarian and Romanian peoples.[68]

The talks and the agreements reached between the two leaders gave
rise to expectations in Hungary that there would be closer contacts
with the Hungarians in Romania. As subsequent developments in the
last decade have indicated, these hopes were short-lived. The Romanians in Hungary continued to play a role in Hungary's attempts to
build the bridge on the foundations that Romania had accepted, at
least on paper, in 1977. *Foia Noastră* intensified its friendly coverage of events from Romania, but the Romanian media—especially
the Hungarian–language press—did not change its policy of minimal
reporting on Hungary, and items linked to the national minorities.
Neither did the media in Romania show any greater interest in the
lives of the Romanians in Hungary than it had done before 1977,
although Hungary did not miss any opportunity to this effect. The
Hungarian reminders were well timed, provoking more polemics with
the Romanian comrades on the delicate issues. Thus, in the guidelines of the 13th Congress of the HSWP, and in speeches by Kádár and
other leaders in 1985, Hungary reiterated its positions on the external
role of the minorities, stressing the need for practical cooperation and
mutual contacts between the nationalities and their mother–tongue
countries.

Hungary often carried its message to Romanian soil, to the evident embarrassment of their hosts, as was the case of the HSWP
greetings to the 13th Congress of the Romanian CP in 1984,

It is a historical fact that citizens of Romanian nationality
live in the Hungarian PR and that a large number of Hungarians are living in the Romanian SR. The national minorities
are becoming true followers of our society by keeping their
language and culture and developing them and by promoting
relations with the nations speaking the common language.[69]

With a positive record to its credit in its policies toward the Ro-
manians, Hungary could carry on playing a safe card in its hands.
Speaking in a Bucharest factory, the Hungarian delegate to the RCP
Congress, Lajos Méhes, Politburo member of the HSWP, declared
Hungary's stand:

> We want whoever claims to be a member of a nationality
> group in Hungary to be able to maintain the inner and outer
> signs of that nationality group, and we want the Hungarians
> living in Romania to do everything possible to help Romania
> flourish.[70]

The continuing strains in Hungarian–Romanian relations clearly demonstrated the failure of Hungary's policy to market the Romanian minority. The change in Hungary's policies in the last few years—more
open and blunt criticism of Romania's nationality policies—serve as
evidence that reciprocity, as viewed by Hungary, was rejected by the
Romanians, and no effort by the Hungarians to encourage the ethnic
identity and the rights of the Romanians in Hungary will be answered
by a change in Romania's policies to the Hungarians. This of course
does not mean that Hungary will choose in the future to "divest"
in its minorities, should reciprocity be rejected by its neighbors, as
Romania has done. Hungary will keep up its positive policies to all
the nationalities as a proof that it has cleared up its own back yard
of remnants of nationalism and chauvinism.

The Minorities as an International Issue

From an early stage on Hungary's emphasis on the role of the
nationalities as connecting bridges of friendship between neighboring
states, it has linked its own minority policy and the situation of the
Hungarians abroad with a wider conception—that of the role of the
minorities in modern international relations. Hungary presents itself,
and rightly so, as the nation with the largest number of its people
living as minorities in Europe. According to Hungarian statistics,
some 3 million Hungarians live abroad—a point frequently repeated
by its spokesmen. Thus, Hungary sees itself as a self-made expert on
the nationality question in Europe and elsewhere, one that has the
moral right to assess and judge the record of the other states. The
obvious aim of this policy is to serve as yet another weapon by means
of which the regime attempts to prove that it is acting adequately on
behalf of the Hungarians in the neighboring countries.

By turning the issue into an international one, Hungary also seeks
to shift its polemics with problematic neighbors to a new and higher
ground—displaying it, as it were, to international public opinion. By
taking the Romanians to such "higher courts," Hungary has exposed
some of the delicate aspects of its relationship with Romania, reassert-
ing its constant interest in safeguarding the rights of the nationalities,
thus seeking a legitimation for reaching out to the Hungarians abroad.

Hungary sees the national minority issue as an international one,
and as György Azcél explained,

We do not look on indifferently when national minorities
are discriminated against, when they are hindered in using
their native tongue, or being educated in it, when they are
unable to maintain contact with their kin in other countries.
We desire in the name of universal interest of socialism that
every national minority, whatever the country, be free to
assert its economic, political, and cultural rights.[71]

The nationality question had both national and international implications, and in the Hungarian view the protection of minorities'
rights and the interest shown by the states in this issue should not
be interpreted as an interference in internal affairs. Such a position
is often voiced by Hungary in order to refute Romanian accusations
that Hungary is interfering in Romania's internal affairs.

The keynote of the Hungarian position in the international aspect
of the minorities' rights is the contention that the nationality question
has not been solved in Eastern Europe. In numerous publications
during frequent Hungarian–Romanian polemics, Hungary has called
attention to what is seen as failure of the Communist regime to solve
this problem once and for all.

Hungary pushes its point on the international implications of the
minority issue by several means. Its media treats the issue frequently,
promotes publications, sponsors research on the topic, and champions
various international organizations. Such Hungarian researchers as
László Kővágó and Rudolf Joó, present the nationality question as a
universal phenomenon with deep historical roots and they argue that
the nations of the world should cope with the issue through understanding and cooperation.[72] In the European, especially the Central
and East European context, the nationality question is seen as one of
the most crucial issues that the nations of the area have to live with.
The nationalist tides are regarded as destructive agents, which have
brought misery and discord to the nations of the area. The mistakes
of the past are highlighted for the nations to learn from them. This
is the predominant message in some Hungarian studies,[73] which have
treated the issues both from a historical and a contemporary perspective. There is also a growing literature which analyses and compares
the positions taken by the East European states on the nationality
issue. Kővágó built up his thesis on the right of Hungary to follow
the developments among the Hungarians abroad by comparing the
definitions and interpretations to the issue of the national minorities
in various socialist states,[74] reaching the inevitable conclusion that
although all the socialist countries profess to adhere to the Leninist
principles of solving the nationality question, there are differences in
the implementation of the principles, especially between the percep-

tions of Romania and Hungary. In describing Romanian perceptions of the nationality issue, the Hungarian researchers are not too far from one Western view, which sees the nationalities in Romania as more "coinhibited" than "coinhabiting."[75]

A major landmark in Hungary's involvement in the international aspect of the minority rights' issue was its participation in a series of international meetings devoted to the issue. Hungary has not only been seeking partners for the endorsement of its policies, but has also been playing an active role in initiating moves at such meetings. The 1974 conference organized by the United Nations in Ohrid in Yugoslavia, became one of the first such forums. The seminar dealt with the protection of human rights of national, ethnic, and other types of minorities. In the debate Hungary joined Yugoslavia in formulating the contemporary aspects of the minorities' lives. Yugoslavia's delegation, warmly supported by Hungary, on the basis of the Universal Declaration of Human Rights of the United Nations, underscored the legitimate interest of the mother–tongue nation in the situation of its national minority in another country.[76] Thi tenet coincided with Hungary's position and its media reiterated Yugoslatia's and Hungary's common views on the concern for the well–being of their national minorities abroad.[77]

Hungary put forward its policy, virtually identical to the Yugoslav position, by urging the states to admit to the existence of the problem and to discuss openly its various aspects, since the silence about the nationality issue between two states was detrimental to good relations between them. In Ohrid, and in the followup conference in Trieste, Hungary drew encouragement for its policy of presenting its own nationalities as a model and example to be emulated.

Yet another type of international activity was the holding of international conferences with participants from abroad, in which Hungarian experts displayed the ample research done in Hungary on the various aspects of the life of the minorities. One such conference was held in Békéscsaba in 1975, attended by 150 researchers from several East and West European countries. Significantly no Romanians appeared.[78] While the scientific work presented and discussed at the conference on the ethnography and the methodology of minority research should not be underestimated, the politically motivated aspects of the conference are also noteworthy. The Hungarian media expounded the international angle of the minority question, and in its coverage of the conference highlighted Hungary's involvement in this issue. Thus, *Népszabadság*[79] quoted statements made by Gyula Ortutay, President of the Society of the Dissemination of Scientific Knowledge, to the effect that "a scientific approach to the national minority question could contribute much to the easing of political tensions."

In the long run, perhaps the best thing that happened to Hungary's policy in regard to the international aspects of the minority question is the Helsinki process. Kádár's address at the Helsinki Conference in 1975, in which he reminded the audience of Hungary's territorial truncations and the existence of a part of the Hungarian nation in the neighboring states, was to elicit in the years to come allegations by Romania that Hungary was again playing with the fire of revisionism. The far-reaching importance of Kádár's speech in Helsinki was the broaching of the "Hungarian question" in a Communist version before the East–West forum. Since then Hungary has proceeded to interpret in a most convenient fashion the clauses relating to human rights and its implications on the minorities.

The selective reading of the Helsinki Final Act in Hungary's view does not necessarily imply that the "Helsinki process" is becoming a platform for the continuing polemics with Romania and for airing its complaints against the Romanian policy toward the Hungarians.

Since the Helsinki Final Act, Hungarian policy-makers have frequently referred to the Act's relevancy and implications for their policies. Thus at the Vienna conference at the end of 1986 and beginning of 1987, Hungary enjoyed the sympathetic attention of the Western media, as it lashed out at Romania's nationality policies. Once again the Hungarian position was based on the perception that the Principles of the Helsinki Final Act also referred to the protection of the interests of ethnic minorities. The Hungarian–Romanian clash at the meeting, and Hungary's unprecedented alignment with the West on the issue of human rights, proved Hungary's success in its "internationalization" of the minority issue. Considering that in 1987 the international status of Romania was at a low, subject to international criticism of its record on human rights, the Hungarian counteroffensive on the minority issue was well timed and effectuated.

Hungary's support of the Canadian proposal on the rights of the minorities was the first instance of a Warsaw Pact state cooperating with a Western state on a human rights proposal.[80] Hungary was riding high on the wave of criticism against Romania—including that from the U. S. Congress, which because of extensive pro-Hungarian lobbying suspended for a half a year Romania's most favored nation status.

Hungarian Foreign Minister Peter Várkonyi once again reiterated his country's position at the UN General Assembly in September 1987. He called for international cooperation in safeguarding the rights, cultural heritage, and language of the national minorities.

Yet another Hungarian–Romanian polemic was linked to Hungary's campaign for the raising of the minority issue, when at the Budapest Cultural forum in 1985 Romania came under heavy criticism. Hungary's delegation, on their home ground, denounced Romania's policies, eliciting Romanian rejection of the Final Document of the Forum. A byproduct of this Hungarian line was the even fiercer criticism leveled at the Romanians at the alternative unofficial forum held simultaneously by the dissidents. This criticism of Romania, along with Hungary's official condemnation of the Romanian policies, created a novel situation.

Chapter VII

Socialist Internationalism in Practice: Hungary
and the "Bridges of Friendship"

Institutionalizing the Contacts with the Hungarians Abroad

The change in Hungary's attitude toward the Hungarians in neighboring states, prominent from the end of 1967, was accompanied by what William F. Robinson described as an "equally surprising turnabout" in the regime's policy toward emigre cultural figures in the West.[1] Actually, the turnabout was much wider in its spectrum,heralding a policy of rapprochement with the Hungarians living abroad. The regime's policies vis–à–vis the Hungarian diaspora, drawn from internal and external sources, represent its attempts to reach a national consensus on "forgiving" the Hungarians who left the homeland in the various waves of emigration, including the "56–ers," and to present a milder, humanistic image of the regime abroad. The emigres, branded for years as traitors and Western spies, were being suddenly courted and invited home by the regime. Such a policy of rapprochement inevitably produced as a side effect the stirring up of arguments among the emigres as to the benefits of conducting a dialogue with the Kádár regime. That may have been one of the regime's aims, as it hoped to break up even further the already politically fragmented Hungarian community in the West.

For the purpose of this study the interesting aspect of the turn–around in the regime's policies is the connection with the regime's interest in the Hungarians living in the neighboring socialist countries. These two lines, often interlinked, represent a clear attempt at institutionalizing the contacts with the Hungarians in the West and the East. Moreover, the policy of acting as interested party in the lives of the Hungarians in the neighboring states could only benefit the search for a rapprochement with the Hungarians abroad.

The main instrument of the regime in carrying out its policy toward the Hungarians abroad is the World Federation of Hungarians (WFH), first established in 1939, and reactivated under its present form in 1957. The Federation intensified its activities after the emigration of some 200,000 Hungarians during and in the wake of the Hungarian Revolution of 1956. The regime followed a very careful path to link the Hungarians everywhere with the motherland, yet distinguished between those living in the neighboring countries and those who left Hungary for the West.

Hungary has not set up a special body to deal with the Hungarians over the borders, and is not expected to do so, as such a step would clearly be interpreted as an interference in the internal affairs of the neighboring states and would evoke historical memories of the revisionist Hungary's government agencies carrying out propaganda to the Hungarians abroad.

The precise limits of the WFH's range of activities in reaching out to the Hungarians in the socialist states have never even been defined, so as not to create the impression that the Federation is in charge of such contacts. As József Bognár, President of the WFH and one of the leading figures in Hungary's ties with its diaspora, explained,

> The Federation is concerned, in the first place, with the problems of emigrants, and in the nature of things, less so with those of the Hungarian minorities in neighboring states, since questions of our relations with them are, as a rule, regulated by bilateral agreements. Of course, this is no rigid position on our part, we follow with attention the life of the Hungarians living in the neighboring countries for it is obvious that the language and Hungarian culture in the life of these communities do not only mean the preservation of traditions but are also effective media of the requirements of modern development.[2]

Nevertheless, as it is evident, the WFH does deal with the Hungarians living in the neighboring countries even if "less so" than with the emigrants. But at the same time its involvement seems to be additional or complimentary to the interstate agreements. The WFH does not function in the neighboring states as a kind of "British Council" or "Goethe Institute," yet it does supply educational material prepared by the Federation.

The differences in the Hungarian approach to the Western diaspora and to the Hungarians in the neighboring countries are often highlighted in order to avoid misinterpretation by Hungary's neighbors. Thus, János Gosztonyi, Secretary of State in the Ministry of Education, explained the differences before the third Hungarian Native Language Conference organized by the WFH in August 1977,

> From the point of view of the native language movement, we must clearly distinguish between the situation of the Hungarians in the neighboring countries and of those in other

parts of the world. The Hungarian speaking inhabitants in the neighboring countries are not immigrants but natives. Their ancestors have lived for centuries—for a thousand years—in what is their native land. It was not their fault, that in the course of history, frontiers shifted.

Gosztonyi added some significant comments on the institutional limits faced by Hungary in dealing with the Hungarians over the borders:

The preservation of their native language and the furthering of their folk culture and national heritage is the business, in the first place, not of some sort of a movement but rather of the laws, institutions or rather network of institutions in which they live. This is how Hungary understands its role.[3]

In spite of this perception, in one major area Hungary makes use of the WFH as an agency to credit, or discredit as in the case of Romania, the nationality policy of a neighboring state. This area is the "mother– tongue movement" (*Anyanyelv*) or "native language movement," as it appears in some Hungarian sources published in English in Hungary, and whose conferences are organized under the auspices of the WFH. The conferences have been held every three to four years since 1970, and have been widely publicized by the Hungarian media.[4] The programs of the mother–tongue movement are aimed at fostering the preservation and teaching of the Hungarian language abroad, and coping with the issue of bilingualism among the Hungarians abroad.

The first two conferences, held in 1970 and 1973, clearly indicated Hungary's policy of rapprochement with the Magyar diaspora in the West, yet there was a surprise in store during the third conference held in August 1977 in Budapest. It was the first such conference to which representatives from neighboring countries were invited as observers. They came from Czechoslovakia, Yugoslavia, and the Sub–Carpathian *oblast* of the Soviet Union. Conspicuous by their absence were Hungarian observers from Romania, The organizers were delighted by the presence of Hungarian observers from the above–mentioned states, as well as the numerous delegates from Western countries, as their presence confirmed the success of the multilateral contacts that Hungary was developing with its diaspora near and afar. The absence of the Romanians was very adroitly taken advantage of by the Hungarians, who could boast the attendance of the representatives from Socialist countries.

In his closing address János Gosztonyi stressed that,

For the first time, new representatives of Hungarians living in neighboring socialist countries have participated in

the work of the Native Language Conference. We welcomed
them with great pleasure and we sincerely regret that there
were no representatives of the Hungarians living in the Socialist Republic of Romania among them. In the future, too,
we shall attribute great importance to the participation in
our work of the representatives of the Hungarians living in
the neighboring countries. We shall do our best to ensure
that they should take part.[5]

There is no doubt that Gosztonyi's words were aimed at the Romanians. As the Conference treated issues linked to the problems of
bilingualism, and the preservation of the Hungarian language, the Romanian attitude indicated their sensitivity to the nature of contacts
between the Hungarians in Romania and Hungary.

The third Mother Tongue Conference discussed issues which should
have been essential to the Hungarians living in Romania, had Romania accepted Hungary's involvement in the life of the Hungarians
abroad. The issue of bilingualism was raised by the organizing hosts
and also discussed by the observers from the socialist countries. The
author of an essay published in Hungary which reviewed the topics of
the conference hinted that Romania should have been an interested
party at the Conference. The author quoted from Ernö Gáll, editor–
in–chief of Cluj based *Korunk*, on the "bilingual characteristic of the
majority of the Hungarians in Romania."[6] The noteworthy aspect of
Gáll's article was its very publication in the August 1977 issue of
Korunk, the same month that observers from Romania failed to attend the Mother Tongue Conference in Hungary. Was Gáll's article,
quoted by *Kortárs* in Budapest, a sad reminder that while the Hungarians in Romania were facing situations similar to those inevitably
experienced by all national minorities living among majority peoples,
they were being denied the opportunity to discuss these issues in the
forums organized by Budapest?

The most important aspect of the absence of the Hungarians
from Romania may have been Hungary's attempt to test Romania's intentions following the June 1977 summit between Ceauşescu
and Kádár, which was supposed to constitute a breakthrough in
Hungarian–Romanian relations, as both sides recognized the role of
the national minorities as bridges of friendship and cooperation between the two states. The Mother Tongue Conference in August 1977
may well have been the first Hungarian challenge to test Romania's
implementation of the accords and agreements reached between the
two leaders less than two months before the Conference.

Romania's signal to Budapest came clear and loud. It would not
agree to the institutionalizing of Hungary's ties with the Hungari-

ans abroad. If the Hungarians in Romania were bilingual—as indeed they obviously were—then the educational and cultural implications of this situation would fall to Romania and not to Hungary. It was this message which Ceauşescu intended to bring home to the Hungarians in 1977–1978, in connection with the renewed Hungarian–Romanian polemics at the time. None of the media in Romania, not even the Hungarian–language press, reported on the Mother Tongue Conference. This seemed standard procedure, as the Hungarian–language press in Romania rarely reports on events taking place in Hungary, especially those related to the nationality issue. At the period when the Mother Tongue Conference was in session in Hungary, the Romanian media did devote considerable space to the coverage of a folkloristic gathering of the Balkan nations, stressing the beneficial role of the cooperation between the Balkan peoples for the peace and stability of the area. It was, of course, much more convenient to cover the Greek folk dances as a means of friendship between the Romanian and the Greek peoples, than to deal with socialist Hungary's attempts to have a say in the education of Romania's Hungarian citizens.

The participation of observers from Czechoslovakia and Yugoslavia at the Mother Tongue Conference certainly testified to these two states' positive attitude to most of the Hungarian initiatives in the nationality domain. But, the Hungarian organizers' chief prize was the participation of the Soviet observers for the first time. Their presence at the Conference should be seen in the context of Soviet policy to promote the small Hungarian minority in the Soviet Union, which could be used as a card in the game the Soviets were playing with the Romanians. After all, if the Soviets could approve their own Hungarians' ties with Hungary, why should Romania be resentful? Naturally, this Soviet–Hungarian logic had one flaw—the size of the Hungarian community in the Soviet Union—less than 200,000—was so minuscule that Moscow could well afford to be generous without compromising its nationality policy toward the other much more numerous ethnic groups living within its borders.

The Hungarian observers from Trans–Carpathia were so keen to play a role at the Conference that they raised the point that in some areas, as in their region, the Hungarians were not only bilinguals, but trilinguals. They also had knowledge of Ukrainian.[7]

The fourth Mother Tongue Conference was held in Pécs in August 1981.[8] There were 200 participants from eighteen states, who continued their tasks as a vehicle for the institutionalizing of Hungary's contacts with the Magyars abroad. The "mother tongue movement" was fulfilling its mission in implementing the regime's policies toward the diaspora. At the same time its role in supporting the ways and means of educating the Hungarians in the West should not be underestimated, as it certainly brought closer to Hungary members of the new generation, the children of former emigres from Hungary.

Public Opinion and Concern for the Minorities

Western experts have been aptly monitoring the pulse of Hungarian society. A "substantial proportion feels that a third of the body of the nation . . . has been cut off from it [but] there is nothing that Hungary can do about this overriding problem of the Hungarian nation."[9] While such feelings of hopelessness have been manifested in Hungarian public opinion, the trends in the last few years have indicated a certain change in its nature and intensity as well as its effects on the policy of the regime. More and more blame is laid at the door of the regime for not doing enough for the Hungarians abroad. This increased pressure is being countered by an attempt to substantiate how much is being done for Hungarians abroad—especially in Romania. At the same time the regime refutes accusations from the opponents of the system, as well as from emigre circles in the West.

The main problem is to try to set limits to the amount of public pressure it is prepared to tolerate, and to prove that it is doing something on behalf of the Hungarians abroad—not because of public pressure but out of a principled policy. Any recognition by the regime that it is bowing to public pressure would naturally be interpreted as a sign of weakness, although it is ready to acknowledge that such a pressure does exist. Hungarian leaders often admit that the issue of the minorities affects Hungary's national mood, as János Gosztonyi related to the problem at the third Mother Tongue Conference in 1977:

> How could one be indifferent when hundreds and thousands of kin and friends live on this and the other side of the frontier. Their lives, fate and situation influence the mood of Hungarians in Hungary—just like the situation and destiny of national minorities here affect their own mother nations.[10]

The problem of the regime consists not so much in recognizing the impact of the Hungarian minority question on the public awareness, but rather in finding the most appropriate mode to denounce the manifestations of "nationalism" in expressing concern about the lot of the Hungarians abroad, especially in Romania, while at the same time defending the regime's record on the issue. This line found expression in unequivocal terms by György Aczél at the National Conference on Information and Culture in January 1973, who stated that

> In earlier years it often happened that the "concern" felt by Hungarian nationalism for the future of the nation in

general, and in particular for the fate of the Hungarian population beyond our frontiers, attempted to throw doubt on the policy of the Party. It is necessary to emphasize that there still are manifestations of this phenomenon.

Aczél dwelt on the dangers of nationalist revival in expressing such —unofficial—concern for the Hungarians abroad. In such cases,

> With a sense of internationalist responsibility towards our people, our nation, we raise these questions always at the most appropriate forums and reject the irresponsible demagogy which—in opposition to the Party, the government and socialism—and incidentally, also harming those whom it wishes to defend—attempts to voice at times a brand of nationalism which it regards as justified. It has to be emphasized: there cannot be any justification for allowing the re–emergence of nationalistic, chauvinistic views.[11]

Aczél was being optimistic when in 1973 he mentioned that "there still are manifestations" of nationalism. Since that time Hungary has had to lend an ear to the ever louder voices from ever wider sections of the population expressing concern for the Hungarians abroad. Thus, at the height of one of the periodical polemics with Romania in late 1986, *Népszabadsag* attempted, almost apologetically, to refute the charges from Hungarian emigres, from the domestic "nationalist opposition" that the regime was not doing enough for the Hungarians abroad.[12] The paper forcefully rebutted the "ill intentions" of such charges whose aim was to increase tension with the neighboring socialist states, and to stir up nationalism at home. Hungary responds to such accusations by actively pursuing the matter with the respective governments, while making sure not to interfere in their internal affairs. The question arises how to discern when the concern for the Hungarians abroad is a "nationalist, chauvinist" phenomenon, and when it is a positive manifestation of warranted care. The answer of the Hungarian regime is the delimitation between positive "official" concern and harmful, unofficial worry about the interests of the Hungarians living abroad. Yet, at times the borderline between what the regime propagates and what the opposition demands may be somewhat blurred.

Since the late sixties there has been a revival of studies dealing with the number of Hungarians abroad, especially in the neighboring states. As often reiterated by the regime's spokesmen, there are close to 3.5 million Hungarians living in the neighboring states. But to "think big" is not always a welcome way of expressing concern for Hungarians abroad, for such a way of thinking may be harmful, unless it originates from the regime. An indication of this approach was evident in an article in *Magyar Hirlap* on the occasion of the fourth Mother Tongue Conference, in 1981. The author, Miklós Szabó, warned about the fallacies of megalomania, although he did not use the term.

> Some features of a search for a new national awareness which is developing out of ethnic awareness also indicate an illusory and harmful way of thinking. According to some people, Hungarians who live within our borders are a small nation but together with all the Hungarians who live outside the borders, we can consider ourselves a great nation.[13]

The sense of greatness, stressed the author, is "anti–democratic and harmful." Such a position, voiced on various occasions, indicated the fear of the regime that things would get out of control because of public pressure, and would thus be considered abroad as manifestations of Magyar nationalism—as Romania indeed assesses them.

From time to time, the Hungarian media do acknowledge the intensity of public pressure. The most explicit reference to its vehemence and the possible consequences was published in an indirect way. *Mozgó Világ*, which has often clashed with the regime on issues of artistic freedom, carried in June 1986 an interview with Béla Köpeczi, the controversial Minister of Culture,[14] and editor of the three–volume *A History of Transylvania* that was published in 1987. Köpeczi has become one of the most outspoken critics of Romania's policies toward the Hungarians, and indeed he was singled out in Romania for his tough positions. Köpeczi no doubt is very much aware of the level of intensity of Hungarian public opinion on this issue, and his open treatment of the divergencies between Hungary and Romania bears out to this awareness. However, the interview was dominated by *Mozgó Világ's* aggressive interviewer, whose Western technique made the questions longer and seemingly more interesting than the answers. At points the interview turned into a duel with the journalist's accusations that the regime was not doing enough for the Hungarians, countered by Köpeczi's defense of the government's record.

Köpeczi was told, rather than being asked, that the concern for the Hungarians abroad embraced "rapidly growing segments of society," and the feeling was that the government's policies were not yielding any results. Moreover, the interviewer implied that the non-policy of the regime was aggravating the situation of the Hungarians abroad by hinting at the situation in Romania. The intensity of the public pressure featured prominently in the interviewer's warning that "valuable members of the Hungarian intelligentsia might turn against the government because of the state of Hungarian–Romanian relations." He admonished the regime that something should be undertaken, and the sooner the better. Köpeczi's answers were very important not only for the insight he gave into the state of relations with Romania but also for his perceptions of the limits of Hungary's intervention on behalf of the Hungarians abroad.

Köpeczi reiterated that Hungary had little latitude in influencing the nationality policy of neighboring states. However, such a pessimistic approach was by no means a policy of "giving up" on this issue—Hungary was indeed conducting a dialogue with the respective countries. Köpeczi acknowledged the public pressure on the government by condemning dissidents who were agitating against the government and seeking to turn the public against the regime. The ongoing debate in Hungarian society would take place with only those, according to the Minister of Culture, who did not assume that the nature of public pressure and concern for the Hungarian minority is the frequent raising of the subject in the popular phone–in programs on TV and radio. In the last decade or so, these programs have taken quite a Western form, with frequent discussions, perhaps even initiated by the regime, on some delicate internal and external affairs. The question of the situation of the Hungarians in Romania, and the overall aspects of relations between the two states have been frequently broached, much more than the sporadic references to the Hungarians in Czechoslovakia, the second main area of concern relating to the Hungarians abroad. Although the tone of the questions in such phone–in programs, or in regular interviews in the media with top leaders, is not provocative, as was the case in the interview with Köpeczi carried in *Mozgó Világ*, the very questions certainly indicate the "public mood" with regard to the issue.

Interestingly enough the government is perpetuating some of these public queries and official responses on the nationality question. One such case is the inclusion of two questions on relations with Romania asked in a phone–in program of Mátyás Szürös, Secretary of the CC HSWP in connection with the publishing of his book *Our Country and the World* in 1985.[15] The program mentioned that the volume included two conversations over *Radio Budapest* on Hungarian–Romanian relations. To make sure that the issue was raised once again, the interviewer asked Szuros to review the state of these relations. In yet another interview with Szüros in the beginning of 1988, the questions were phrased in a way which clearly implied public interest in the fate of the Hungarians in Romania, especially with the deterioration of the economic situation in that country:

Szecsi: Our next theme is Romania. This is not the first time this question has cropped up. . . . Many listeners have dictated questions about waiting times at the border.

The listeners' questions were put by Éva Szecsi and András Kerekes, who went on phrasing the questions:

Kerekes: [a listener asks] . . . when are we going to be able to hear on Hungarian radio and TV and read in the press an official stance regarding the matter of the Hungarians in Transylvania?

Szecsi: Yes, this is not the first time this question has cropped up. So what does the Hungarian government intend to do for the Hungarians living in Romania? Last year you stressed that we were very resolute to act. Do we now have suitable means at our disposal?[16]

Public interest is also reflected in the readers' letters to the newspapers, a phenomenon which the regime openly acknowledges. Thus, reviewing the letters sent to *Népszabadság*, the paper wrote that

Letters also testify to the extent of the interest with which public opinion follows the fate of the Hungarians that live beyond Hungary's borders. Concrete cases show that the interest and the occasional anxiety are justified.[17]

In this case, the paper not only reviewed and classified the letters according to their topics but also expressed a political opinion on the anxiety of the letter writers when justified.

In 1986–1987 the most significant addition to the conflict with Romania was the Church's blunt condemnation of Romania's nationality policies, which was initiated and encouraged by the regime. After all, what could be more popular in Hungary than the Church's concern for the Hungarians in Romania? One of the first indications of the Church's growing involvement in the minority issue was given in an interview in *Magyar Nemzet* with József Cserháti, the Bishop of Pécs.[18] He declared that the Church felt responsibility for Hungarians in all parts of the world, and added,

We wish we could do more for them. . . . What we know about them is far from enough, and what we do for them is far from sufficient. . . . I know that the Hungarian state makes very big sacrifices for the cause of Hungarians living beyond our borders, but I must honestly say that despite all our efforts and all our endeavors to quiet our conscience, what we are doing is not enough.

The statement issued at the end of 1986 by the religious establishment, the Ecumenical Council, and the Roman Catholic Episcopate, on the plight of the Hungarians in Romania, revealed not only the point of no return that Hungarian–Romanian relations had reached at the time, but was also significant evidence of how much public pressure had influenced the government.

The statement by the church leaders was preceded by a series of petitions signed by numerous believers, calling on the country's religious leaders to express at Christmastime solidarity with the Hungarians in Romania. The inducement for pastoral letters was certainly welcomed, if not initiated by the government, which could only benefit and gain support from such a manifestation of solidarity with the Hungarians in Romania.

The statement issued by seven churches, members of the Hungarian Ecumenical Council,[19] was almost a verbatim quotation from official government statements on Hungary's position on the ties with the Hungarians in the neighboring states,

> We declare that they are part of our Hungarian culture, which they support and upheld. This is why we feel responsible for their fate. Based on this responsibility, we wish them to be good citizens of their states so they can be bridges of friendship between Hungary and their countries.

In recruiting the Church in the campaign against Romania, the Hungarian government indicated that there was a national consensus on the issue.

Naturally, Romania stepped up its version of national unity in the face of the danger from Hungarian "nationalists and chauvinists," a campaign into which religious bodies in Romania are increasingly drawn in. It would be indeed quite ironical if neighboring socialist states were to conduct their polemics under the Church's cloak.

The opposition in Hungary is, of course, the place to look for expressions of dissatisfaction with the regime's policies in regard to the Hungarians abroad, and for signs of public pressure. Covering the wide spectrum of opposition, Hungarian dissidents by and large share the concern for the Hungarians over the borders, as can be seen in one of the major meetings of opposition groups, in June 1985, in Monor near Budapest. Sándor Csoóri, a writer with outspoken, often nationalist, views was the main spokesman for the Hungarians over the borders.[20] Csoóri followed with great concern the plight of these Hungarians, especially in Romania. He spoke, referring to polemics and debates of recent years, of the "psychological and political warfare between the two states." Csoóri emphasized that questions were being raised in Hungary, and there was mounting pressure to "do something" for the Hungarians abroad. Interestingly, no one dares to suggest explicitly "what *is* to be done," but in the opposition's view the Kádár regime's mentality was hindering any attempt to openly challenge the Romanians. Csoóri denounced the policy of silence that characterized the regime's approach and accused its passivity as a cause for further deterioration of the situation.

The Monor meeting was not the only forum in which the regime's policies were censured. Dissident circles have for years dwelt on various aspects of the situation of the Hungarians abroad, and their voices have either been heard in Hungary, through their *samizdat* publications, or brought in through the emigre papers from the West that always manage to circulate despite the attempts of the authorities to suppress them.

The issue of the Hungarians in the neighboring states figures also at the presentations delivered at the Lakitelek meeting of intellectuals in September 1987, which surprisingly was attended by Imre Pozsgay, the General Secretary of the Patriotic People's Front. The situation of the Hungarians in Romania came up on several occasions and was presented by the dissenting intellectuals as further evidence for the regime's passivity in face of the plight of the Hungarian minority in Romania. It can be expected that the newly formed Hungarian Democratic Forum will press on with the issue, along with its more general aims related to the participation of the members of the society as true partners in the political process. A dialogue between the regime and the progressive–minded opposition may in the long run contribute to the formulation of a common strategy in regard to the fate of the Hungarians in the neighboring states, especially Romania. If so, such a trend will represent an innovation in the regime's dealing with the issue of the Hungarians abroad, and with the role on noncomformist elements in its policy.

Building the "Bridges of Friendship" with the Neighboring States: the Case of Yugoslavia and Czechoslovakia

The changes in Hungary's policy with regard to the Hungarians abroad have brought since 1968 a new dimension to its relations with the neighboring socialist states. The nationality factor became the most important component of the bilateral relations, excepting, of course, Hungarian–Soviet relations. Starting from its relations with Romania, through Yugoslavia and Czechoslovakia, Hungary has since 1968 implemented its principles, which have remained unaltered throughout the last twenty years—to monitor the fate of the Hungarians in these countries closely, and to use the nationalities on both sides of the borders as bridges of friendship. As already indicated, this policy met with overt opposition from Romania, while Yugoslavia and Czechoslovakia acquiesced for the most part, albeit with mild reservations, especially by Czechoslovakia.

The most divisive issue to this day remains the Hungarian–Romanian one, as it involves not only the nationality component but the much more complex problem of the fate of Transylvania, which has continued to embitter the relations between the two states. The forthcoming parts of this study will attempt to review the main trends in Hungary's relations with its neighbors in the light of the changes in Budapest's policies since 1968, and the attitudes of the respective countries to Hungary's unilateral "bridge building" initiative.

Yugoslavia

Relations with Yugoslavia returned quite smoothly to their normal course after the difficult, but short–lived period of strain in the wake of the Soviet led invasion of Czechoslovakia. With some ups and downs, Hungarian–Yugoslav relations have remained friendly, as both sides showed interest in fostering their ties. The national minorities have served as a very convenient vehicle for the expression of two nations' common desire for friendly relations. Both countries have a long tradition of agreeing to disagree, and for the most part to push aside sensitive, delicate issues likely to hamper their friendly course. There is no reason even to hide some fundamental, divisive points. Kádár and Tito kept up very efficient working relations, and "acknowledging the experiences of the past," were able to recognize and "define common denominators which dictated the individual characteristics and differences, while at the same time striving actively to identify ways for improved understanding and cooperation."[21]

The "acknowledgement of the experiences of the past" may also imply some unpleasant memories from the history of both countries in the last half century, such as remembering that

> Hungary was one of the countries that occupied parts of Yugoslav territory. And not to be ignored either, is Hungary's participation in the Cominform campaign against Yugoslavia.[22]

While the insertion of this passage in a Yugoslav article was well intentioned, as the author went on to explain the positive sides of what is termed as "model neighbors," the truth of the matter is that these two topics can be evoked whenever something goes sour in their relationship.

In sharp contrast to the pattern of Hungarian–Romanian relationship, the Hungarians and the Yugoslavs are both eager to avoid

unnecessary controversies and polemics, emphasizing the common denominators and not the divisive issues. Although there have been
short outbursts of tension, linked either to issues of the Communist
movement or to the nationality issue, they have been kept on a low
key by both sides, who are careful not to allow their differences to
influence the overall patterns of bilateral relations. Criticism, when
unavoidable, is much more restrained than in the case of Hungarian–
Romanian relations, and without so much of its emotional tone.

At all contacts between the two states there is mention of their
mutual satisfaction over the situation of the respective national minorities, with special emphasis on their bridge–building role in bilateral relations. Both states frequently express their satisfaction that
the nationality question is not a divisive one. As Hungary's Foreign
Minister, Frigyes Puja, expressed it during a visit in Hungary of his
Yugoslavian counterpart, Milos Minic, in 1977, "it is fortunate that
the existence of the nationalities is not a source of discord between
us."[23]

In order to assess the role of the national minorities in the relations between the two states, and Hungary's position in regard to the
life of the Hungarians in Yugoslavia, some of the trends and developments in the life of the Hungarians in Yugoslavia should be reviewed.
According to the 1974 Constitution, the Hungarians, who numbered
426,865 in the 1981 census, belong to the "nationalities,"[24] among
which they are second largest after the Albanians. This designation
for the non–South Slav "nations," such as the Serbs, Croats, and
Slovenes, was an innovation of the new Constitution.

The most significant trend among the Hungarians in Yugoslavia
is the demographic development which indicates a decline in their
number, a fact noticed by Hungary. Numerically this was very evident in Vojvodina, where the largest concentration of Hungarians live.
Between 1963 and 1981 the number of Hungarians in the autonomous
province declined from 435,345 to 335,356 and their proportion in the
population dropped from 24.5 percent to 16.5 percent.[25] This trend
is due to the widespread assimilation which, similar to the minorities in Hungary, is often voluntary and should be seen as a natural
development.

Another factor is the dispersion of the Hungarians through other
parts of Yugoslavia, where many of the Hungarians, whose number
is unknown, prefer to declare themselves as "Yugoslavs." As some
167,215 citizens in Vojvodina declared themselves as "Yugoslavs," it
could be surmised that most of the "missing" Hungarians, numbering
more than 38,000—i.e., the difference between the number of Hungarians in 1971 and in 1981—were in fact those who had become

"Yugoslavs." But most of the "Yugoslavs" were found to be Serbs, so it seems that the number of Hungarians who declared themselves as Yugoslavs is smaller than previously thought. This factor should not, however, be taken into consideration in discussing the decline in the number of the Hungarians in Vojvodina, Slovenia, and Croatia, where other concentrations of Hungarians are living.[26] There are some Hungarians—and their number is not known—who "opt" for yet another solution: that of declaring themselves as belonging to one of the South Slav nations, especially the Serbs, a peculiar phenomenon which may also be ascribed to the process of assimilation.

The decline in the number of Hungarians in Vojvodina is obviously also a reflection of the political role of the Hungarians in the Autonomous Provinces. For years there has been a perceptible decline in the number of Hungarians in the higher local bodies of the League of Yugoslav Communists and other decision–making bodies. The rising number of Serbs in Vojvodina, 54.4 percent of the Province's 1981 population, could alter the character of the area in due time and could even engender second thoughts as to the need for a Hungarian Autonomous Province. Although such thoughts have not yet found expression, at least officially, the status of the Province is often a cause for friction between the Province authorities and Belgrade. Ludanyi's analysis pointed to the "second rate status of the Autonomous Provinces"[27] and to manifestations of "practical inequality," when the situation of the Provinces and the Republics is compared in relation to the federal authorities. But this "original sin" is not about to change, and in the case of Vojvodina, a further decline in the number of Hungarians could endanger the present constitutional arrangements.

Moreover, the events in Kosovo in 1981, and especially in late 1987, may have an unwanted effect on the political role of the Hungarians, who did not manifest irredentist claims—although such accusations have been leveled against them in Yugoslavia since the beginning of the eighties. They fear that they may become victims both of the federal regime's trend, in face of Serbian pressure, to centralize its authority, and of the Republican government in the management of the affairs of the Autonomous Province, as in the case of Kosovo. Such a trend may be turned into a precedent.

Although the difficulties in the Serbian SR with Kosovo differ in nature from some disagreements with the leadership of Vojvodina, the Hungarians in the Province are carefully watching the developments related to the situation in Kosovo. According to some reports in 1981, the case of the Albanians in Kosovo aroused sympathy among the Hungarians. One such report mentioned the warm welcome given by Hungarians to Albanian folk dancers from Kosovo at a festival in Vojvodina, where the Hungarians expressed their sympathy by cheers and clapping.[28] At the time, the Serbian authorities lashed out more strongly at alleged Hungarian nationalism in order to discredit any manifestations of Hungarian sympathies with the Albanians in Kosovo. *Borba* warned of the dangers of Hungarian nationalism "that engages in tactical games and calculates and waits to see whether another nationalism that is rising might perhaps benefit it in some ways."[29]

Hungarian participation in the Yugoslav political system was questioned by such researchers as Ludanyi,[30] who stressed the mostly "symbolic" nature of the Hungarian participation in the government and other decision–making bodies. The ethnic imbalance in the various authorities within the Province has often been pointed out, and the Hungarian language press has been treating these issues in a keen and open manner, in spite of Serbian accusations of "nationalism." It seems that this issue is a crucial problem in the life of the Hungarians in Yugoslavia—more so than the issue of their practical participation in the system.

Naturally, mutual suspicions, remnants of the traumas of World War II, are also linked to Yugoslavian sensitivity to the role of the Hungarians in the political system. Hungarian politicians in Yugoslavia are known defenders of the rights of the autonomous provinces and the republics vis–à–vis the federal authorities. One forthright spokesman for this view is István Rajcsán, who in 1984 as President of the National Assembly in Vojvodina criticized "centralism and isolationism." Rajcsán suggested that not force, as some colleagues in Belgrade proposed, but the further development of self–management was the key to correct policy. The ensuing debate in 1984, in the course of which *Magyar Szó* condemned some Serbian advocates of what it branded as the "Rankovitch type unitary state," highlighted the Hungarians' sensitive position whenever there is a crisis in the system linked to the nationality question.

During the Croatian crisis in 1971, the Hungarians were apprehensive that the Croats' nationalist demands would reflect unfavorably on their own rights, just as they were afraid of the revival—or as some presented it the continuation—of the Great–Serbian pressure. Since the beginning of the eighties a rising number of incidents have occurred involving accusations of Hungarian nationalism and irrendenta, and there seems to be more friction between the Hungarians and the regime than before. Although overall the state of the Hungarians is good—the best among the three states neighboring Hungary—the manifestations of friction have also placed Budapest in a delicate situation.

The charge of Hungarian nationalism in Yugoslavia was brought up in the early eighties in conjunction with the events in Kosovo. These accusations were aimed generally against those defined by the regime as "nationalists," but not specifically against the Hungarians. One forum which expressed concern over nationalist manifestations in the light of the events in Kosovo was the session of the Intra-National Relations Committee of the Praesidium of the Vojvodina LC in 1981. The connection between the events in Kosovo and some signs of nationalism in Vojvodina were presented by the Party leaders.

The Committee stated that,

> Counterrevolutionary events in Kosovo, which have been sharply condemned everywhere, have at the same time prompted the basic unit of the Vojvodina LC to carry out a deeper, fuller and more critical appraisal of their state of awareness and activity in implementing the policy of national equality.[31]

Concerning the intensity of nationalism in the area, the document issued by the Committee specified that nationalism "has not manifested itself so acutely as in the organized activity in Kosovo." It mentioned manifestations of Serbian nationalism while Serbian voices speak about the "threat to Serbdom," and Hungarian voices speak of "inadequate conditions for the development of the Hungarian nation in Yugoslavia."

Much of the criticism and condemnation of Hungarian nationalism in Yugoslavia is linked to the events from the area's history and the Magyars' role in it. Some of the allegations are not unlike those raised in Romania in connection with the polemics with Hungary. The difference here is that Hungary is involved only indirectly, if at all. Hungary, for example, reports factually on polemics that are taking place in Yugoslavia between the Hungarians and Serbo-Croat elements. The main allegation brought up against the Hungarians since the early eighties—and there has been a marked uneasiness in this respect since Tito's death—is the fact that Hungarian "nationalists are still expressing their regret over the 'unjust' Treaty of Trianon, which caused the 'annexation' of the former territory of Hungary."[32]

Like the Romanians, the Serbs and Croats are suspicious that many Hungarians are still harboring dreams from the past, an approach that was reflected in one of the bitter controversies at the beginning of 1983 over Hungarian aspirations. The debate was sparked off by the late Gyula Illyés who, at the time of heightened Hungarian-Romanian polemics over the nationality issue and the fate of Transylvania, gave an interview to the *Frankfurter Rundschau*,[33] in which, among others, Illyés accused the Yugoslavs of carrying out a policy of "de–Magyarization."[34] Illyés's sharp comments immediately drew fire from some of the Serbian newspapers. Thus, *Vecerni Novosti* titled its article "Empty Nostalgia Dreams of Austro–Hungary" denouncing "individuals among the Hungarian intellectuals in Yugoslavia" and also a section of priests inbued with "Hungarian nationalism and irredenta," who according to the paper had joined forces with the Croatian Ustasha and the Albanian irredentists.[35]

One of the more interesting points about the debate the Illyés' interview sparked off in Yugoslavia was its similarity to a scandal likewise triggered by an article of Illyés in December 1977, condemning Romania's nationality policies. The debate between Hungary and Romania at the time was quite similar to that which took place within Yugoslavia in 1983, in the wake of Illyés's interview. It seems that the Yugoslav media took in this case a page from Romanian pronouncements, as some Romanian papers wrote at the beginning of 1978 on the "nostalgia" felt by some in Hungary for the days of the Monarchy and for the days of the "Admiral without a fleet"—Horthy.

The Hungarian media in Yugoslavia rejected Illyés's attempted defense of the Hungarians in Yugoslavia, and *Magyar Szó* gave voice to its indignation over the feeling expressed by a Belgrade paper that some Hungarian intellectuals were adhering to nationalist–irredentist perceptions. In attacks against alleged Hungarian nationalism, the Catholic Church is often mentioned as one of the hotbeds of such an agitation. As one of the speakers at the session of the Provincial Committee of the Vojvodina LC put it, "to a great extent the nationalist expressions are also encouraged by the Church."[36] A similar line was taken by an article in *Vecerni Novosti* to the effect that "a section of the Hungarian priests in our country imbued with Hungarian nationalism and irredentism" cooperated with the Croatian Ustasha and the Albanian "irredentists."[37]

The Yugoslav media did not show consistency in the accusations against the Hungarian Catholic Church and its cooperation with Croat nationalist elements. It would seem rather absurd to take to task the Hungarian nationalists for cooperating with the Croat nationalists, as their ultimate goals would be quite different. Another Yugoslav source, *Politika*,[38] was even more evenhanded when it reported on rivalry between Croatian and Hungarian priests for posts in Subotica. Such a situation is often reported from areas where Hungarians and Croat populations live side by side. The paper, in reporting on this struggle for power—and jobs—in the Church hierarchy, did not accuse the Hungarians of cooperating with the Croats;

on the contrary, its judgment was equal to both sides: the Hungarian Catholic priests were "imbued with Hungarian nationalism" and the Croatian clergymen were filled with "Croatian nationalism." The denunciation of Hungarian–Croatian clerical-nationalist cooperation, on the one hand, and the frictions between the two sides, on the other hand, represent a relatively new phase in the intensifying Yugoslav campaign against alleged Hungarian nationalist activity in the country. It is a sensitive issue, due to the deep religious feelings both among the Croats and also among the Hungarians. The Hungarian Catholics in Croatia seem to be more active than in Vojvodina. They are in a defensive position facing the strong Croatian religious establishment.

Signs of friction among the Hungarian and Croat Catholics were also evident during the 1970–1971 commemoration of the one thousandth anniversary of the birth of Saint Stephen. At the time the central authorities gave permission for celebrations on both sides of the border, in Vojvodina and Baranya, but these celebrations were put off because of the hesitations of Croatian religious leaders.[39]

The role of Hungary—and of individual Hungarians—in the fate of Yugoslavia during World War II still constitutes a very sensitive issue, which has captured public attention in recent years. Yugoslav sources often mention the burdens of the past "just in case," when for political reasons the issue might be used either in relations with the Hungarians in Yugoslavia or with Hungary itself. The Hungarian occupation of areas of Yugoslavia, the atrocities committed by Hungarian forces against local populations, and the vicious circle created by retaliatory actions against local Hungarians as soon as the fate of the war had taken a turn left a traumatic imprint on the Hungarians' relationship with the inhabitants of the area. There was no doubt that to a certain extent, as Ludanyi put it, at the end of the hostilities the Hungarians in Vojvodina remained a minority that had attempted to "desert" Yugoslavia during the Partisans' fight for Yugoslavia's preservation.[40] The role of the Hungarians during the war, and especially the degree of their "constructive" contribution to the liberation of Yugoslavia, has often been brought up by the regime in order to counterbalance the negative impressions of the nefarious behavior of the Hungarians in the invading forces, of the regime Hungary had imposed, and of the attitude of the local Hungarians, many of whom, if not most, welcomed the occupation by Hungary.

A renewed and bitter debate on this issue was touched off in 1983 during a historical symposium in Sarajevo, at which one of the participants, Slobodan Nesovic, a well-known Serbian journalist, minimized the role of the Hungarians in the liberation of Yugoslavia, and considered their participation as insignificant.[41] Hungarian responses in Yugoslavia, especially those by Ida Szabo, one of the old–timers of the Yugoslav Communist movement, emphasized the role of the Hungarian communists in Vojvodina, their suffering at the hand of the occupying Fascist Hungarian authorities, and the part played by the Hungarian partisan detachment, 'Petöfi Sándor," which had grown into a brigade by the end of the war. In the ensuing debate the Hungarian–language daily in Novi Sad, *Magyar Szó*, published articles by Serbian authors bitterly criticizing Nesovic's thesis. The suggestion that Nosovic's position represented an attempt by some Serbs to curtail the autonomy of Vojvodina by disparaging the role of the Hungarians in the liberation of Yugoslavia is fairly plausible, considering that some circles in Belgrade, both in the Federal government and at the Republican level, are concerned about Hungarian demands for more autonomy. Even if the Hungarian pressure in this direction is not forceful, the wartime record of the Hungarians in Yugoslavia could become the trump card of the Serbs.

In marked contrast to the debate that has been going on for years between Hungary and (for the most part) Romania over the fate of Northern Transylvania under the Horthyst rule, both sides have acted to limit and to tone down the polemics, and not to allow it to interfere in their relations. The most significant expression of this attempt is the joint work effectuated by the Military History Museum of the Hungarian People's Army with the Military History Institute of the Yugoslav People's Army. The outcome of this collaboration was the joint publication of a collection of documents on *The Participation of Horthy Hungary in the Attack and Occupation of Yugoslavia, 1941–1945*. As a Yugoslav review of the volume commented, the facts presented in the volume are

> inseparable parts of the history of the two countries and constitute the historical foundation and source of friendship and cooperation of their peoples, who are building a socialist society.[42]

The volume also highlights those aspects of the Hungarian occupation of parts of Yugoslavia which were denounced in 1983—namely, the role of the Hungarian Communists in the Partisan movement. Likewise, the positive role of the "Petöfi" brigade, which initially had been formed on Hungarian territory, was also emphasized.

The well–known cases in the last two decades illustrate the extent of the conflict between the Hungarians and the Yugoslav regime over the alleged nationalist activities: the so–called "Rehák" case of 1967, and the regime's campaign against *Új Symposion* in 1983. When

László Rehák, the foremost authority on the life of the Hungarian minority in Yugoslavia, activist in the Vojvodina LC and member of the Serbian Republic's Assembly, complained in the Assembly of the delay in setting up a Hungarian Studies Institute at the University of Novi Sad, he was taken to task as a "nationalist" and was not elected to the vice presidential post of the Serbian Republic Executive Committee.[43] Rehák's grievances in 1967 were an expression of the Hungarian intellectuals' frustration over the unfulfilled promises by the authorities to set up the Institute, which was eventually founded in June 1968. The Institute was the continuation of the Chair for Hungarian Language and Literature established at the University of Novi Sad in 1959. The Chair lived up to its expectations, was engaged in fruitful work, but was restricted in its activities by its very character, which has limited means at its disposal to carry out various educational and scholarly tasks in certain areas of Hungarian studies.[44] The "Rehák affair" was interpreted by Pedro Ramet as "the beginning of breakdown in the Serbian–Hungarian equilibrium."[45]

Although Serbian ethnocentric attitudes have been evident since the late sixties, most noticeably during the Croatian crisis in 1971, the Rehák affair did by no means signal a new era of breakdown, but rather indicated a new stage of growing national awareness by the Hungarians and a tougher Serbian response to alleged manifestations of "Hungarian nationalism." The "Rehák affair" also had a Hungarian aspect, inasmuch as his publications on the nationality question in Yugoslavia were widely reported in Hungary, yet no specific mention was made of the criticism against him. By publishing positive reviews of his study, Hungary may have intimated that it related merely to the scientific achievements of the person, while shunning the man himself. Neither was there mention in Hungary of the polemics between *Magyar Szó* and Serbian papers, as the Hungarian–language paper overtly defended Rehák, clearing him of any nationalist feelings and even hinting that those who criticized and accused him of nationalism were actually the ones who harbored such views.

The second major crisis in the Hungarian–Serbian relations was the fate of the Novi Sad based *Új Symposion*, an avant–garde magazine with a long tradition of outspoken views appealing to a wide readership, especially among the younger generation of Hungarian intellectuals. The journal was closed down by the authorities and its editorial board dismissed in May 1983, but it renewed publication with a new editorial board with a January–February 1984 issue. The crisis around the journal was yet another stage in a long series of conflicts with the authorities. In the late sixties *Új Symposion* had rather bluntly and candidly given voice to Hungarian dissatisfaction

with their status and situation in Yugoslavia. During the days of
the Croatian crisis in 1971, the paper published a story by a student, Rózsa Sándor, giving vent to the frustration of his generation.
Working at the time as the Hungarian–language program coordinator
of the Novi Sad Youth Council, Rózsa bitterly labeled the Hungarians as the "niggers" of Yugoslavia,[46] and gave a candid account of
some of the problems facing the minority. Rózsa was jailed for three
years, while Ottó Tolnai, the journal's editor, was also convicted; his
one–year sentence was later suspended.[47] Under a new editorship, *Új
Symposion* had to apologize for Rozsa's story.

After more than twelve years of relative quiet in the relations between the authorities and the journal, the crisis erupted anew in 1983,
when the Praesidium of the Vojvodina Socialist Youth Association,
which publishes the journal, dismissed its editor, János Sziveri, and
the editorial board, on charges of "ideological–political deviations."
The paper published

> poems containing unacceptable ideological–political messages
> . . . it allowed anti–self management, and new leftist ideas
> to find their way into the columns of the periodical, which
> was often permeated by a certain degree of opposition.[48]

Although the clampdown on *Új Symposion* came shortly after
the bitter exchange of articles in the Serbo–Croatian and Hungarian-
language press in the wake of Illyés Gyula's comments on the Hungarians in Yugoslavia, it seems that the monthly had not necessarily been involved in so–called "nationalist" activities. Rather, the
authorities took a defensive preemptive action against this outspoken mouthpiece of the Hungarians, which in the past had combined
grievances on the nationality issue with a broader vision of artistic
liberty than permitted by the regime. Yet, the crisis around *Új Symposion* did have implications on Hungarian–Serbian relations, as the
ousted members of the editorial board argued that the monopoly of
the Hungarian language publishing house in Novi Sad, Forum, which
is safely under Party control, is to blame for the situation. In other
words, the Hungarian editors resented their own publishing house's
monopoly because it was under a centralized Serbian control. The
reappearance of *Új Symposion* under a new editorial board in 1984,
and the tone of the journal since then, indicate that the new line will
deal less with sensitive issues of the Hungarians in Yugoslavia, and
will adhere more to the norms or artistic freedom as perceived by the
regime.

Hungarian cultural life in Yugoslavia is presented by the regime
as one of its main achievements. Indeed, the educational and cultural

opportunities available in the Hungarian language are the best among the three Successor States under discussion. While there are well-founded complaints on the limited openings available for Hungarian students graduating in the various educational facilities in Romania and Czechoslovakia, the situation in Yugoslavia is much better. Currently there are more than 40 daily, weekly, and other periodicals in the Hungarian language. The Hungarian–language publishing house, Forum, accused by Hungarian intellectuals because of its monopoly, is bringing out a wide variety of journals and books. It is also engaged in the distribution of Hungarian–imported books and periodicals from Hungary, on a much wider scale than in the other two neighboring socialist states.

Radio and TV programs in Hungarian are also best developed in Yugoslavia, and cooperation with Hungary assures a steady flow of programs and information in the Hungarian language. In spite of the absence of a strong Hungarian intelligentsia in Yugoslavia (and in this respect the situation is similar to the one in Slovakia) the Tito regime encouraged the rapid growth of a Hungarian intelligentsia through its nationality policy, promoting Hungarian writers and scholars. Since 1969 the Novi Sad University has published regularly the Papers of the Institute of Hungarian Studies, under the aegis of the Hungarian Institute at the University, whose establishment was the subject of the "Rehák affair." The *Magyar Szó*, published in Novi Sad, is the main political organ aimed at the Hungarian population, and on the cultural scene, the monthly *Hid (The Bridge)*, holds a prominent position.

As to the available number of educational facilities at all levels of instruction, the situation among the Hungarians in Yugoslavia is similar to some extent to the one in Slovakia. The Vojvodina authorities often complain that the minority composition of the university students in Vojvodina is not proportionate to the ethnic makeup of the province. Likewise, there was a downward trend in the number of Hungarian students that chose to study in the Hungarian language. Certainly this reflects the tendency to assimilation, which both Yugoslavia and Hungary have called attention to.

In the framework of its policy of "responsibility" for the Hungarian culture in the neighboring states Hungary shows a marked interest in the cultural scene of the Hungarians in Yugoslavia. The literary press in Hungary usually praises the achievements of Hungarian cultural life in Yugoslavia, and some of their publications are published jointly with Hungary. Such was the publication in Hungary of an essay by István Széli on the recent history of Hungarian culture in Yugoslavia.[49] Széli is at the Chair of Hungarian Studies in

Novi Sad, along with Ervin Sinko, the veteran Communist writer and essayist. Szeli surveyed in his book the multilateral development of Hungarian culture in Yugoslavia, treating, besides Vojvodina, the developments in Croatia and Slovenia. Reviews published of the book in Hungary did not imply any criticism of present–day Yugoslav nationality policy, and in fact conveyed the message that Hungary endorsed neighboring Yugoslavia's line.[50]

The relations between Hungary and Yugoslavia do not reflect the occasional periods of strain, such as whenever there appear numerous instances of condemnation in Yugoslavia of "Hungarian nationalism." Hungary's practice has been to minimize the account of events in Yugoslavia, so as to avoid polemics on topics which are likely to lead to a sharper exchange of words. Hungary usually reacts only in instances where it is directly involved, as was the case during accusations in 1983 of Hungarian nationalism in Yugoslavia. The Belgrade *Politika* reported, without comment, on a local Party committee in Subotica, which in its session claimed that "some citizens of the Hungarian People's Republic had spread the view that the area of Vojvodina was once Hungarian, and that it would become Hungarian again."[51] Around the same time other Yugoslav newspapers, such as *Vecernje Novosti*, reported that many irredentist incidents were taking place in Subotica, located on the Hungarian–Yugoslav border, involving visiting Hungarian citizens.[52] The media in Hungary rejected these accusations, but instead of refuting them directly, supplied evidence of the close relations of collaboration between Subotica and the border towns on Hungarian territory. Since 1981, and especially in 1983, the media in Hungary have merely touched upon accusations in Yugoslavia of the awakening of Hungarian irredentism, cautiously limiting the report to factual accounts and refraining from commentaries. Yet, with all this, the media in Hungary emphasized that the Yugoslav allegations were false, resorting for this purpose to quotations from the Yugoslav press items, especially from the Hungarian–language press, which rejected all these allegations. Such an approach was also adopted by Hungary during the removal of the editorial board and the closing down of *Új Symposion* in 1983. The media in Hungary reported very briefly on the event, and a week later *Népszabadság* printed a very short account of the events, taken over without comment from *Magyar Szó*.[53]

The most striking feature of the reflection of the nationality issue in the relations between the two states is their very frequent lavishing of mutual praises for their respective achievements in the solution of the nationality question, and for the successful implementation of the "bridge" theory initiated by Hungary. As one Yugoslav paper expressed it:

> If a Hungarian, coming to Yugoslavia, feels very much at ease, I may add that the same applies to the way a Yugoslav feels in Hungary. This says a great deal about the relations between the two countries: good neighbor relations in practice.[54]

Even so, occasional "skirmishes" on delicate issues do crop up here and there but they are usually brushed off without any long range influence on the course of bilateral relations. Such was the sharp Yugoslav criticism in April 1981 of a Hungarian press report, in which, according to the Yugoslavs, *Népszabadság*[55] did not treat the Kosovo disturbances in a correct way. The main Yugoslav papers reproduced in *Magyar Szó's* rebuttal to Budapest. It was a rare case where the Hungarian–language press in Yugoslavia served as a "model" for criticism of Budapest. Yet, the polemics over the style of Hungarian approaches to the nature of disturbances in Kosovo petered out before long, and several weeks after the sharp exchange of words, Lazar Mojsov, the President of the Praesidium of the CC LYC, visited Budapest, and was engaged in an "extremely useful dialogue." Both sides at the time made a point of emphasizing the continuity in their relationship in the post–Tito era, a fact highlighted at all high–level contacts that followed Tito's death in 1980.[56] Kádár's visit to Yugoslavia in March 1984 also symbolized continuity in their relationship, and on the eve of his arrival the Yugoslav media printed Kádár's statements after Tito's death on his relations with the late leader. According to the Hungarian perception, and reiterated by Kádár during his 1984 visit, the cordial relations between the two countries and the two Parties were based on the "bridge of friendship" created by the national minorities in both countries. This line was once again reconfirmed during the visit of the Yugoslav Prime Minister, Milka Planinc, in Hungary in December 1985. Both sides expressed their belief that the solution of the national minority question was "exemplary" in the two countries, and that the nationalities constituted an important factor in promoting friendship and cooperation.[57] Likewise, Hungary maintains relations with the various republics in Yugoslavia, a developing feature in their interstate relations. In 1985 the Prime Ministers of Croatia and Montenegro visited Hungary, and Hungary's Deputy Prime Minister, József Marjai, visited Bosnia–Herzegovina and Macedonia. Such ties are developing beside the ties based on the local nationalities.

The Yugoslavs, for their part, are also satisfied with the fate of the South Slavs in Hungary, and this too finds expression in the joint communiqués following high–level meetings, and in the well-established, multifaceted border trade. Common projects, mentioned before in this study, assure a steady flow of information and mutual exchange of views on the nationalities' lives. Such is, for example, the joint Hungarian–Slovene cooperation on the situation of the rural areas on the territories along the frontier, established between the ethnic research group of the Gorky State Library in Budapest and the Institute for the Study of the Nationality Question in Ljubljana. Although the project "does not intend to analyze the Hungarian and Yugoslav nationality policies" it is motivated by the understanding and the good will of both sides.[58]

Occasionally, some critical comments do pop up in Yugoslavia on the state of the South Slavs in Hungary. One such comment in 1985 referred to the Slovenes, numbering some 5,500 and constituting the smallest among the three major South Slav groups in Hungary (the Serbs, Croats, and Slovenes). The President of the Slovenian Republic, France Popit, declared that the Slovenes in Hungary had not yet achieved "economic and educational emancipation," and he expressed only partial satisfaction with the position of the Slovene minority in Italy, Austria, and Hungary.[59]

Public pressure in Hungary on behalf of the Hungarians in Yugoslavia is relatively mild, especially compared with the anxiety over the fate of the Hungarians in Czechoslovakia and Romania. Even the dissident groups acknowledge that Yugoslavia's minority policy is positive, and the Hungarians there enjoy more rights than in the two other states. Yet opposition groups in Hungary frequently express their concern about the future of the Hungarian existence in Yugoslavia, because of the trends of assimilation and what they present as a decline in the Hungarian school system, especially in Vojvodina. Thus, *Beszélő* criticized the situation of the Hungarians in Vojvodina and presented evidence on the lack of autonomy of the Hungarian sector and its complete dependence on the province's political bureaucracy.[60]

In spite of these assessments, the Hungarian regime does not have to prove to the nation that it is "doing something" for the Hungarians in Yugoslavia, except for what the Hungarians call a "close monitoring" of the situation. Once Yugoslavia accepted the theory of the "bridges of friendship" the show is on, and will be going on in the future. The danger, as many opponents of the regime in Hungary see it, is that under the more or less smooth surface, the Hungarian minority in Yugoslavia is losing its place and role, due not only to natural trends of assimilation, but also to the policies of the Belgrade regime. As one Western researcher summed up:

The situation of the Hungarians in Yugoslavia is perhaps the best of all Hungarian residents in the successor states, even so they are exposed to continuous pressure of denational- ization and to ever–returning communist and Great Serbian oppression.[61]

Yet, from Hungary's point of view, there is no doubt that it is gener- ally very satisfied with the treatment of the Hungarians in Yugoslavia, and its nationality policy can be considered exemplary, compared with Czechoslovakia and Romania.

An unexpected recent development in Yugoslavia's role in the "Magyar question" in the Danube Basin has been the presentation of the Hungarian–Romanian polemics. Since 1967 the media in Yu- goslavia have been reporting differences between Hungary and Roma- nia on the nationality issue. Such reports are usually published in the *Magyar Szó* or other Hungarian–language organs in Yugoslavia. The tone of such items leaves no doubt that, even if it is only unofficial, the Hungarians in Yugoslavia are clearly on Hungary's side. In the last few years there has been a growing trend on the part of Yugoslavia to "monitor" the bitter dispute between the two states, in a way which even created tension between Romania and Yugoslavia. Yugoslav re- ports often present the issues in veiled terms, from which the reader can deduce his own conclusions. Thus, one Yugoslav weekly wrote in connection with Hungarian–Yugoslav relations that

> The Hungarian nation, a specific ethnic (sic) oasis surrounded by Germanic, Romanic, and Slavic peoples, has encountered a number of problems involving its survival, as attested by the existence of a large Hungarian minority in Romania (Erdely–Transylvania).[62]

The "Yugoslav connection" has two main aspects: one is the Yugoslav presentation and comments on issues involving Hungarian–Romanian relations, and the other is the way Hungary makes use of such Yu- goslav comments, or other relevant items from the Yugoslav media which are linked to Romania.

The Yugoslav viewpoint is presented either as factual reporting on the issues involved or quite frank discussions on the intensity and the acerbity of the Hungarian–Romanian polemics. During 1985, the Yugoslav media in several instances painted a picture that amounted to a tacit agreement with Hungary's complaints on the treatment of the Hungarians in Romania.[63]

Romania's sensitivity to the "Yugoslav connection" was borne out in polemics that involved the two states following Romanian accu- sations that Yugoslavia was supporting the Hungarian claims against

Romania on Transylvania. The short-lived debate was sparked by an item in the "Daily Lexicon" column of the Zagreb *Vjesnik*.[64] which gave a description of Transylvania apparently offensive to the Romanians, whereupon they published a strong criticism in *Romania Literară*.[65] According to the Romanian authors, *Vjesnik* wrote that "some observers and experts on Hungarian–Romanian relations note the fact that Hungary is dissatisfied with the general situation of its conationals in Romania." The Romanian critics took to task the "reactionary, slanderous" tone of the items in *Vjesnik*, which in their view "supported the lost case of revisionists." Romanian susceptibilities were laid bare by the fact that while the item in *Vjesnik* was unsigned, anonymity was not the issue here. Rather, as *Vjesnik* replied to the Romanian charges, it was a "short item . . . in a modest column on a page filled with articles designed to entertain our readers."

The Romanian response was a barrage by "heavy artillery" — fired by two professors. Although *Vjesnik* considered the argument closed in this issue of June 11, 1986, there can be no doubt that Romania continues to monitor the Yugoslav angle in the Hungarian–Romanian dispute. Romania's involvement, or rather Yugoslavia's keen reporting on, especially, the delicate issues of the Transylvania question, touched upon yet another aspect of the complex nationality question in this area—the functioning of the Budapest-initiated "bridge theory."

Romania, which fosters traditional, amicable ties with Yugoslavia— from the point of view of both countries' leadership, their friendship is a keystone of their regional foreign policy—was ready to acknowledge the positive role of the nationalities in the two states with much more ease than in the case of Hungarian–Romanian relations. In Romania there are about 44,000 South Slavs, mostly Serbs and Croats, while some 38,000 Romanians live in Yugoslavia, mostly in Vojvodina. In mutual contacts the nationalities are presented as playing a positive role,[66] and both countries reported joint projects on the two sides of the border, involving the nationalities.

Yugoslavia's quite unequivocal sympathy with the Hungarian side in Hungarian–Romanian polemics is rather surprising for several reasons. Hungary was never involved in the Yugoslav–Bulgarian polemics over Macedonia, and perhaps was never requested by Yugoslavia to side with it against Bulgaria. In addition, Hungary never expressed its intention to support the Yugoslav case. It seems that Yugoslavia has been mildly supportive of Hungary because the Hungarian position on the role of the minorities fits into the Yugoslav conception better than do Romanian policies and practices. Yugoslavia,

which has a very good record on the treatment of the Hungarians—
a policy openly sanctioned by Hungary—feels that Hungary's complaints in regard to Romania's nationality policy are justified and
are aimed at providing the same liberties that it provides to the minorities. On the other hand, the situation in this intricate web of
Hungarian–Romanian–Yugoslav relations has a certain irony in it,
one which is often found in the Balkan political tradition. Yugoslavia
condemns Hungarian nationalism and irredentism at home, and logically should see eye to eye with the Romanians, who are now denouncing the Hungarian government for revisionism. Nevertheless, it
champions Hungarian national rights in Romania—or at least toler-
ates criticism of Romania in the Hungarian–language media in Yugoslavia. Hungary's role in these developments is one of a smiling
bystander—after all, sympathetic Yugoslav reports on the differences
with Romania add more weight to Hungary's own claims.

One aspect of Hungary's involvement in this web is a relatively
new feature—one not linked directly to the nationality question. It
is the Hungarian publication of Yugoslav complaints about difficulties in traveling to Romania. This issue is related to the problems
in Hungarian–Romanian travel arrangements at the borders, and the
point is that the bureaucratic difficulties raised by the Romanian customs and other border officials at the entry points between Hungary
and Romania have been felt also by Yugoslav travelers, who gave
vent to their annoyance in the Yugoslav media.[67] The Yugoslav papers have printed some very curious details about the behavior of the
Romanian border guards, the tone of which is, "we have told you with
whom you are dealing." In some cases newspapers in Hungary have
published the same items that appeared in the Hungarian–language
press in Yugoslavia but added a certain angle to the effect that the
media in Hungary understand only too well the complaints against
the Romanians published by Hungarians in Yugoslavia. The article
in *Heti Világgazdaság*[68] reinforced to the readers in Hungary the image long projected by Hungary that not only were the Romanians
misbehaving toward the nationalities, but their other policies were of
a negative character as well.

Summing up the role of the Hungarian minority in Yugoslavia, in
Hungary's perception, the positive attitude by the Yugoslav regime
serves Hungary's cause well by pointing an accusing finger at the
Romanian regime.

Czechoslovakia

Hungarian–Czechoslovak relations since 1969 have been affected
only to a certain degree by the situation of the Hugarians in Slovakia.

In spite of the Hungarian interest in "monitoring" the developments in the life of the Hungarians there, overall the principle that the national minorities should play the role of "connecting bridges" has been implemented, although one can often feel that the underlying tensions have not been eliminated, and that the "bridge" is often lip–service paid to an idea. Yet while the course of Hungarian–Czechoslovak relations on the nationality aspect has not been as smooth as that with Yugoslavia, it has undoubtedly been more unruffled and more unperturbed than relations with Romania. Political factors, in particular the conditions within the Warsaw Pact and the character of interstate relations in the area, have favored a close relationship between the two states, in spite of the evident differences in the approach of the regime toward the patterns of the necessary reform. Hungary is viewed by Czechoslovakia as a model for reform, especially since the emergence of the post–Husak leadership in late 1987, but at the same time a model which should be emulated with caution. Hungarian foreign policy initiatives, especially Hungary's perceptions on the need for a continuing East–West dialogue in Europe, and Hungary's role in this process were being watched with a suspicious eye in Prague, until Gorbachev's line gave an even greener light to the positions long favored by Hungary.

Hungarian pragmatism and open–mindedness was mostly alien to the arch–conservative Husak and his comrades. Yet since 1968 the two states have continued to foster and to stress their good relations and their multilateral contacts. Certainly the nationality question is vital to both countries. Differences are usually successfully eliminated from the course of relations between good neighbors, and those small differences that remain are usually toned down. In this respect the Hungarian–Czechoslovak relations may seem even more unperturbed than the Hungarian–Yugoslav relations due to the occasional polemical outbursts on some sensitive issues between the latter. However, on a deeper level there are more indications of dissatisfaction on the state of the Hungarian minority in Czechoslovakia than in Yugoslavia among the dissidents in Hungary, and this is also reflected, albeit covertly, in the attitude of the Hungarian regime to the issue.

There are two main problems which cloud the life of the Hungarians in Slovakia, and are revealed through Hungary's monitoring of the situation: the educational–cultural opportunities available for the minority and its political representation before the authorities. Linked to these issues appear the growing manifestations of Hungarian dissidence in Slovakia, and its contacts with the opposition in Hungary. Czechoslovakia's nationality policy toward the Hungarians, and the other minorities as well, since the Minorities Statute went into effect in January 1969, has been based on the regime's recognition that national consciousness among the Hungarians is strong and alive, and that their integration into the system, as Prague would like to see it, is rather difficult, if not impossible.

The Leninist nationality policy, so often quoted and praised in joint official communiqués of the two states, does provide the Hungarians with rights granted, according to Juraj Zvara, with a view to fostering internationalism in accordance with the formula that, "not enough internationalism means estrangement from the fatherland, but much internationalism means attachment to it."[69] As to the attachment to the fatherland, and according to Hungarian emigre and dissident sources inside Hungary and Czechoslovakia, the identity of the fatherland is by far not an easy question; there are signs for the strong identification of the Hungarians in Slovakia with Hungary—not necessarily with the Budapest regime but with the "idea" of Hungary. This issue places the Hungarian government in a delicate situation.

The policies of the Prague regime, along with the strong national feelings among the Hungarians, represent a contradiction to which the official sources refer as "national manifestations" among the minority. Most of the grievances about the life of the Hungarians in Czechoslovakia have centered around the cultural–educational domain, in which a struggle seems to be going on between the Hungarian minority and the authorities. The right of the Hungarians to be educated in their mother tongue, a policy that the regime guaranteed and implemented for years after the adoption of the Minorities Statute, encountered a setback by the late seventies, when the authorities started to limit, or even gradually to dismantle, the educational–cultural facilities of the minority.[70]

This policy is an obvious result of the slow pace of the desired integration and assimilation of the Hungarians in Slovakia. Zvara's studies have shed some light on the rationale of the regime in coping with the problem of bilingualism and the effects of instruction in the Hungarian language.[71] Thus, in accordance with its nationality policy the regime allows education in the mother tongue. As Komensky's dictum goes: "Every nation can become erudite in its mother tongue"; but as Zvara clearly stated, there are practical problems deriving from the instruction in the mother tongue. The principle of fostering education in Hungarian goes

> together with the consistent realization of learning and teaching Slovak, and is the basis of enabling students growing up in mostly Hungarian environments to hold their own, in jobs and higher education, anywhere in the country.[72]

The "consistent realization of learning and teaching in Slovak" was not at all interpreted in this positive way by the Hungarians, who unexpectedly showed strong opposition to the proposed measures which, if implemented, would have meant a reduction in the number of Hungarian schools, amalgation into Slovak schools, and an increase in the subjects taught in the Slovak language. The first steps in this direction appeared by the late seventies, when plans were published to the effect that as of the fifth grade all subjects—except for the Hungarian language, history, and geography—would be taught in Slovak. This step was rationalized by the need for the Hungarian pupils to be able to cope with their future university studies, a sensitive issue among the Hungarian minority in Czechoslovakia. As only 5.6 percent of college and university students in Slovakia are Hungarians, while their share in the population is about twice as high, a problem certainly exists, but the tough Hungarian responses to the Slovak attempts at changing the educational system stem from the realization of the regime's motives of not only aiding the Hungarian students, but also curtailing the Hungarians' educational opportunities.

The educational issue is much more complex than presented either by the regime or by the Hungarian dissidents in Slovakia and abroad. The problem starts at a much more basic level, embracing the instruction in Hungarian in elementary and secondary education. Complaints on the problems facing Hungarian education have long been voiced by Hungarian spokesmen and in the meetings of CSE-MADOK. The shortcomings in the training of teachers in Hungarian and the low standard of instruction given in the Hungarian language have become a matter of grave concern for the Hungarians and not only among their dissident circles. There have also been some echoes in Hungary. Suspicions are rampant, as the Hungarians see an attempt of Slovak encroachment behind every step, and it just may be that their susceptibilities are understandable and justified in view of the Slovak authorities' determination to stamp out the vestiges of Hungarian nationalism, viewed as a "relic of the past." Procedures to integrate the educational system by gradually curtailing available facilities, and by infusing more courses in the Slovak language, are seen by the authorities as a necessary means to further the integration of the Hungarians into the system.

With all this, the Slovak authorities have acted with a certain measure of caution on this issue and with much more circumspection than the Romanian authorities. The first suggestions were aired in 1978 and later shelved until the end of 1983, when the Slovak government approved a proposal, not yet incorporated into the new draft law on education, that would empower the local national councils to change the language of instruction into Slovak, provided that the parents of the children in the minority schools agreed. The proposed amendment has been shelved yet again, because of the unexpectedly strong opposition among the Hungarians.

The resistance shown by the Hungarians was unprecedented in any socialist country with a Hungarian minority, and it surprised both the Slovak authorities and the Hungarian government. The nature of the Hungarian opposition evinced the strong sense of identity of this minority, and has certainly brought home to the regime that some of their apprehensions concerning the Hungarians were well-founded. The protest movement involved a few notable dissident individuals, the most prominent being Miklós Duray, and according to some sources it encompassed as many as 10,000 Hungarians, most of whom were not associated with any oppositionist activity in Slovakia. Moreover, the protest movement boiled over to Hungary, adding a new dimension to the issue involved.

The activities of Miklós Duray, in what has become the "Duray Case," very rapidly turned into an international human rights case, which was seen by the Western media as yet another step of the dissident movement in Czechoslovakia in the wake of the Charter 77 movement.[73] For the first time an unofficial Hungarian body was formed in 1978—the Committee for the Legal Rights of the Hungarians in Slovakia—of which Duray, a geologist by profession, became the main spokesman. Duray sent a petition to the Slovak government on the issue of Hungarian schooling, and organized wide-scale activities through the Committee. An analysis of the situation of the Hungarians in Czechoslovakia and proposals for the improvement of their situation were submitted to the Helsinki follow-up meeting, as well as to the Madrid meeting of the CSCE. These activities received wide publicity not only in such emigre papers as the prestigious *Irodalmi Ujság*, but also in the western media. Duray was arrested twice, in 1982 and 1984, and freed without trial in 1985, in the framework of the amnesty granted on the occasion of Czechoslovakia's Liberation Day.

Duray's activities brought together the Czechoslovak human rights movement and the Hungarian activists. The incongruous coalition once again surprised the authorities. In 1983 Duray joined the Charter 1977 movement, and from then on the campaign against him waged by the regime was incorporated in the overall pattern of clampdown on dissidents at the time. His arrest in 1984 was also linked to the publication in the West of his autobiography *The Dog Trap (Kutyaszorito)* prefaced by one of the prominent dissidents in Hun-

gary, Sándor Csoóri. The book was very well received by Czech intellectual emigre publications, once again highlighting the common goals
of the Czech and Hungarian human–rights movements. The echoes
of the Duray case in Czechoslovakia were resounding, and prominent
Czechoslovak dissidents appealed to the Slovak CP leadership expressing their solidarity with Duray and demanding a "public discussion
on the issue, and on the position of the Hungarian minority in our
society, that Miklos Duray raised." [74]

Duray succeeded in bringing his message to the Czechoslovak dissidents that his activities and those of his colleagues were not aimed
specifically to benefit the Hungarians, but were rather motivated by
the desire to safeguard the human rights in the country and to strive
for a free and democratic society. A main feature in Duray's activities was his call for collaboration between the nations involved and
their organizations in exile: "I would be glad if the Hungarian exile
committees and associations in Western Europe and overseas found
it possible to shake hands with the Slovak and Czech emigrees." [75]

The opposition in Hungary set up the Duray Committee, which
included some of the foremost intellectuals in Hungary. Not all of
them had previously been active in dissident activities. The Committee sent informative letters and memoranda to the Hungarian leadership and promoted grass–roots activities among the public, which
responded very favorably to the Committee's call to express support
for Duray. One of the Committee's main achievements in Hungary
was to cast a shadow over Husák's visit in Hungary in November 1984.
The Committee held a news conference in a private apartment where
it distributed a statement to the Western media representatives. The
Committee argued that Duray's activities "took place within a constitutional framework, and that his eventual conviction would seriously
infringe upon human and civil rights." [76] The Committee correctly
stated that "Hungarian public opinion, too, has been aroused," and
recounted their pleas to the Czechoslovak leadership.

Hungary's government was placed in a delicate situation: it was
trying not to bow to public pressure while the regime's policies in supporting the cultural and educational rights of the Hungarians abroad
were being put to test. Duray, after all, was the champion for the
safeguarding of these rights in Slovakia. There were rumors that the
Hungarian government had intervened in Prague on behalf of Duray,
and that the topic had come up for discussion in several high–level
meetings between the two states. Hungary's intervention, if it had
taken place at all, was not motivated by the endeavor to support
a persecuted Charter 77 human rights movement, but by the steps
suggested by the Slovak authorities to expand the teaching of Slovak

which, with the effects such measures would have on education and culture, would be a slap in the face to Budapest's policies.

It seems that Hungary's intercession may not have been directed at freeing Duray, but rather to bring about a change in the Slovak authorities' approach to the educational problems of the Hungarians. Such a Hungarian intervention, or at least the broaching of the issue, took place during the visit to Czechoslovakia of Hungary's Deputy Minister of Education, Jozef Drecin, in March 1983. He held talks with the Czech and Slovak Ministers of Education. At the same time, the strong support for Duray in Hungary, and the activities of the opposition, may have prompted the government to intervene in Duray's fate. The determination with which the Slovak authorities treated the case indicates the differences between Czechoslovakia and Hungary on such other issues as the nature of the Hungarian economic reforms and foreign policy initiatives by Hungary. There was no doubt that the Duray case, as a symbol of the problems facing the Hungarians in Slovakia, clouded interstate relations between Hungary and Czechoslovakia.

The Duray case and the crisis around the planned changes in the educational structure available to the Hungarians in Slovakia coincided with another issue which, while not directly linked to the nationality question, added fuel to the protests in Hungary. It was the agreement between Czechoslovakia and Hungary to build the Gabickov–Nagymaros hydroelectric system, a project which was the outcome of years of planning and negotiations between the two countries. The proposed system raised heavy opposition both in Hungary (where it was even criticized by the media) and in Slovakia on the grounds that the system would cause irreparable ecological destruction affecting the landscape in areas of Northern Hungary. Prominent Hungarian scientists and intellectuals appealed to the government, and thousands signed petitions in Hungary against the plan.[77] It appears from the joint communiqué published after the visit of Czechoslovak Prime Minister Lubomir Strougal to Hungary in August 1987 that Hungary intended to speed up the construction of its part of the power project, as soon as the government experts give some assurances regarding the protection of the environment. That this environmental crisis in Hungary, along with the pressure of public opinion, took place simultaneously with the Duray case added weight to the opposition's activities.

CSEMADOK's role in the last few years, and its educational–cultural activities, rank second after the problem of bilingualism and the teaching of Slovak in the schools to the Hungarian minority in Slovakia. The Fourteenth National Conference of CSEMADOK heralded

a new era in the organization's activity, along with its readmission,
at the beginning of 1987, to the Slovak National Front, from which
it had been expelled in 1971. The media in Hungary did not elaborate much on the nature of the changes in the regime's attitude to
CSEMADOK, and attempted to avoid any open discussion on the
period of the purges in 1968–1972. Radio Budapest's correspondent
to the Fourteenth National Conference mentioned that the organization was "once again a member of the National Front from which
it was expelled under the charge of national activities following the
crisis of 1968."[78] At the time of CSEMADOK's expulsion, the media
in Hungary kept a very low profile, reporting only in passing that the
Hungarian organization had come under fire for presenting "right–
wing, nationalistic and petty bourgeois trends."

The organization's activities since 1972 have not in fact changed
very much—only its status has. During these years CSEMADOK
fulfilled its role as the cultural association of the Hungarians, without benefiting from the financial–organizational support of the Slovak
National Front, which encumbered such activities as the publication
of its weekly, *Hét*. The problem until its readmission into the Front
was one of image and prestige, as the status of the Hungarians was
reflected in the lack of support from the official bodies. As Zoltán
Sido, CSEMADOK's National Chairman, reported to the National
Conference, until its readmission the organization "could only undertake to meet the already existing demands in areas populated by
Hungarians, but it had no resources for raising them."

CSEMADOK increased its membership considerably between 1982
and 1987 from 15,000 to more than 90,000. Its range of activities was
summed up by Radio Budapest's reporter as "carrying out general
educational activity, thus helping to preserve and develop nationality
consciousness and the mother tongue."[79] Some of the issues raised
at the Fourteenth National Conference may serve as an indication
to the problems facing the Hungarians in Czechoslovakia: some of
the speakers complained that guidelines relating to bilingualism were
not consistently implemented and "nationalist phenomena can be observed, both on the Slovak and Hungarian side, which is harmful to
both sides."

Hungary has, of course, been monitoring the cultural life and
other aspects of the existence of the Hungarians in Czechoslovakia,
especially since the beginning of the crisis marking the attempts of
the Slovak authorities to curtail the Hungarian–language education.
The very presence of a Hungarian radio reporter at the CSEMADOK
National Conference is an indication of the interest shown by Hungary
in the topic. Such a reportage presents an opportunity to air issues

which otherwise would not have been dealt with in the Hungarian media. For example, Radio Budapest mentioned the criticism by some speakers of the Czechoslovak TV's Hungarian–language program for not having dealt sufficiently with the life of "Southern Slovakia"— in other words, with the life of the very audience to which it was intended.

One interesting development in Hungary's attitude to Czechoslovakia's nationality policy is its taking a comparative viewpoint in respect to the other states' nationality policies. Thus, Zoltán Sido, Chairman of CSEMADOK, wrote in the Budapest daily *Magyar Nemzet*, also quoted by Radio Budapest, that "neither in Romania nor Yugoslavia are so many Hungarian cultural commodities and services available as in Czechoslovakia."[80] Although Sido does not represent Hungary's viewpoint, but that of his organization in Czechoslovakia, the comparison in itself is interesting to the public in Hungary.

Hungary has never criticized the educational–cultural aspects of Czechoslovakia's nationality policy, nor has it expressed its views on the accusations that in Slovakia there are still manifestations of Hungarian nationalism. Indirectly, however, the Hungarian media have attempted to calm down the public concern for the minority in Slovakia. During the height of the Hungarian protest in Slovakia against the proposed changes in the school system, Radio Budapest reported from Slovakia an interview with the Minister of Education, who declared that the composition of the students admitted to the universities and colleges must reflect in its nationality composition the "structure of society" as a whole.[81]

Hungary's contact with the Hungarians in Slovakia are much more open than with Romania, and they seem to be almost on the same level as the situation in Yugoslavia. There are no problems in importing books and periodicals from Hungary into Slovakia, and the Hungarians in Czechoslovakia are exposed to cultural developments in Hungary. This was also stressed by Zoltán Sido's interview with the Hungarian media in which he expressed his satisfaction that "very many people" in Slovakia listened to Hungarian radio or watched Hungarian television. Yet often Hungary hints that perhaps there are not enough cadres to teach the Hungarians and neither are there enough books. During the visit to Czechoslovakia of Hungary's Minister of Education, Béla Köpeczi, in 1985, the guest handed out books printed in Hungary to students and teachers, as if spreading the good news of the mother–tongue culture. This gesture was reported to the Hungarian public too.[82]

Overall, the image presented by the media in Hungary on the cultural life of the Hungarians in Slovakia is a positive one, and it leaves the impression that the favorable presentation is also aimed at covertly criticizing the Romanian attitude to the cultural ties between the Hungarians in Romania and Hungary. Satisfactory reports on the state of the Hungarian culture in Slovakia were published in Hungary during 1987, at the height of the Hungarian criticism of Romania's nationality policy. This was evident in an interview in *Élet és Irodalom*[83] with a Hungarian writer in Slovakia, Gyula Hodosi. He outlined the multifaceted Hungarian–language activity in Czechoslovakia, including the results of the joint publishing agreements between the two states. As yet another sign for the atmosphere of thaw in Czechoslovak–Hungarian relations is Hungary's frequent mention of the activities of the Hungarian Cultural Center in Prague.[84] Though active in a geographical area not inhabited by Hungarians, it deals with the dissemination of Hungary's culture in the capital, a form of cooperation nonexistent between Hungary and Romania. Moreover, a higher form of such cooperation was reached with the agreement on establishing a Hungarian cultural center in Bratislava, signed in September 1987.[85] Radio Budapest did mention that the establishment of the center was reached "after years of negotiations"—a clear indication of the reluctance of the Slovak authorities to allow the functioning of such an establishment, which naturally will attract numerous Hungarians.

The premises will be opened in 1989, and unlike other Hungarian institutions in Slovakia will be built with Hungarian money, by Hungarian contractors, and will be the property of Hungary—an interesting legal arrangement which almost amounts to a diplomatic and ex–territorial basis for the Center. Once again, the agreement with Czechoslovakia, reached at the height of the Hungarian–Romanian polemics, added more weight to Hungary's claims against the curtailing of Hungarian rights in Romania. Hungary may have eventually to face a slowdown in such steps by Czecholsovakia, which has no interest in adding fuel to the Hungarian–Romanian fires. Certainly it will attempt to distance itself from such an involvement, which to a certain extent has already been made by the Hungarian media's comparisons on the availability of cultural facilities to the Hungarians in Slovakia with those in Romania.

Hungary has emphasized that the Czechoslovak regime has overcome its former negative policies after having cleared itself from the mistakes of the past. Hungary has conceded that the "continuity and the qualitative facet of Hungarian literature in our northern borders is not in danger,"[86] implying perhaps that such a danger does exist along Hungary's other borders. A major source for the understanding of Hungary's attitude to the existing trends among the Hungarians in Slovakia, especially on the cultural level, was the publishing of András Görömbei's book on *Hungarian Literature in Czechoslovakia, 1945-1982*,[87] which was hailed as a "pioneer monograph"[88] and warmly praised in Hungary for its comprehensive treatment of the subject. Görömbei, who lives in Slovakia and is a prolific writer himself, tackled some of the delicate issues of the past history of the Hungarians, and especially their culture in postwar Czechoslovakia. The Bratislava *Irodalmi Szemle* also warmly praised the book, mentioning its pioneering character as the first major publication to deal with the history of Hungarian literature in Slovakia.[89]

The numerous reviews in Hungary of Görömbei's book indicated the public's interest in the topic.[90] Some of the reviews published in Hungary made use of the occasion to discuss the political storms that bettered the Hungarian culture in postwar Czechoslovakia, emphasizing Hungary's close monitoring of its trends in the last years. That the "bad old days" were over and that the Czechoslovak system had learned from its past mistakes was one of the leading ideas in the Hungarian reviews of Görömbei's book. This position, along with the Hungarian reviews of Zvara's critical studies on the nationality question in Czechoslovakia, were yet one more aspect of Hungary's endorsement—albeit often with a critical view—of Hungarian cultural possibilities in Slovakia.

On a more academic level, but with wider implications, are the research possibilities involving the nationalities on both sides of the border. Such academic ties are of course illustrative of a more general pattern of relationship. Some Hungarian journals responded with keen interest to an article in the Bratislava *Slovenske Pohl'ady* by Rudolf Chmel, on "New Ties—Old Problems,"[91] in which the Slovak author pointed to the diminishing number of new researches into Slovak Hungarology and Hungarian Slavistic–Slovak studies, which in his view was detrimental to the further development of Hungarian–Slovak relations. The Hungarian review of this study concurred with the main conclusions, but stressed that fruitful work was being done in translating current Hungarian literature into Slovak ,and Slovak literature into Hungarian. At the same time the Hungarian source deplored that the furthering of Slavic studies in Hungary left much to be desired, just as on the Slovak side there was a certain crisis in Hungarian oriented studies.

István Fried's article in *Tiszatáj* also touched on a sensitive issue through which the author connected his theme—Slovak and Hungarian literary contacts—with a wider theme: that of Hungarian–Romanian contacts. Fried wrote that in the process of mutual acquaintance by both sides, there was an urgent need for more literary contacts such as the translations of each others' works—hinting that in this respect the state of Hungarian–Slovak relations was better than the Hungarian–Romanian one.

It should be noted that on the issue of Hungarian culture in Slovakia, Hungarian dissident and emigré sources are of course pessimistic as compared to the optimistic line of the regime.[92] Such sources point to the "thousands of cases of discrimination against Hungarian language and letters in Slovakia,"[93] but still acknowledge that the situation is better than in Romania.

The place and role of the minorities in Hungarian–Czechoslovak relations can be best observed through their reflection in interstate relations. All joint communiqués between the two states refer to the "Marxist–Leninist solution of the nationality problem," which makes a "vital contribution to the friendship and cooperation between the two."[94] Such reference also came up during periods when some tension was evident in their relationship, such as during Gustav Husák's one–day visit to Budapest in December 1984 at the height of the Duray case, when Hungary reportedly was intervening on his behalf in Prague. In bilateral talks both sides emphasize the importance of the minorities living on both sides of the border, and their role in implementing the bridge theory. Although at times it seems that Czechoslovakia has been less enthusiastic about the whole range of ties between the nationalities, as suggested by Hungary.

Compared with Romania's lack of interest in the fate of the small Romanian minority in Hungary, Slovakia does show interest in and keeps up contacts with the Slovaks in Hungary, but does so to a lesser extent than does Hungary with the Hungarians in Slovakia. Such Hungarian leaders as Prime Minister Grosz reiterated in his meeting with Czechoslovak Premier Strougal in September 1987 his country's position that there is a need for "deepening of cultural contacts between the nationalities living in the two states as well as mutual respect for our historical past." It was significant that Strougal dwelt less than his Hungarian counterpart on the role of the nationalities, referring to "socialist internationalism in practice" in a less enthusiastic tone than Grosz.

Indirectly, Hungary's "good–neighbor" relations with Czechoslovakia may serve, as in the case of cultural relations, as a reminder to the Romanian colleagues. Thus, when Ceauşescu and Kádár issued their communiqué on the role of the nationalities as bridges of friendship in June 1977, the first time the Romanians had agreed to the inclusion of the nationalities in such a document—it was in some parts almost a verbatim repetition of similar lines in joint Hungarian–Czechoslovak and Hungarian–Yugoslav communiqués. As the perception of the nationalities as bridges of friendship had been mentioned for the first time in October 1967 in a joint Hungarian–Czechoslovak communiqué, it took some ten years for Hungary to reach the same level of agreement and understanding with Romania. It seems that the relations with Czechoslovakia and Yugoslavia were used by Hungary as a leverage on Romania. Thus, in September 1977, Hungary held highest level talks with Czechoslovakia and Yugoslavia, first during Husak's visit in Hungary, shortly followed by Kádár's visit to Yugoslavia. These two meetings took place three months after what seemed at the time a breakthrough in Hungarian–Romanian relations. The communiqué with Czechoslovakia and Yugoslavia elaborated to a larger extent on the need to expand bilateral relations, and to involve the nationalities in these relations, than in previous documents. It was as if Hungary were raising the stakes on its line toward the next phase of relations with Romania.

Hungarian–Czechslovak agreements cover a whole range of subjects, such as the recognition of the importance of tourism in bilateral relations, a point stressed in the 1977 talks between Husák and Kádár, but absent from the Kádár–Ceauşescu agenda in the same year. In marked contrast to the state of individual contacts between Hungary and Romania (especially in the light of the restrictions by the Romanian authorities on visitors from abroad, in particular Hungary, and a virtual ban on visitors from Romania to Hungary, Hungarian–Czechoslovak ties are much smoother. Hungary is considered the most popular foreign destination for Czechoslovak tourists. Numerous Czechoslovak citizens, including many Hungarians, visit Hungary. One major crisis which erupted between the two states on the issue of travel was caused by travel restrictions to Hungary imposed by the Czechoslovak authorities at the beginning of 1986, due to economic considerations.

The restrictions on the foreign exchange allowances to Hungary were neither connected with political motivations, nor with the nationality aspects of the ties between the two states, although they may well have served the aim of the Czechoslovak regime to reduce the exposure of its citizens to the more consumer oriented Hungarian market. These steps certainly affected the Hungarians from Slovakia, but the restrictions did not add up to a systematic curtailing of contacts between Hungarians on both sides of the border.

In spite of Czechoslovakia's almost open reservations over the Hungarian regime's economic reforms and some aspects of Hungary's foreign policy, there is a smoothly running mechanism which assures the airing of various issues—including the more sensitive ones—similar to the relations with Yugoslavia. Yearly meetings take place between the leaders of Hungary and Czechoslovakia, either on the level of Party leaders or between the Premiers, who deal with the more practical aspects of bilateral relations. Such meetings are of course conspicuously lacking in Hungarian–Romanian relations.

Summing up the state of Czechoslovak–Hungarian relations and their reflection on the nationalities, Hungary considers Czechoslovakia as a "quiet front," with some occasional flareups,. Hungary is thus able to devote more attention to the main issue—that of the relations with Romania. Both Hungary and Czechoslovakia are keen to preempt any tension over the minorities question, and whenever differences arise they are able to localize the divisive issues and prevent their spilling over to different aspects of their bilateral relations. The occasional complaints in Hungary among dissidents on the life of the Hungarians in Czechoslovakia, especially during the Duray case, have placed the Budapest government in a delicate position, compelling it to do something about the problem and to produce results. But overall, the issues seem much simpler and easier to cope with than those with Romania.

Transcarpathia—"Bridge between Peoples"

One of the most interesting features of Hungary's relationship with its kin beyond the borders are the ties with the approximately 200,000 Hungarians who live in Transcarpathia—or, as it is officially called, the Zakarpatskaya Oblast of the Ukrainian SSR, with Uzhgorod (Ungvár) its capital. The area is an ethnic patchwork and crossroads of the various cultures and regimes which have clashed over it. Under Czechoslovak rule between the two world wars, it was inhabited by people that the Czechoslovak census vaguely defined as "Russians": actually they were Great Russians, Ukrainians, Carpatho–Russians, Hungarians, Jews, and a small minority of Czechs and Slovaks. The Czechoslovak leadership in World War II, under Beneš, attempted to reach an agreement with Stalin on the continuing incorporation of Carpatho–Ruthenia into postwar Czechoslovakia; but by late October 1944, when the Soviet forces were in full control of the area, it was only natural—in the spirit of Soviet policy—that the "unanimous" will of the local masses should decide for the area to become a part of the Soviet Union, a step which was legalized by the signature of the Czechoslovak and Soviet governments in Moscow on June 19, 1945.[95] Hungarian historiography very rarely touches on the circumstances that brought the area under Soviet rule, and a pronouncement like the "Liberation of Uzhogorod on October 27,1944 opened the way for its peaceful development"[96] is the most far reaching and explicit one that such sources would venture to utter. It avoids the delicate issues of the attempts of Czechoslovak Communists in late 1944 to keep the area under their rule.

For years the area was shrouded in a rather mysterious atmosphere. Information was very scarce, and Western sources had a difficult time in assessing the developments in the Oblast, especially the social–economical and cultural trends among the Hungarians living there. Thus, RFE's research paper on the area concluded that "relatively little is known about the Hungarian minority in that part of Eastern Europe" and stressed that "reliable information about the years between the incorporation of the territory into the USSR and the early 1960s is scant."[97] In a similar tone, the *Oxford History of Hungarian Literature* wrote that "very little is known about cultural life in Kárpátalja. . . . Whatever cultural life exists there is noticeably limited in appeal and significance."[98]

In the last twenty years there has been a marked change on the nature of information emerging from the area which is reported by the media in Hungary. More details appear on the life of the Hungarians there. Even more significantly, there are emerging patterns of contact between Hungary and the Hungarians in the area, thus lending support to the Hungarian policy that nationalities should play the role of connecting bridges between neighboring states (although there are no significant Russian or Ruthenian minorities living in Hungary). Because of the sensitivity of the topic, Hungary treated the fate of the area in the Rákosi–Stalin years as a taboo, with only rare references to the developments there, and there was practically no human contact between the two sides of the border. The fact that Uzhgorod lies only 26 kilometers from the border of Hungary was not mentioned in Hungarian media until the eighties. For years the impression had been prevalent that "Kárpátalja" was situated in some faraway corner of the Earth.

Until the late sixties there were not even references to the "Leninist–nationality policy" in regard to the Hungarians in the area. Most of the items in the Hungarian media concentrated on the cultural aspects of the Transcarpathian Oblast. Thus, *Szabad Nép*[99] quoted a member of the Ukrainian Supreme Soviet who during a visit to Budapest spoke on the Hungarian–language teaching and other educational and cultural activities. According to the media in Hungary, by the mid–fifties the language instruction was Hungarian in some thirty–five elementary schools, eleven high schools, one teachers' training institute, and a Hungarian section functioned at the teachers' training department of the University of Uzhgorod.[100] The media in Hungary emphasized that the Hungarian minority in the USSR also had its own press, the main daily being the *Kárpáti Igaz Szó* issued in

Uzhgorod, and the *Vörös Zászlo* issued in Beregovo (Beregszász), but it was not until at least 1965 that it was made clear that the *Kár'pati Igaz Szó* was a translation of the Ukrainian paper of the area, the *Zakarpatskaya Pravda*.

In spite of the near–complete news blackout from the Oblast, the events of October 1956 in the area were widely published in the West, mostly through emigre groups, and some Western correspondents' details bore out the severe measures taken against the Hungarians as reprisal for the disturbances during October.

The past quarter century has brought numerous changes into the situation of the Hungarians in the area. The key to the change lies in the correct perception of Moscow and Kiev of the role of the Hungarians in interstate relations with Budapest and the potential benefits for both regimes from a positive attitude toward the Hungarians in Transcarpathia. From a Soviet point of view the Hungarians are too small a minority to pose any nationalistic challenge. It would not be in the interest of the Soviets to promote Ukrainization nor Russification, although emigre groups, including the very active Ruthenian activists in the United States and Canada, have frequently suggested that the Hungarians are exposed to strong assimilatory pressures, as in Romania or even Czechoslovakia. In spite of the incontestable tendencies to natural assimilation, there is not enough evidence to prove that the authorities are pursuing a deliberate policy of denationalization of the Hungarians. On the contrary, they actually seem to be interested in promoting Hungarian existence in the area and in allowing contacts with Hungary in order not only to demonstrate the success of the "correct Leninist nationality policy" but also with a view to helping the Budapest regime in its attempts to present the Soviet Union in a positive way, and thus indirectly fueling the anti–Romanian positions of Budapest. The Soviet line toward the Hungarians can be viewed under two main aspects: the ties between Hungary and the Hungarians over the border, and the cultural, educational developments in the area.

Since the mid–sixties wide ranging cultural contacts have been built up between the Hungarians in Transcarpathia and Hungary, followed by more open borders and tourism on both sides of the border. Hungarian students at the University of Uzhgorod were permitted, albeit in small numbers, to attend courses in Hungary, at the University of Debrecen, and a growing number of Hungarian academics have been invited to the University of Uzhgorod.[101] Some of these scientific contacts are channeled through the Hungarian section of the Philosophy Department of Uzhgorod University, which has functioned since 1963; it is the main center for the training of Hungarian–language teachers. The Soviet authorities do not impose any limitations on the import of textbooks from Hungary, and joint publication projects are one of the main pillars of the good relationship. The Kárpáti Kiadó, the Hungarian language publishing house in Uzhgorod, was established in 1945, and since 1958 has concluded numerous joint book publishing agreements with publishing houses in Hungary, especially Europa and Kossuth.[102] Naturally, a sizable part of the 500 publications published in cooperation with Hungary until 1985 are of a political nature, and as the Director of the Kárpáti Kiadó declared in an interview with the Budapest *Könyvilág* "it is our tradition to publish yearly 1–2 works of Lenin." But beyond the required dose of Marxist–Leninist classics and other political topics, the cooperation between the Hungarian and Kárpáti Kiadó publishing houses has indeed brought the two sides closer, and has spread Hungarian literature (without, of course, the more avant–garde type of works) into the Ukrainian SSR.

To a large extent Hungarian–language publishing in the area is quite dependent on agreements with Hungary, and about a quarter of all books published by Kárpáti are brought out in cooperation with publishing houses in Hungary. Many works by the not so numerous Hungarian men of letters from the Oblast are distributed in Hungary, along with Hungarian translations of Ukrainian writers transmitted through Kárpáti. The media in Hungary widely praise these Hungarian works from the Ukraine, which are presented as a proof of the lively Hungarian life over the border. Although most Hungarian critics would agree, off the record, that these works are of lower quality than those from the other three socialist states, if one takes into account the backward development of the area, and the small number of the Hungarian minority, devoid of an intellectual tradition, it seems that Hungary is keen to "upgrade" the Hungarian culture in the Oblast.

There is also a constant stream of artistic delegations on both sides and it is noteworthy that more such groups from Hungary visit Transcarpathia than Transylvania. Likewise, numerous and various delegations visit each other along the border areas, in a pattern reminiscent of the Hungarian–Yugoslav border trade. Szabolcs–Szatmár County in Hungary is engaged in multifaceted cooperation with Transcarpathia, and the two countries are linked in a "socialist competition" with the aim of improving their economic performance. This aspect highlights another feature of the Soviet–Hungarian cooperation on the nationality level: the Soviet side benefits economically from Hungary's more developed economy. One such example of economic cooperation is the building in Ushgorod of the most modern hotel in the Oblast, the Zakarpaty, built with Hungarian investment, contractors, and workers.[103] Tourism has become a regular feature. A tourist bus service regularly runs from Hungary into Transcarpathia, and possibly also the other way around.

Another interesting feature of these relations is the Hungarian oriented cooperation, encouraged by the Soviets, between Hungary, Slovakia, and the Soviet Union. This is effectuated especially on the cultural level, and there are several publishing projects also aimed at the Hungarian public in Slovakia. Thus, the Bratislava–based Madách publishing house cooperates with Kárpáti Kiadó and with publishers from Hungary. Such activities, in the eyes of Kárpáti's Director, "contribute to the friendship between the neighboring peoples."[104] The Soviet side does not impose any limitations on the import of newspapers and periodicals from Hungary, and in Uzhgorod the same day's *Népszabadság* is on sale, a simple fact of "socialist cooperation" which Hungarian readers in Translyvania are not allowed to enjoy.

There are, of course, some limitations on the ways Hungary presents this satisfactory relationship between Hungary and the Hungarians in Transcarpathia. In contrast to the criticism leveled at the nationality policies of the other three neighboring states in various periods, Hungary could never afford any disapproval of Soviet policies, not even about the dark years of postwar Stalinism when all traces of alleged Hungarian nationalism were brutally erased. Neither did Hungary ever find fault with the slow development of Hungarian educational and cultural facilities in the area, as evident until the mid–fifties. Another delicate feature of this relationship is Hungary's wary caution in making use of the slogan of the bridge–building role of the nationalities—not only because there are no Ukrainians or Russians in Hungary, but also because Hungary realizes quite well that Moscow is not eager to implement such a relationship between some of its nationalities and the neighboring socialist states.

Yet, overall, the Soviet furtherance of the small Hungarian minority has clearly paid off from Budapest's point of view. It can safely label the Soviet nationality policy as "Leninist," and it can boast about the frequent contacts with the Hungarians there. From Moscow's angle, such an investment into the minuscule Hungarian minority is certainly a cost–effective project.[105]

Chapter VIII

Between Crisis and Détente: Hungarian–Romanian Relations, 1969–1977

The Romanian regime's policies to ameliorate the situation of the national minorities lasted at least until 1971, when Ceauşescu's drive for recentralization changed the previous more moderate policy.[1] The Romanian effort does not seem to have impressed Hungary very much. On the contrary, the relationship between the two countries went on a collision course, not necessarily because of developments in Romania's nationality policy toward the Hungarians, but rather because of the continuing attempts by Hungary to press Romania for an inclusion of the minorities in their relations, and because of Hungary's continuing role as the primary critic of Romania's foreign policy.

Hungarian–Romanian relations in the seventies passed through three distinct stages: (1) the major crisis in the summer of 1971, (2) the signing of the Treaty of Friendship and Cooperation in 1972, and (3) the 1977 (supposedly landmark) agreements between Kádár and Ceauşescu on the role of the nationalities in their relations. Since then, Hungarian–Romanian relations have gone downhill, reaching the lowest ebb since the end of World War II. In retrospect, the crises of the seventies were only preparatory stages for the full–blown renewal of old rivalries over the fate of Transylvania.

The Crisis of the Summer of 1971

The events of 1971 are seen by Western analysts as the "most overt attempt by the Soviet Union and Hungary to use the national question as a means of exerting pressure on Romania."[2] The "main event" of the crisis—the one which took the foreign observers by surprise—was the Hungarian side's raising publicly for the first time the issue of the Hungarian minority in Romania, thus inaugurating a new era in Hungarian–Romanian relations—open polemics on this sensitive issue.

For the Hungarians the road to the heart of the issue passed through Beijing. The occasion was the unprecedented Soviet criticism of Romania's foreign policy, and especially its rapprochement with China which, along with Yugoslavia's détente with China, appeared to Moscow and to Budapest as a clear step toward the formation of a pro–Beijing axis in the Balkans.[3]

Ceauşescu's visit to China in June 1917 was the first by an East European leader, excepting the Albanians, since the Chinese–Soviet rift. Naturally the Soviets were infuriated, and they instigated Hungary to settle some accounts with the maverick Romanians. The tough Soviet line stood in stark contrast to the joint Romanian-Soviet efforts to normalize their relationship in the post–August 1968 period, after the initial crisis had subsided. The Soviets' outbursts at Ceauşescu's policies in the wake of his visit to China bore out their determination to thwart any Romanian (or for that matter any Romanian–Yugoslav) attempt to sneak in China through the back door of the Soviet Bloc. Nevertheless for the Soviets, as for Hungary, the maverick Romanian policy also served as a convenient pretext to settle some further accounts with the Romanians, in light of Bucharest's determination to keep reminding the Soviets to whom Bessarabia historically belonged.

The very day that Ceauşescu returned home there were already some signs of a crisis brewing. One indication was the two and one-half year period from November 1968 through May 1971 during which no significant high–level contacts had occurred between Hungarian and Romanian leaders other than those during festive occasions or Party conferences. In addition, both sides, as we have noted, kept silent over the need to renew their Treaty of Friendship. Along with occasional comments in the Hungarian media on the situation in Romania (such as the poor functioning of the Council of the Workers of Hungarian Nationality) Budapest hinted that in spite of the normalization reached several months after the crisis of August 1968, things were not getting better in Hungarian–Romanian relations. Although Romania's nationality policy was more lenient, in two respects Hungary could not be satisfied with the situation in Romania: one was Romania's stress on the separate development of the Hungarian minority's culture in Romania, a line contrary to Budapest's perceptions, and second, Romania's continuing refusal to include the national minorities in interstate relations.

In May 1971 two high–level Hungarians, Zoltán Komócsin and György Aczél, finally visited Bucharest for talks with some of their Romanian counterparts—Paul Niculescu–Mizil, Manea Mănescu, and other Party officials. Within several weeks, two prominent leaders from both sides, Komócsin and Niculescu–Mizil, were engaged in a bitter polemic on the nationality issue. The talks in May 1971 should therefore be seen as a significant step toward the buildup of the imminent crisis. The communiqué published after the talks in Bucharest shed no light on the precise topics discussed,[4] but it could be inferred from the text that there was no agreement on the renewal of the Treaty, and that relations between the two Parties were dealt with.

The Hungarian delegation to Bucharest was well-versed in the terminology of the Romanian CP, and their talks in Bucharest were held shortly after a renewed onslaught by Ceauşescu on all manifestations of nationalism. The occasion was the meeting of the CWNH, in which the Romanian leader acknowledged that there were some remnants from the past, and that nationalist phenomena continued to exist.[5] Coming precisely when Romanian nationalism, as propagated by the RCP, had reached new heights, the Romanian leaders' recriminatory remarks were obviously directed against Hungarian nationalism.

Another issue of that period, which may have had an indirect effect on Romania's relations with Hungary, was the German emigration from Romania. In view of the close relations between Bonn and Bucharest, especially economic ties important for the Romanian side, and considering the Polish decision reached in late 1970 to allow some German emigration, some Germans in Romania requested permission to emigrate to West Germany. Ceausescu rejected such ideas, declaring that "there is not now, nor will there ever be, any agreement or understanding with anyone on the removal of the population of German or any other nationality."[6] The only possible candidates among "any other nationality" for such emigration agreements were the Hungarians. There were certainly no such problems with Jewish emigration to Israel.

The Soviet reprimand of Romanian foreign policy started on the eve of Ceauşescu's visit to China. The Soviets criticized the "nationalist and anti-Soviet manifestations in the policies of some states, and the unfounded theories of limited sovereignty."[7] Some of the critical anti-Romanian notes in the Soviet media were those broadcast from Moscow, in Romanian and Hungarian, and beamed at audiences in those countries, stressing Soviet support for the Hungarian line against Romania's foreign policy. At the same time the Soviet broadcasts repeatedly reminded the Romanians that they owed their liberation to the Soviet Union—a major Soviet propaganda argument against Ceauşescu's maverick diplomacy in the Soviet Bloc.

The Soviet-inspired campaign against Romania, and for that matter also against Yugoslavia, was handed over for execution to Hungary, which not only faithfully followed the Soviet line but also carried it much further, touching on the nationality issue between Hungary and Romania. Hungary's criticisms of Romania were more intense than were those of the Soviet Union, which confined itself more to the criticism of Romania's relations with China and its negative

effects on the unity of the socialist camp. The Hungarian reference to
the nationality issue was, however, carefully restricted to Romania.
Hungary refrained from any critical reference to the situation of the
Hungarians in Yugoslavia, while it criticized its policy of supporting
a pro–Beijing axis in the Balkans.

The Hungarian criticism of Romania was delivered in a speech
by Zoltán Komócsin in the Hungarian National Assembly on June 24,
1971. Komócsin mentioned the difficulties in relations that Romania
had caused by the differences in their foreign policies. His references
to the nationality issue was ambiguous, and in retrospect rather mild
compared with recent Hungarian expressions of indignation over Romania's nationality policies. Komócsin stressed that:

> We are fundamentally interested in having the inhabitants of
> both our country and Romania—including those of the Hun-
> garian nationality living there—come to understand that
> the fate and destiny of our peoples are inseparable from
> socialism.[8]

The Romanian response was not late in coming. On July 9, *Scînteia*
published a 5,000 word reply by Komocsin's counterpart in the Party
hierarchy, Paul Niculescu–Mizil. He rejected all Hungarian attempts
to interfere in Romania's internal affairs, using a tough tone virtually
unheard until then in Hungarian–Romanian polemics. Mizil warned
those who were trying to pursue a policy based on national hatred,
and thus fostering nationalism. Romania, went on Mizil, "cannot
permit any attempts at nationalism or chauvinism–mongering, no
matter where they come from."[9]

One of the noteworthy themes in Mizil's article was the contention that "outside elements"—meaning the Soviets and Hungarians—
were bluntly intervening in Romania's internal affairs. Mizil stressed
that such a state of affairs would not be tolerated, and pointed out
that Romania never even attempted to grade the performances of
other states in building their socialist societies. Overall, at that stage
Romania was not interested in a flareup with Hungary, especially as it
would have entailed the worsening of relations with Moscow. Romania
was keen to bring home to the Bloc member–states the achievements
of its foreign policy, and not to aggravate its relations with them.

Following Mizil's article the Hungarian side continued to pursue
its critical line toward Romania, encompassing all elements of Romania's foreign policy, but referring only by inference to the differences
over the nationality issue. Hungary condemned the attempts to form
a pro–Chinese "Bucharest–Belgrade–Tirana Axis" in the Balkans[10]
and some Hungarian articles ridiculed Romania's policy of "small

states—big policies."[11] Hungary compared its own policy of loyalty to the principles of socialist internationalism to those of Romania, overtly emphasizing the deep differences between the two on a whole range of fundamental issues, such as the role of the nation under socialism, a favorite theme resorted to by both sides to highlight their dissension.

During the crisis with Hungary and with the Soviet Union, the Romanian leadership continued its policy of stressing the close links between the coinhabiting nationalities living in the country. There was an added emphasis on the need for cooperation and understanding between all components of the "Romanian socialist nation," as well as a strong protest against any attempts by outside elements to interfere in Romania's internal affairs. Yet the Romanian regime felt, and Hungary appeared only too keen to exploit, Ceauşescu's dilemma—that more extensive rights to the Hungarians might in the long run lead to that minority's wish to establish closer links with Hungary, especially in view of Budapest's policy of monitoring the life of the Hungarians abroad. Romania was indeed apprehensive at the time of Hungary's attempts to interfere in its internal affairs, considering that Hungary, with the Soviets' backing, was evidently eager to link the nationality issue with other divisive issues in the relations between Romania and the other states loyal to Moscow's line.

The significance of the 1971 crisis consists in its being the first major crisis in which Hungary played the role of the most outspoken critic of Romania's foreign policies, linking it with the nationality issue. Actually, from then on Hungary was to concentrate rather more on the nationality issue, pressing the Romanians to accept its perceptions on the role of the nationalities in bilateral relations. Romania, for its part, was interested in a freer hand in dealing with its nationality problems, without the scrutinizing critical eyes of Hungary watching its steps. The renewal of the Treaty of Friendship and Cooperation in 1972 was a milestone which both parties had to pass in their own interest, so that both sides could present a normalization in their relations.

The Renewal of the Treaty of Friendship and Cooperation

The renewal of the Treaty, the last to be renewed between the East European states among themselves and with the Soviet Union, was in itself indicative of the divisive issues clouding their relations even as it evidenced the normalization of their relations. From September 1971 a rapid succession of visits and high-level talks took place between the Hungarian and the Romanian leaderships, a characteristic pattern between Communist states in time of crisis or during

attempts to defuse tensions. Thus, shortly after the climax of the
polemics, a high–level Romanian delegation arrived at the International Hunting Exhibition in Hungary. Ilie Verdeţ, a member of the
Presidium RCP, Dumitru Popescu, and Vasile Pantilet. secretaries
of the CC RCP, and Defense Minister Ion Ioniţă numbered among
the renowned Romanian hunting experts. The hunting team was followed by several visits and contacts between economic ministers and
leading functionaries. In late September 1971, *Népszabadság's* editor
István Sarlós visited Romania, invited by *Scînteia.* It was significant
to the atmosphere of détente that he was also received by Nicolescu–
Mizil, who led the anti–Hungarian campaign in   Scînteia in July.

The other high–level talks paved the way for Kádár's visit to Romania in February 1972. Two secretaries of the CC RCP, Niculescu–
Mizil and Manea Mănescu, held talks in Budapest in late October,
during which Niculescu–Mizil held long talks with Zoltán Komócsin.
The meeting between the two leading Party leaders, who in their
speeches and articles characterized the tension between the two sides,
made keen efforts to reduce the tension even further.

Hungary's Foreign Minister, Péter János,held talks in Romania
in late November, raising expectations that the groundwork for the
signing of the renewed Treaty had been prepared, and there were even
some suggestions that the Treaty may have been renewed in principle,
pending the official signing by the two leaders.[12] The official communiqué after János's visit did refer to the importance of the Treaty in
deepening relations, but no further details were given.[13]

The Soviet leadership was interested at that stage in defusing the
crisis within the Bloc in the wake of Romania's and Yugoslavia's rapprochement with China. Moscow felt that the Romanians were well
aware of the limits of autonomy and deemed that the strings should
not be overstrung. This cautious Soviet stand was evident both from
the highest level contacts between the Soviet Union and Yugoslavia,
and a series of talks between Romanian and Soviet leaders. Moscow
was keen on a Hungarian–Romanian rapprochement, realizing, correctly, that Romania had understood only too well that the nationality issue would be brought up in connection with Bucharest's maverick policies. In the wider regional and inter–Bloc context, the Soviet
Union could not tolerate the apparent strain in the relations between
two Warsaw Pact states, especially as evidenced by the nonrenewal
of the Friendship Treaty. Moscow also had to present a unified position in face of the talks preparing the Conference for Security and
Cooperation in Europe (CSCE).

Some ten days before Kádár's visit to Bucharest in February
1972, during which the Treaty of Friendship was renewed, Kádár

made an unexpected visit to Moscow. According to some observers the visit was also linked to the state of Hungarian–Romanian relations, a topic also raised during the Kádár–Brezhnev talks.[14]

The Soviet media not only warmly praised Hungary's foreign policy and its loyalty to the principles of socialist internationalism, but also went beyond the customary eulogies and recalled Hungary's determined struggle against "nationalism," commending its record in combatting nationalism at home.[15] Even more meaningful was *Pravda's* emphasis that the national minorities in Hungary enjoyed complete rights, certainly a point aimed at justifying Hungary's broaching the nationality issue with Romania. This was a most unusual reference, a topic which the Soviet media did not find especially interesting, except when there was need to back Hungary against Romania on this issue.

One clear linkage between the Hungarian–Romanian relations and Soviet attempts to convince both sides that it was time to normalize their relations was the presence in Moscow, when Kádár arrived on February 11, 1972, of a Romanian delegation led by Gizella Vas, member of the CC RCP, of Hungarian origin. Vas was engaged in talks with Katushev and subsequently participated in the talks with Kádár.

On the eve of Kádár's arrival in Bucharest, the media of both states warmly acclaimed the relations of friendship, completely overlooking the sharp exchanges of words in the summer of 1971. The Romanian media especially stressed the positive developments in their economic relations, thus somewhat downgrading the political–ideological relations.[16] During Kádár's visit both leaders raised, in their own ways, the existing differences, which the media tried to smooth over. In one of his major speeches at a "friendship rally" in Bucharest, Ceauşescu referred to the "different ways in solving the tasks of socialist construction," which in his views should not obstruct the relations of friendship between the two neighbors.[17] The problem of the national minorities was brought up by Kádár, while Ceauşescu passed over it. In one of his speeches, quoted by *Scinteia*, Kádár emphasized the equal rights of the Germans, Slovaks, South Slavs, and Romanians in Hungary and the support given by the regime in fostering their languages and cultures. He evidently expected the Romanian leader to refer to the Hungarians in Romania in the same positive way as he had done, but Ceauşescu preferred to ignore the hint. The very mentioning of the Romanians in Hungary in *Scinteia* was rare. The Romanian press seldom does so.

During the talks that led to the renewal of the Treaty of Friendship, Kádár attempted to include the minorities issue in the docu-

ments between the two delegations, but the Romanian side refused.[19]
This and other signs indicated that the rapprochement between the
two would be short–lived, and that not all divisive issues had been
solved. Telltale clues also point to last–minute differences, and the
communiqué issued prior to the publication of the Treaty was not
labeled a "joint" one, as is customary at such high–level meetings.
Yet another sign for the strained relations was the difference between
some of the articles in the Hungarian–Romanian Treaty and parallel
ones in similar treaties between Hungary and other East European
states. The differences were on the avoidance of Romania and Hungary to commit themselves to "joint actions."[20]

The Road to the Ceauşescu–Kádár Summit in 1977

Within five years after the renewal of the Treaty of Friendship
and Cooperation, Romania, albeit hestitantly, agreed to include the
national minorities issue in an interstate document. Thus, at least on
paper, it accepted Hungary's perceptions on the bridge of friendship
between neighboring socialist states. In this period Hungary brought
the nationality issue to the forefront, giving expression to its determination to follow more closely the life of the Hungarians in Romania.

The relations between the two states did not improve significantly
in this period. It was rather surprising that, after the signing of the
treaty, there were no significant high–level contacts between the two
states for two years. In February 1974, the Romanian Premier Ion
Gheorghe Maurer visited Hungary while in the same period both
states' leaders had conferred with Party or Government leaders of all
the other Bloc states.

Some details on the continuing stagnation in the relations between the two states demonstrate that the rapprochement reached in
1972 was not long lasting. For example, both sides acknowledged in
various forms that more could have been done in expanding economic
ties. The Hungarians were frank in publishing details of the problems
encountered in their economic relations, such as Romania's delays
in supplying agreed upon merchandise or products.[21] On the eve of
Maurer's visit to Hungary, a Hungarian economic weekly published
pessimistic details on the state of economic relations, intimating once
again that the blame lay with the Romanian side.[22] As to tourism,
following the rapprochement of 1972 both sides reported an increase
in visitors. The data supplied by Hungarian sources is clearer in assessing the number of tourists from Romania. In 1971 some 250,000
Romanian citizens visited Hungary while in 1973 the number was increased to 370,000.[23] Once in a while the Hungarian media hinted
vaguely that there were also numerous visitors of Hungarian origin

among those Romanian citizens.[24] Likewise, the number of Hungarian citizens visiting Romania grew from 110,000 in 1970 to 239,000 in 1975.

Romania followed with great interest the development of Hungary's policy toward the Hungarians abroad, and in general Hungary's perceptions of the national interest and its relation to internationalism. By 1972–1973 Hungary intensified its ideological campaign, led by György Aczél, whose numerous speeches on the issue (as well as those of Zoltan Komocsin until his early death) served as the foundation for the regime's line. The Romanians discussed several times Hungary's perceptions on such topics, and one main occasion was the working visit to Budapest of Romania's Deputy Prime Minister, János Fazekas. An ethnic Hungarian, he held talks with Aczél in August 1973.[25] The Romanians knew only too well that Aczél was the main address for any of their complaints on Hungary's drive for a closer relationship with the Hungarians abroad.

The Romanian Premier's visit to Hungary in February 1974 failed to contribute significantly to the improvement of relations between the two states. Much lip service was paid to the friendly relations but there were no signs of Romania's willingness to accept Hungary's policies.[26] Overall, on Hungary's list of foreign policy priorities, Romania retained a special place, unchanged for years, hinting at continuing differences on various issues between the two.[27]

There were clear indications that Hungary was pressing the Romanians for a clearer inclusion of the issue of the national minorities in their relations, in spite of Romania's refusal to do so. The Hungarian tactics were manifested during the Eleventh Congress of the RCP in November 1974. In that forum Hungary had brought home again to the Romanian leadership its perception of the role of the minorities contained in the HSWP's message to the Romanian comrades:

> An important factor in the further development of our friendship is a consistent implementation of the Leninist policy of nationalities; this policy considers the nationalities as a living bridge among socialist states.[28]

The Romanian leaders did not reply directly to the Hungarian message nor to Aczél's reiteration at the Congress of Hungary's views; but Ceaușescu stressed once again the equality of rights enjoyed by the coinhabiting nationalities in Romania, and refuted complaints that there were not enough educational facilities for the minorities, a point that he had been emphasizing on several occasions. At the same time Ceaușescu continued to stress the importance of learning Romanian—a hint that perhaps for the sake of learning the Romanian language, some educational facilities of the nationalities would have to be sacrificed.[29]

At the Eleventh Congress of the RCP the line pursued by Romania and Hungary on the external aspects of the nationality question was evident: Romania dismissed any external role of the nationalities in interstate relations, while Hungary stressed the need to include the issue in bilateral relations. The cat and mouse game was continued on Hungarian soil several months later. In March 1975, at the Eleventh Congress of the HSWP, Kádár stated in unequivocal terms Hungary's own nationality policies and its perception on the external role of the nationalities. While publishing excerpts from Kádár's speech at the Congress, the Romanian media completely ignored any reference to the national question.[30] So did Romania's representative to the Hungarian Party Congress, Ilie Verdeţ, who mentioned only Romania's positive policies toward the nationalities.

It should be noted that during this period Romania stepped up its campaign aimed at clarifying the regime's nationality policies, endeavoring to provide evidence of friendship between the Hungarians and the Romanians, yet keeping clear of any reference to the external role of the nationalities.[31]

While Romania attempted to present at the Helsinki Conference a spotless record on the nationality issue, it was Hungary that stole the show among the East European states. Kádár's address on Hungary's losses of territory and population in the upheavals of this century were met with indignation by Romania, and was openly repudiated in later years, in Lăncrănjan's book *A Word on Transylvania*, and numerous times during the Hungarian–Romanian polemics in 1987.

As a result of the expectations raised among the Hungarians and the Germans in Romania, despite all their differences, in the wake of the "spirit of Helsinki," the Romanian leadership forcefully combatted any attempts to stir up "nationalist–chauvinist agitation." The forum for Ceauşescu's tough speeches was the meeting of the nationality councils of the Germans and the Hungarians, and although some of his more specific remarks were aimed to dispel any illusions among the Germans that emigration to West Germany might be increased, his line was also intended to dampen expectations among Hungarians that the new spirit in East–West relations might also have a favorable effect on their situation, especially on matters related to contacts with Hungary.[32]

Shortly after Ceauşescu's speeches on the nationality question in December 1975, the Romanian Foreign Minister, Gheorghe Macovescu, held talks in Hungary about issues related to the "socialist construction" in the two states; but there were indications that the nationality problem also came up for discussion.[33] The spirit of Helsinki was a rather haunting one, at least in Hungarian–Romanian relations, and within a year after the Helsinki Conference, at the Berlin meeting of the Communist Parties, Kádár gave assurances that Hungary had no territorial demands from any of its neighbors and that it would respect the European borders as agreed by the participants of the Helsinki Conference. This time Kádár's declaration was good news, and the Romanian media published excerpts from his speech relating to the borders.[34] Romania made the same commitments regarding the borders hinting at Soviet Moldavia, just as Kádár was hinting at Transylvania. The air of détente also reached the relations among the socialist states, and in August 1976 Ceauşescu visited the Moldavian SSR, followed three months later by Brezhenev's visit in Bucharest, the first formal visit by a Soviet leader in Romania in a decade.

The "spirit of Helsinki" was one of the main reasons for Romania's gradual—if reluctant—acceptance of Hungary's demands to include the nationalities in its interstate relations with Hungary. Soviet pressure to do so was also a major factor in the Romanian change of attitude. Moreover, after both Yugoslavia and Czechoslovakia had accepted the Hungarian principles, Romania could not persist in refusing a similar process with Hungary. The Hungarian insistence that Romania include the minorities in their relations was also motivated by the precedent of Romanian–Yugoslav relations. During their meeting in July 1974, Ceauşescu and Tito agreed that the correct nationality policy contributed to the strengthening of relations between the two states.[35] Hungarian statements from 1974–1975 onward leave no doubt that Hungary was pressing the nationality issue on the Romanians by all possible means. As indicated, the Hungarian references to the life of the Hungarians abroad were presented in the wider context of the Helsinki process and the other international activities to the minorities.

The Hungarian–Romanian breakthrough on the nationality issue came in two stages of high–level talks: the visit of Hungarian Premier György Lázàr to Romania in December 1976, and the Ceauşescu–Kádár summit in June 1977. Something was already moving in Hungarian–Romanian bilateral talks at the end of October 1976, when Romanian and Hungarian teams conferred on ideological relations between the two Parties.[36] One such round of talks took place in the two capitals within a few days with the participation of leading experts on inter–Party affairs in both Central Committees. The two teams were evidently paving the way for Lázàr's visit to Romania and the planned meeting between Ceauşescu and Kádár.

Lázár visited Romania some two months after his visit to Yugoslavia, where the cooperation between the states on the nationality issue constituted an important part of the Hungarian–Yugoslav talks. The Hungarian Premier's visit to Belgrade was deemed a success, as both sides committed themselves to the bridge principle in their relations.

The Hungarian media stressed that Lázár's visit was aimed at expanding cultural relations with Romania.[37] Officially both sides acknowledged that they had discussed the opening of cultural centers in both capitals, a very minor Hungarian achievement considering Bucharest's small Hungarian population. Hungary sought to inaugurate cultural centers, or facilities, in cities as densely inhabited by Hungarians as Cluj. Furthermore, by that period both Czechoslovakia and Yugoslavia had agreed to such reciprocal arrangements with Hungary. As a further step in expanding relations, Romania and Hungary reached agreements related to tourism. In the wake of the Lázár visit, the Romanian media warmly praised relations with Hungary, characterizing them as "ascending"; but there was no specific mention of cultural agreements, which were one of the main objectives of the Hungarian side.

The Ceauşescu–Kádár meeting was probably agreed upon during Lázár's visit in Romania, and the Romanian side, in anticipation of the high–level talks, intensified its campaign of publicizing the successful solution of the national question in Romania. There were also some tough words of warning from Ceauşescu in April 1977 rejecting "voices from the West" that were agitating for Hungarian emigration from Romania, and the meeting of the CWHN as well as the parallel organization of the Germans sent a telegram to Ceauşescu in which they condemned the "attempts by irredentist–chauvinist elements to break up the integrity of the homeland." Although the accusations were aimed at Western emigré groups and Hungary was not targeted directly, in light of subsequent Romanian criticism of Budapest's policies, it can be assumed that to Romania the "irredentist–chauvinist" circles were just over the Hungarian border.

This was the immediate backdrop to the Ceauşescu–Kádár meeting in Oradea and Debrecen on June 15–16, 1977, one of the most interesting in the annals of Communist interstate relations. The meeting on the two sides of the frontier was presented as a clear indication of the deep feelings of friendship between the two peoples, but Western sources also surmised that Kádár had refused to go to Bucharest. His presence in Oradea was his first among the Hungarians in Romania since February 1958. Most of the members of the Hungarian and Romanian teams at the Ceauşescu–Kádár meeting

were those who had led the preparatory talks some months before,
such as András Gyenes, Dumitru Turcuş, and Constantin Oancea.
The Hungarian–language press in Romania closely followed the discussions, this time publishing details in honor of the Romanian guests
on the Hungarian side, which provided more information on Hungary
than the Hungarian–language media in Romania had published for
years.[38]

The significance of the high-level meeting lay in one paragraph
of the communiqué—not a joint statement—published at the end of
the talks. For the first time it mentioned the existence of Hungarians
in Romania, and Romanians in Hungary. As to the wording of
the communiqué and the agreements reached in the talks, both sides
could present it as a victory for their respective position. Hungary
had achieved Romania's acceptance of the nationalities as bridges of
friendship, while Romania had succeeded in including the sentence on
the solving of the question of the nationalities as an internal problem
of every state. Hungary could also interpret the agreements reached
as a recognition of its status among the Hungarians in Transylvania,
an interpretation rejected from the beginning by the Romanian side,
most overtly expressed by the foot–dragging in the implementation of
the accords, for example on the opening of a Hungarian Consulate–
General in Cluj and other agreements aimed at promoting cultural
contacts.

The media in Romania wished to minimize the nationality issue
in the agreements reached between the two leaders, a point highly
publicized by the Hungarian side. Except for quoting the part of
the communiqué relating to the minorities, the Romanian media did
not discuss the issue before, during, and after the Oradea–Debrecen
talks. *Lumea*, for example, singled out those aspects of the agreements which did not entail any Romanian commitment as the promotion of means intended to strengthen the relations between the two
states, but refrained from any discussion of the minorities.[39] The main
Hungarian language daily, *Előre,* chose to underscore Ceauşescu's argument that the issue was an internal one for every country to solve
without interference,[40] lest the talks raise some expectations among
the Hungarians in Romania.

From today's perspective, the talks proved to be a total failure,
inasmuch as the agreements reached in 1977 were never implemented
by Romania—as Budapest has repeatedly pointed out. The 1977
talks became a kind of reference point to which the Hungarian side has
always referred as an evidence for Romania's conduct, while Romania,
it seems, would rather have forgotten the whole set of commitments
agreed upon at the Ceauşescu–Kádár meeting.

Chapter IX
A Decade of Crisis: Hungarian–Romanian
Relations, 1977–1987
New Beginning, Old Problems

The intensity of the Hungarian–Romanian polemics on the nationality issue and on the historical aspects of the fate of Transylvania surprised those observers who may have taken at face value the agreements reached in the June 1977 meeting between Ceauşescu and Kádár. It was not only the Western observers who were confused. The public in both states—and especially the Hungarian minority in Romania—did not foresee such a rapid deterioration in the relations between the two states, at a time when their leaders were welcoming the turning point in their relations, and characterizing them as being continuously on an "ascending course." In fact, that ascent soon turned out to be a downhill slide.

Hungary's main complaint, which was to be frequently voiced in the forthcoming years, was Romania's failure to implement the agreements reached in June 1977, while Hungary's efforts were directed at securing the implementation of the accords in all senses—from the theoretical perception of the role of the nationalities as bridges of friendship to the practical steps envisaged in the agreements. Among these, the Hungarian side perceived the opening of the Hungarian consulate in Cluj as one of the main test cases of Romanian intentions. Although this bone of contention was removed with the opening of the Hungarian Consulate in April 1980, Hungary continued to refer to the Romanian foot–dragging in the effectuation of the agreements. Earlier, in December 1978, Hungarian Foreign Minister Frigyes Puja characterized the relations between the two states as "developing well," but emphasized that in certain respects progress was not satisfactory and called for a speedier implementation of the 1977 agreements. Puja outlined some of the major problems confronting the relations with Romania at the time, "We should like travel, that is human contacts, communication between the two peoples to be placed on a broader basis," and after reiterating the essential tenets of the agreements, Puja expressed his country's desire to see these points of the communiqué put into practice as soon as possible.[1]

The Romanian side did not wish to dwell on the issue of the implementation, or rather the nonimplementation, of the 1977 agreements, concentrating instead on refuting Hungarian claims against Romania's nationality policy and other issues raised by Hungary. Within a year of the 1977 meeting between the two leaders, their relations reached one of their lowest points ever. The major reason for the mutual leveling of a chain of charges and countercharges on the nationality issue and the fate of Transylvania can be sought in the blunt Hungarian accusations published in Hungary against Romania's nationality policies and in the growing manifestations of unrest among the Hungarians in Romania—especially the "Király affair"—which in turn prompted a closer monitoring by Budapest of the situation in Romania.

While the crisis was brewing in Romania around the dissatisfaction among the Hungarians, as evidenced by the first two letters sent by Károly Király, Budapest struck first. Gyula Illyés, Hungary's leading poet and "Grand Old Man of Hungarian letters," published two articles in the Christmas and the New Year 1978 issues of *Magyar Nemzet*, which became collectors items in Hungary because of their inordinately harsh condemnation of Romania's nationality policies. The "Illyés crisis" was not defused until the second half of 1978, and it left a very bitter taste among Romania's leaders, who, in the wake of the Hungarian stand as manifested by Illyés and openly supported by other intellectuals in Hungary, felt beleagured by what was seen as a harbinger of renascent Hungarian revisionism.

Illyés, who in his last years had become Hungary's most outspoken critic of Romanian policies toward the Hungarians, certainly did make some very unpleasant accusations. Illyés, who in the words of a Hungarian journal "is and has always been deeply concerned about the integrity of his language and culture,"[2] made in his two articles a *tour d'horizon* of the past and the present of the Hungarian nation in the light of Herder's pessimistic assessments published in 1791 to the effect that the Hungarians, small in number and wedged between others, would disappear in the centuries to come. Illyés's articles represented an intellectual endorsement of the regime's policy toward the Hungarians abroad, in a style and content much more dramatic than the customary line often repeated by the official spokesmen of the regime. Illyés could afford in this instance to play the role of *enfant terrible*, as this time there was much closer affinity between his views and those of the regime than had been the case in the past. Illyés wrote not only about the fate of the Hungarians in Romania, but also the overall problems confronting the Hungarian nation in Hungary and abroad and the preservation of its cultural heritage. On the international aspect of the minority question he did not depart from the official party line, but championed agreements between states on the national minority issue and on the preservation of the cultural values of the minorities.

The surprise in Illyés's articles lay in his outburst against "a nation" where

> a Hungarian speaking population of a million and a half faces grave problems as in the elementary schools small children are taught in their own language that their ancestors were barbarian invaders and inferior devastators.

He stressed that more than 20 percent of the "children of the largest minority in Europe are not even taught the alphabet in their own language." Illyés used the term *apartheid* in referring to the withdrawal of children from Hungarian–language schools by their parents,

> from a fate closer to apartheid. The intelligentsia have vanished from vast regions, moreover, all cultural minority activity has come to a standstill in a large number of nationality cities.[3]

This policy in Illyés's eyes was a "violation of basic human rights." His blunt articles actually contained all the grievances that had been voiced until then in private in Hungary about the fate of the Hungarians in Romania. His list of complaints amounted to an "everything you wanted to know about the plight of the Hungarians in Transylvania but did not dare to ask about openly."

When the Romanians counterattacked, it was not lost on them that Illyés's two articles were in fact a part of a whole series of references to Romania's nationality policies, although most were written in a milder tone than the poet's fulminations. The articles in *Magyar Nemzet*, along with details on the plight of the Hungarians in Transylvania as reported from the Király letters and other similar documents, were amply publicized by the Western media.[4] Naturally the topic was also discussed in the emigré press, both Hungarian and Romanian, which added new fuel to the otherwise heated passions flaring up in the polemics between the two states.

The Romanians responded with an unprecedented campaign to stress the rights of the minorities in Romania and to emphasize their equal participation in the life of the country. Then, beginning in May 1978, they aimed a forceful assault directly at Hungary's criticism of Romania's policies. The Romanian response was also intended to keep in check any further complaints from inside Romania on the nationality issue.

The Romanian switch to the offensive was evident from the numerous articles and other publications that appeared following the Ceauşescu–Kádár talks and before Illyés's articles, and in the period after the beginning of January 1978. Thus, for example, an article in *Era Socialistă*, written before the outbreak of the vehement polemics, stressed the historical roots of the fraternal ties between the coinhabiting nationalities in Romania, and mentioned, in the light of the June 1977 meeting, the existence of a Romanian minority in the neighboring socialist countries,[5] without giving any special details about the Romanian nationality in Hungary.

The following May the same journal published an article by Ion Mitran, editor of *Scinteia*. It reiterated the standard themes to the effect that the nationality question had been solved once and for all in socialist Romania, but then went on to attack those who spoke of "cultural genocide." Such persons, Mitran's message implied, play into the hands of revisionist elements and of the Hungarian reactionaries and emigré circles.

Ceauşescu found a forum for the transmission of the Romanian response to Illyés's and other Hungarian accusations against Romania. He delivered a major speech at the Council of the Working People of the Hungarian and German nationalities, in which he lashed out against the attempts made by "some ultrareactionary, neo–fascist, revisionist circles," who were sowing divisions with the poisoned weapon of nationalism and chauvinism.[6]

Stefan Péterfi, the Chairman of the CWPHN, raised a rhetorical question in a similar vein, asking what "rights and humanitarian judgments are some people trying to interfere in our internal affairs, trying to give solutions to our problems?"

The Hungarian–Romanian flareup came at a rather sensitive moment from a Romanian point of view, and this is precisely what Hungary was bent upon exploiting. The key to the understanding of the polemics at the beginning of 1978 should be sought not solely in the course of Hungarian–Romanian relations, but also beyond, in trends in their relationship with the West, and especially with the U. S. Since the end of 1977 Hungary had been riding high on a wave of improving relations with the U. S., highlighted by the return of the Crown of St. Stephen to Hungary in January 1978, a gesture of good will accompanied by warm, mutual praises between the two sides. President Carter's campaigning for human rights was a convenient vehicle for broaching the minority issue with Romania, considering that after all Hungary could present itself as the side which was implementing the Helsinki agreements, and was advocating human rights related to the national minorities.

With the intensified activities in the U. S. by Hungarian emigré organizations on behalf of the Hungarians in Romania, a campaign which met with some understanding and sympathy in U. S. political circles, Romania found itself on the defensive. Among the documents circulated in the U. S. by such groups as the Committee for Human Rights in Romania, was the widely publicized 40–page document on "Romania's Violations of the Helsinki Final Act Provisions Protecting the Rights of National, Religious and Linguistic Minorities." Such leading U. S. politicians as Dante B. Fascell, the Chairman of the U. S. Commission on Security and Cooperation in Europe, labeled the document as "extremely well documented and a substantive work."

Romania was evidently annoyed by the Hungarian claims voiced in the U. S., and by the media's reporting of the protest documents emanating from Transylvania. It was against this irritating background that Ceauşescu's visit to the U. S. took place in April 1978. The Romanian leader reacted very bitterly to the noisy interruptions by Hungarians and pro–Hungarian demonstrators in New York and Washington, and attempted to halt them by means which to say the least, were highly undiplomatic.[7]

It was not only the Hungarian side that irked President Ceauşescu. At the time when Romania was waging its own public relations campaign in the U. S., President Carter himself was stressing the need for "strengthening human rights." The clear inference was that the issue was not necessarily to be raised only in the Soviet Union.[8]

One week after Ceauşescu's visit to the U. S. the Washington connection was highlighted by the meeting of the CC HSWP at which the Kádár leadership evinced its determination to thrust the minority issue forward with the Romanian side. It was after Ceauşescu's return from Washington that Romania stepped up its campaign against the Hungarian version of the nationality issue and of the state of the Hungarian minority in Romania. The campaign that stressed the cultural–educational rights of the Hungarians was intensified, while simultaneously straightforward answers were given to the allegations from Hungary.

Romanian sources repeatedly elaborated on the equal opportunities enjoyed by the coinhabiting nationalities, and their "active participation" in the socialist transformation of Romania.[9] The number of Hungarian deputies in the Grand National Assembly, 29 out of 349, and their share in the local and regional bodies was also featured prominently. Likewise, the Romanian campaign concentrated on the cultural facilities and press in the languages of the national minorities. In 1978 there were 32 Hungarian–language periodicals that printed a total of 633,000 copies, 8 dailies in counties with a large Hungarian population, as well as the daily *Előre*, issued in Bucharest.[10] The Romanian sources also reported that besides the 210–220 titles published each year in the Hungarian language, a large number of books were also imported from Hungary. That figure was about 280–300 titles a year, amounting to 350,000–400,000 copies a year. The figure for 1977 was a record 328 titles with 453,000 copies imported from Hungary.[11] This increase was a reflection of the atmosphere following the Ceauşescu–Kádár talks in June 1977. The Romanian susceptibility to the issue of the books and other publications available to the Hungarians was undoubtedly due to the allegations from Hungary, not yet officially brought up at the time, that the Romanian authorities were limiting the number of books from Hungary. The Romanian media did not respond to the complaints from Hungary that the import of newspapers and journals from Hungary was being curtailed.

Likewise details were given on the educational opportunities available to the Hungarians, such as the number of students at all levels of education.[12] Such informative data were given without specifically mentioning the allegations from Hungary.

The human rights campaign in the West, and Hungary's position in the matter, including such manifestations as the Illyés articles in the Budapest press, coincided with growing signs of dissent from Transylvania, which also influenced the course of Hungarian–Romanian relations. The Király affair was one of the most important such dissonant voices from Romania. Member of the CC RCP and Vice President of the CWHN, Károly Király protested several times in letters to Ceauşescu and the Party leadership on the state of the Hungarian minority. Király alleged a whole series of discriminatory measures against the Hungarians, in education and employment. He outlined his own endeavors and those of his other colleagues to improve the situation of the Hungarians—attempts which were rejected by the regime. Király found fault especially with the functioning of the Council of the Hungarian Workers, which had no real functions, and fulfilled the task of acting as mere puppets of the regime, without any substantial contribution to the life of the Hungarian minority in Romania.[13]

The Király affair was not an isolated case of a dissonant voice form Transylvania in a period that was critical of Romania's relations with the West, especially with the U. S. Several more manifestations of protest became known at the time, which augmented the Romanian regime's dilemmas on its way to cope both with the rising tension with Hungary and with the Hungarian dissidence in

Transylvania itself. At least three voices of protest were widely publicized at the time in the West: that of Lajos Takács, the former Rector of the Bolyai University in Cluj (which at the time had already been merged with the Romanian–language Babeş University), of the restrictions on Hungarian–language education, and of János Fazekas, member of the Political Executive Committee of the RCP and First Deputy Prime Minister, the most prominent ethnic Hungarian in the Party leadership.[14] All these grievances–which were of course not publicized in Romania and were referred to only in very vague terms by Ceauşescu—certainly caused deep concern among the Party leadership—in particular Király's claims that he enjoyed the support of some key figures among the Hungarian minority. The subsequent protests indeed bore out his point.

The Romanian leadership opted for a double course: a mildly apologetic tone, acknowledging that some mistakes and abuses had regrettably taken place, and even promised that the Party would hold open debates on some of the unspecified issues raised by those persons whose identity was not openly revealed by the Romanian media. At the same time a vehement campaign against Hungary's positions was initiated, which provoked an immediate flareup of polemics on a scale unprecedented until then in the history of the relations between two socialist states. The opening salvos for the anti–Hungarian campaign were the numerous references by Ceauşescu and the other leaders to "outside interference" in Romania's internal affairs, which "violate the interest of the Romanian people."

While some accusations were leveled against Hungarian emigré circles it was rapidly becoming obvious that what Bucharest had in mind was not only emigré circles in the West but also—and more important—the Budapest regime itself. The latter was acting, according to the Romanian version, in cooperation with the darkest forces of reaction outside Hungary.

The direct Romanian response to Illyés's articles, published in the May 6, 1978 issue of the weekly *Luceafărul,* came after several attempts by both states to lower the tone of the polemics. One such attempt was the visit of Ştefan Andrei, alternate member of the Political Executive Committee, to Budapest in February 1978. Such contacts became a standard procedure during periods of crisis in Hungarian–Romanian relations, and besides the laconic expression that the two sides had "exchanged information on the results of building socialism in Romania and Hungary," the two sides also discussed the "significance of the agreements reached in Oradea and Debrecen"—a mild reference that the agreements were not exactly implemented. It was significant that Andrei's visit was accompanied by historiographical salvos (another standard procedure in times of crisis), this time with some bitter Romanian remarks on Hungarian historical works.

Apparently Andrei's visit failed to ease the mounting tension between the two sides, and on April 4, Hungary's Liberation Day, Romania found itself in the embarrassing position of having to convey its friendly greetings to brotherly Hungary, at a time when Ceauşescu and the Romanian media were lashing out at "foreign interference" in Romania's internal affairs.

Scînteia presented a line which ignored the crisis between the two states on the nationality issue, referring to the "continuously upward evolution of relations," which, of course, lest Budapest should forget, were based on the "firm foundations of principles of national independence and sovereignty."[15]

One month later, the Romanian media presented a different picture of the issues between the two states. The article in *Luceafărul*, written by Mihnea Gheorghiu, President of the Academy of Socio-Political Science, was a reply in kind to Illyés's articles and contained several tough passages leveled against not only Illyés, but also those who approved of his line.[16]

The Romanian answer to Illyés was clearly prompted by the attention focused in the West on the Hungarian problem in Romania. Gheorghiu emphasized that Illyés's articles in *Magyar Nemzet* "were taken over and extensively commented on by certain foreign newspapers and radio stations." Gheorghiu does believe Illyés's statement, in a BBC interview, that his articles had not been cleared with the authorities beforehand, but Gheorghiu still makes the connection between Illyés and the regime:

> there is probably something or someone interested in heating up the gunpowder keg again, and in putting the bourgeois-nationalist apple of discord back into the basket of timeliness.

Thus, Gheorghiu assumed the double task of destroying the credibility not only of Illyés as a person, but also of those who may have been behind him. While Illyés did not single out any Romanian personality, but wrote on the nationality policies of the regime, Gheorghiu made a character assassination through which he reached those who may have commissioned Illyés to write his anti–Romanian polemics. Illyés is "most angry with the results of the latest two world wars"—a contention that has often been heard since then in Romania against Hungarian official circles. Illyés is also "proud of his origin, maybe full of nostalgia for the collapsed dual [Austro–Hungarian] Empire and of the memory of the Admiral without a Navy" [Horthy].

Gheorghiu speculates that Illyés, who in an interview with Reuters took upon himself the responsibility of having disclosed the "worsening situation of the Hungarians in Romania," does have influence over others, since "backward minds can still be seduced by *vivere pericolosamente*—living dangerously—in shirts of discrediting colors." In order to hammer into the Romanian public opinion Illyés's grave allegation, the *Luceafărul* had to print some rather delicate passages from the articles. Thus, Romanian readers could learn that Illyés had reached the conclusion that the "treatment of the national minorities in Romania amounts to an apartheid on a South African scale, and if not ethnocide, then to definite ethnic oppression."

Gheorghiu stated that there were no issues between Hungarians and Romanians, and went on to wonder about the identity of those who "can benefit from all these improper provocations and hits below the belt." Gheorghiu's article was followed by similarly worded articles in all the other major Romanian newspapers and periodicals. However, these publications did not pursue a personal vendetta against Illyés, but accused in quite clear terms those behind him. In a long exposé under the headline "The RCP—A Consistent Fighter Against National Enmity and for Brotherhood Among Peoples," *Scînteia* referred to the imperialist circles who make use of a large variety of means, as "pressure, interference in the internal affairs of various states, use and threat of force and application of economic and political levers." This policy of divide and rule had, according to *Scînteia's* hints, some adherents closer to the region, among those who were "still propagating chauvinism and racism."[17]

As the other Romanian publications, *Scînteia* emphasized the Horthyst occupation of Northern Transylvania after August 1940, and this point, along with extensive historiographical debate going on between the two states, amounted to a rather explicit Romanian criticism of Hungary's intervention into Romania's internal affairs. The "defamatory and slanderous irredentist blows intended against Romania by insignificant fascist and Horthyst groups across the ocean are doomed to utter failure and sound like a voice in the desert," claimed *Scînteia*. But actually the publication was revealing the anxiety among the Romanian leadership over the developments from three areas: the protests from inside Transylvania, Hungary's accusations against Romania, and the loud and quite effective Hungarian emigré activity in the West, which could not be counterbalanced by pro-Romanian activities.

Scînteia also referred to Romania's relations with the Socialist states which were based, among others, on "noninterference into the internal affairs of other states and renunciation of the use and threat of force," but there was no other more explicit criticism of Hungary's role in the crisis. More direct, albeit veiled references to Hungary's position were published in *Era Socialistă*, which attacked those who spoke of "forced assimilation" and about "cultural genocide." Such elements, warned the Romanian Party's theoretical journal, served the cause of "fascist and Horthyst elements."[18]

By then the Romanian public was well aware of Illyés's aspersions, so the veiled references in *Era Socialistă* and *Scînteia* to the "real culprits" in Budapest was an attempt to keep the polemics at a more or less civilized level, especially considering the wide attention the polemics were receiving in the Western media.

As usual, historical anniversaries provide ample forums for the airing of the regime's policies, and such occasions are in abundance in Romania. Ceauşescu chose the mass rally in Bucharest commemorating the 130th anniversary of the 1848 Revolution in the Romanian lands as a platform to launch one of the his more resentful attacks against the Hungarian position, and to defend Romania's record on the minority issue. Romania,

> is doing everything to ensure the full assertion of each nationality and citizen of the Fatherland in the spirit of the revolutionary humanism characteristic of our socialist society . . . and rejects all attempts by reactionary foreign circles to denigrate our nationality policy.[19]

Then, the Romanian leader made one of his most vehement statements against foreign interference in Romania's internal affairs. He did so with a rare reference to the Romanians living in the neighboring countries:

> The existence of a Romanian nationality in the neighboring countries, as well as the existence of Hungarian, German, Serbian, and other nationalities in our country demands that we act continuously to strengthen the cooperation and friendship between our peoples and countries.

However, his forceful protestations against any attempts to interfere in Romania's affairs was made in a way that left no doubt as to the severity with which Romania viewed Hungary's policies:

> I would like to stress the fact that the problems of the Romanian nationality in Hungary, Yugoslavia and other countries are not solved in Budapest, Belgrade and other capitals of the respective countries. Likewise the problems of the Hungraian, German, Serbian and other nationalities in Romania are not solved in Budapest, Berlin, Bonn, Belgrade, or elsewhere, but here in Bucharest by our Party. . . . As far as we

are concerned we will never make use of the existence of the Romanian nationality on the territory of various countries to interfere in the affairs of those states. At the same time, I wish to state firmly that we will not allow anybody to use the nationality problem to interfere in any way in Romania's internal affairs.

As the ball passed into the Hungarian court, *Élet és Irodalom*, a counterpart of the Romanian *Luceafărul*, published a long article by Zsigmond Pál Pach, head of the Institute of History of the Hungarian Academy of Sciences, entitled "Along the Danube: Here You Must Live," which can be seen as one of the most pessimistic assessment yet that emerged from Hungary on the divisive national issues between Hungary and Romania.[20] After Illyés's articles and Gheorghiu's response, Pach opened, or rather reopened, a Pandora's box of accusations and counteraccusations on the minority issue, the territorial disputes in Southeastern Europe, and the role of the nationality question in the relations between the socialist states.

First of all, Pach came to the defense of Illyés, after his character assassination at the hands of Gheorghiu. Evoking passages from Illyés's works, Pach took to task the Romanian historian for misinterpreting Illyés, and asked bluntly, "can one insinuate that the Hungarian writer is full of nostalgia for the Dualist and the Horthy era, for the memory of the admiral without a navy."

Pach presents Illyés as one of the staunchest supporters of friendship between the nations of the Danube Basin, and clears him of any suspicion of revanchist feelings. Naturally Pach aimed not merely to "exculpate" Illyés, but also to air some crucial points regarding the Romanian position on the nationality question. Pach outlined the tragic results of the cycle of hatred between the nations of the area, instigated by the ruling classes—a position not very different from that of his Romanian colleagues—but then he painted in very bleak colors a picture of the post–World War II developments, emphasizing that the "total defusion of mines laid in the course of centuries cannot be executed immediately." Moreover, "problems do not cease to exist if we do not talk about them" —which was the tactic of Gheorghiu according to Pach.

Indeed, the essential point of Pach's message was, and has been repeated several times since then by leading intellectuals from Hungary, that a problem really existed between the Romanians and the Hungarians, which was also related to the historical dispute over Transylvania. Pach called for a sober, open minded debate between the two sides, a friendly exchange of views, and even more, for "persistent, ardous daily deeds, in order that no nationality should feel even the slightest sign of discrimination." The subsequent developments in Hungarian–Romanian relations certainly proved that Pach was correct in his assessment that it was naive to think after the Liberation that the socialist transformation would in itself automatically solve the national problem in the Danube region.

Parallel to the continuing historiographical polemics, concentrating on the Romanian publications about the crimes committed during the Horthyst occupation in Northern Transylvania, the two sides attempted more or less successfully to ease the tension between them. Once in a while, there was a short lull, followed by a new round of bitter polemics. The endeavors to keep up a modicum of cordiality were doomed to failure, as Romania remained adamant in its refusal to implement the agreements reached in the Ceaușescu–Kádár talks concerning the expansion of communication between the two sides, involving the national minorities.

Hungary kept up the pressure on Romania to implement the agreements, and this became the topic of several high–level contacts, among them a visit of a high ranking Hungarian Party delegation to Romania in November 1978, made up of three secretaries of the HSWP, Miklós Ovári, András Gyénes, and Ferenc Havasi. These talks, as well as the lower level consultations that followed Ştefan Andrei's visit to Budapest in February 1978, failed to advance the state of relations between the two countries. More than a year and a half after what was described as a historical meeting between the two leaders, relations were at a stalemate, as Hungary was urging the Romanian side to mend its ways on the nationality issue.

The Saga of the Hungarian Consulate in Cluj–Napoca

Hungary attached a crucial importance to the opening of its Consulate General in Cluj–Napoca, which was seen by Budapest as the first test case in Romania's implementation of the 1977 agreements. As the official opening of the Consulate General did not take place until April 11, 1980, foot dragging on the part of Romania can be assumed. Hungary showed open displeasure at the delay, while the Romanian side kept completely silent over the matter. The first hints of Hungarian displeasure came in a TV interview given by Foreign Minister Frigyes Puja, who complained, without specifically mentioning the issue of the Consulate, that the overall development of Hungarian–Romanian relations was good but the evolution in several aspects "is not sufficient." [21]

The Hungarians were eager—too eager—to announce the implementation of the agreement reached on the Consulate in Cluj. As early as January 1978, the Hungarian Ambassador to Romania visited Cluj and declared that the Hungarian Consulate there and the Romanian Consulate in Debrecen would be inaugurated "in the near future"; a day later, the Hungarian Presidential Council published the decree on the establishment of the Consulate General in Cluj.[22]

It seems that the "Illyés crisis" contributed to the slowdown in the process of implementing the agreement on the Consulates.

Puja's references almost a year later indicated that not much progress had been made, so the issue of the consulate may serve as a barometer for the state of relations between the two sides. Hungarian pressure to open the Consulate was carried to the Romanian side by Puja's visit to Bucharest in April 1979, intended to relax their strained relationship. Although there were no references to the divisive issues, the press in Hungary emphasized that both sides advocated the "complete" implementation of the 1977 agreements. Puja's visit paved the way for the return visit by the Romanian Prime Minister, Ilie Verdeţ, in July 1979. This was the highest level contact between the states in two years. While polemical salvos between historians of both states continued to preoccupy their respective media, some headway was made on the political level. In what almost amounted to a provocation by Hungary, Foreign Minister Puja received Dr. István Szepes, who was appointed Consul–General in Cluj, on the very first day of Verdeţ's visit in Hungary, and during his stay in Budapest the Hungarian government announced officially that their Consul would take up his office in the near future.[23]

The official communiqué published in both capitals on July 18, 1979 characterized Verdeţ's talks in Budapest as "open, friendly and held in a businessslike atmosphere." On the whole it dealt with the bilateral relations, and the two sides clearly saw the results of the talks as a balance sheet of the two years since the supposed breakthrough in their relations. It was in this document that for the first time since 1977, Hungary and Romania discussed and agreed on steps to facilitate the contacts between the two sides of the border. The opening of a new border point for international traffic in Csengersima–Petea was agreed upon, as well as the improvement of small border traffic at various crossing points, a step similar to the one taken along Hungary's border with Yugoslavia. The joint communiqué was the first one to deal publicly with the issue of the Hungarian and the Romanian consulates on each others' territory, stating that they would open "in the near future"[24] which was an obvious indication that all roadblocks had been removed.

Hungary continued to emphasize its perceptions on the role of the nationalities in interstate relations, and while this point was being made clear enough in numerous articles by writers and historians,

Verdeț's visit was an appropriate occasion to remind the Romanian side of it once again. While most of the dailies in Hungary did not elaborate on this point, beyond quoting from the official communiqué, *Magyar Hírlap* did refer to the nationalities as "bridges of friendship" between neighboring states.[25] It was very noticeable that the press in Romania, while devoting due attention to Verdeț's visit to Hungary, did not refer to the "bridge of friendship."

One major issue which preoccupied the public in Hungary but was not discussed publicly in Romania at all was the territorial extent of the Hungarian consular district in Romania. This was indeed a sensitive issue, as the extent of the territory   would, theoretically, mean a possibility for a closer involvement by Hungary in the life of the Hungarians in the area. In July 1979 the Hungarian public was told in a radio program that six counties in Transylvania would be under the jurisdiction of the Consulate in Cluj, and it was evident that only a part of the Hungarians living in Transylvania would be covered. In several instances the issue was brought up by the media in Hungary. Thus, in the popular *Foreign Policy Forum* on TV, some questions were asked about the Consulate, to which one of the panel members replied:

> As for the implementation of the Debrecen–Oradea agree-ment, concluded two and a half years ago, it is partly on the way to being realized. For example, the Consulate–General in Cluj is able to carry out its activities, our Consul–General is now making his introductory calls on the Party and State leaders of the consular district, and has begun to carry out part of the usual activities.[26]

As part of the political détente, and in an effort to ease the tension between the two states, Hungary refrained from any criticism of Ro-mania's policies during the Twelfth Party Congress. The head of the Hungarian delegation, Antal Apró, did not elaborate too much on the nationality issue in the relations between the two parties, and in general his greetings were friendly and warm.[27] Several months later, at the Eleventh Congress of the HSWP, the head of the Ro-manian delegation, Iosif Banc, warmly praised the relations between the two states, mentioned the significance of the Kádár–Ceaușescu agreements of 1977, and stressed the need to adhere to the principles of noninterference in other states' internal affairs,[28] a mild reference to Romania's hints that Hungary was attempting to interfere in its internal affairs. Interestingly, at both Party conferences the two sides tried to avoid any further complications in their relations, and seemed to close their eyes to assessments of certain events on the part of the other side, if they diverged essentially from their own. Thus, news about the Romanian opposition to the Soviet invasion of Afghanistan was not publicized by the Hungarian media—a sensitive issue indeed, taking into consideration the Hungarian public's feelings toward Soviet invasions of other countries.

The official opening of the Hungarian consulate in Cluj was held on April 11, 1980 amidst extensive coverage by the media in Hungary—including a live report carried by Radio Budapest—and a much more restrained presentation in the Romanian media. Thus the *Scînteia* report[29] was terse, while that of *Népszabadság* was more detailed.[30] It included the names of the counties under its jurisdiction—Kolozs, Szatmár, Szilàgy, Bihar, Arad, and Temes—a piece of information not specified by the media in Romania. An important feature of the Hungarian presentation of the opening of the Consulate was the repeated references to the "bridges of friendship"—a point consistently disregarded by the Romanian side.

Romania did not publicize many details about the opening of the Romanian consulate in Debrecen in December 1981, and tried to evade any signs of the reciprocity which in fact had been the idea behind the Oradea–Debrecen agreements of 1977. After a period of low-key activities, Romania closed down its consulate for "financial reasons,"[31] so that the Hungarian expectations for reciprocity in this matter were not fulfilled. Apparently the Hungarians did not suffer from financial straits as they kept open their Consulate in Cluj at 16 Mureşan Street—the address mentioned in the press in Hungary but not in Romania.

The end of the consular test–case should also be seen against the wider context of the echoes of the spirit of Helsinki among the East European states. Both Hungary and Romania had to give proof of at least the successful implementation of agreements between themselves, before professing their adherence to the provisions of the Helsinki agreements. The Helsinki followup Conference held in 1980 in Madrid, and the continuing pressure by the Carter administration on human rights, was certainly a factor in both states' determination to ease the tension between them, although the continuing historiographical debates, which were in fact much more than debated between historians, indicated that the lull was not to be a lasting one.

The "Lăncrănjan Crisis"—Attacks and Counterattacks

The "ascendant course of relations" between Hungary and Romania, to use the expression frequently adorning the official communiqués after high–level talks, was in fact very "descendant," judging from the frequency and the intensity of the polemics, involving the historians and the intellectuals of the two states as well as the media, and well reflected in the public appearances of both leaderships. As in the past, several issues were intertwined into one, seemingly never-ending polemic. However, the treatment of the issues became more passionate, words were no longer chosen with care to avoid bitterness in their relations, old taboos were lifted, and the polemics reached more and more into the very heart of the matter—not only into the fate of the Hungarian minority in Romania, for whose welfare Budapest was willing to challenge the Romanian regime, but also into the age–old problem of Transylvania itself.

One of the more acrimonious controversies was the "Lăncrănjan affair," which opened up long–standing disputes. The crisis was centered around the publication of *A Word on Transylvania*[32] by Ion Lăncrănjan, a writer of mixed reputation, a nonconformist whose works were often banned or delayed in publication.[33] Nevertheless, his proximity to the highest echelons of the Party was well known.[34] Lăncrănjan, it seems, was often more than a few steps ahead of the leadership. His survey on Transylvania received due attention not only in Romania, but also—and especially—in Hungary. Its tone was vehement and its forceful anti–Hungarian theme was aimed against the Hungarian minority in Romania as well as Hungary itself.

Judging from allegations that revisionism was being reawakened by the highest circles in Budapest, as Romania claimed after the publication of the *History of Transylvania* in 1987, the Lăncrănjan affair is somewhat overshadowed by the resurgence of the historiographical debate after 1987, but *A Word on Transylvania* still remains the most severely criticized Romanian book by Hungarians, whereas the *History of Transylvania* published in Hungary is the other way around.

Lăncrănjan berated in his book various works on Transylvania, censuring everything written on the issue, by Hungarian emigres living in the West, by authors from Hungary, and, surprisingly, by Hungarian writers in Romania—among them József Méliusz—and a publication by the Kriterion Publishing House, *The Hungarian Nationality in Romania*. Lăncrănjan's book can be classified as one of the heaviest salvos in the historical debates between the two states, although not written by a professional historian, nor claimed to be a historiographical book.

Finding fault with publications from Hungary on the ancient history and the origins of the Romanians, Lăncrănjan proceeds to present a rather competitive history of the two nations, in which the Romanians are the bearers of a humanitarian heritage, while the Hungarians do not seem endowed with such qualities. The more Lăncrănjan approaches the recent turbulent history of the area, the more critical he becomes of the Hungarians and the regime in Hungary itself, and ultimately of some of his fellow Hungarian compatriots.

Lăncrănjan actually reiterated the main tenets of Romanian historiography with regard to the essential divisive issues, thus rejecting the Hungarian notion that the peace settlements after World War I were of an imperialist character, and that Romania's war for achieving national unity was an imperialist war. While repeating the well-known Romanian arguments, he did so in an unprecedented vociferous tone, and broached some sensitive issues which had been taboo until then. Thus, he emphasized the differences between the Hungarian and the Romanian Communists' attitudes to the existence of the Romanian state between the two world wars, accusing the Hungarians of a "Cominternist" attitude. The Romanian criticism of the Comintern's policies toward Romania and its integrity became a favorite theme of Ceauşescu after 1965, but Lăncrănjan was specifically finding fault in the attitude of the Hungarian Communists. On this topic, Lăncrănjan drew a clear line to present–day Hungary, implying that Hungary could be considered as a revisionist state, and quoted from Kádár's speech at the Helsinki Conference in 1975. Lăncrănjan made an innovation in this respect, too, inasmuch as Kádár's speech, which Lăncrănjan took out of context, later became a target of Romanian criticism of Hungary, especially after the publishing of the *History of Transylvania*.

Perhaps his most outspoken words—and they are echoed nowhere else—were written about the period 1945–1958, when, according to the author, during the period of the class struggle, there was no Romanian persecution of Hungarians, but rather the reverse.

Lăncrănjan declared, and the reviews in Romania echoed his claim, that he was motivated by his friendly feelings toward the Hungarians, and that his pleas in the book were made for the sake of fraternal feelings for the Hungarians. Yet, as the Romanian reviews of the book also emphasized, Lăncrănjan felt that he ought to respond to the revisionist tones voiced from abroad. Overall the Romanian criticism of the book was positive. One reviewer in *Anale de Istorie* labeled the book

> One of the most significant testimonies on the topic, a true hymn, a song to this ancient Romanian land, written by a person who felt that he must express his love for his native land.[35]

A Word on Transylvania was published at the height of the polemic on that region and during a period of tension in Hungarian–Romanian relations, and the tough language of the book was carried on by other

writers, who either based themselves on Lăncrănjan, or tried to sub-
due the tone of the polemics without losing any of its essentials. Thus,
Mihnea Gheorghiu, the Chairman of the Academy of Social and Political Sciences, an old hand in polemics with Hungary, who had responded in 1978 to Illyés's accusations against Romania's nationality
policy, called for a less emotionally charged involvement in presenting
the relevant arguments.[36]

The Hungarians in Romania were less enthusiastic about the
book, and for that matter, about the intensification of the polemics
on Translvania and Lăncrănjan's   criticism of prominent Hungarian writers. Reportedly at a meeting of the Cluj section of the
Romanian Writers' Union, three Hungarian writers condemned the
book as fascist, and demanded its withdrawal. In Transylvania, the
samizdat publication *Ellenpontok (Counterpoints)*, which during 1982
had carried several memoranda on the situation of the Hungarian minority in Romania, drew the attention of its readers in Hungary to
Lăncrănjan's book before official responses had been given in the Hungarian media. The smuggled copies of *Ellenpontok* were important in
the formulation of a Hungarian response to the book. The first discussion of the book in a very bitter tone appeared in *Tiszatáj*, published
in Szeged.[37] The author, Pal Köteles, used a caustic language that
was much more polemical than that of György Száras, a well-known
writer and essayist, whose articles and interviews at a later stage can
be seen as an official Hungarian response to *A Word on Transylvania.*

Köteles treated Lăncrănjan's theses one by one, taking the author to task for not bothering to check the facts and for being driven
by his preconceptions. He also dwelt on an issue which was gradually
being raised more and more frequently by Romanian historians—the
atrocities committed against the Jews by the Hungarians in Northern Translyvania during the Horthyst occupation of the area. This
aspect of the history of the Holocaust should be viewed as more than
a historiographical polemic, as it represents a segment of the dispute
about the inherent humanism of the Romanian people, as presented
by Romanian historians. On this point, Köteles agreed with Lăncrănjan
that the Hungarians had committed terrible crimes against the Jews,
but he revealed that Romanian authorities also took part in the persecution and murder of Jews in Romania during the war. In addition,
Köteles mentioned the Romanians' participation in the Axis war effort against the Soviet Union.

As to the allegations that socialist Hungary opposed the Treaty
of Trianon, the Hungarian reviewer forcefully denounced Lăncrănjan
for his attack against Kádár's references to Trianon at the Helsinki
Conference. The overall impression created by this Hungarian review

of Lăncrănjan's book was that it was a vehemently anti–Hungarian, Romanian nationalist work, which undermined the friendship between the two peoples and states. And if Lăncrănjan felt that "here in Hungary we often worry without any basis about the fate of the Hungarians in Romania," this book "is a proof that no anxiety is exaggerated, nor is it superfluous."

In case not all Hungarians read *Tiszatáj*, along came György Száraz's article in *Valóság*, and also a radio interview[38] in which he responded cynically to the "odd sort of book on Transylvania," in which "myth and reality are mixed up." Száraz, who later published a book on Transylvania, parts of which appeared in full–page articles in *Népszabadság*, became one of the most prolific writers in Hungary to participate in the polemics with Romania. He rejects the allegations of modern postwar Hungarian irredentism, and attacks Lăncrănjan, as Köteles had done, for mentioning—without name—Kádár's speech in Helsinki, taken out of context. Száraz summed up his contention stating that "Janos Kádár did speak about the *diktat* in Trianon, and I believe we have no reason to disagree with Lenin, who branded the peace settlement at Versailles as a cruel violence against weak nations." And here, Száraz emphasizes, Lăncrănjan has a "high-handed attitude to history, failing to distinguish between facts and myths."[39] In Száraz's eyes Lăncrănjan represents "something that would be good to overcome quickly," but as he himself explained in the radio interview, Lăncrănjan was not easy to overcome quickly; and he conveyed the feeling that this phenomenon should be confronted to the fullest possible extent. In the interview Száraz gave some indication of the reaction to the book in Hungary, as "some aspects created a fair amount of astonishment and unease among public opinion in Hungary." Lănacrănjan's style was also criticized as being "full of repetitions, and its prose is studded with romantic phraseology."

Once again the political implications of the book became evident in Száraz's interview—he took up Lăncrănjan's treatment of alleged passages from Kádár's speeches and interviews over the years. In this case the Romanian "either turned them upside down or he simply fabricated a 'quotation' which cannot be found anywhere because it does not exist."

And if Lăncrănjan's treatment of Kádár were not enough to emphasize the political implications of the book, Száraz was asked over the radio, "How far does this approach, which Lăncrănjan presents in this work, agrees with the official Romanian approach?" Száraz answered by verbal acrobatics, quoting from Ceauşescu's remarks that "anyone who tries in this or that way to harm the cooperation and unity of the citizens of the country, inevitably becomes the servant of

the country's enemies and enemy of those who are building socialism."
To which Száraz added, "I think this is sufficiently clear."

The Lăncrănjan affair did in fact come to an end with Száraz's
replies. From that point on the "multilateral polemics" took over the
debate about the specific book, involving the Party leadership as well
as the intellectuals in both countries. Another heavy salvo was fired a
year later with the renewal of the Lăncrănjan–Száraz polemics, upon
the publication of Lăncrănjan's new book *Vocaţia consructivă (Constructive Vocation)*, in August 1983, to which Száraz replied in an essay entitled "Yet Another Odd Book Has Appeared."[40] Lăncrănjan's
new book was an open polemic with Száraz, in which the Romanian author, reinforced at the time by the "descending" rather than
the "ascending" course in Hungarian–Romanian relations, reiterated
point by point his theses from *A Word on Transylvania*, interspersed
with long quotations from Száraz's articles, and in turn Száraz's reply
included long passages from Lăncrănjan. The message of this revived,
almost personal debate, was the obvious awareness on both sides of
the rapid deterioration of the polemics and their entry into what had
been a most forbidding, and virtually forbidden territory in the history of Hungarian–Romanian polemics: the troublesome relationship
between the two nations throughout the centuries.

Hungary and the Developments in Romania's Nationality Policy

We have seen that the concern shown by Hungary for the fate
of the Hungarians abroad, especially in Romania, became the most
important feature in Hungary's relationship with the respective countries. The rising public pressure to do something about the Hungarians over the borders was prominent in the Hungarian media, as well
as in reports by Western correspondents describing the atmosphere
in Hungary. According to such reports the misery of the Hungarians
in Romania was the "number one topic discussed by the Hungarian
public."[41] The activities of the dissidents in Hungary as well as the
smuggling of *Ellenpontok* from Transylvania into Hungary intensified
the pressure on the government.

A vicious circle evolved as the Romanian authorities showed more
anxiety over the signs of discontent among the Hungarians in Romania and over Hungary's growing involvement and concern over the
developments, while the Hungarian regime found itself under mounting pressure to demonstrate the falsity of the allegations and warnings from Romania, during the historical polemics from 1982 on, that
Hungary was not reacting with indifference to the fate of the Hungarian minority in Romania. It counterattacked and initiated polemics

on the issue of Transylvania and on the rights of the Hungarians in Romania to thwart off an alleged Hungarian revisionism and nationalism.

Hungarian nationalism, real or alleged, was countered or preempted by heavy doses of Romanian nationalism. In seeking popular support, and in order to rally the nation behind the Party, Ceauşescu intensified the Romanian nationalist campaign. His assessment that the Hungarian card was worthwhile playing proved once again to be a correct one. Yet, Romania may have misjudged Hungary's determination to pursue the matter of the Hungarian minority. Among emigré circles in the West, as well as in Western public opinion, the pro–Hungarian presentation of the case had the upper hand.

Less than a month after the opening of the Hungarian Consulate–General in Cluj–Napoca, Ceauşescu delivered in May 1981, on the occasion of the 60th anniversary of the RCP, one of his toughest speeches on the role of the nation and the Party under socialism, along with a *tour d'horizon* of the history of the Romanian nation and the RCP. Ceauşescu attacked foreign hisotrians who disagreed with the Romanian perception of the continuity of the Romanian nation, which had inhabited Transylvania since ancient times. Against the background of the crisis in Poland and evident signs of a "Romanian malaise," not unlike the Polish one, Ceauşescu lashed out at the enemy, unspecified, which might attempt to destabilize the country. Such counterrevolutionary elements could, according to the Romanian leader, penetrate from the outside or be reactivated by the forces of the dark past from inside.[42]

The discontent among Hungarians in Transylvania reached a new dimension after the first expression of protest became known—in the wake of the Király letters sent to the Romanian leadership. The eight issues of the samizdat *Ellenpontok* published since 1981 could only increase the anxiety of the Romanian regime, at a time when the crisis in Poland was preoccupying the Eastern bloc.

On the diplomatic front, Romania was in difficulty as well. In the U. S., it was faced with a campaign over the renewal of Romania's most favored nation status. In Madrid, there was the matter of the presentation of the human rights record before the followup conference on the Helsinki agreements. On both fronts Romania was facing criticism due to strong pro–Hungarian pressure. In response, it conducted a strong offensive back home, clamping down on Hungarian activists and intensifying the campaign against Hungary.

In the summer of 1982 the U. S. pressure on the human rights issue, as manifested in a letter signed by 51 Senators and addressed to Ceauşescu, dealt with concerns over Romania's emigration policies—

especially regarding Jewish emigration, the problems facing some of the Christian groups, and the decline in the number of educational facilities for the Hungarian minority. The report submitted by the State Department to the House of Representatives' Committee on Foreign Relations dealt a heavy blow to Romania's position, as it singled out grievances which reflected not only the views of Hungarian activists in Transylvania but also some of those voiced by Hungary over the merger of the Bolyai Hungarian–language University in Cluj with the Romanian one.

Yet another blow to the Romanian line at the time was an article "In Darkest Transylvania," in the *New Republic* written by John Lukacs, a well–known historian.[43] The article severely criticized Romania's nationality policies toward the Hungarians, describing various anti–Hungarian measures in force in the area, such as the lack of educational facilities, the lack of bilingual signs, and the "distressingly brief" Hungarian–language broadcasts. Lukacs described the long waiting lines along the Hungarian–Romanian border, a situation which was increasingly criticized at the time by Hungary. The enormous differences between the two socialist states were in Hungary's favor, according to the author, who summed up his reportage in a very pessimistic way.

Lukacs's article could well have been added to a growing list of such articles published in the Western media and naturally picked up by the Hungarian emigre press, or other anti–Communist, pro–Hungarian publications.[44] But this piece had a different fate. U. S. Senator Daniel Patrick Moynihan (Democrat of New York) asked that the article be printed in the Congressional Record as it "provides rare and valuable insight into the Romanian Government's persecution of 2.5 million Hungarians, and should be read by every Senator."[45] It was no surprise that Lukacs was branded by the Romanian poet Adrian Păunescu as "scoundrel, a fool, whom not even the dogs would care to bite out of disgust."[46]

Against the background of the rising criticism of Romania in the Western media on its record of human rights, Hungarian activists in Transylvania drew attention to the Western media to the samizdat *Ellenpontok*, which contained a memorandum and a proposal regarding the Hungarians in Romania as an indissoluble part of the entire Hungarian ethnic body—a point which was in fact the policy of the Budapest regime, although with a milder definition: for the cultural autonomy, coequality of the Hungarian language, and the preservation of Hungarian ethnic and cultural sites.[47]

The Hungarian dissident activity in Transylvania was immediately followed by a clampdown on Hungarian intellectuals there, who were accused of being behind the *Ellenpontok* memorandum and other illegal activities. Among those arrested were Attila Ara–Kovács, a writer; Attila Kertész, actor; Géza Szöcs, poet; and Károly Toth, teacher.[48] The arrests of November 1982 not only focused the attention of the Western media on the issue of human rights in Romania, but also became an instant topic of discussion in Hungary, where intellectuals embarked on the most outspoken criticism of Romania's policies up to that date, placing the regime in an embarrassing position, thus creating a situation reminiscent of the Duray case in Czechoslovakia. Some 71 leading Hungarian intellectuals signed a letter addressed to Premier György Lázár, in which such personalities as the historian Péter Hanak, the philosopher Mihaly Vajda, László Rajk, one of Hungary's leading "professional dissidents," Miklós Haraszti, well known writer, and others complained about the persecution of the Hungarian intellectuals in Transylvania. The letter called upon "everybody who is able to help to protest against the procedure of the Romanian authorities." The protest action was accompanied by some verbal addenda, such as Gyula Illyés's interview to the French media, in which he accused the Romanian regime of "outrageous attitude toward the Hungarian minority in Romania," and described its situation as "unbearable."[49]

It was against this background of growing official and nonofficial concern in Hungary over the rights of the Hungarians in Romania, and the Budapest regime's dilemma over how to present the case to "our Romanian friends" that two leading Hungarian Party leaders, György Aczél and Péter Várkonyi, visited Romania at the end of November 1982. The atmosphere was tense not only because of the above–mentioned events preceding the visit of the two Hungarian leaders, but also because of the overall trend—the exacerbation of the historiographical debates, the bitter dispute over Lăncrănjan's book, and Hungary's hints that Romania was not fulfilling its obligations under the June 1977 agreements.

In the midst of the historiographical polemics focusing on such divisive issues as the Daco–Roman continuity in Transylvania, a theory rejected by Hungarian historians, Hungary introduced a new element in its campaign against Romania—satire. *Népszabadság* published "The Identity," which in allegorical terms held up to ridicule the Romanian perceptions of the past and the present; the full–page story was illustrated with a drawing depicting somebody very similar to Ceauşescu.[50] Written by Zoltán Galabardi, not one of the well-known writers in Hungary, the satire must have immediately caught the attention of the Romanians, who in turn settled accounts with the publication of an unflattering photograph of Aczél and Várkonyi photographed during their visit to Romania in November 1982.

Aside from the satirical interlude, all aspects of the Hungarian–Romanian relations were being affected by the deep differences over the nationality issue, as well as by the continuing polemics on the past of Transylvania. At certain stages both sides attempted to project a make–believe image of "business as usual." Hungarian Premier Lázár visited Romania in July 1982, at the height of the Lăncrănjan controversy, and his visit may have been one of the most uneventful ones, as both sides avoided the discussions on the real issues confronting the relations between the two states. New economic agreements were presented as proof for the "ascending course" in their relations, and although a stalemate in the economic relations often serves as an indication of the other divisive issues, in this case the economic relations were boosted as a tactical device meant to defuse the tension.

Aczél and Várkonyi's visit in Bucharest highlighted the deep crisis, as it came only a few days after the protest letters signed by Hungarian intellectuals. The visitors and their hosts dealt with the nationality issue between the two sides, and there were two separate communiqués, which reflected the deep divergences in their viewpoints. The Romanian communiqué did not refer to the nationality issue as a topic in the discussions, and described the talks as having passed in "comradely atmosphere of sincerity, of mutual esteem and respect"; the Hungarian communiqué was more outspoken on some of the divisive issues. It stated that,

> In order to promote cooperation between the Hungarian and Romanian peoples it is indispensable to develop continuously the political, economic, scientific, educational, and cultural relations and the communication of the citizens of the two countries. An important incentive role is played by the Romanian nationality in Hungary and the Hungarian nationality in Romania.[52]

Hungary intensified its pressure on Romania to the effect that there must be progress on the level of "communication" between the two sides, which in fact was a clear hint that Romania was continuing its policy of limiting the contacts between the Hungarians in Romania and Hungary. On the occasion of the anniversary of the signing of the Treaty of Friendship and Cooperation signed in January 1948, *Népszabadság* wrote on the "unexplored possibilities for a more complete expansion of relations," and specifically mentioned the area of cultural links and tourism, both major points which were frequently raised by Hungary. It was significant that *Népszabadság's* tone, and

that of the other Hungarian media, was increasingly candid in referring to such "unexplored" possibilities, which in fact were suggested
by Hungary but rejected by Romania.

Hungary's expectations from the Romanian side, and Romania's
position on this matter, were once again highlighted during the visit of
Romanian Foreign Minister Stefan Andrei to Budapest in late February 1983. Hungary restates its views on the role of the nationalities
between the two states, and writing on Andrei's visit, *Népszabadság*
once again emphasized that "there is still a lot to do" in Hungarian–
Romanian relations, and the paper expressed its hope that Andrei's
visit would serve as an opportunity to "work out methods to settle open and unsolved questions,"[53] the nature of which was elaborated on by the Hungarian source. However, in January 1983, György
Aczél, who had on his mind the unsuccessful visit to Bucharest with
Peter Varknoyi, spoke on the concern felt in Hungary over forcible
assimilation in an unspecified country, where "false historical justification is given" in order to justify current policies.[54] Once again,
there were two communiqués. Romania once again ignored the minorities issue and emphasized the economic aspects, while Hungary
mentioned once again that the respective minorities were a factor in
the relations between the two states.

The strained relations over the nationality issue were reflected
in several more ways, giving evidence to the failure in the political
contacts between the two sides by Party and State leaders. Romania was increasingly on the offensive, charging outside interference in
its internal affairs. Romania not only incessantly reiterated its positions on the solving of the nationality issue in Romania, but also
openly rejected some of Hungary's main positions. The main speakers
at the Council of the Hungarian nationality in April 1983 protested
against the "attempts by international reactionary forces to interfere
with Romania's internal affairs," and also condemned the voices from
abroad, which evidently were very close geographically, and whose
"deeds cannot but serve the enemies of socialism," and whose "pieces
of advice are a direct form of interference in the internal affairs of our
socialist, united, free, independent and sovereign nation."[55]

Likewise, in one phase of the long debate raging between experts
and leaders of both states on the role of the nation—namely Lászlo
Kövágó's works—it was stressed, quoting Ceaušescu, that "we would
be happy if nationalities would enjoy in each country advantages at
least equal to those of the coinhabiting nationalities in Romania."[56]
Then there was a three–part article by Florescu, which reached

its climax in the third installment. There, for the first time, a Romanian publication criticized Hungary's perception that the nationalities should play the role of bridges of friendship, a principle accepted by Ceauşescu in his meeting with Kádár in 1977. Florescu disputed the emphasis placed on the role of coinhabiting nationalities as "unique bridges of friendship," a perception which distorted the true nature of relations between states. Such "marginal bridges" should be placed, according to the Romanian author, in their proper context. Further on in his article Florescu refuted the notion that a so-called "mother nation" had the right to play the role of an interested party in the affairs of a nationality living in another state.

Such rejections of the main principles of Hungary's policies were only bound to intensify the criticism leveled against Romania's nationality policies, and were to carry the historiographical disputes further. At a time when Hungary itself was publicizing its own model of nationality policy, the overt Romanian criticism of the bridge theory came out into the open precisely at a time when it would have been in Romania's best interest to quietly damp down the foreign criticism of its policies. Florescu's articles and several other similar Romanian pronouncements were ill timed, when the regime was waging a campaign in the West to explain its record on human rights. The bitterness of the Romanian reaction toward the positions and policies of Hungary at such a time could only indicate the anxiety felt among the Romanian leadership over the "destabilizing" effects of Hungary's activities and their impact on the Hungarians in Romania.

Hungary continued, and intensified, its warning that Romania was pursuing a nationalist line, and the flareup in Hungarian–Romanian relations at the end of 1983 with the full-page interview in *Népszabadság* with Zsigmond Pál-Pach, Vice-President of the Hungarian Academy of Sciences,[57] marked a worsening trend in their relations. Even more forceful than the interview with Pach was an editorial in *Új Tükör (New Mirror)*, which accused the Romanian leadership of pursuing a nationalist and chauvinist policy. This article was considered by one well-known Western observer as a novelty, considering that "never since the Communists came to power, has the Hungarian press so openly criticized the nationalist course of the Romanian leadership."[58] Such a step, according to this assessment, "should have been impossible without the consent of the Politburo of the HSWP." Likewise, the almost instant Romanian reply in *Scînteia*[59] was a very resentful piece with accusations of "revanchism and nationalism" not only against Hungarian historians but also against Hungary's regime as a whole. In this polemical atmosphere, it was only a matter of time before Hungary raised officially some of the issues confronting relations with Romania, and its complaints on the fate of the Hungarians in Romania. The platform chosen by the Hungarian leadership to air some of the problems concerning the Hungarians in Romania was a rather undiplomatic one—a festive "friendship" rally in Budapest on the occasion of Romania's Liberation Day in August 1984. Deputy Prime Minister Lajos Faluvégi not only praised Romania's achievements in building socialism—and after all this was the leitmotif of the rally—but also answered one by one Romania's allegations against the Hungarian position on the nationality issue. Faluvégi strongly defended his country's right to monitor the fate of the Hungarians abroad, rejecting the charges that such an activity represented an interference in another country's internal affairs.[60] Referring to the subject of human contacts between the two states—one of the more sensitive points in Hungary's list of demands from Romania—Faluvégi defended the right of people to "cultivate friendship and family ties [and] . . . visit each other," and that the proper conditions should be provided for this. Faluvégi not only repeated almost verbatim the known position of Hungary on communication between the two states but also quoted from the Helsinki Accord and the opinions voiced at the follow-up discussions and meetings in Europe. It was a clear and open hint that Romania was not behaving in accordance with the international agreements to which it was a signatory.

Faluvégi also touched on the point that the national minorities should be able to feel that they were able to preserve their own language and culture, and to establish contacts with the nations speaking the same language. Faluvégi's allusions that the human contacts along the border between the two states were being hindered by the Romanian authorities reflected the growing concern in Hungary over this issue, as well as the impetus of public opinion to exert pressure upon the Romanians to relax their measures. Western press reports, quoting Hungarian dissident sources in Transylvania, revealed that Romania had refused to allow some 3,000 visitors from Hungary to enter Romania during 1985.[61] Such reports were confirmed by the media in Hungary, which during the summer of 1985 opened up a "new front" against Romania, heralded by Faluvégi in August 1984.

In a campaign begun by some Hungarian provincial papers, which gained momentum in the leading newspapers, attention was drawn to the plight of Hungarian citizens kept for hours under "intolerable" situations.[62] The details given in the Hungarian media were utterly distressing, and the tone of the articles toward the Romanians was full of unrestrained indignation, in a vein similar to that of the Western media.

Faluvégi's rating and scolding of the Romanian side for the difficulties in the relations between the two states have to be seen also against the background of more news from Transylvania on a crackdown on Hungarian activists. Although not reported by the media in Hungary, it was of course known either through the efficient underground rumor pipeline, or through some of the main Western radio stations.

Another indication of the continuing strain in Hungarian–Romanian relations was the cautious greetings of Hungary to the Thirteenth Congress of the RCP in November 1984. In spite of Ceauşescu's emphatic reassurances on the rights enjoyed by the coinhabiting nationalities in Romania, and his strong condemnation of all manifestations of "nationalism, chauvinism, anti–Semitism and other forms of humiliation of man," the head of the Hungarian delegation to the Congress, Politburo member Lajos Méhes, made a point of reiterating in Bucharest that the Hungarians in Romania should preserve their ethnic identity and be proud of it.[63]

Romanian hints at the Congress that Hungary was interfering in its internal affairs, a message carried by several speakers, did not seem to have made much of an impression on the Hungarian leadership. A month later, in the guidelines published for the forthcoming Thirteenth Congress of the HSWP, it dealt publicly, for the first time in such a document, with the nationality issue, emphasizing Hungary's right to ensure that Hungarians living in the neighboring states be able to develop their culture, language, and foster their national heritage.

Although discussions preparing the guidelines to the Thirteenth Congress of the HSWP had lasted for some time before their publication in December 1984, the publication coincided with one of the most vehement polemics between the two sides—one sparked off by an article in the August 1984 issue of *Kritika* concerning Vilmos Nagy, the Hungarian Defense Minister in World War II. The article was branded by *România Literară* in December 1984[64] as "fascist, reactionary and chauvinist," a text which according to the Romanian weekly was aimed at "rehabilitating Horthysm."

In whatever form the two countries phrased it, the nationality issue loomed menacingly over their relations—whether it was at the top of the agenda in official talks, or evident in the polemical articles in the press of the two countries when it was not on the agenda. At the end of 1984 the Romanian side showed anxiety over the intensification of the polemics fueled by a more overt approach of Hungary to the delicate issues. It reiterated again and again the basic tenets of its nationality policy, but the tone became more anti–Hungarian than ever. Thus, speaking at the plenary meetings of the Councils

of Working People of Hungarian and German nationality Ceauşescu
declared that:

> Our people, the nationalities in Romania rejected and will
> reject resolutely any attempt of the reactionary, imperialist
> forces, of outside circles to undermine the unity, brother-
> hood, independence and sovereignty of Socialist Romania.

Likewise, declared the Romanian leader,

> we give a firm riposte to all nationalistic, chauvinistic, revi-
> sionist and revanchist outlooks and positions. . . . Socialist
> Romania does not come up with recipes and we do not teach
> lessons or how to resolve the national question. . . nor can
> we bear to be given advice, nor to be taught lessons by any-
> body as concerns the resolution of the national question.[65]

Ceauşescu did not accuse Hungary openly, but taking into consideration that three weeks before his speech, *Romania Literară* had written
on the rehabilitation of Horthy, his words on the "most reactionary
imperialist neo-fascist, Horthyst circles," which "slander and back-
bite realities in Romania," there was no doubt where his words were
aimed at. There are also people, warned Ceauşescu, who "mystify
history. . . . they go as far as praising former empires, the policy of
domination and oppression of other peoples."

Such a diatribe could hardly have been seen as a welcoming
speech in anticipation of Hungarian Foreign Minister Péter Várkonyi's
visit to Romania on January 21-22, 1985. For the third year, both
sides issued their own separate communiqués. Thus the Hungarian
news agency, MTI reported that "Péter Várkonyi invited Ştefan Andrei to visit Hungary. Ştefan Andrei was pleased to accept it,"[66] but
the AGERPRES version of the Romanian communiqué was not aware
of the Hungarian invitation to Andrei, nor the Romanian Minister's
pleasure to accept the invitation. In a by now customary procedure
the Romanian version did not report the MTI's version that besides
bilateral relations, the two Foreign Ministers conferred on their minorities, which "are destined to play a stimulating role" in the friendly
relations between the two states. Although *Scînteia* gave a wide coverage of Várkonyi's meeting with Ceauşescu, the essence of the talks
was not reported in the manner of the Hungarian media.

Some light on the state of relations during Várkonyi's visit was
shed during a phone-in program with the participation of Mátyás
Szürös, Secretary of the CC HSWP, who answered listeners' questions about Várkonyi's visit. Szürös estimated that "basically things
are all right, but from time to time, serious problems and even tension arise in Hungarian-Romanian relations which we would not like

to overdramatize."[67] This was a very rare mention of the term "tensions" in describing relations between the two states—a sad reality of which both sides were well aware but had hitherto refrained from mentioning openly. Szürös reiterated Hungary's position on the role of the "bridges of friendship," a term long forgotten and never much used in any case by the Romanian side.

In spite of the tension and the vitriolic polemics, both sides kept up the channels of dialogue, a usual pattern in periods of tension. During Várkonyi's visit the way was paved for a higher level meeting: the visit of Romanian Prime Minister Constantin Dăscălescu to Hungary in April 1985. The visit was another failed mission in a strained dialogue, despite the sincere readiness on both sides to continue the dialogue and to defuse the tension as far as possible. Internal and external considerations in Romania necessitated a prudent and discreet line both with regard to the Hungarian minority in Romania, and to Hungary's involvement in their fate. While nationalism served as a well tested way to stir up emotions and increase popular support for the regime, at the same time the intensifying condemnation of Romania in the West, and the concentrated pressure on the minorities question, were placing Romania in a vulnerable position.[68] Consequently, any further signs of unrest in Transylvania, and the continuing harassment of the Hungarian activists there, could only be counterproductive to Romania's image abroad.

Thus, Dăscălescu's visit was yet another attempt to continue the dialogue and to improve relations. However, as long as Romania rejected the inclusion of the national minorities in their bilateral relations, as agreed upon in 1977, chances for a meaningful dialogue were nil. Indeed, Kádár stressed in his talks with Dăscălescu, reported by the media in Hungary but not in Romania, that the minorities had a vital role to play in strengthening the relations of friendship. In an apparent attempt to ease the tension, the Hungarian side agreed to delete any explicit reference to the national minorities and to the bridge theory, although these points were reiterated during the talks with the Romanian guests. The communiqué—this time a joint one— did refer to the agreements reached in 1977, without elaborating on the national aspect.

The Hungarian gesture to avoid any further deterioration only went halfway, as during the Thirteenth Congress of the HSWP in March 1985, the Hungarian side, both in the guidelines and in the speeches and debates, expressed its concern in the strongest terms for the safeguarding of the ethnic identity of the Hungarians abroad, their culture, and their ties with Hungary.[69] If the Romanian side could feel satisfaction that the communiqués issued at the end of

Dăscălescu's visit were less representative of Hungary's viewpoints, there were other ways and means through which Hungary could indicate that nothing had changed in Budapest's basic attitude to the Romanian handling of the issues involved.

The Hungarian side emphasized the need to strengthen tourism, border trade, and other means of human contact between the two sides. Although Hungarian sources produced evidence of a renewed flux in tourism between the two states—and these reports were published on the eve of Dăscălescu's visit—they became obsolete very soon, as in June 1985 Hungary launched its protest at the Romanian vexations of Hungarian tourists wishing to cross into Romania.

Facing a barrage of criticism by Romania on a multitude of issues, being accused among others of nothing less than rehabilitating the Horthy regime, Hungary continued its own offensive, designed both for internal and external consumption. Following Pál Pach's pessimistic assessment of the present impact of past forces in East Central Europe, the Hungarian policymakers presented their viewpoint on the influence of the debate with Romania on Hungary's foreign policy. In one of the more comprehensive surveys of Hungarian foreign policy, Mátyás Szürös writing in *Külpolitika*,[70] linked up the past with the present, acknowledging the past's impact on current affairs:

> The hostilities inflamed in the course of history between the Hungarians and the peoples and nationalities living in the surrounding Danube Valley, but primarily the consequences of the Trianon Peace Treaty—considered by Marxist–Leninist analysis as unjust and of an imperialist character—represent a particular range of problems for our foreign policy to this day. . . . in shaping its foreign policy [toward] Hungarians living abroad, Hungary believes that the existence of nationalities is not an obstacle but one more reason for our cooperation with our neighbors to develop dynamically.

Certainly in many points Szürös's article was meant as a response to the constant stream of allegations from Romania on outside interference in its internal affairs, and an indication that Hungary's foreign policy would persist in focusing on the national minorities' role in international affairs, while at the same time proffering Hungary's own nationality policy as a model for a correct "Leninist nationality policy."

It should be emphasized that Szürös's article and other similar statements by Hungarian leaders stressed, as already indicated, that the minority issue is an international one, pertinent not only to matters of foreign policy in interstate relations, but also to elementary human rights. It was in this spirit that the Hungarian delegation presented its case at the Ottawa Human Rights Conference in May 1985.

The events at the Budapest Cultural Forum in November 1985, whose final document Romania refused to sign, as well as the accusations against Romania at the unofficial meeting of the Forum in Budapest further strained Hungarian–Romanian relations, in spite of the occasional attempts to defuse the crisis by means of direct talks between the Party and Government leaders. Hungary was increasingly and openly reproaching the Romanian side for the unsatisfactory state of relations, and the popular radio phone–in programs became the platform for the airing of such complaints with the participation of leading personalities like Mátyás Szürös and Béla Köpeczi, who defended the regime's activities on the issues dealing with Romanian relations. In such programs and in newspaper articles the Hungarian public was informed that regrettably the Romanian side was not implementing the 1977 agreements, and also that Hungary was expressing its unconcealed dissatisfaction over the situation of the Hungarian minority in Romania.[71] Quotations from Kádár's condemnation of nationalism and chauvinism served as a reply to the Romanian accusations that the Hungarian side was making use of methods of the past to revive hatred between the peoples of the area.

The official complaint voiced by Hungary at the Budapest Cultural Forum and the Vienna meeting of the conference on Security and Cooperation in Europe in March 1987 on the Romanian treatment of the minorities represented an intensification of the open campaign against Romanian policies. Thus, Hungary complained that there was no reciprocity between the two states in the free flow of information, and that the availability of Hungarian journals in Romania was restricted in marked contrast to matters between Hungary and the other socialist states. Such grievances were voiced for the first time in clear terms in October 1986 by Rezsö Bányász, State Secretary of the Information Office.[72] The date, provided by *Magyar Hirlap*, confirmed the observations of foreigners and of dissident sources both in Hungary and Romania that the Hungarians in Transylvania had no free access to publications from Hungary. Once again Hungary could prove that it was the Romanian side which was not behaving in accordance with the Helsinki spirit.

Hungary's official complaints never referred to the dissident documents circulating in Hungary on the situation, but there seems to be a linkage between the official and unofficial condemnation of Romania. The regime in Hungary continued to face tough criticism from dissidents that Budapest was only paying a weak lip service to the idea of championing the rights of the Hungarians abroad. Among the main documents circulating from Romania, and which must have come to the attention of the Hungarian regime, was the appeal of journalist–poet Géza Szöcs and Károly Király addressed to the United Nations.[73] The document included complaints on the state of neglect of Hungarian cultural sites and decline in the number of Hungarian educational facilities. A stronger letter was addressed to Ceauşescu by Király, which became known in Hungary through the *samizdat* publication of *Erdélyi Magyar Hirügynökség (Hungarian Press Agency of Transylvania)*. It concentrated on criticism of Ceauşescu's style of rule and on the economic conditions, and was immediately used in Hungary in what seemed by the beginning of 1988 as a national protest movement against Romania developing in Hungary.[74] There was no doubt that such voices emerging from Transylvania posed a new challenge to Budapest's policies.

Hungary's monitoring of the cultural developments among the Hungarian minority in Romania served as a trigger for another flareup in the mutual accusations. This time Hungary took the offensive. In January 1986 all the major dailies in Hungary, as well as Radio Budapest, reported that *Müvelödés*, a Hungarian–language periodical in Romania, which had been published for 38 years, would be replaced by a Romanian journal, *Cîntarea României (Ode to Romania)*, which would have a section in Hungarian.[75] *Magyar Nemzet* was most critical of the intended Romanian step, and insisted on Hungary's right to monitor and to express concern about such developments in the Hungarian minority's cultural life.

Élet és Irodalom, the weekly of the Hungarian Writers' Union carried an interview about *Müvelödés* with János Kovács, its last editor–in–chief.[76] The Hungarian weekly made a point of informing its readers that for the last three years the journal had been functioning without an editor–in–chief, and the Hungarian interviewer, Erzsébet Almási, opened the questions by stating that

> I could just as easily put the question in the past tense, since on the first of January 1986 the minority organ called *Müvelödés* ceased publication. More precisely, it appears in Romanian under the title *Cîntarea României*.

The Romanian news agency, AGERPRES, denied that the journal had vanished, and referred to "news items published by the press in Hungary, which circulates the quite groundless assertion that a Hungarian language publication in Romania, *Müvelödés*, 'vanished.' "[77] Quoting the assistant chief editor of *Cîntarea României*, the Ro-

manian news agency justified the reorganization which had incorporated *Müvelödés* into the Romanian journal. The assistant editor,
József Mezei, noted for those who "ignore" or "pretend to ignore,"
that some 32 periodicals with a total circulation of 83.7 million copies
a year are published in the Hungarian language in Romania.

The different versions on the fate of the Hungarian periodical in
Romania were being spread at a time when Romania was once again
under criticism, this time by the PEN Club, an international writers'
organization headquartered in New York. The head of its Hungarian delegation, Istvan Bart, offered a resolution (although a milder
version of the one originally proposed) which condemned Romania in
very strong terms. It mentioned the hindering of the free flow of information from Hungary into Romania, the closing down of *Müvelödés*,
and other steps that were infringing upon the cultural rights of the
Hungarian minority in Romania.[78]

The continuing Hungarian criticism of Romanian policies has
been gradually centering around other aspects, such as the alleged
forced assimilation to which the Hungarians are exposed. Since the
beginning of 1987, the Hungarian media have openly treated the issue
of the assimilationist trends in a tone which is increasingly similar to
that of oppositionist circles.[79]

The publication in Hungary of the three–volume *History of Transylvania* caused the most vehement flareup in years. It seemed to
symbolize the breakdown in communication between the two sides.

However, that the routine of the Hungarian–Romanian polemics
was disturbed by the growing impact of Gorbachev's *glasnost* on the
area. After a successful visit by Gorbachev to Hungary in 1985, where
he was seemingly impressed by Budapest's showcase Váci Street with
its fashionable boutiques, Romania's turn came in May 1987, amidst
a clear sign that the Soviet leadership was not very enthusiastic about
the stagnation in Romania, and about Bucharest's cool reception of
the winds of change blowing from Moscow. Gorbachev also showed interest in Romania's nationality policy, and urged it to follow Leninist
principles.[80]

Obviously, the Soviets were interested in keeping up the Hungarian –Romanian dialogue. In Gorbachev's speeches during his visit
to Buch- arest, he called for the intensification of consultations between the sister parties of Eastern Europe. Soviet involvement in the
problems between Hungary and Romania came up in a very overt way
during Politburo member Igor Ligachev's visit in Budapest in April
1987. At a news conference Ligachev said that the problems ought to
be settled by the two sides, and that the Soviet Union would not act
as a judge in the dispute.

Against this background, another round of high–level contacts took place between the two sides. A top–level Romanian delegation, composed of Emil Bobu, member of the Political Executive Committee and Ioan Stoian, alternate PEC member and in charge of the Party's foreign relations, visited Budapest on June 4–5, 1987. Once again, separate communiqués were issued. The Hungarian one was, as quite customary, more detailed and revealing than that of the Romanian side. Once again Hungary reiterated its commitment to the 1977 agreements and in the spirit of Hungary's performance in 1986–1987 in international forums, the Hungarian side emphasized that although it was an internal matter for Romania to solve its nationality problem, this issue also had international implications and an impact on Hungary itself. Hungary also called for the clarification of their different views of history through a comradely exchange of opinions, which, judging from both countries' publications following the publishing of the *History of Transylvania*, was far from comradely. As to practical steps taken to defuse the tension, the Hungarian statement was rather vague, and referred to proposals aimed at removing "unfavorable manifestations"; in other words, no progress was made to defuse the crisis despite Soviet pressure to do so. The Romanian version of the talks emphasized, as usual, the points which Romania kept reiterating, namely the "mutual confidence and respect," and, of course, the "observance of sovereignty, independence and noninterference in each other's internal affairs."[81]

The sensitivity of the public in Hungary to the fate of the Hungarians living in Romania was once again demonstrated in a new development which will have inevitable effects on the relations between the states: the growing number of refugees from Romania wishing to settle in Hungary, or to continue their way to the West through Hungarian territory. These refugees are mostly ethnic Hungarians, but some of them are Romanians. By the end of 1987 their case was being transformed into a political issue, which complicated the relationship between the regime and the opposition in a period of growing assertiveness by oppositionist groups. The Hungarian authorities have not released exact figures on the number of such cases, but according to Western sources their number is on the increase, and unofficial estimates put it around 10,000. Rumors, some of them based on solid facts and circulated in Romania, reported that Hungarian border guards have closed their eyes to refugees crossing into Austria. The whole situation placed the Hungarian authorities in an unexpected and embarrassing situation.[82] Officially they gave the travelers from Romania the choice of either returning to Romania or leaving for another country. This possibility may further complicate the Hungarian attitude, as Hungary wishes to avoid aiding such refugees crossing into the West. The embarrassment of the Hungarian authorities was only increasing in face of usual pressure from the public. This time the Hungarian authorities are being pressed to aid not only ethnic Hungarians, but also ethnic Romanians wishing to leave Romania. Some of the latter are turning Budapest into the center of anti–Ceaușescu activities, adding further fuel to the Hungarian–Romanian dispute.

In January 1988 the Aliens' Branch of the Hungarian Police decreed the return of some 160 refugees to Romania. Twelve were returned before, under mounting protest, the decree was rescinded. Such dissidents as Sándor Csoóri and Pál Bodor contended that the problem for the Hungarians was not only political, but also moral.[83] This placed the whole issue within the wider framework of the situation of the Hungarians in Romania in a period of worsening economic crisis and mounting opposition to the regime. The Hungarian dissidents charged that the Romanian government wanted to curb the number of refugees from Romania. The problem was increasingly mentioned in the Hungarian media, although without exact data on the numbers involved. At least, the regime was openly admitting the existence of the problem. Thus in a phone–in program on Radio Budapest, Matyás Szürös was asked by the moderator on the "legal regulations in our country for the humane settlement of the refugee question" after "a tremendous number of questions have raised the issue."[84] Surprisingly, Szürös expressed some understanding for those wishing to reach Hungary,

> in recent years foreign citizens, mainly of Hungarian nationality, have to a growing extent asked permission from our authorities for temporary legal residence in Hungary. Their action is perfectly natural, since people who have been wounded in their Hungarian identity, or else in general injured people who are Hungarians, where else could they turn to but to the Hungarian People's Republic. After all, there is one Hungary in the world.

This statement was one of the most outspoken ones in translating into practical terms Hungary's care for the Hungarians abroad, reminding them that the mother country was a haven for the "injured" Hungarians abroad—certainly an innovation on the principles of socialist internationalism.

There were also signs that Hungary would be ready to involve the International Red Cross in solving the problems of Hungarian nationals with Romanian citizenship wishing to settle in Hungary.

Asked about the matter by a BBC correspondent, State Secretary of the Ministry of Foreign Affairs, Gyula Horn, declared that "should the international organization take the initiative, such advances probably would not be rejected." [85]

Ten years after the Ceauşescu–Kádár summit, the spirit of that meeting was absent from the high–level talks and contacts between officials of both countries. In those ten years there was no summit meeting between the leaders of the two states, an unprecedented situation in relations between the East European socialist states. Both sides, especially the Hungarian one, frequently refer to the agreements of 1977, yet on the occasion of the meeting's tenth anniversary the media in both states recalled the event without presenting significant change in their relationship. On the contrary, that was the worst since the end of the war.

Some Aspects of the Historiographical Debates between Hungary and Romania

The 1964 debates between Hungarian and Romanian historians on the formation of the national states in the wake of World War I became an integral part of their relationship. [86] Both leaders, but especially Ceauşescu, frequently resort to historical themes to condemn the other side's positions on a variety of issues. As the relations were becoming more and more strained, the historical aspect assumed a more prominent role, shifting the contest to the academic arena.

The institutional ties between the historians of the two states are far from friendly, and the experts from both sides are very bellicose in presenting their case before local and foreign academic forums, publishing their findings not only in the specialized journals of the trade, but also in the mass media.

Historians of the East European countries meet and discuss topics of mutual interest in the mixed commissions of historians, which also often coordinate to a large degree the visits by historians and their research. Likewise, the historical institutes of the Communist parties keep up close organizational ties. There are joint meetings, and researchers often from several or all the East European states participate in conferences or meetings with the aim of exchanging opinions on the work done in the respective historical institutes.

The Hungarian–Romanian joint commission of the historical sciences was formed in 1970, and in 1971 it issued its first, and seemingly last, volume of joint papers on the development of the Hungarian and Romanian historical sciences since 1945. [87] One Hungarian review of the volume presented some of the apparent difficulties in the ties between the historians of the two states, who made every effort to reach a common denominator in their meeting in July 1971 on the eve of one of the fiercest Hungarian–Romanian polemics on the nationality issue. According to the Hungarian review, there were difficulties, especially for foreigners, in gaining access to Romanian archives, and in both Romania and Hungary the libraries and bookstores did not have enough of each other's historical publications. The tone of the review implied that the situation in Romania regrading Hungarian books was more difficult than that of obtaining of Romanian books in Hungary.[88]

Various appraisals published in Hungary on the external ties of the Hungarian historical bodies, such as the Institute of History of the Hungarian Academy of Sciences, overtly indicate the "special" relationship with their Romanian colleagues—not always with a positive connotation. Thus, a survey of the external ties of the Hungarian historical institutions and organizations in 1977 presented a list of priorities on the relations with foreign historians, in which the Romanians, as in reviews of Hungary's foreign relations, occupied a special place. The Hungarian document referred to "publicistic and professional debates which accompany our relations with the Romanian and Slovak colleagues," and suggested that more joint meetings would contribute to the mutual acquiescence of the sides involved.[89] Romania very rarely refers to the activities and significance of the joint commission of the historians and its role in the relations between the two states. Hungarian sources, however, used to mention, at least until the bitter polemics since the late seventies, the contribution of the joint commission to their bilateral relations.[90]

The historical journals of the Party institutes for historical research are also actively involved in the attempts to reach a meaningful cooperation between the two sides. The respective journals frequently publish articles by each other's researchers,[91] or write informative pieces on each other's activities. Such articles usually do not refer to the ongoing bitter debates on a wide variety of issues between the historians of the two states.[92] The leading Party historians are involved in the ups and downs of the relations, as exemplified by the visit in Budapest of Ion Popescu-Puţuri, head of the Social–Historical Institute of the CC RCP, immediately following the Ceauşescu–Kádár summit in 1977. He met with his counterpart, Henrik Vass, in an attempt to bring about détente in the historiographical debates. The accommodation reached then was ephemeral; a week after the summit, Péter Hanák, one of Hungary's most noted experts on the Austro–Hungarian Empire, wrote on the "after–life of the Monarchy," criticizing the Romanian positions—overwhelmingly negative—on the Monarchy. In Hanák's view the Dual Monarchy had its positive sides—a topic debated by historians of both states.[93]

Hungarian historians often do not hide their disappointment and deep differences with their Romanian colleagues. Such was the tone of Academician Lajos Elekes in an interview with Radio Budapest following the seventh meeting of the Hungarian–Romanian joint commission of historians, which dwelt on the 1848–1849 Revolutions. Speaking on the divergences between the two sides, Elekes remarked that "there are here and elsewhere remnants of the ideology of earlier periods, let us be blunt about it: remnants of nationalism. . . . I cannot deny that even historians are influenced by this to some extent.[94]

Historical conferences are a favorite battleground for the Hungarian and Romanian historians. While bilateral conferences can be presented as "all in the family," clashes at conferences attended by participants from other countries assume political significance as well. Such was the case at the Fifteenth International Historians' Conference held in Budapest in August 1980, attended by more than 2,700 scholars from 66 countries. Long before the Congress, Romania had expounded its historical and political views on such issues as the Daco–Roman continuity, the development of Romanian national identity, the formation of the national state in 1918, and Romania's history during and following World War II. In countless articles preparing public opinion for the Congress, the Romanian media made clear that for centuries the Romanian nation had faced the expansionist policies of empires and big powers.[95]

Hungary sent a strong delegation of 70 historians led by Dezső Nemes, member of the CC HSW and President of the National Committee of Historians. The Hungarian media covered the debates between Hungarian and Romanian historians, and more information was published after the end of the Congress. Some of the prominent members of the Hungarian delegation, such as Pál Zsigmond Pach, the Vice–President of the Hungarian Academy of Sciences and Director of the Institute of Historiography, and the late György Ránki, Director of the Institute of Historical Sciences of the HAS, were interviewed in the major dailies, which brought more details of the debate with the Romanian colleagues at the Congress. Pach spoke of the nationalist views presented at the Congress, hinting at the identity of those holding such views,[96] and Ránki outlined the major areas of clashes over Transylvania during World War II,[97] one of the more divisive and emotionally laden topics.

In a report written by Ránki for *Történelmi Szemle*, he stressed that the debates between the Hungarian and Romanian scholars did not dominate the Congress, but it is significant that the report dwelt to a large extent on these supposedly marginal debates. Ránki correctly predicted that the open debates between the Hungarian and Romanian historians "will continue in the future."[98]

The deterioration in the historical debates and their political significance, borne out especially by the publication of the three-volume *History of Transylvania*, harmed the institutional contacts between the historians of the two sides. The debates have been assuming more and more the form of relentless bitter polemics in the mass media and professional papers, instead of taking place in an atmosphere of true scholarship at scientific meetings which, as the Hungarian side has frequently pleaded, should be the norm between the historians of the two neighboring states.

All the major divisive points in the historical debates are related to the national question and to the past and present of Transylvania. The issue of Daco–Roman continuity is one of the major topics—one that assumes a political significance. The Romanian view of the circumstances of the formation of the Romanian people and the claim to an unbroken continuity in inhabiting the area is challenged by Hungarian historiography, which asserts that the Magyars found the area of Transylvania unpopulated when they arrived in the tenth century. In June 1979 the issue came up in a conference of Hungarian and Romanian historians, and the Hungarian position was reiterated at the 1980 Congress in Bucharest. In all these debates the two sides did not refrain from underscoring the current political importance of the debate. The events in Romania marking the 2050th anniversary of Burebista's Kingdom, the "first centralized Dacian state," were of a highest political significance, with speeches delivered by Ceauşescu stressing the continuity of the Romanian nation. Hungarian scholars, like Péter Hanák, rejected the Romanian notions, and stated that the "international and domestic balance of power will not be decided upon the merits of debates about indigenousness and historic priority."[99] That is wishful thinking in face of the bellicose answers to the Hungarian rejection of the Romanian theories. In contrast to the rather low-key Hungarian campaign on the issue, the Romanians worked themselves up into a frenzy with such nonhistorical contributions as Adrian Păunescu's poem "The Free Dacians," according to which "Transylvnia and the Banat are full with free Dacians" and "Decebal's blood flows in the Prut and Tisza rivers."[100]

In spite of Ceauşescu's dictum in 1976 that

> we believe that one of our national and international duties is
> to do everything to see that certain problems inherited from
> the past, created by the policy of the oppressing classes, do
> not affect the cooperation and solidarity between our Parties

and peoples, this was precisely what was happening in the historical polemics between Hungary and Romania.

It was this contradiction between theory and practice that was evident in Ştefan Paşcu's criticism of Hungarian historians around the arguments relating to the origins of the Romanian nation and the history of Transylvania. He cautioned that

> by its essence history is a revolutionary, humanist science, which must not, under any circumstances, sow distrust between the peoples or working people of different nationalities.

But at the same time he took to task

> certain historians, who push aside facts and do not hear the voice of time, a time calling for collaboration in the interest of peace and progress, they raise all kinds of theories, ignore historical truth and alter the mission of a science having a profound human significance.[101]

The arguments around the theory of Daco–Romanian continuity are just one face of the historical polemics, and the image presented by Romania of the Hungarian historians is one of a long list of falsifications, in which the

> inadmissible omission and the obvious distortions are not accidental, of course, they pursue goals having nothing in common with historical truth and the ethics of historical research.[102]

The overall Hungarian presentation of the past of Transylvania, and of the national liberation movement is challenged by Romania. Usually Romanian historians show a greater concern and sensitivity when Hungarian theses are published abroad and the Hungarian version of the dispute is disseminated among a Western readership. In a highly polemical study, the late Romanian historian Constantin C. Giurescu rebuffed the treatment of Romanian history as presented in the book *History of Hungary*,[103] but the attack was against the English and French versions of the book, which had been published several years earlier in Hungary in the Hungarian language.

Likewise, an article in the Spanish edition of the monthly *Hungaria*, was attacked by the two prominent Romanian historians, Ştefan Ştefănescu and Nicolae Petreanu, entitled "Hungarian Revisionists and Chauvinists Are at It Again."[104] The Romanian historians charged that the Hungarian article, written by Péter Ruffy, contained old chauvinist, revisionist, and revanchist themes taken from the interwar arsenal of Horthyist propaganda.

Romanian historians are also sensitive to publications by Hungarian emigfes in the West, implying that they represent Budapest's line. The Bucharest review *Săptămîna Culturală a Capitalei, (The Cultural Weekly of the Capital),* chose to criticize a book published in Canada by Endre Haraszti, on the *Origins of the Romanians,* on the very day that Ştefan Andrei visited Hungary in February 1978.[105] The connection between the emigré historians and their motherland was made in veiled terms, and a week earlier *Contemporanul* had criticized an article from *Magyar Hirlap* on the origins of the Romanian people, which according to the Romanian review, was full of distortions.[106] The Romanian historians condemned the "erroneous ways in which the history of the peoples' origin is presented" in terms which were very similar to the criticism leveled against Haraszti's book published in Canada.

The relationship between nationalism and internationalism remains one of the most disputed topics between Hungarian and Romanian historians. It is a topic which also serves well the leaders of the two sides in their arguments against each other's positions. The Hungarian position for more than a decade has been that nationalism should not be ignored, and that "old habits have not lost their effect"—as expounded by Zsigmond Pál Pach in one of his polemical articles against the Romanian perception of the post–World War I Peace Treaties.[107] The author stressed that while fighting remnants of nationalism at home, it was the task of Hungarian historians to unmask "those manifestations of nationalism that occur elsewhere, that arise in the historiography of the neighboring countries." This was also emphasized in an interview given by Zsigmond Pál Pach to *Népszabadság,*[108] which caused one of the vehement flareups between the two sides, as the Hungarian historian very bitterly remarked on the disappointment that socialist transformation of society had not solved the nationality issue in the Danube area. In other words, the Romanian answer to the Hungarian pessimism on the presence of nationalism in Eastern Europe, and its effects on the nationality issue is a simple one—that the Hungarians are still playing with the fire of nationalism, and it is they who are pursuing a policy which is bound to lead to the revival of hatred between nationalities.

The issue of disintegration of the Habsburg Monarchy, the Peace Treaties, and the formation of the national states have continued to be one of the most debated topics in recent years. In contrast to the Romanian view, which sees a fundamentally positive nature in the peace treaties following World War I, and emphasizes that for the first time, peoples, independent of the great powers, forced their will on the Paris Peace Conference, the Hungarian side stressed the imperalist nature of the Peace Treaties, including the Trianon Treaty.[109]

Romanian leaders and historians show a great sensitivity to the growing number of studies published in Hungary on the circumstances of Trianon, in which they see a trend to justify the nationalist line in opposing the Treaty of Trianon.[110] The strongest words on the Romanian condemnation of the Hungarian position are usually uttered during the commemorations in December, marking the founding of the unified Romanian national state. Such events, especially since 1982, have brought about new and strongly worded polemics centering not only on the circumstances of the founding of the Romanian national unitary state in 1918, but also on the overall conceptions of both sides on the idea and role of the nation.

A new element was added in 1983, when Ilie Ceauşescu, the President's brother, Secretary of the Romanian Army's High Political Council, not only disregarded the formation of the Hungarian Soviet Republic in March 1919, but also wrote on the aggression against Romania in the summer of 1919, which was aimed at reannexing Transylvania.[111] To the dismay of his critics from Hungary, Ceauşescu described the Romanian army's role in crushing the Hungarian Soviet Republic as a patriotic task, in which Romania proved its determination not to allow anybody to challenge the integrity of the Romanian homeland. No wonder that Hungarian historians immediately reacted to this perception, and more works were published. Among them was Ernö Raffay's, which expounded the "Romanian irredenta" and dwelt on such characteristics as the inherent xenophobia in the Romanian perception of the Daco–Roman continuity.[112]

Through the ensuing debates focusing on the problematic relationship between the two Communist Parties between the wars, and on the Comintern's policies toward Romania and the national question, both sides reached perhaps the most difficult, if not the most traumatic, theme in their disputes. It had clear political implications: the fate of Hungarian–occupied Northern Transylvania following the Vienna *Diktat* of 1940. The arguments in this case are very bitter. Not only is the very definition of the Hungarian occupation, the nature of the *Diktat* arbitration under dispute, but also is the charge by the Romanian side that Hungary is whitewashing the Horthyst regime and rehabilitating its main personalities. Such was the case with the Romanian treatment of a Hungarian study on the resignation of Vilmos Nagy, the Hungarian Minister of National Defense, who in the view of Hungarian historians, took a "national position" in opposing Horthy.[113] In their reply to the Hungarian article, two Romanian historians, Florin Constantiniu and Mihail Ionescu, summed up their view of the Hungarian study, which "brings back in the highlight the Horthy regime and one of its leading representatives, implicitly disseminating anti–Romanian revanchist theses." [114]

The Romanian response to the study in *Kritika* and other similar Romanian studies, including those which were written in answer to *The History of Transylvania*, accuse the Hungarian historians of minimizing the anti–Romanian and anti–Jewish atrocities committed by the Horthyst occupation forces in Northern Transylvania. Thus, *România Literară* wrote on the expulsion of 290,000 Romanians from their homes, the 30,000 Romanians deported to labor camps in Germany, and the

> systematic policy of de–nationalizing of the Romanians, the prohibition to speak the Romanian language, the desecration of their churches. . . . ethnic genocide, aimed at the physical and spiritual extermination of the autochtonous and majority Romanian population. [115]

While Romanian historiography emphasizes the collaboration between the Hungarian and the Romanian democratic forces against the Horthyst occupation, the campaign criticizing the present–day Hungarian historians, and for that matter the Budapest regime, represents a Romanian attempt to delegitimize the Kádár regime, which dared to defend the force of the past and a nationalist–revanchist line.

The Romanian insistence on the Hungarian treatment of the fate of the Jews in Northern Transylvania, as opposed to their fate in Romania, sparked off new rounds of debates, aimed at proving, from the Romanian side, the humanist nature inherent in the Romanian nation in contrast to the Hungarians' criminal deeds, while the Hungarian historians counterattacked by reminding the Romanian historians of the fate of the Jews in some areas of Romania, especially the pogrom in Iaşi in 1941, and the behavior of the Romanian forces in the occupied areas of the USSR after June 1941.

Both sides clearly see the need to respond to each others' allegations. No historical book, essay, or article remains unanswered, especially those dealing with the events of World War II. Thus, the publication of *Horthy's Fascist Terror in Northwestern Romania, September 1940–October 1941* was "required by the situation in which a series of inimical elements imbued with revisionist and revanchist ideas," spread lies about the events of that period. Although this passage referred to the Hungarian emigré historians, the Romanian article went on to explain that the

> volume was also required by the fact that, over the last few years, works and articles were published in the Hungarian

People's Republic trying to rehabilitate Horthy's regime, to absolve it of the crimes and atrocities it committed against the Romanian people.[116]

The words used by the Romanian historians and the warm reviews this book received in Romania could not but indicate the current political implications of the historical debate. The years of the Hungarian domination were

> a terrible Saint Bartholmew's night for the Romanian population . . . in the name of the "most splendid Mongolian race," the descendants of Attila, Arpad and Ghengis Khan tried to turn back the history of human relations to the age of barbarism.[117]

It is only natural that after such publications the Hungarian response is never late in coming. Mátyás Szürös promptly rejected the Romanian allegations and condemned the practice of using "murky darkened episodes and delicate issues of our history on the level of official propaganda."[118]

In moving forward to the immediate postwar events, the Romanian side growingly emphasized Hungary's revisionist claims at a time when the fate of Transylvania was being decided. Such a flareup took place following the publication of a study in *Kritika* on some of István Bibó's perceptions in 1946–1947. The late sociologist and publicist, whose works have lately been rehabilitated and widely published in Hungary, pressed during the Paris Peace Conference for the return of some areas of Transylvania to Hungary. This argument heated up yet another divisive issue between the two states: the decisions of the Paris Peace Conference in 1946–1947, which led to the establishment of Hungary's postwar borders, and the Romanian interpretation that Hungary attempted to gain back the whole, or parts, of Transylvania.

Often the commemoration of events serves as a jumping board into old–new controversies. Such was the case with the Hungarian commemoration in 1984 of Petru Groza's 100th birthday, an event marked by a lower key celebration on the Romanian side. For the Hungarians it was an opportunity to remind the Romanian neighbors that Groza was "a good Romanian," seemingly a rare specimen according to the Hungarian view, who sincerely believed in the granting of equal rights to the Hungarians. The image of Groza which emerged from some of the Hungarian publications was that of someone who believed in and acted for the friendship between peoples. All major Hungarian publications carried articles commemorating and evaluating Groza's activities.[119] At a time when Ceaușescu was rejecting

Hungary's theory on the role of the nationalities as bridges of friend-ship, Hungary reminded Romania that it was Groza who had treated Transylvania as such a bridge. The Hungarian articles commemo-rating Groza were not only written for the sake of the past but the date was also used to list a whole series of complaints on Romania's refusal to behave according to the norms laid down not by a leader from Hungary, but by Romania's own Premier. Hinting at the dif-ficulties in traveling between the two socialist states the Hungarian media reminded the Romanians that Groza had gone as far as to sug-gest doing away with passports and visas altogether. But Groza had disappointments too, as things were not progressing in his own time as he would have liked. Such was the case with shelving of the plan for a customs union between the two states.

The publication of the three-volume *A History of Transylvania* in Hungary was a symbolic ending to the decade that had started with the Ceauşescu–Kádár talks in June 1977. It was marked by the climax of the historical debates, and the opening of a new round which, more than ever, was frought with political implications.

The connection between the past and the present of Transyl-vania is fairly frequent in Hungarian publications of recent years, and one such significant project was the series of long articles writ-ten by György Száraz and published in full page installments in *Népszabadság*.[120] Entitled "On the Past of Transylvania in the Present," the series eloquently outlined the topic. It condemned the erroneous historical perceptions of Hungarian nationalism, and placed special emphasis on such fallacious views held by the Romanians, both in the past and in the present.

The History of Transylvania was edited by Béla Köpeczi, Minis-ter of Culture, and published by the Hungarian Academy of Sciences. The volumes became an instant bestseller, and their 2,000 pages con-tain the findings of the best Hungarian historians on the ancient and the recent history of Transylvania. While not directly confronting the tenets of Romanian historiography, *A History of Transylvania* clearly opposes them, starting from the rejection of the Daco–Roman continuity.

The political implications of the project were quite unequivocal for Romania: the volumes, especially the parts dealing with the recent past, emphasize the connection between Hungarian culture in Tran-sylvania and the totality of Hungarian culture in Hungary. Reaction in Romania was swift and unprecedented. Because of the attention accorded to the book in the West, a public relations campaign was initiated, with such highlights as an ad in the *Times* of London.[121]

At home, from Ceauşescu down, the professional and popular

journals assaulted this latest manifestation of "Hungarian revanchism," this time branding as a "revisionist" the Hungarian Minister of Culture.[122] Ceauşescu attacked the Hungarian historians' work at the plenary meeting of the Council of Workers of Hungarian Nationality, at which, joined by other speakers, he condemned the "irredentist, revanchist" winds blowing from Hungary. "Political and cultural" personalities in Hungary were accused by Ceauşescu of harboring anti–Romanian ideas, which amounted to attacks on Romania's territorial integrity. This severe Romanian judgment on the Hungarian work was also published in the Resolutions of the meeting, and amply reported and analyzed by the Romanian media. The historical debates between the two sides are far from being over, and the next round following *The History of Transylvania* should, of course, be viewed only as the end of one cycle and the beginning of a new one.

Between the tenets of "socialist brotherhood and revolutionary tradition" and the debate on *The History of Transylvania*, there is now a gaping chasm that no bridge can easily span. The foundations of such a bridge were at best washed away by the tides of Communist nationalism; perhaps they were never even laid down.

Footnotes for Chapter I

1 George Schöpflin, "Trianon Two Generations After," in Béla K. Király, Peter Pastor and Ivan Sanders (eds.), *War and Society in East Central Europe*, Vol. VI, *Essays on World War I: Total War and Peacemaking, A Case Study on Trianon* (New York: Social Science Monographs, Brooklyn College, 1982), p. 644.

2 Quoted in the review of Rudolf Fischer of Frigyes Puja, *A felszabadult Battonya* (Budapest: Gondolat, 1979), in *The New Hungarian Quarterly*, no. 78, summer 1980.

3 Olimpiu Matichescu, *Opinia Publică Internaţională Despre Dictatul de la Viena* [International Public Opinion on the Vienna Dictate], (Cluj: Dacia, 1975), p. 232.

4 Josezef Révai using pseudonym Endre Rozgonyi in *Szabad Szó*, November 12, 1938.

5 Berecz János, "Hazánk Nemzetközi Helyzetének Változásai" [The Changes in Our Country's International Position], *Párttörténeti Közlemények*, no. 1, 1985, p. 23.

6 Dániel Csatári, *Forgoszélben: Magyar–Román viszony 1940–1945* [In the Whirlwind: Hungarian–Romanian Relations 1940–1945] (Budapest: Akadémia Kiadó, 1968), p. 410.

7 See for example in Gyula Kállai, *A magyar függetlenségi, mozgalom 1939–1945* [The Hungarian independence movement] (Budapest: Szikra, 1955), p. 203, also quoted in Yehuda Lahav, *Soviet Policy and the Transylvanian Question 1940–1946* (Jerusalem: The Hebrew University of Jerusalem, the Soviet and East European Research Centre, Research Paper 27), p. 16.

8 Zoltán Vas, *Hazatérés* 1944 [Homecoming 1944], (Budapest, 1970), p. 103, also quoted in Sándor Fekete's review of the book in *Kortárs*, no. 6 (1971).

9 For comprehensive historical background see, Stephen Fischer–Galati, "The Great Powers and the Fate of Transylvania Between the Two World Wars" and Stephen D. Kertész, "From the Second Vienna Award to Paris: Transylvania and Hungarian–Romanian Relations During World War II," both studies in John F. Cadzow et al. (eds.), *Transylvania—The Roots of Ethnic Conflict* (Kent State University Press, 1983), pp. 180–189, 190–223.

[10] Berecz, *op. cit.*, p. 23.

[11] Csatári, *op. cit.*, p. 446, see also, Lahav, *op. cit.*, pp. 18–27.

[12] From among the numerous Romanian sources see, for example, László Bányai, *Közös Sors–Testvéri Hagyományok* [A Common Fate–Fraternal Heritage], (Bucharest: Politikai Könyvkiadó, 1973), László Bányai, "In Spiritul Frăţiei Şi Solidarităţii Dintre Toţi Oamenii Muncii," [In the spirit of brotherhood and solidarity between all working peoples], *Era Socialistă* 54, no. 14 (1974): 26–29.

[13] *Új Tükör*, December 16, 1984.

[14] Foreign Office (FO)371, R 6446/219/37, also quoted in Lahav, *op. cit.*, 23.

[15] *Scânteia*, November 15, 1944.

[16] *Scânteia*, February 16, 1945.

[17] Csatári, *op. cit.*, pp. 452–453.

[18] *Scânteia*, March 16, 1945.

[19] For such warnings by the communists, see *Scânteia*, March 19, 1945.

[20] For an interesting testimony of the atmosphere in Cluj at the time, see János Demeter, *Századunk Sodrában* [In the Whirlwind of Our Century], (Bucharest: Kriterion, 1975), pp. 342–355. Demeter, one of the leading progressive Hungarians in interwar Transylvania, served as Deputy Mayor of Cluj, and one of the leaders of the National Democratic Front in Transylvania from ca. late 1944. For a review of Groza's activities and his visit in Cluj, see Gerelyesné Dian Eva, "Petru Groza Politikai Pályája 1945 Utáni Dokumentumok Tükrében," *Századok*, no. 5–6 (1985): 1272–1350, [The Political Activities of Petru Groza in the light of post–1945 documents].

[21] See Le Problème Hongrois par Rapport à la Roumaine (Budapest: Ministère des Affaires Etrangères, 1946), p. 49, also see Stephen D. Kertész, *Between Russia and the West, Hungary and the Illusions of Peacemaking 1945–1947* (Notre Dame, Indiana: University of Nortre Dame Press), 1984.

[22] As reported by the Office of the British Political Representative in Bucharest, FO 371 59145 X/M 07434.

[23] Sándor Balogh, *Parlamenti es Pártharcok Magyarországon 1945–1947*, [Parliamentary and Party Struggles in Hungary 1945–1947], (Budapest: Kossuth, 1975), p. 44.

[24] *A Magyar Kommunista Párt es a Szociáldemokrata Párt Határozatai 1944–1948*, [Resolutions of the Hungarian Communist Party and the Social Democratic Party], (Budapest: Kossuth, 1967), p. 82.

25 *Népszava*, August 10. 1945, also quoted in a report of the British Political Mission in Hungary, FO 371 48645 02396.

26 Ildikó Lipcsei, "Kurkó Gyárfás," *Historia*, no. 5–6 (1984).

27 For the various stages of the Paris Peace Conference and Hungary's position see, Kertész, *Between Russia and the West*, Stephen D. Kertész, *The Last European Peace Conference: Paris 1946— Conflict of Values* (Lanham, New York, London: University Press of America, 1985).

28 Miklós Vásárhelyi, "Az Erdélyi magyarság," *Társadalmi Szemle*, 1, no. 8–9 (1946): 629–634 [The Hungarians in Transylvania].

29 See *Libertatea*, February 3, 1945, *Jurnalul de Dimineață*, February 6, 1945.

30 Mihály Korom, "A magyar népi demokrácia elsö évei" [The first years of the Hungarian people's democracy], *Valóság*, no. 3 (1984):7.

31 Sándor Balogh, *A népi demokratikus Magyarország külpolitikája 1945-1948* [The foreign policy of the Hungarian people's democracy 1945–1947] (Budapest: Kossuth, 1982).

32 For a personal account of the Moscow visit, see Ferenc Nagy, *The Struggle Behind the Iron Curtain* (New York: Macmillan, 1948), Stephen D. Kertész, *Diplomacy in a Whirlpool: Hungary between Nazi Germany and Soviet Russia* (Notre Dame, Ind.: University of Notre Dame Press, 1953).

33 *Szabad Nép*, April 23, 1946.

34 *Ibid.*, May 1. 1946.

35 Béla Fogarasi, "A dunai népek együttmüködése" [The cooperation of the Danubian nations], *Társadalmi Szemle* 1, no. 5 (1946): 346–354.

36 *New Hungary* May 15, 1946. Auer was one of the leading democratic politicians involved in attempts for a rapprochement between nationals of the Successor States. In 1946 he served as Hungary's Minister Plenipotentiary to France.

37 For a detailed analysis of the diplomatic activity at the time see, Kertész, *Diplomacy in a Whirlpool*, ch. X. In modern Romanian historiography the best presentation may be found in Stefan Lache, Gheorge Tuţui, *La Roumanie et la Conférence de la paix de Paris (1946)* (Bucharest: Editura Academiei RSR, 1987).

38 *Dreptatea*, May 9, 1946.

39 *Balogh, op. cit.*, p. 283.

40 Rákosi's visit to the West was one of the first encounters between the new leaders of Eastern Europe and Western leaders at that juncture of the Cold War.

41 *Balogh, op. cit.*, p. 293.

[42] See for example in British diplomatic documents, FO 371 59025 X/M 07529.

[43] See Stanley M. Max, *The United States, Great Britain and the Sovietization of Hungary 1945–1948* (Boulder: East European Monographs, 1985), especially ch. V; Paul D. Quinlan, "The United States and the Problem of Transylvania during World War II."

[44] *Szabad Nép,* June 27, 1946.

[45] *Szabad Nép,* June 16, 1946.

[46] On the importance attached to the 1946 Resolutions in Romanian historiography see, Ioan Ceterchi (ed.), *Naţiunea si Contemporaneitatea,* [The Nation and contemporaneity], (Bucharest: Editura Stiinţifică, 1971), p. 146.

[47] *Szabad Nép,* July 21, 1946.

[48] *New Hungary,* June 9, 1946.

[49] See, for example, *Scânteia,* September 6, 1946.

[50] *Szabad Nép,* August 30, 1946.

[51] Unsigned article, probably written by one of the main Party leaders, *Szabad Nép,* August 13, 1946.

[52] *Szabad Nép,* September 7, 1946.

[53] Kertész, *Between Russia and the West,* p. 134.

[54] Robert R. King, "Eastern Europe," Robert G. Wirsing (ed.), *Protection of Ethnic Minorities* (New York: Pergamon Press, 1981), pp. 94–95.

[55] Quoted in Yeshayahu Yelinek, *The Lust for Power* (Boulder: East European Monographs), p. 112.

[56] Korom, *op. cit.,* p. 6.

[57] On Czechoslovakia's nationality policy until 1948 see, Kálmán Janics, *Czechoslovak Policy and the Hungarian Minority 1945–1948* (New York: Social Science Monographs, distributed by Columbia University Press, 1982). For a periodization of the history of the Hungarians in postwar Czechoslovakia see, George Schöpflin, "Nationalities in Eastern Europe."

[58] *Magyarok Csehszlovákiában,* [Hungarians in Czechoslovakia], (Bratislava: Epocha Könyvkiadó, 1969), pp. 204–206.

[59] *Ibid.*

[60] Quoted in a review of Michal Barnovsky, *Socialne Triedy A Revolucne Premeny Na Slovensku V Rokoh 1944–1948* (Bratislava, 1978), p. 206 in *Századok,* no. 1 (1983), p. 222 [Social classes and revolutionary change in Slovakia 1944–1948].

[61] Oszkár Betlen, "Az új Csehszlovákia és a cseh–magyar viszony," [The new Czechoslovakia and Czech–Hungarian relations], *Társadalmi Szemle* 1 (1946): 56.

62 *Ibid.*
63 Oszkár Betlen, "A nemzetiségek Magyarországon," [The nationalities in Hungary], *Társadalmi Szemle* 1, no. 2 (1946): 115.
64 Kertész, *Diplomacy in a Whirlpool,* pp. 142–143.
65 Sándor Balogh, "Az 1946. február 17-i magyar–csehszlovák lakosságcsere egyezmény" [The Hungarian–Czechslovak population exchange agreement of February 27, 1946], *Történelmi Szemle* 22, no. 1 (1979): 59–87.
66 *Ibid.*
67 *Ibid.*
68 *Ibid.*
69 Magyarok Csehszlovákiaban, p. 211.
70 *Ibid.,* p. 212.
71 *Ibid.,* p. 212.
72 See, for example, *Szabad Nép,* July 3, 1946.
73 See, for example, Oszkár Betlen, "Reszlovákizálás és a szlovákok kényszerü attelepitése," *Társadalmi Szemle,* 1, no. 8–9 (1946): 624.
74 *Magyarok Csehszlovákiában,* p. 211.
75 The essay reprinted in Endre Arató, *Tanulmányok a Szlovákiai Magyarok Történetéböl 1918–1975,* [Studies on the History of the Hungarians in Slovakia 1918–1975], (Budapest: Magvetö, 1977).
76 Quoted in Arató, *op. cit.,* pp. 341–342.
77 For some recent Hungarian views on the population exchange with Czechoslovakia, see Károly Szabó, István E. Szöke, "Adalékok a magyar–csehszlovák lakosságcsere tarténetéhez" [Addenda to the History of the Hungarian–Czechoslovak population exchange], *Valóság,* 10 (1982): 90–93.
78 See Andrew Ludanyi, "Titoist Integration of Yugoslavia: The Partisan Myth and the Hungarians of the Vojvodina 1945–1975, *Polity,* XII, no. 2 (1979); for a comprehensive study of Yugoslavia's policy towards the Hungarians see, Andrew Ludanyi. *Hungarians in Romania and Yugoslavia: A Comparative Study of Communist Nationality Policies,* (Ph.D. thesis, The Louisiana State University and Agricultural and Mechanical College, University Microfilms, Ann Arbor, Michigan, 1971).
79 Ludanyi, "Titoist Integration."
80 Oszkár Betlen, "A nemzetiségek Magyarországon," [The nationalities in Hungary], *Társadalmi Szemle* , no. 2 (1946): 117.
81 Miklós Vásárhelyi, "A párisi békekonferencia eredményei," [The results of the Paris Peace Conference], *Társadalmi Szemle* 1, no. 11 (1946): 812–813.
82 *Szabad Nép,* October 1, 1946.

83 *Ibid.*, October 3, 1946.
84 *Ibid.*, October 11, 1946.
85 *Ibid.*, November 11, 1946.
86 *Ibid.*, November 20, 1946.
87 *Ibid.*, November 21, 1946.
88 *Ibid.*, May 4, 1947.
89 See, for example, Oszkár Betlen, "A nemzetiségek Magyarorszagon," p. 117.
90 See Piotr Wandycz, "The Soviet System of Alliances," *Journal of Central European Affairs,* 16, no. 2 (July 1956): 177–189, Zbigniew Brzezinski, *The Soviet Bloc* (New York: Praeger Publishers, 1966.).
91 See, for example, *Scânteia, Szabad Nép,* January 24, 1948.
92 See, for example, Robert R. King, *Minorities Under Communism* (Cambridge: Harvard University Press, 1973), ch. 2–3.

Footnotes to Chapter II

1 Imre Nagy, *On Communism* (New York: Praeger Publishers, 1957).
2 Elisabeta Petreanu, "Activitatea Internaţională a României Între 1948–1965 (I)" [Romania's International Activities between 1948–1965], *Revista de Istorie,* 31, no. 8 (1978): 1347–1348.
3 *Scânteia,* December 12, 1948.
4 See, for example, *Szabad Nép,* December 25, 1948.
5 *Scânteia,* January 7, 1949.
6 See the analysis in the *samizdat* report from Transylvania, György Lázár, "Jelentés Erdélyböl" [Reportage from Transylvania], in *Irodalmi Ujság* (Paris), March–April 1977.
7 *Szabad Nép,* March 25, 1949.
8 George Schöpflin, *The Hungarians of Romania* (London: Minority Rights Group, Report No. 37), p. 9.
9 For the most comprehensive descriptions of the Romanian purges see Stephen Fischer–Galati, *The New Romania: From People's Democracy to Socialist Republic* (Cambridge, Mass.: MIT Press, 1967), ch. 2; Ghiţă Ionescu, *Communism in Romania 1944–1962* (London: Oxford Unviersity Press, 1962), ch. 9; Robert R. King, *History of the Romanian Communist Party* (Stanford, Calif.: Hoover Institution Press, 1980).
10 *The Hungarian Minority in Romania,* Radio Free Europe, 1959, p. 17.
11 King, *Minorities Under Communism,* p. 149.
12 *Szabad Nép,* July 20, 1952.

13 *The Hungarian Minority in Romania.*
14 *Szabad Nép*, July 20, 1952.
15 *Magyar Hirlap*, February 21, 1972.
16 *Szabad Nép*, November 2, 1954.
17 Mihály Czine, "Az újabb romániai Magyar irodalomról" [On the contemporary Hungarian literature in Romania], *Valóság*, no. 1 (1970): 74–76.
18 For some of these contacts see, *Szabad Nép*, April 14, 1954; see also Elemér Illyés, *National Minorities in Romania—Change in Transylvania* (Boulder, Colo.: East European Monographs, 1982).
19 Robert R. King, "Eastern Europe," in *Protection of Ethnic Minorities*, p. 94.
20 *Új Szó*, December 22, 1953, also quoted in János Ölvendi, *Magyarok Szlovákiában* [Hungarians in Slovakia], Uj Látóhatár, no. 6 (1961).
21 *Új Szó*, June 5, 1951.
22 *Magyarok Csehszlovákiában*, p. 217.
23 *Ibid.*, p. 221.
24 *Ibid.*, 220.
25 Arató, *Tanulmányok a Szlovákiai. . ..* p. 355.
26 For details on the activities of CSEMADOK, see Radio Free Europe, Czechoslovak Situation Report 6, June 4, 1987.
27 Arató, *Tanulmányok a Szlovákiai . . .*, pp. 356–357.
28 *Ibid.* p. 357.
29 *Kritika*, no. 12 (1973), pp. 5–6.
30 On the state of Hungarian culture in Slovakia at the time see, András Görömbei, *A Csehszlovákiai Magyar Irodalom 1945-1980* [The Hungarian Literature in Czechoslovakia] (Budapest: Akadémiai Kiadó, 1982). Fábry's fate is treated in numerous reviews of the book, for example in *Tiszatáj*, no. 1 (1984).
31 Quoted in András Károly, "Egy szálingben—Magyar írók magyar irodalom Csehszlovákiaban" [In a shirt—Hungarian writers, Hungarian literature in Czechoslovakia], *Új Látóhatár*, no. 2 (1982).
32 *Magyarok Csehszlovákiában*, p. 243.
33 Arató, *Tanulmányok a Szlovákiai*, p. 341.
34 For some of CSEMADOK's activities in the fifties, see *István Révay*, "A Csehszlovákiai Magyarság Élete 1959-ben." [The life of the Hungarians in Czechoslovakia in 1959], part I, II *Katolikus Szemle*, no. 2, 3 (1960).
35 *Új Szó*, March 18, 1954.
36 *Ibid.*, April 23, 1955.

37   *Magyarok Csehszlovákiában,* p. 245.
38   Arató, *Tanulmányok a Szlovákiai,* p. 245.

Footnotes for Chapter III

1   *Szabad Nép,* September 9, 1956.
2   Andrew Ludanyi, "The Revolution and the Fate of the Hungarians in Neighboring States," Béla K. Király, Barbara Lotze, and Nándor F. Dreisziger (eds.), *The First War Between Socialist States: The Hungarian Revolution of 1956 and Its Impact* (War and Society in East Central Europe, vol. XI (New York: Social Science Monographs, Brooklyn College Press, 1984), p. 400.
3   *Hungarians in Czechoslovakia* (New York: Research Institute for Minority Studies, 1959), p. 90.
4   See Stephen Fischer–Galati, "The Revolution and the Hungarian Question in Romania," Béla K. Király et al. (eds.), *The First War between Socialist States.*
5   *Scânteia,* November 7, 1956.
6   *Ibid.*
7   *Scânteia,* December 22, 1956.
8   *Új Szó,* October 30, 1956.
9   See, for example, *Newsweek,* November 11, 1956.
10   Ludanyi, *The First War between Socialist States,* pp. 397–399.
11   *Népakarat,* May 24, 1957.
12   *Népszabadság,* August 22, 1957.
13   *Népszabadság,* September 22, 1957.
14   *Ibid.,* October 27, 1957.
15   *Élet és Irodalom,* May 10, 1957.
16   *Népakarat,* August 24, 1957.
17   *Népszabadság,* November 9, 1957.
18   *Ibid.,* February 27, 1958.
19   *Népszabadság,* February 27, 1958.
20   *Ibid.,* March 4, 1958.
21   Ferenc Baktai in *Népakarat,* March 30, 1958.
22   Dániel Csatári, *Román–Magyar Kapcsolatok,* [Hungarian–Romanian Relations] (Budapest: Kossuth, 1958).
23   *Népszabadság,* December 10, 1958.

Footnotes to Chapter IV

1   George Schöpflin, "National Minorities in Eastern Europe" (Facts on File, 1986).
2   *Scînteia,* February 20, 1959, see also, Ionescu, *Communism in Romania.*

3 Miklós Tomka, "A kisebbségek Jugoszláviában" [The minorities in Yugoslavia], *Valósag*, no. 9 (1969), p. 106.

4 *The Times* (London), June 24, 1959.

5 *The New York Times*, June 11, 1959.

6 *TASS*, March 26, 1959, quoted in *East Europe* 8, no. 5 (1959): 42–43.

7 *Népszabadság*, August 23, 1959.

8 See, for example, the editorials in *Népszabadság* and *Magyar Nemzet*, August 23, 1960.

9 King, *Minorities under Communism*, pp. 156–157.

10 Radio Budapest, December 24, 1960, in *REF Monitoring*, December 24, 1960.

11 *Csongrád Megyei Hirlap*, January 3, 1961.

12 King, *Minorities under Communism*, p. 157.

13 This viewpoint is presented in Révay István, "A nemzeti kérdés éve 1968" [1968—The Year of the National Question] *Katolikus Szemle*, XXI, no. 4 (1969): 311.

14 *Élet es Irodalom*, September 16, 1961.

15 See Elemér Illyés, "Education and National Minorities in Contemporary Romania," *Transylvania–The Roots of Ethnic Conflict*, pp. 245–268; see also Elemér Illyés, *National Minorities in Romania*.

16 For such reports see, for example, George Bailey, "Trouble over Transylvania," *The Reporter*, November 1964: 25–30.

17 Quoted by Elek Telegdi, "Position of the Hungarian Minority in Romania," *The Review* (Brussels), 5, no. 2 (1963).

18 Quoted in István Révay, "Az Erdélyi helyzet" [The situation in Transylvania], *Katolikus Szemle* 18, no. 3 (1966).

19 See, for example, David Binder, "Romanian National Feelings Rise," *The New York Times*, July 16, 1964, and Thomas Schreiber, "La situation de la minorité Hongroise en Roumanie," *Le Monde*, July 26, 1964.

20 *RFE*—Item 1481/64.

21 *RFE—Hungarian Situation Report*, February 18, 1964. For other aspects of Romania's rift with the Comecon, see John Michael Montias, "Background and Origins of the Romanian Dispute with Comecon," *Soviet Studies* 16, no. 2 (October 1964): 125–151, Randolph L. Braham, "Romania and the Comecon 1960–1963)" *The Journal of Social Sciences*, XXI, no. 1 (Winter 1966): 3–18, James F. Brown, "Romania Steps Out of Line," *Survey*, no. 49 (October 1963).

22 See *RFE—Hungarian Situation Report*, February 18, 1964.

23 The criticism was leveled against B. V. Ushakov's work "On the Foreign Policy of Hitlerite Germany," *Anale de Istorie*, no. 6 (1962).

24 *Népszabadság*, August 23, 1964.

25 For various analyses of the April 1964 Statement see, Ghiţă Ionescu, "Communist Romania and Nonalignment," *Slavic Review* 24, no. 2 (June 1965): 241–257; Graeme J. Gill, "Romania: Background to Autonomy," *Survey* 21, no. 3 (Summer 1975): 94–113.

26 Peter Pastor, "Official Nationalism in Hungary Since 1964," George W. Simmons (ed.), *Nationalism in the USSR and Eastern Europe in the Era of Brezhnev and Kosygin* (Detroit: University of Detroit Press, 1976).

27 For some Hungarian press reports, see *East Europe*, 13, no. 6 (1964).

28 Kállai's speeech in *Társadalmi Szemle*, no. 7 (1964), *Népszabadság*, June 25, 1964; for aspects of Hungarian foreign policy, see William F. Robinson, *The Pattern of Reform in Hungary* (New York: Praeger Publishers, 1973).

29 *RFE—Hungarian Situation Report*, July 7, 1964.

30 *Népszabadság*, July 28, 1964.

31 See *Pravda*, October 25, 1964. The article was published on the occasion of the Romanian Army Day.

32 *Népszabadság*, January 24, 1965.

33 For some aspects of Romania's foreign policy in the Balkans, see Aurel Braun, *Romanian Foreign Policy Since 1965* (New York: Praeger Publishers, 1978).

34 See "An alternative foreign policy for Hungary," *RFE—Hungarian Research*, March 29, 1966; see also William F. Robinson, "Hungary's Turn to Revisionism," *East Europe*, 16, no. 9 (1967): 14–17.

35 *Népszabadság*, December 13, 1964.

36 *Tiszatáj*, no. 3 (March 1966).

37 *Pravda*, July 21, 1965.

38 The two were Jenö Fock and József Sándor, see *Scînteia*, July 18, 1965.

39 See, for example, Kállai's article in *Népszabadság*, January 16, 1965.

40 *Csongrád Megyei Hirlap*, January 19, 1966.

41 On Maurer's visit see, *Hungary 1967* (Budapest: Pannonia, 1967), p. 256.

42 For the Hungarian version of the speech, see *Népszabadság*, March 5, 1966.

43 Robert R. King, *Minorities under Communism*, p. 171.

44 See Stephen Fischer–Galati, "The continuation of nationalism in Romanian historiography," *Nationality Papers*, VI, no. 2 (1978), pp. 179–184.

45 See the discussion on aspects of Romanian nationalism and historiography in George Schöpflin, "Romanian Nationalism," *Survey*, 20, no. 2/3 (Spring–Summer 1974),pp. 77–104.

46 Among the analyses presenting this view, see François Fejtö, *A History of the People's Democracies* (London: Penguin Books, 1974), p. 163.

47 For the elaboration of the Romanian view, see Stephen Fischer–Galati, "The Romanians and the Habsburg Monarchy," *Austrian History Yearbook III* (1967), part II, pp. 430–439.

48 For an overall view of Hungarian historiography's position, see Imre Gonda, "Problems of the Austro–Hungarian Monarchy," *Magyar Tudomány*, no. 10 (1964).

49 *Ibid.*, p. 11.

50 The Hungarian position is also summed up in Zoltán Horváth, "After–Thoughts on the Habsburg Monarchy," *The New Hungarian Quarterly*, 5, no. 16 (1964).

51 *Esti Hirlap*, May 6, 1964.

52 *Contemporanul*, May 29, 1964.

53 See, for example, Péter Hanák, "Problems of East European History," *East European Quarterly*, 1, no. 2 (1967), pp. 136–139; see also Robert R. King, *Minorities under Communism*, ch. 9.

54 László Kövágó, "The events of the 1918 Revolution in the works of Czechoslovak, Yugoslav, and Romanian historians," *Valóság*, no. 10 (1966).

55 Andrei Oteţea, P. Schwann, and Karl Marx: *Insemnări Despre Români* (Bucharest: Editura Academiei R. P. R., 1964).

56 See, for example, Aladár Mód, "The Significance of the National Question," *Új Irás*, no. 5 (1966); see also Andrew C. János, "Nationalism and Communism in Hungary," *East European Quarterly*, V, no. 1 (1971), pp. 74–101.

57 For the Hungarian and Romanian perceptions at the time see Gabriel Fischer, "Nationalism and Internationalism in Hungary and Romania," *Canadian Slavonic Papers*, X, no. 1 (1968), pp. 26–41.

58 *Népszabadság*, October 22, 1966.

59 *Ibid.*, October 8, 1966; see also the discussion in George Barany, "Hungary: from Aristocratic to Proletarian Nationalism," Peter F. Sugar and Ivo L. Lederer (eds.), *Nationalism in Eastern*

Europe (Seattle: University of Washington Press, 1971), pp. 307–309.

60 *Scînteia,* October 8, 1966.

61 *Elet és Irodalom,* May 21, 1966.

62 *Népszabadság,* August 2, 1966.

63 George Schöpflin, *National Minorities in Eastern Europe,* p. 310.

64 See, for example, in *Elöre,* August 16, 1966.

65 *Ibid.*

66 Robert R. King, *History of the Romanian Communist Party,* p. 131.

67 For some aspects of Romania's nationality policy see, Trond Gilberg, *Modernization in Romania Since World War II* (New York: Praeger Publishers, 1975); Trond Gilberg, "Modernization, Human Rights and Nationalism: The Case of Romania," G. Klein and M. J. Reban (eds.), *The Politics of Ethnicity in Eastern Europe* (New York: Columbia University Press, 1981).

68 *Kritika,* no. 1 (1965), p. 58.

69 Mihály Czine in *Valóság,* no. 1 (1970), pp. 74–76.

70 See *Kritika,* no. 6 (1966), pp. 32–35.

71 Paul Lendvai in *Die Presse* (Vienna), August 6, 1966; see also *The New York Times,* May 14, 1966.

72 Quoted in Radio Free Europe, Hungarian Situation Report, May 30, 1967.

73 *Magyar Nemzet,* October 15, 1967.

74 See *Népszabadság, Magyar Nemzet,* August 23, 1967.

75 *Pravda,* September 17, 1967.

76 For some commentaries on the Romanian walkout see, "Romania Does It Again," *New Statesman,* March 8, 1968; George Urban, "Divisions deepen," *Communist Affairs,* no. 1 (1968), p. 10.

77 *Népszava,* March 5, 1968.

78 Radio Budapest quoted in *East Europe,* no. 5 (1968).

79 János Kádár, *For a Socialist Hungary* (Budapest: Corvina, 1954), p. 54.

80 Robert R. King, *Minorities Under Communism.*

81 *Ibid.*

82 *Ibid.*

83 George Schöpflin, "National Minorities Under Communism," in Kurt London (ed.), *Eastern Europe in Transition* (Baltimore: John Hopkins Press, 1966), pp. 126–127.

84 Milan J. Reban, "Czechoslovakia: The New Federation," George Klein and Milan J. Reban, *The Politics of Ethnicity in Eastern Europe,* p. 224.

85 Arató, *Tanulmányok a Szlovákiai Magyarok,* p. 359.

[86] For an analysis of the changes, see Robert R. King, *Minorities Under Communism*, p. 112.

[87] Arató, p. 359.

[88] *Új Szó*, May 12, 1960, see also János Ölvendi, *Új Látóhatár*, no. 6 (1961).

[89] *Új Szó*, February 24, 1959.

[90] *Pravda* (Bratislava) April 15, 1962, quoted in George Schöpflin, *National Minorities Under Communism*, p. 140.

[91] Ölvendi in *Új Látóhatár*, no. 6 (1961), George Schöpflin, *National Minorities Under Communism*, p. 128, *Új Szó*, July 8, 1961.

[92] *Magyarok Csehszlovákiában*, p. 240.

[93] *Új Szó*, August 1, 1959, also quoted in István Révay, *Katolikus Szemle*, no. 2 (1960).

[94] *Magyarok Csehszlovákiaban*, p. 240.

[95] Robert R. King, "Eastern Europe," *Protection of Ethnic Minorities*, p. 95.

[96] *Új Szó*, May 18, 1964.

[97] Arató, p. 359.

[98] *Kulturny Zivot*, no. 24 (June 1965), quoted in Radio Free Europe, Czechoslovak Situation Report, February 28, 1979.

[99] Kalman Janics, *Czechoslovak Policy*, p. 215.

[100] Arató, p. 350.

[101] Quoted in *Kritika*, no. 2 (1965).

[102] *Ibid.*

[103] *Népszabadság*, October 3, 1964.

[104] *Ibid.*, October 15, 1967.

[105] István Révay in *Katolikus Szemle*, no. 3 (1969).

[106] *Magyarok Csehszlovákiában*, p. 243.

[107] *Kritika*, no. 2 (1965).

[108] For the Hungarian–Slovak polemic, see Robert R. King, *Minorities Under Communism*, pp. 176–186.

Footnotes to Chapter V

[1] George Schöpflin, "Hungary: An Uneasy Stability," Archie Brown and Jack Gray (eds.), *Political Culture and Change in Communist Systems* (London: Macmillan, 1979), p. 145.

[2] William F. Robinson, *The Pattern of Reform in Hungary*, pp. 299–300.

[3] Robinson, pp. 298–301; also see *Népujsag*, October 26, 1967

[4] *Élet és Irodalom*, March 30, 1968.

[5] See, for example, *Magyar Nemzet*, May 11, 1968.

6   *Népszabadság*, May 12, 1968.

7   *Élet és Irodalom*, May 18, 1968.

8   János Szász in *Gazeta Literară*, July 25, 1968.

9   *Népszabadság*, December 31, 1967.

10 These views were expressed in several articles in the summer 1968 issue of *Uj Symposion*.

11 *Magyar Hirlap*, April 5, 1969.

12 Robert R. King, *Minorities Under Communism*, p. 120.

13 Arató, *Tanulmányok a Szlovákiai*, p. 364, see also Elemér Hommonay, "The Hungarians in the Communist Successor States Since 1964," in George Simmons, *Nationalism in the USSR and Eastern Europe*, pp. 421–422.

14 Robert R. King, "Eastern Europe," in *Protection of Ethnic Minorities*, p. 95. *Magyarok Csehszlovákiában*, pp. 265–266.

15 Hommonay, p. 421, *Új Szó*, March 27, 1968.

16 *Ibid.*, April 27, 1968.

17 Arató, p. 364.

18 *Magyarok Csehszlovákiában*, p. 270.

19 *Pravda*, (Bratislava), May 17, 1968.

20 *Praca*, May 21, 1968 cited in *Magyarok Csehszlovákiában*, p. 269.

21 Robert R. King, *Minorities Under Communism*, p. 121.

22 *Népszabadság*, June 15, 1968, for some aspects of Hungarian–Czechoslovak relations, see Bennet Kovrig, *Communism in Hungary, From Kun to Kádár* (Stanford: Hoover Institution Press, 1979), p. 410.

23 Robert R. King, *Minorities Under Communism*, p. 119.

24 For some assessments of Hungary's policies and public attitudes to the invasion, see "Hungary—What now?" Radio Free Europe, Hungarian Research Report, no. 18, October 28, 1968; Rudolf Tőkés, "Hungarian Intellectuals' Reaction to the Invasion of Czechoslovakia," E. J. Czerwinski, Jaroslav Piekalkiewicz, *The Soviet Invasion of Czechoslovakia* (New York: Praeger Publishers, 1973), pp. 134–154.

25 "Hungary—What now?" *ibid.*

26 *Népszabadság*, August 30, 1968 and *Új Szó's* reply, September 10, 1968.

27 See, for example, in *Társadalmi Szemle*, no. 8–9 (1968).

28 *Népszabadság*, September 27, 1968.

29 Arató, p. 367.

30 Robert R. King, "Eastern Europe," in *Protection of Ethnic Minorities* p. 96; see also Milan J. Reban, "Czechoslovakia: The New Federation," in George Klein, *The Politics of Ethnicity in Eastern Europe*, pp. 215–246.

31 CSEMADOK was readmitted into the Slovak National Council in 1987.
32 Arató, p. 365.
33 George Schöpflin, *National Minorities in Eastern Europe*, p. 310.
34 George Schöpflin, "The Hungarians in Romania," p. 10; see also Elemér Illyés, *National Minorities in Romania*, p. 129.
35 *Scînteia*, August 24, 1968.
36 *Esti Hirlap*, August 24, 1968.
37 See, for example, *Magyar Hirlap*, August 24, 1968.
38 *Magyar Nemzet*, August 24, 1968.
39 *Esti Hirlap*, August 24, 1968.
40 *Népszabadság*, August 27, 1968.
41 *Ibid.*, August 29, 1968.
42 *Le Monde*, August 31, 1968.
43 See Radio Free Europe, Hungarian Situation Report 75, November 14, 1968.
44 *MagyarNemzet*, October 8, 1968.
45 See Ala Yazkova, "Imperialism and Eastern Europe," *New Times*, November 29, 1968.
46 *Népszabadság*, December 5, 1968.
47 *Ibid.*, February 16, 1969.
48 For the council's role according to the official Romanian view, see Eduard Eisenburger, *Egalitate Reală, Participare Activă* [Real Equality, Active Participation] (Bucharest: Editura Politică, 1978), Full Harmony and Equality between the Romanian People and the Coinhabiting Nationalities (n.d.); see also Michael Shafir, *Romania—Politics, Economics, Society* (London: Frances Pinter, 1985), pp. 158–168; Trond Gilberg, "Ethnic Minorities in Romania under Socialism," B. L. Faber (ed.), *The Social Structure of Eastern Europe* (New York: Praeger Publishers, 1976).
49 *Scînteia*, September 2, 1968.
50 *Népszabadság*, January 11, 1969.
51 *Magyar Hirlap*, July 16, 1968 in Radio Free Europe, Hungarian Press Survey no. 1940.
52 *Valóság*, no. 9 (1968).
53 Tomka's review also included some references to this effect on Romania's nationality policy.
54 *Magyar Szó*, August 26, 1968, also cited in *Hungary—What Now?* Radio Free Europe, Hungarian Research Report 18, October 26, 1968.
55 *Népszabadság*, August 27, 1968.
56 *Magyar Szó*, August 29, 1968.

Footnotes to Chapter VI

1 László Kövagó, it Nemzetizégek a mai Magyarországon (Budapest: Kossuth, 1981), p. 46; see also, Raphael Vago, "Nationality Policies in Contemporary Hungary," *Hungarian Studies Review*, XI, no. 1 (Spring 1984), pp. 43–60.

2 For a characteristic reference to the total number of 450,000, see for example, *MTI*, January 23, 1985 in *Summary of World Broadcasts*, Eastern Europe of the BBC (SWB/EE), January 26, 1985.

3 László Tripolszky, "Promoting Ethnic Culture," *The New Hungarian Quarterly* XXI, no. 77 (Spring 1980), p. 133.

4 Ivan Volgyes, "Legitimacy and Modernization: Nationality and Nationalism in Hungary and Transylvania," George Klein, *The Politics of Ethnicity in Eastern Europe*, p. 140; *Tripolszky*, p. 133.

5 Volgyes, p. 140.

6 Ferenc Herczeg in *The New Hungarian Quarterly*, no. 7 (1978), p. 91.

7 *Ibid.*, p. 91.

8 For a discussion on postwar Hungarian Jewry, see András Kovács, "The Jewish Question in Contemporary Hungary" in Randolph L. Braham and Bela Vago (eds.), *The Holocaust in Hungary: Forty Years Later*, (East European Monographs, 1985), pp. 205–232.

9 Ferenc Herczeg, p. 89.

10 László Kövágó, *Nemzetiségek a mai*, p. 39.

11 Ferenc Herczeg, p. 90.

12 *Magyarország*, May 4, 1980.

13 Ferenc Herczeg, p. 94.

14 *Magyarország*, May 4, 1980.

15 Oszkár Betlen, "A nemzetisegek Magyarországon," *Társadalmi Szemle*, 1, no. 2 (1946), p. 116 [The Nationalities in Hungary].

16 László Kövágó, "Népköztársaságunk nemzetiségi politikájáról" [On the nationality policy of our People's Republic], *Társadalmi Szemle* 11, no. 11 (1968), p. 31; see also László Kövágó, "A szocialista nemzetiség politika kialakitásának útjan," *Párttörténeti Közlemények*, XXVI, no. 3 (1980) [The development of the Socialist nationality policy].

17 László Kövágó, *A szocialista nemzetiségpolitika*, p. 78.

18 Martin L. Kovács, *National Minorities in Hungary*, pp.162–163.

19 Lázló Kövágó, *A szocialista nemzetiségpolitika*, p. 85.

20 *Ibid.*

21 On the Romanians in Hungary, see Radio Free Europe, Hungarian Situation Report/5, April 28, 1986.

22 *Magyarország*, May 4, 1980.

23 Ferenc Herczeg, "Nemzetisegi politikánk eredményei és feladatai" [The results and tasks of our nationality policy], *Pártélet*, no. 4 (1978), p. 39.

24 See Radio Free Europe, Hungarian Situation Report/1, January 1984.

25 László Kövágó, *A szocialista nemzetiségpolitika*, p. 85.

26 *Nemzetiségi kérdés–nemzetiségi politika* [Nationality question–nationality policy] (Budapest: Kossuth, 1968).

27 *Ibid.*

28 László Kósa, "Status of Minorities in Hungary," *Valóság*, no. 4 (April 1969), in Radio Free Europe, Hungarian Press Survey no. 2036, August 20, 1969. For a discussion on the status of the minorities in Hungry, see also Martin L. Kovács, "National Minorities in Hungary, 1919–1980," Stephan M. Horak, *Eastern European National Minorities 1919–1980* (Littleton, Colorado: Libraries Unlimited, 1985).

29 Kövágó László, "Népköztársaságunk nemzetiségi politikájáról [On the nationality policy of our People's Republic], *Társadalmi Szemle*, no. 11 (1968).

30 Tripolszky, *Promoting Ethnic Culture*, p. 136.

31 On problems of bilingualism, see Martin L. Kovács, National Minorities in Hungary, Herczeg, p. 95.

32 Tripolszky, *Promoting Ethnic Culture*, p. 132.

33 Kósa, *Status of Minorities in Hungary.*

34 Ivan Volgyes, *Legitimation and Modernization*, p. 142.

35 *Magyar Nemzet*, January 21, 1981.

36 Radio Budapest in English in *SWB/EE*, February 2, 1985.

37 László Kövágó, "Public Education for Ethnic Minorities," *Kortárs*, March 1973, Radio Free Europe, Hungarian Press Survey no. 2288, June 15, 1973.

38 *MTI* in English, January 19, 1985 in *SWB/EE*, January 26, 1985.

39 Martin L. Kovács, *National Minorities in Hungary.*

40 *TANJUG* in English, January 25, 1985 in *SWB/EE*, February 2, 1985.

41 *MTI*, January 24, 1985 in *SWB/EE*, January 26, 1985.

42 *MTI*, January 22, 1985 in *SWB/EE*, January 25, 1985, on the Romanian minority in Hungary; see also, Hungary's Treatment of Its Ethnic Minorities, Radio Free Europe, Hungarian Situation Report/5, April 28, 1986.

43 *Pravda* (Bratislava), September 23, 1983 in Foreign Broadcast Information Service (FBIS), Daily Report (DR), Eastern Europe (EE), October 7, 1983.

44 For reports from the Conference, see *Tiszatáj*, no. 11 (1984).

45 See Ethnic Minorities Encouraged to Assert Identity, Radio Free Europe, Hungarian Situation Report/6, March 8, 1978.

46 Radio Free Europe, Hungarian Stiuation Report, July 22, 1976.

47 *Népszabadság*, November 27, 1983.

48 *Dunántúli Napló*, October 31, 1978.

49 *Együtt a nemzetiségekkel*, p. 74.

50 *Nemzetiségi kérdés–nemzetiségi politika*, p. 10.

51 Ferenc Herzceg, p.93.

52 Kádár at the Twelfth Congress of the HSWP, *SWB/EE*, March 26, 1980.

53 Lászó Kővágó, *Nemzetiségek a mai Magyarországon*, p. 168.

54 George Schöpflin, *Hungary an Uneasy Stability* p. 145.

55 László Kővágó, *Nemzetiségek a mai Magyarországon*, p. 172.

56 *Ibid.*, p. 172.

57 *Népszabadság*, December 4, 1985.

58 *MTI*, October 12, 1977 in *FBIS–DR/EE*, October 15, 1977.

59 László Kővágó, *Nemzetiségek a mai Magyarországon*.

60 *SWB/EE*, March 26, 1980, *Le Monde* March 26, 1980; also see László Ribansky, Nationalities in Hungary: Few in Number But Pampered, Radio Free Europe, RAD Background Report/259, October 28, 1980.

61 László Kővágó, *Nemzetiségek a mai Magyarországon*.

62 *Békés Megyei Népujság*, March 30, 1960.

63 *Ibid.*, April 19, 1969.

64 *Ibid.*, February 16, 1971.

65 *Népszaa*, October 26, 1973.

66 Radio Free Europe, Hungarian Situation Report/10, April 19, 1978, citing Világgazdaság, March 17, 1978.

67 *Magyar Nemzet*, April 19, 1983.

68 See *Népszabadság, Elöre, Scînteia*, June 19, 1977.

69 *Népszabadság*, November 20, 1984; also see Radio Free Europe, Romanian Situation Report/16, December 29, 1984.

70 *Ibid.*

71 György Aczél, "The challenge of our change," *The New Hungarian Quarterly*, no. 90 (1983), p. 23.

72 Joó Rudolf, "Nemzetiségi Kérdés" in *Együtt a nemzetiségekkel*, p. 355.

73 *Ibid.*, p. 355.

74 László Kővágó, *Nemzetiségek a mai Magyarországon*, pp. 28–41.

75 For a discussion on Romania's nationality policy, see Shafir, *Romania*, p. 158.

76 *Kommunist* (Belgrade), July 22, 1974.

77 *Magyar Szó*, August 18, 1974.

78 Radio Free Europe, Hungarian Situation Report/49, November 28, 1975.

79 *Népszabadság* November 4, 1975.

80 See Radio Free Europe, Hungarian Situation Report/9, August 14, 1987.

Footnotes for Chapter VII

1 William F. Robinson, *Pattern of Reform in Hungary*, p. 301.

2 "Hungarians in the World—A Conversation with József Bognár," *The New Hungarian Quarterly*, 19, no. 69 (1978), pp. 98–99.

3 János Gosztonyi, "Hungarians at home and abroad," *The New Hungarian Quarterly*, no. 69 (1978), p. 19.

4 For reports on some of the conferences, see Radio Free Europe, Hungarian Situation Report 28, August 7, 1973, RFE/HSR 28, August 24, 1977.

5 Gosztonyi, p. 18.

6 Károly Nagy, "Gondolatok hüközvetitése," *Kortárs*, no. 3 (1978), pp. 473–474.

7 *Ibid.*, p. 474.

8 Radio Budapest, August 3, 1981, in *SWB/EE*, August 5, 1981.

9 Schöpflin, *Hungary: An Uneasy Stability*, p. 144.

10 Gosztonyi, p. 19.

11 For parts of Aczél's speech, see *The New Hungarian Quarterly*, no. 52 (1973), pp. 73–74.

12 *Népszabadság*, October 29, 1986; see also Radio Free Europe, Hungarian Situation Report/12, November 21, 1986. For characteristic accusations in the Hungarian emigre press that the Kádár regime is to blame, see for example issues of *Irodalmi Ujság*.

13 Radio Budapest, August 3, 1981, in *SWB/EE*, August 5, 1981.

14 *Mozgó Világ*, June 1986, pp. 4–17.

15 Radio Budapest, November 14, 1985, in *FBIS-DR/EE*, November 15, 1985.

16 Radio Budapest, January 25, 1988 in *SWB/EE*, January 28, 1988.

17 Lászlo Ujlaki in *Népszabadság*, January 11, 1988.

18 *Magyar Nemzet*, February 1, 1986; also reported by *MTI*, February 1, 1986 in *SWB/EE*, February 24, 1986.

[19] See Radio Free Europe, Hungarian Situation Report 1, January 31, 1987.

[20] On the Monor meeting, see Radio Free Europe, RAD Background, February 24, 1986.

[21] *Review of International Affairs* (Belgrade) February 20, 1977.

[22] "Model Neighbors," *Review of Intenational Affairs*, July 20, 1987.

[23] *TANJUG*, January 31, 1977 in *FBIS-DR/EE*, February 1, 1977.

[24] See Zdenko Antic, "Yugoslavia's Position on the Minority Issue," Radio Free Europe, RAD Background Report/289, December 1983.

[25] See Hungarian Minority in Yugoslavia, Radio Free Europe, RAD Background Report/252, December 1, 1982.

[26] See Vojvodina, *A Paradise for National Minorities?*

[27] Andrew Ludanyi, "Titoist Integration of Yugoslavia: The Partisan Myth and the Hungarians of the Vojvodina, 1945–1975," *Polity* 12, no. 2 (1979), p. 248.

[28] Pedro Ramet, *Nationalism and Federalism in Yugoslavia 1963–1983* (Bloomington, Indiana: Indiana University Press, 1984), p. 168.

[29] *Ibid.*, p. 168.

[30] Ludanyi, *Titoist Integration*, p. 249.

[31] *TANJUG*, September 14, 1981 in *SWB/EE*, September 17. 1981.

[32] Remarks made by Gen. (ret.) Rudolf Jontovics, who served as the political commissar of the Petöfi Brigade, the remarks made in March 1985, see Radio Free Europe, Hungarian Situation Report/4, April 6, 1985.

[33] *Frankfurter Rundschau*, December 21, 1982.

[34] Illyés's accusations were one of the rare comments made in Hungary to the effect that the Yugoslavs are pursuing a policy of "de–Magyarization."

[35] See Radio Free Europe, Situation Report/4, March 2, 1983.

[36] *Ibid.*, April 6, 1985.

[37] *Ibid.*, March 2, 1983.

[38] *Politika*, February 21, 1983, cited in *ibid.*, March 2, 1983.

[39] Hommonay, *The Hungarians in the Successor States*, p. 430.

[40] Andrew Ludanyi, *Titoist Integration*, p. 230.

[41] For a review on the issue, see Polemics over the Wartime Role of the Hungarians in Yugoslavia, Radio Free Europe, RAD Background Report/281, December 29, 1983.

[42] *Socialist Thought and Practice*, no.3–4 (1987), p. 128.

[43] Andrew Ludanyi, *Titoist Integration*, p. 250.

[44] On some of the activities of the Hungarian Chair, see *Hommonay*, p. 430.

45 Pedro Ramet, *Nationalism and Federalism*, p. 122.

46 Andrew Ludanyi, *Titoist Integration*, p. 251, *Uj Symposion*, no. 8 (1971).

47 Pedro Ramet, *Nationalism and Federalism*, p. 122, Hommonay, p. 431.

48 *Magyar Szó*, May 12, 1983, cited in Radio Free Europe, Hungarian Situation Report/8, May 30, 1983.

49 István Széli, *A magyar kultúra útjai Jugoszláviában* [The Paths of Hungarian Culture in Yugoslavia] (Budapest: Kossuth, 1983).

50 See, for example, József M. Pásztor, "A jugoszláviai magyar kultúra" [The Hungarian Culture in Yugoslavia], *Könyvilág*, no. 4 (1983).

51 *Politika*, June 23, 1983, cited in Radio Free Europe, Hungarian Situation Report/10, July 11, 1983.

52 *Vecernje Novosti*, June 23, 1983, cited in Radio Free Europe.

53 See, for example, *Népszabadság*, May 20, 1983.

54 "Model Neighbors," *Review of International Affairs*, July 20, 1987.

55 The Yugoslav media criticized an article in *Népszabadság*, April 9, 1981.

56 See, for example, the visit of Yugoslav Premier Veselin Djuranovic in Hungary in July 1980, as reported in *Népszabadság*, July 16, 1980.

57 *Népszabadság*, December 11, 1985.

58 Joó Rudolf, "A joint Hungarian–Slovene research report concerning the situation of rural national minorities," *Canadian Review of Studies in Nationalism*, XIII, no. 2 (1986), pp. 271–274.

59 *Tanjug*, March 30, 1985, cited in Radio Free Europe, Hungarian Situation Report/4, April 6, 1985.

60 Beszélö, cited in *ibid*.

61 Hommonay, p. 431.

62 "Model Neighbors," *Review of International Affairs*, July 20, 1987.

63 See *NIN*, May 19, 1985; *Politika*, August 1, 1985. On the deep differences between Romania's and Yugoslavia's nationality policies, see Andrew Ludanyi, "Socialist Patriotism and National Minorities: A Comparison of the Yugoslav and Romanian Theory and Practice," Steven Bela Vardy and Agnes Huszar Vardy (eds.), *Society in Change—Studies in Honor of Béla K. Király* (Boulder, Colo: East European Monographs, 1983), pp. 557–583.

64 *Vjesnik*, February 24, 1986.

65 *Românîa Literarâ*, May 29, 1986.

[66] See, for example, *Scînteia,* November 11, 1981.

[67] *NIN,* January 4, 1987.

[68] Cited in Radio Free Europe, Hungarian Situation Report/1, January 31, 1987.

[69] Quoted in *Új Szó,* January 17, 1986, in Joint Publications Research Service, East Europe Report (JPRS/EER), April 10, 1986. See also E. Fehér Pál's article on Zvara's studies, *Népszabadság,* April 3, 1983.

[70] See George Schöpflin,*National Minorities in Eastern Europe,* p. 305.

[71] *Új Szó,* January 17, 1986.

[72] *Ibid.*

[73] For details of Duray's activities, see Mary Hrabik Samal, "The Case of Miklos Duray," *Cross Currents,* 4 (1985), pp. 39–45.

[74] *Ibid.* p. 42. The Slovak support took the Hungarian dissidents by surprise, as borne out in an appeal letter sent on the Duray case from Slovakia and published in *Irodalmi Ujság,* 1 (1985), an appeal of support by Slovak intellectuals was also published in *Irodalmi Ujság,* no. 4 (1984).

[75] *Ibid.,* p. 44.

[76] The text of the statement by the Duray Committee published in Radio Free Europe, Hungarian Situation Report/15, December 7, 1984.

[77] For the text of the protest letter signed by 50 Hungarian intellectuals, see *Irodalmi Ujság,* no. 3 (1984).

[78] Radio Budapest, April 12, 1987, *SWB/EE,* April 20, 1987.

[79] *Ibid.*

[80] Cited in Radio Free Europe, Czechoslovak Situation Report/6, June 4, 1987.

[81] Cited in Radio Free Europe, Hungarian Situation Report/15, December 7, 1984.

[82] See Radio Free Europe, Czechoslovak Situation Report/13, August 13, 1985.

[83] Radio Budapest, April 14, 1987, *SWB/EE,* April 20, 1987.

[84] See, for example, *Népszabadság,* January 28, 1981.

[85] Radio Budapest, September 3, 1987, *SWB/EE,* September 7, 1987.

[86] *Élet es Irodalom,* November 14, 1981.

[87] András Görömbei, *A csehszlovákiai magyar irodalom 1945–1980* (Budapest: Akadémiai Kiadó, 1982).

[88] See, for example, Csaba Gy. Kiss, in *Tiszatáj,* no. 1, (1984).

[89] *Irodalmi Szemle,* no. 4 (1984).

[90] Some of the reviews published in *Kritika,* no. 8 (1984).

91 See, for example, István Fried, "A szlovák–magyar irodalmi kapcsolatok jellegéhez," [On the characteristics of Hungarian Slovak literary ties] *Tiszatáj*, no. 7 (1984).

92 See, for example, Magda Bokodi, "Szlovákiai magyar irodalom," *Új Látóhatár*, no. 2 (1984).

93 *Ibid.*

94 See, for example, the communiqué issued after Husak's visit in Hungary, *Népszabadság*, September 17, 1977.

95 For the phases of the Soviet takeover, see Paul Robert Magocsi, *The Shaping of a National Identity—Subcarpathian Rus, 1848–1948* (Cambridge: Harvard University Press, 1978), ch. 13; see also Robert R. King, *Minorities Under Communism*, pp. 27–31.

96 *Magyar Nemzet*, July 16, 1980.

97 See Small Concessions to the Hungarian Minority in Transcarpathia, Radio Free Europe, Background Report/219, September 9, 1980.

98 Loránt Czigány, *The Oxford History of Hungarian Literature* (Oxford: Clarendon Press, 1984), p. 475.

99 *Szabad Nép*, September 23, 1950.

100 *Népszava*, August 19, 1956.

101 See, for example, Hommonay, p. 423.

102 *Kritika*, no. 5 (1981).

103 *Magyar Nemzet*, July 16, 1980.

104 *Kritika*, no. 5, (1981).

105 For the Soviet view of the past and the present of the area, in the Hungarian language, see *A boldogság felé* [Towards Happiness] (Uzhgorod: Karpati, 1975).

Footnotes to Chapter VIII

1 See Shafir, *Romania*, pp. 158–168; Schöpflin, *National Minorities in Eastern Europe*, p. 310; Illyés, *National Minorities in Romania*, ch. 4.

2 Robert R. King, *Minorities Under Communism*, p. 165.

3 Fejtö, *A History of the People's Democracies*; Robert R. King, "Romanian Foreign Policy," *Survey* 20, no. 2/3 (1974).

4 *Scînteia*, May 5, 1971.

5 *Scînteia*, March 13, 1971, Ceauşescu's speech was reprinted without any comments in the Hungarian foreign policy journal, *Nemzetközi Szemle* 5 (1971), pp. 20–27.

6 *Scînteia*, February 20, 1971.

7 See, for example, *Krasnaya Zvezda*, June 1, 1971.

8 *Népszabadság*, June 26, 1971.

9   *Scînteia*, July 9, 1971, *International Herald Tribune*, July 10. 1971.

10 *Magyar Hirlap*, August 13, 1971.

11 The cynical reminder was made close to Romania's Liberation Day in *Népszava*, August 20, 1971.

12 *Le Monde*, November 17. 1971.

13 *Népszabadság*, November 24, 1971.

14 See, for example, *Le Monde, International Herald Tribune*, February 25, 1972.

15 *Pravda*, February 3, 1972.

16 See, for example, *Lumea*, 9 (1972), p. 10.

17 *Ibid.*, p. 2.

18 *Scînteia*, February 27, 1972.

19 *Christian Science Monitor*, March 23, 1972.

20 The text of the Treaty, in *Scînteia*, February 27, 1972. See also Romanian–Hungarian Relations: Friendship with Reservations?, Radio Free Europe, Eastern Europe/5, March 10, 1972.

21 *Világgazdaság*, October 1974.

22 *Figyelö*, February 27, 1974.

23 *MTI*, January 22, 1974 in *FBIS/EE*, January 23, 1974.

24 *Magyar Nemzet*, March 5, 1974.

25 *Scînteia*, August 8, 1973.

26 The text of the joint communiqué, *Népszabadság*, March 3, 1974.

27 See, for example, in Puja Frigyes, "One Year of Hungarian Foreign Policy," *The New Hungarian Quarterly*, no. 3 (1974), p. 12.

28 *Népszabadság*, November 26, 1974.

29 Shafir, *Romania*, p. 162.

30 For parts of Kádár's speech as presented in Romania, see *Era Socialista*, no. 7 (1975), pp. 49–52.

31 See Ionel Nicolae, "Politica PCR in problema naţională" [The RCP's Policy on the National Problem] *Era Socialistă*, vol. LV, 1 (1975), pp. 30–34.

32 *Frankfurter Allgemeine Zeitung*, November 21, 1975.

33 *Yearbook on International Communist Affairs 1977* (Stanford, Calif.: Hoover Institution Press), p. 52.

34 *Scînteia*, June 30, 1976.

35 *Ibid.*, July 14, 1974.

36 Radio Budapest, October 28, 1976 in *SWB/EE*, October 30, 1976.

37 *Nepszabadág*, December 21, 1976.

38 See *Elöre*, June 15–19, 1977.

39 *Lumea*, June 16, 1977.

40 *Elöre*, June 19, 1977.

Footnotes to Chapter IX

1 See the interview with Puja in *The New Hungarian Quarterly*, vol. XX, no. 74 (1979), p. 85.
2 For a summary of the Hungarian–Romanian polemics following Illyés's articles, see "At the Danube," *The New Hungarian Quarterly*, vol. XIX, no. 72 (1978).
3 Interestingly, the Hungarian media refrained from quoting Illyés on *apartheid*. See *ibid.*
4 See, for example, *Le Monde*, January 25, 1978.
5 *Era Socialistă*, no. 23 (1977).
6 For Ceauşescu's speech, see *Hungarians and Germans in Romania Today* (Bucharest: Meridiane Publishing House, 1978); also in *SWB/EE*, March 15, 1978.
7 See Ion Mihai Pacepa's version in his *Red Horizons* (Washington, D.C.: Regnery Gateway, 1987).
8 *Le Monde*, April 15, 1978.
9 See, for example, Gheorghe Unc in *Anale de Istorie*, no. 2 (1978).
10 "Papers in the Languages of the Coinhabiting Nationalities," *Romania Today*, no. 5 (1978).
11 *AGERPRES*, February 20, 1978 in *SWB/EE*, February 22, 1978.
12 *AGERPRES*, March 10, 1978, in *SWB/EE*, March 13, 1978.
13 Among the numerous sources on the Király affair, see Shafir, *Romania*, p. 159; *The New York Times*, February 1, 1978, *The Christian Science Monitor*, May 2, 1978.
14 *The Christian Science Monitor*, May 2, 1978.
15 *Scînteia*, April 4, 1978.
16 The *Luceafărul* article published by *AGERPRES*, May 6, 1978 in *SWB/EE*, May 9, 1978.
17 *Scînteia*, May 13, 1978.
18 Ion Mitra in *Era Socialistă*, May 1978.
19 For Ceauşescu's speech, see *SWB/EE*, June 13, 1978.
20 *Élet és Irodalom*, July 8, 1978; for an English version, see *SWB/EE*, July 11, 1978.
21 See Radio Free Europe, Romanian Situation Report/4, April 18, 1978.
22 *Ibid.*
23 *Ibid.*
24 *Népszabadság*, July 18, 1979.
25 *Magyar Hirlap*, July 18, 1979.
26 See *SWB/EE*, October 20, 1979.

27   *Magyarország*, no. 48, December 2, 1979.

28   *Népszabadság*, March 26, 1980.

29   *Scînteia*, April 12, 1980; *Le Monde*, April 16, 1980.

30   *Népszabadság*, April 12, 1980.

31   Mátyás Szürös declared in a phone–in program over Radio Budapest that "according to official information received from our Romanian friends, the Consulate in Debrecen as well as a number of other missions have been closed down for financial reasons." *SWB/EE*, February 14, 1985.

32   Ion Lăncrănjan, *Cuvînt despre Transilvania* (Bucharest: Editura Sport–Turism, 1982).

33   See G.Cioranescu, "An escalation of polemics over Transylvania," Radio Free Europe, RAD/162, August 11, 1982.

34   See Shafir, *Romania*, pp. 149–150.

35   Ion Bulei, in *Anale de Istorie*, no. 3 (1982).

36   *Luceafărul*, May 29, 1982.

37   Pál Köteles, "Töprengés egy torzkép elött" [Pondering over a Distortion], *Tiszatáj*, October 1982.

38   György Száraz, "Egy Különös könyvröl," [About an odd book], *Valóság*, no. 10 (1982), pp. 95–104; the radio interview on October 25, 1982 in *SWB/EE*, October 28, 1982.

39   György Száraz in *The New Hungarian Quarterly*, no. 89 (1983).

40   See György Száras, *Valóság*, no. 3 (1984).

41   Paul Lendvai in Vienna Domestic Service, December 21, 1983 in *FBIS-DR/EE*, December 23, 1983.

42   *Scînteia*, May 9, 1981.

43   *New Republic*, February 3, 1982.

44   See, for example, Lukács's article reprinted in the *Carpathian Observer*, vol. 10, no. 1 (1982).

45   *Congressional Record*, U. S. Senate, March 3, 1982, S1573.

46   *România Liberă*, May 29, 1982.

47   For the text of the memorandum, see Radio Free Europe, Hungarian Situation Report/18, December 15, 1982.

48   *Le Monde*, December 11, 1982.

49   Cited in Radio Free Europe, Hungarian Situation Report/18, December 15, 1982.

50   *Népszabadság*, April 24, 1982.

51   *Scînteia*, December 1, 1982; Shafir, *Romania*, p. 186.

52   On the Hungarian–Romania talks, see *Le Monde*, December 11, 1982.

53   *Népszabadság*, March 1, 1983.

54   *Ibid.*, January 12, 1983.

55 *Scînteia*, April 1, 1983.
56 *România Liberă*, April 25, 1983.
57 *Népszabadság*, December 3, 1983.
58 Paul Lendvai, Radio Vienna, December 21, 1983 in *FBIS–DR/EE*, December 23, 1983.
59 *Scînteia*, December 6, 1983.
60 *Népszabadság*, August 23, 1984.
61 See, for example, *AFP*, August 1, 1985 in *FBIS–DR/EE*, August 2, 1985; *The New York Times*, July 28, 1985.
62 *Hajdú Bihari Napló*, July 23, 1985.
63 *Népszabadság*, November 22, 1984, Radio Budapest, November 21, 1984 in *SWB/EE*, November 23, 1984.
64 *România Literară*, December 6, 1984.
65 *AGERPRES*, December 26, 1984 in *SWB/EE*, January 1, 1985.
66 See *MTI*, January 23, 1985 in *SWB/EE*, January 25, 1985.
67 Radio Budapest, February 11, 1985, in *SWB/EE*, February 14, 1985.
68 See, for example, *Financial Times*, December 4, 1984, December 28, 1984.
69 The media in Romania did not mention that the nationality issue was raised at the Congress of the HSWP. See, for example, *Elöre*, March 28, 1985.
70 *Külpolitika*, no. 4 (1985).
71 See, for example, *Népszabadság*, October 29, 1986.
72 *Magyar Hirlap*, October 23, 1986.
73 *Kurier*, (Vienna), June 25, 1986.
74 See Radio Free Europe, Romanian Situation Report/1, January 13, 1988.
75 Radio Free Europe, Hungarian Situation Report/3, February 25, 1986.
76 *Élet es Irodalom*, January 17, 1986.
77 *AGERPRES*, January 21, 1986 in *FBIS–DR/EE*, January 24, 1986.
78 See *Irodalmi Ujság*, no. 2 (1986).
79 See, for example, Szürös's radio interview, February 9, 1987 in *SWB/EE*, February 13, 1987.
80 See George Schöpflin, "Gorbachev, Romania, and 'Leninist Nationalist Policy'," Radio Free Europe, RAD Background Report/96, June 12, 1987.
81 *Scînteia*, June 6, 1987.
82 *The Jerusalem Post*, April 13, 1988.
83 Radio Vienna, January 21, 1988 *FBIS–DR/EE*, 21 January 1988.

84 Radio Budapest, January 25, 1988 in *SWB/EE*, January 28, 1988.

85 *MTI*, March 1, 1988 in *SWB/EE*, March 8, 1988.

86 The aim of the discussion is to outline some of the main features in the continuous Hungarian–Romanian historiographical debates, and to present their relevance to the minorities' question and to the Transylvanian issue in the relations between the two states.

87 *A Magyar es a Román Törtenettudomány Negyedszázados Fejlödése* (Budapest: Akadémai Kiadó, 1971).

88 *Magyar Tudományos Akadémia* II Osztály Közleményei, vol. 24 (1975).

89 Rottler Ferenc, "A Történettudományi kutatások helyzete" [The state of research in historical sciences], *Századok*, vol. III, no. 1 (1979), p. 9.

90 See, for example, references to the Commission on the eve of Ion Gheorge Maurer's visit to Hungary and on the eve of the Kádár-Ceauşescu talks, *Magyar Nemzet*, February 26, 1974, *Népszabadság*, June 15, 1977.

91 See, for example, Henrik Vass, "Problems of the Hungarian revolutionary working class movement," *Anale de Istorie*, vol. XVI, no. 3 (1970), pp. 19–40.

92 An article devoted to 25 years of *Anale de Istorie* was published in *Párttörténeti Közlemények*, vol. XXVI, no. 4 (1980), pp. 211–217.

93 *Élet es Irodalom*, June 25, 1977.

94 Radio Budapest, July 9, 1979 in *SWB/EE*, July 11, 1979.

95 *Scînteia*, August 10, 1980.

96 *Népszabadság*, August 24, 1980.

97 *Magyar Nemzet*, August 15, 1980.

98 György Ránki, "Gondolatok a bukaresti történészkongreszusról" [Thoughts on the historians' conference in Bucharest], *Történelmi Szemle*, vol. XXIV, no. 2 (1980).

99 The first issue of *Historia* in 1979 carried a round table debate on the pre–history of the Hungarians and of the nations in the Carpathian basin, refuting the Romanian claims.

100 *Luceafărul*, July 14, 1979.

101 Ştefan Paşcu, "Who Benefits By It," *Romania Today*, no. 4 (1980), p. 28.

102 The passage is from a long Romanian review of the *Historical Atlas* published in Hungary in 1984, severely censured by the Romanian critics for gross falsifications. See *Contemporanul*, December 27, 1985.

[103] *Revista de Istorie*, no. 6 (1975), pp. 941–948.

[104] *România Literară*, December 5, 1985.

[105] *AGERPRES*, December 17, 1978 in *SWB/EE*, February 20, 1978.

[106] *Contemporanul*, February 10, 1978.

[107] *Magyar Hirlap*, October 31, 1976.

[108] *Népszabadság*, December 3, 1983.

[109] On the background of the Romanian views of Trianon, see Stephen Fischer–Galati, "Trianon and Romania," *Essays on World War I: Total War and Peacemaking, A Case Study of Trianon*, pp. 422–437.

[110] For such a Hungarian study, see Mária Ormos, *Pádovától Triánonig 1919–1920* (Budapest: Kossuth, 1983).

[111] *Scînteia Tineretului*, November 21, 1983.

[112] Ernö Raffay, *Erdély 1918-1919-ben* (Budapest: Magvetö, 1987).

[113] *Kritika*, August 8, 1984.

[114] *România Literară*, December 6, 1984.

[115] *Ibid*.

[116] *Contemporanul*, January 10, 1986.

[117] *Saptămina*, December 27, 1985.

[118] Radio Budapest, January 28, 1986, cited in Radio Free Europe, Hungarian Situation Report/3, February 25, 1986.

[120] *Népszabadság*, December 24, 1983; July 31, 1984; December 31, 1984.

[121] *Erdély Története* (Budapest: Akadémiai Kiadó, 1986).

[122] For some of the main Romanian replies, see the issues of *Anale de Istorie, Magazin Istoric, Revista de Istorie* in 1987. Some of the issues contained at least one, but often three or four, studies answering the Hungarian work on Transylvania.

Selected Bibliography

Aczél, György. "Cultural Policy and Social Progress," *The New Hungarian Quarterly*, 14, no. 52 (1973): 69–74.

Arató, Endre (ed.). *Tanulmányok a Szlovákiai Magyarok Történetéböl 1918–1975* (Budapest: Magvetö, 1977).

Balogh, Sándor. *A népi demokratikus Magyarország külpolitikája 1945–1948* (Budapest: Kossuth, 1982).

———. "Az 1946 február 27-1 magyar–csehszlovák lakosságcsere egyezmény," *Történelmi Szemle* 22, no. 1 (1979): 59–87.

———. *Parlamenti es Pártharcok Magyarországón, 1945–1947* (Budapest: Kossuth, 1975).

Bányai, László. *Közös Sors—Testvéri Hagyományok* (Bucharest: Politikai Könyvkiadó, 1973).

Berecz, János. "Hazánk nemzetközi helyzetének változásai," *Párttörténeti Közlemények*, no. 1 (1985).

Bondor–Deliman, Ecaterina. "Nationalităţile conlocuitoare in istoria si viata politică–economică a României socialiste," *Lupta de Clasă*, no. 7 (1971).

Braham, Randolph L. "Romania: On the Separate Path," *Problems of Communism*, no. 3 (1964).

Braun, Aurel. *Romanian Foreign Policy Since 1965: The Political and Military Limits of Autonomy* (New York: Praeger Publishers, 1978).

Brown, F. James. "Romania Steps Out of Line," *Survey* no. 49 (October 1963).

Cadzow, John F., Andrew Ludanyi and Louis J. Elteto (eds.). *Transylvania: The Roots of Ethnic Conflict* (Kent, Ohio: Kent University Press, 1983).

Ceterchi, Ioan. *Naţiunea si Contemporaneitatea* (Bucharest: Editura Ştiintifică, 1971).

Cohen, Lenard J. "Federalism and Foreign Policy in Yugoslavia: The Politics of Regional Ethnocentrism," *International Journal* XLI, summmer 1986, pp. 626–654.

Csatári, Dániél. *Román Magyar Kapcsolatok* (Budapest: Kossuth, 1958).

———. *Forgó Szélben: Magyar–Román viszony 1940–1945* (Budapest:

Akadémiai Kiadó, 1968).

Daicoviciu, Constantiniu F. H. "Historical Considerations On a Book of Antihistorical Ethnography," *Romania—Pages of History 2*, no. 3–4 (1977): 155–169.

Eisenburger, Eduard. *Egalitate Reală, Participare Activă* (Bucharest: Editura Politică, 1978).

Fischer, Gabriel "Nationalism and Internationalism in Hungary and Romania," *Canadian Slavonic Papers*, X, no. 1 (1968): 26–41.

Fischer-Galati, Stephen. *The New Romania: From People's Republic to Socialist Republic* (Cambridge, Mass.: MIT Press, 1967).

_____. "The continuation of nationalism in Romanian historiography," *Nationality Papers* VI, 2 (1978): 179–184.

_____. *Twentieth Century Romania* (New York: Columbia University Press, 1970).

_____. "Smokescreen and Iron Curtain: A Reassessment of Territorial revisionism vis-à-vis Romania Since World War I," *East European Quarterly*, XXII, no. 1 (1988): 37–53.

Fischer-Galati, Stephen et al. (eds.). *Romania Between East and West: Historical Essays in Memory of Constantin C. Giurescu* (New York: Columbia University Press, 1982).

Fogarasi, Béla. "A dunai népek együttmüködése," *Társadalmi Szemle*, 1, no. 5 (1946): 346–354.

Gerelyesné, Dian Eva. "Petru Groza Politikai Pályája 1945 Utáni Dokumentumok Tükrében," *Századok*, no. 5–6 (1985): 1272–1350.

Gilberg, Trond. *Modernization in Romania Since World War II* (New York: Praeger Publishers, 1975).

_____. "Ethnic Minorities in Romania Under Socialism," in B. L. Faber (ed.), *The Social Structure of Eastern Europe* (New York: Praeger Publishers, 1976).

Görömbei, András. *A Csehszlovákiai Magyar Irodalom 1945–1980* (Budapest: Akadémiai Kiadó, 1982).

Gosztonyi, János. "Hungarians at home and abroad," *The New Hungarian Quarterly*, no. 69 (1978).

Graeme J. Gill. "Romania: Background to Autonomy," *Survey*, 21, no. 3 (Summer 1975): 94–113.

Horak, M. Stephan et al. *Eastern European national Minorities 1919–1980* (Littleton: Colo.: Libraries Unlimited, 1985).

Hungarians and Germans in Romania Today (Bucharest Meridiane, 1978).

Illyés, Elemér. *National Minorities in Romania: Change in Transylvania* (Boulder: East European Monographs, 1982).

Janics, Kálmán. *Czechoslovak Policy and the Hungarian Minority*

1945-1948 (New York: Social Science Monographs, distributed by Columbia University Press, 1982).

Janos, Andrew C. "Nationalism and Communism in Hungary," *East European Quarterly*, V, no. 1 (1971): 74–101.

Joó, Rudolf. "A Joint Hungarian–Slovene Research Report Concerning the situation of rural national minorities," *Canadian Review of Studies in Nationalism*, XIII, no. 2 (1986): 271–274.

———. "A nemzetiségi kérdés az 1945 utáni europai államközi dokumentumokban, *Külpolitika*, no. 2 (1977): 79–91.

Jowitt, Kenneth. *Revolutionary Breakthroughs and National Development: The Case of Romania, 1944–1965* (Berkeley and Los Angeles: University of California Press, 1971).

Kertesz, Stephen D. *Diplomacy in a Whirlpool, Hungary between Nazi Germany and Soviet Russia* (Notre Dame, Ind.: Notre Dame University Press, 1953).

———. *Between Russia and the West—Hungary and the Illusions of Peacemaking 1945–1947* (Notre Dame: University of Notre Dame Press, 1984).

King, Robert R. *A History of the Romanian Communist Party* (Stanford, Calif.: Hoover Institution Press, 1980).

———. "Eastern Europe, Robert G. Wirsing (ed.), *Protection of Ethnic Minorities* (New York: Pergamon Press, 1981).

Kiraly, Bela, K, Peter Pastor and Ivan Sanders (eds.). *Essays on World War I: Total War and Peacemaking, A Case Study of Trianon* (War and Society in East Central Europe, Vol. VI, New York: Social Science Monographs, Brooklyn College, 1982).

Kiraly, Bela K, Barbara Lotze, and Nandor F. Dreisziger (eds.). *The First War between Socialist States: The Hungarian Revolution of 1956 and Its Impact* (War and Society in East Central Europe, Vol. XI, New York: Social Science Monographs, 1984).

Klein, George and Milan J. Reban. *The Politics of Ethnicity in Eastern Europe* (Boulder: East European Monographs, 1981).

Korom, Mihály. "A magyar nepi demokracia elso evei," *Valosag*, no. 3 (1984).

Kövágó, László. "A szocialista nemzetiségi politika kialakulásának utján," *Párttörténeti Közleméneyek*, XXVI, no. 3 (1981).

Kövari, Attila. *The Antecedents of Today's National Myth in Romania, 1921–1965* (Jerusalem: The Hebrew University of Jerusalem, The Soviet and East European Research Centre, 1983).

Kovrig, Bennett. *Communism in Hungary from Kun to Kádár* (Stanford, Calif.: Stanford University Press, 1979).

Lache, Ştefan and Gheorghe Ţuţui. *La Roumanie et la Conférence de la paix de Paris, 1946* (Bucharest: Editura Academiei RSR,

1987).

Lahav, Yehuda. *Soviet Policy and the Transylvanian Question 1940–1946* (Jerusalem: The Hebrew University of Jerusalem, The Soviet and East European Research Centre, 1977).

Lăncrănjan, Ion. *Cuvînt despre Transilvania* (Bucharest: Editura Sport Turism, 1982).

Lipcsei, Ildikó. "Kurkó Gyárfás," *Historia*, no. 5–6 (1984).

Ludanyi, Andrew. *Hungarians in Romania and Yugoslavia: A Comparative Study of Communist Nationality Policies* (unpublished Ph.D. thesis, The Louisiana State University and Agricultural and Mechanical College, 1971).

_____. "Socialist Patriotism and National Minorities: A Comparison of the Yugoslav and Romanian Theory and Practice," Steven Bela Vardy and Agnes Huszar Vardy (eds.), *Society in Change: Studies in Honor of Bela K. Kiraly* (Boulder: East European Monographs, 1983).

_____. "Titoist Integration of Yugoslavia: The Partisan Myth and the Hungarians of Vojvodina," *Polity*, XII, no. 2 (Winter 1979): 225–252.

A Magyar Kommunista Párt és a Szociáldemokrata Párt Határozatai 1944–1948 (Budapest: Kossuth, 1967).

Magyarok Csehszlovákiában (Bratislava: Epocha Konyvkiadó, 1969).

Max, Stanley M. *The United States and the Sovietization of Hungary 1945–1948* (Boulder, Colo.: East European Monographs, 1985).

Minda, Tibor. "A nemzeti kisebbségek helyzete Vajdaságban," *Hid* (Novi-Sad), January 1963: 102–107.

Molnár, Miklos. *A Short History of the Hungarian Communist Party* (Boulder: Westview Press, 1978).

Nagy, Ferenc. *The Struggle Behind the Iron Curtain* (New York: Macmillan, 1948).

Ölvendi, János. "Magyarok Szlovákiában," *Új Látohatár*, no. 6) (1961).

Ramet, Pedro. *Nationalism and Federalism in Yugoslavia 1963–1983* (Bloomington, Indiana: Indiana University Press, 1984).

Révay, István. "A nemzeti kérdés éve 1968," *Katolikus Szemle*, XXI, no. 4 (1969).

Robinson, William F. *The Pattern of Reform in Hungary* (New York: Praeger Publishers, 1973).

Samal, Hrabik Mary. "The Case of Miklos Duray," *Cross Currents*, 4 (1985): 39–45.

Schöpflin, George. "Hungary between prosperity and conflict," *Conflict Studies*, no. 136 (1982).

_____. "Romanian Nationalism," *Survey*, 20, no. 2/3 (Spring–Summer

1974): 77–104.

―――. "National Minorities under Communism," in Kurt London (ed.), *Eastern Europe in Transition* (Baltimore: Johns Hopkins Press, 1966).

―――. *The Hungarians of Romania* (London: Minority Rights Group, Report no. 37).

Simmons, George W. *Nationalism in the USSR and Eastern Europe in the Era of Brezhnev and Kosygin* (Detroit: University of Detroit Press, 1976).

Shafir, Michael. *Romania–Politics, Economics and Society* (London: Francis Pinter, 1985).

Száraz, György, "Egy különös könyvröl," *Válóság*, no. 10 (1982).

Széli, István. *A magyar kultúra útjai Jugoszláviában* (Budapest: Kossuth, 1983).

Vago, Raphael. "Nationality Policies in Contemporary Hungary," *Hungarian Studies Review*, XI, no. 1 (Spring 1984): 43–60.

Wolfe, Thomas. *Soviet Power and Europe 1945–1970*. (Baltimore: Johns Hopkins Press, 1970).

Yelinek, Yesheyahu, *The Lust for Power* (Boulder, Colo.: East European Monographs, 1983).

Index

:zél, György, 70, 142, 151, 160, 161, 202, 209, 236, 237
lied Control Commission, 28
ndics, Erzsébet, 84
ndrei, Ştefan, 220, 221, 238, 242, 255
pró, Antal, 73, 74
ier, Pál, 21

icilek, Karol, 50, 94
ilogh, Edgár, 44, 45, 88, 106
ittonya, 6
íkes County, 130
:regovo, 199
»ssarabia, 13, 84
»niuc, Mihai, 72
iszku, Béla, 76
ɔbu, Emil, 248
obnár, József, 155
ɔlyai University, 68–70, 72, 87, 88
ikovina, 84

:eauşescu, Ilie, 256
:auşescu, Nicolae, 78, 85, 89, 90, 106, 117, 139, 143, 194, 195, 202, 207, 212, 223, 242
hisinevschi, Iosif, 61
luj, 14, 18, 46, 61, 68, 214, 225
ɔuncil of Workers of German Nationality (CWGH), 120
ɔuncil of Workers of Hungarian Nationality (CWHN), 120, 121
:atári, Dániél, 66, 67, 85
SEMADOK, 108–116, 137, 186, 190

Csográd County, 131
Csoóri, Sándor, 165
Czechoslovakia, 10, 15, 22, 26, 29–35, 40, 41, 108, 117, 183–196
Czine, Mihály, 88

Daicoviciu, Constanti, 83
Dăsălescu, Constantin, 243, 244
Dinnyes, Lajos, 39, 40
Doboz, István, 103
Dubček, Aalexander, 113
Duray, Miklós, 187–189
Élet és Irodalom, 84, 85, 104, 105

Fábry, Zoltán, 55, 90, 110
Faluvégi, Lajos, 240, 241
Fazekas, János, 61, 65, 69, 91, 209, 220
Foaia Noastra, 136, 146
Fogarisi, Béla, 21, 22

Gerö Ernö, 19, 21, 25, 37
Germans, in Hungary, 126, 154
Georghiu–Dej, Gheorghe, 12, 24, 42, 43, 45, 68, 71, 82
Gorbachev, M. S., 247
Gosztonyi, János, 155–158
Grosz, Károly, 194
Groza, Petru, 13–16, 20, 24, 39, 40, 45, 47, 68, 258–259
Gyöngyši, János, 19
Hanák, Péter, 251
Hungarian Autonomous Region, 46–49, 59, 69–71, 91

Hungarian Communist Party (Hungarian Socialist Workers' Party), 7, 10, 15, 26, 32, 36, 38, 86, 130, 131, 148, 209, 210, 243
Hungarian People's Alliance (MNSZ), 11-16, 43-45, 59
Husák, Gustav, 26, 34, 57, 187, 194

Ilyés, Gyula, 171, 172, 176, 215, 217, 221
Ionţă, Ion, 206
Irodalmı Szemle Bratislava), 98, 110, 193

Joó, Rudolf, 151

Kádár, János, 66, 78, 80, 86, 90, 100, 113, 120, 139, 143, 153, 179, 195, 206, 207, 211, 212, 230, 235
Kállai, Gyula, 9, 65, 76
Kárpáti Igaz Szó. 197
Katus, László, 197
Katus, László, 82
Khruschev, N. S., 69
Király, Károly, 121, 124, 219, 234, 245
Komóscin, Zoltán, 76, 77, 80, 90, 118, 202, 204
Köpeczi, Béla, 162, 163, 191, 245
Korunk, 45, 87
Kosovo, 169
Kövágo, Lászlo, 133, 135, 143, 144, 151
Kurkó, Gyárfás, 16, 44

Lăncrănjan, Ion, 229, 230, 233
Lázár, György, 211, 212, 236, 237
Lörincz, Gyula, 110, 112
Luca, Vasile, 12, 37, 38, 43, 45, 46, 47, 48

Magyar Szó, 174-178
Manescu, Manea, 202, 206

Maniu Guards, 10-14
Marosán, György, 71
Maurer, Ion Gheorghe, 80, 208
Méhes, Lajos, 148
Méliusz, Jozsef, 44, 64
Mihnea, Gheorghiu, 221, 222
Moghioro‚s, Alexandru, 61
Molnár, Erik, 82, 83
Münnich, Ferenc, 67, 99

National Democratic Front, 13, 15
Nagy, Ferenc, 19-22, 39, 40
Naby, Imre, 42
Nemes, Dezsö, 118, 252
Niculescu, Mizil, Paul, 90, 118, 120, 202, 206
Novotný, Antonín, 100

Ortutay, Gyula, 153

Pach, Pál Zsigmond, 224, 239, 252
Pandi, Pál, 59
Paris Peace Conference, 18-23, 31, 37-38
Paşcu, Ştefan, 254
Patriotic People's Front, 104
Pauker, Ana, 39, 40, 48
Pănescu, Adrian, 253
Péter, János, 76
Petrescu, Titel, 18
Pozsgay, Imre, 166
Puja, Frigyes, 6, 16, 168, 214, 225, 226

Radio Kossuth, 6, 8
Rajk, Lászlo, 43, 44, 47
Rákosi, Matyás, 8, 20-23, 43, 48
Ránki, György, 252
Răutu, Leonte, 61
Rehák, Lászlo, 123, 174, 175, 177
Révai, Jozsef, 8, 20
Romania, 6-26, 61-67, 117-122, 201-261
Romanians in Hungary, 125, 145-150
Rónai, Sándor, 71

Sălăjan, Leontin, 77
Scînteia, 12
Sidó, Zoltán, 190
Slovakia, 7, 16, 17, 26–31, 41–59,
    91–101
Slovak Communist Party, 28, 32, 33,
    94, 96
Slovaks, in Hungary, 125–144
Slovak National Council 55, 58
Social Democratic Party (Romania),
    18
Soviet Union, 12, 15, 74, 75, 77, 83,
    84, 119, 120, 203, 205–207
South Slavs in Hungary, 124–144
Stalin, 19, 22, 38, 43
Strougal, Lubomir, 189, 194
Sütér, Istvan, 84
Szabad Nép, 38, 39, 60
Szabédi, Laszlo, 88
Száraz, György, 232, 233, 259
Szász, Janos, 105
Szilágyi, Péter, 146, 147
Szirmai, István, 63, 76
Szürös, Mátyás, 163, 244, 245,
    258

Tătărescu, Gheorghe, 21, 25, 39
Tîrgu–Mureş, 61, 65, 68, 91
Tito, Iosip Broz, 29, 42, 77, 179
Tomka, Miklos, 123
Transcarpathia, 41, 159, 196–200
Transylvania, 10–26, 46–49, 61, 69
Trianon, Treaty, 5

Új Symposium, 107, 174, 176
Új Szó, 56, 58, 94, 95
Uzhgorod, 197, 198, 199

Valoság, 84
Várkonyi, Péter, 153, 236, 237,
    241, 243
Várkonyi, Tibor, 120, 121
Vas, Gizella, 207
Vas, Zoltán, 9

Vass, Henrik, 251
Verdet, Ilie, 206, 209
Vienna Diktat, 8
Vojvodina, 62, 168, 171, 173, 175
Yugoslavia, 10, 15, 35, 36, 41, 77,
    122, 152, 159, 167–183, 195
Zvara, Juraj, 35, 98, 185, 193